The Historical Evidence for Jesus

G. A. Wells

Prometheus Books

700 East Amherst Street
Buffalo, N.Y. 14215

Library of Congress Card Catalog No. 82-60381
ISBN: 0-87975-429-X

To anyone

δεομενῳ, εγειρεσθαι
υπο μυωπος Τινος,

but more particularly to four
who have no such need:

Elisabeth, Carl, David and Derek

Contents

Statement of My Thesis
and Acknowledgments

Of the many criticisms which were made of my first book on Christian origins, *The Jesus of the Early Christians* (London, 1971), three were substantially just: (1) The work relied more on the pioneer critics of the nineteenth and early twentieth centuries than one would expect of a book published in 1971. (2) It gave too much attention to (and was not entirely accurate in its representation of) the pagan background of earliest Christianity, thus neglecting some of the Jewish factors in the origin of this undoubtedly Jewish sect. (3) It too readily posited interpolation (rather than redaction of traditions of different provenance) to account for unevennesses and contradictions in early Christian documents.

I was able to profit from these criticisms when I wrote the sequel volume, *Did Jesus Exist?* (London, 1975). In the present volume I shall try to answer criticisms of that book and to come to terms with some of the substantial body of apologetic and critical literature concerning the New Testament that has appeared in the meantime. There is inevitably some overlap between this present book and its two predecessors (particularly in Chapter 1), but most of what I say here either is not in them at all or develops more fully points only adumbrated in them.

My fundamental theses remain the same: namely, the earliest references to the historical Jesus are so vague that it is not necessary to hold that he ever existed; the rise of Christianity can, from the undoubtedly historical antecedents, be explained quite well without him; and reasons can be given to show why, from about AD 80 or 90, Christians began to suppose that he had lived in Palestine about fifty years earlier.

The subtitle of this book indicates that it is addressed particularly to those who feel some skepticism toward the claims of Christianity and would welcome an account, written without religious commitment, of the kinds of documents the twenty-seven books of the New Testament are. I have tried to avoid the rancor which mars much that atheists have written on Christianity.

In J. M. Robertson's account of its rise (published early in the twentieth century) the only motives that appear to play an important part in Christianity's development are greed, superstition, jealousy, and the quest for power. But the motives and ideals of many Christians in more recent times are clearly of a different character, and it is reasonable to suppose that generous tendencies have played a part at all times. Robertson leaves unexplained the qualities of courage and independent thought which called forth persecution and then enabled the early Christians to endure it.

One can perhaps excuse the bias, for or against their subject matter, which historians commonly display, on the ground that the immense application and industry demanded of them cannot easily be sustained without the impelling force of some moral emotion. And it seems often to have been supposed that it was the historian's duty to vindicate the good and chastise the wicked. But serious historians must surely rise above this simple dualism. Religion has been the source of many evils, but religion itself is a product of the same human nature that is the source of whatever good has appeared.

Nearly all the authorities whose views I quote in this book are New Testament scholars; they are Christian theologians writing in standard Biblical commentaries or in theological journals. My purpose in quoting them is not to settle any issue by a mere appeal to their authority, but to show that many, indeed most of the propositions on which I build my case are not laymen's aberrations, but are accepted—even widely accepted—by scholars who are within Christianity. Many such scholars have had the detachment and objectivity to study the books of the New Testament as historical documents, just as one would any records of a bygone age. In the few instances where I have been able to meet some of these theologians personally, I have learned to respect them not only as scholars but also as men.

Perhaps my deepest debt (certainly in what I write about the gospels and Acts) is to Ernst Haenchen, whom I never met. This great scholar wrote with a humor, clarity, shrewdness, and thoroughness that I have seldom found elsewhere. I have drawn very fully on the books and papers he published before his death in 1975, and I have also consulted his commentary on the fourth gospel, which appeared posthumously in 1980, thanks to the devoted efforts of his wife and one of his pupils.

I have also referred to a number of theological writers whom I regard as quite unhelpful except insofar as they draw attention to the fact that many positions I regard as indefensible are nevertheless still defended. Such writers are often unaware of the difficulties their views present to an uncommitted outsider.

I have given particular attention to Dr. J. A. T. Robinson's recent attempts to establish what are by now minority views among New Testament scholars, namely that all four canonical gospels were composed before AD 70 and that the Acts of the Apostles give a broadly reliable portrait of the first-century church, compatible with what we learn from Paul's letters on that subject. Robinson is sufficiently well-known to warrant this attention, even though many of his colleagues in New Testament studies justly regard his views as conservative.

I have throughout kept in mind the warning of Loisy: *"il ne faut pas s'improviser historien des origines chrétiennes"* (see References entry no. 134, p 244). He meant, as is clear from what he said elsewhere (133, p 6), not that the field is to be barred to all but professional theologians, but that assimilation of all the relevant evidence is the indispensable basis of any worthwhile opinion.

I do not of course claim to have proved my views correct. If the evidence were such that one theory could be established to the exclusion of all others, the whole question would have been settled long ago. Whether my hypothesis is preferable to others will depend on whether it makes the best sense of the greatest number of details.

A NOTE ON QUOTATIONS AND ABBREVIATIONS

For ease in reading and to minimize footnotes I refer to the works of other authors by the numbers these works are given in the References (pp 239 ff). Abbreviations used only there are listed at its head.

I refer to my two previous books on Christian origins as JEC (*The Jesus of the Early Christians*) and DJE (*Did Jesus Exist?*).

The New Testament quotations are (except when otherwise indicated) from the Revised Standard Version of the Bible (RSV), copyrighted 1946, 1952 © 1971, 1973 by the Division of Christian Education of the National Council of the Churches of Christ in the U.S.A., and used by permission. I refer to the Revised Version of the King James Bible of 1611, published in 1881, as RV, and to the New English Bible (2nd ed., 1970) as NEB. The Old and New Testaments are sometimes designated OT and NT.

I follow the usual terminology in calling the first three of the canonical four gospels "the synoptics." The traditional term *synoptic* means "what can be seen at a glance," and owes its origin to the fact that these three gospels are so alike that, if they are put side by side in parallel columns, one can see immediately what material has been added to, omitted from, or adapted in each.

The books of the NT are referred to by means of the following abbreviations (given here in alphabetical order):

Acts	The Acts of the Apostles
Coloss.	Paul's Epistle to the Colossians
1 and 2 Cor.	Paul's Epistles to the Corinthians
Ephes.	The Epistle to the Ephesians, ascribed to Paul in the canon

Gal.	Paul's Epistle to the Galatians
Hebrews	The Epistle to the Hebrews
James	The Epistle of James
1, 2 and 3 John	The Epistles ascribed in the canon to John
Jn.	The Gospel According to John
Jude	The Epistle of Jude
Lk.	The Gospel According to Luke
Mk.	The Gospel According to Mark
Mt.	The Gospel According to Matthew
1 and 2 Peter	The Epistles ascribed in the canon to Peter
Philem.	Paul's Epistle to Philemon
Phil.	Paul's Epistle to the Philippians
Rev.	The Revelation to John (the New Testament Apocalypse)
Rom.	Paul's Epistle to the Romans
1 and 2 Thess.	The Epistles to the Thessalonians, ascribed in the canon to Paul
1 and 2 Tim.	The two Epistles to Timothy
Titus	The Epistle to Titus
	(The last three are known as the Pastoral Epistles and are ascribed in the canon to Paul.)

Introduction

I THE NEW TESTAMENT TEXT

The Four Principal Textual Families

Reconstituting Christian origins from the New Testament depends on establishing a reliable text. None of the original documents is extant, and the oldest existing copies, made by hand before the invention of printing, differ at some points. We know from the apocryphal gospels, as well as from statements of orthodox and heretical Christians, that in the second century gospel texts were altered and combined. This was particularly likely to occur in those early days, when the documents were not regarded as authoritative and definitive, and when there was no central organization to secure and enforce uniformity.

It is for those early days that the manuscript tradition is defective. The oldest extant fragment of the New Testament (P^{52}, the Rylands papyrus, consisting of a few verses of *John*) is dated not later than AD 150. But this is about sixty years after the gospels were written, and, as a recent authority has noted, it is probable that most of the significant variations in the text had arisen by then (89, pp 84–8).

New Testament manuscripts earlier than the tenth century are written in *uncial* letters, almost identical with the stiff capital letters (not connected to each other) used in stone inscriptions. There is no division between words and practically no punctuation. A cursive style (where the individual letters are connected) had long been used for non-literary purposes such as private correspondence, but only in the ninth century was it formalized into a *minuscule,* or small-letter, style, which within a century replaced the uncial hand in literary writing.

1

In the early Christian centuries, each main center (Alexandria, Antioch, etc.) supplied local churches with Christian writings in the form current locally, and the text in one region was not absolutely identical with that in another. "In the earliest period," says Black, "these writings in use in Church and Synagogue were subject to the most radical change and alterations in both their subject-matter and text, with little regard for the author's original work" (18, pp 279–80). The idiosyncrasies of a local text would be retained and even increased as further copies were made, so that eventually a type of text grew up which was peculiar to that locality.

Metzger and others believe that it is possible today to assign most extant manuscripts to a locality, by comparing their characteristic readings with quotations of these passages in the writings of Church Fathers who lived in a particular area (139, p xvii). On this basis, four principal textual types have been recognized. Some quite early manuscripts admittedly consist of mixed texts that cut across these divisions; therefore this grouping into four has not remained unchallenged.[1] Here as elsewhere the student of the New Testament must resign himself to the fact that there is some doubt and uncertainty about even the most fundamental propositions of his science.

Two of the four principal local textual types can be proved to have existed as early as the second half of the second century:

1. The *Alexandrian* text. Its principal witnesses were for long two fourth-century codices (Codex Vaticanus and Codex Sinaiticus), but recent papyrus discoveries have proved these to be accurate copies of much earlier documents. Thus P[75], the Bodmer papyrus of *Luke* and *John* published in 1961, is dated AD 175–225, and is in essential agreement with Codex Vaticanus.

2. The *Western* text, widely used in Italy, Gaul, and North Africa. There is no manuscript evidence for it earlier than AD 300 (P[38] and P[48]), and the principal codex (Codex Bezae) is as late as the fifth or sixth century. Nevertheless, a number of second- and third-century Church Fathers quote this textual type.

The other two main types cannot be proved to be so ancient. The *Caesarean* mixes readings of Alexandrian and Western textual types and may have originated in the third century; and the *Byzantine* is represented by a fifth-century codex, by later uncials, and by most minuscules. Its earliest witness is Chrysostom, bishop of Constantinople in the late fourth century. One of its characteristics is to combine divergent readings into one expanded reading. Distributed quite widely through the Byzantine Empire, it was the most generally accepted text from the fifth century until the rise of textual criticism in the nineteenth.

When Erasmus produced the first printed copies of the Greek New Testament in Basel in 1516 he used Byzantine-type manuscripts, and these also underlay almost all translations into modern languages until the nineteenth century. Modern printed texts, both in Greek and in translation, are however based on the oldest available manuscripts, the various readings of which have been critically sifted according to certain principles—long-established in editing the Greek and Latin classics—which include the following:

(1) A scribe tends to change a word or phrase he does not understand into one that makes sense to him. Hence the reading which is at first glance harder to understand in the context is likely to be the original.

(2) The reading from which one can understand how others developed is to be preferred.

(3) Intentional changes are likely to be additions (explanations, supplementary material from other traditions). Sometimes marginal comments giving such explanation or supplementation were incorporated into the text by a later copyist. For these reasons, a shorter reading is generally preferable.

The Western Text

In the process of sifting, scholars and editors of the late nineteenth and early twentieth centuries accorded material of the Alexandrian type more weight than material from the other most-ancient textual family, the Western type. Haenchen notes (94, pp 47–53) that discussion of the Western text has been bedeviled by failure to distinguish three senses of the term. First, the Western witnesses of the gospels, Acts, and the Pauline letters introduce a great number of variants that aim at smoothing and clarifying the text and which sometimes add pious phrases. All the witnesses do not include all these variants, and so in this sense the Western text is not a standardized one. Second, there are variants peculiar to the Western text of Acts. These were introduced by someone working on a copy of the Western text in the first sense, and whose revisions in time came to be incorporated into nearly all the Western witnesses of Acts, making its text nearly 10 percent longer than the Alexandrian. Third, there are yet other variants which are characteristic only of Codex Bezae, the principal uncial witness to the Western text. Haenchen regards many of these as mere scribal errors. Let us study in some detail the text in the second and third senses of the term, namely the revision of the Western text of Acts and the readings peculiar to Codex Bezae.

The reviser pursues a clear doctrinal bias by introducing anti-Jewish and pro-Gentile readings. Whereas, for instance, Codex Vaticanus says that the Jews, when they crucified Jesus, "acted in ignorance" (Acts 3:17), Western witnesses add *evilly* in order to stress that their action was nevertheless a crime. In the previous chapter, the "holy spirit" enables the apostles to "speak in tongues," and Peter explains to Jewish onlookers that this fulfils the prophecy of Joel: "I will pour out my spirit upon all flesh" (Acts 2:17). Codex Bezae puts the noun for *flesh* in the plural in order to emphasize that the promise was not made merely to the Jews. (Although other extant Western authorities do not give this reading, the Codex is here following a theological tendency of the Western text generally.) This reading cannot be original. The author of Acts represents Peter as only later persuaded to extend the Christian mission to include Gentiles, and therefore he would not have made him preach the Gentile mission in his address to the Jews in chapter 2. Numerous other examples of the anti-Jewish and pro-Gentile stance of the reviser have been specified in recent work.[2]

The reviser also added historical, biographical, and geographical details, some of which show that he had a more accurate knowledge of Jerusalem than did the author of Acts. For instance, Acts 3:8 describes how the paralytic healed by Peter and John went with them "into the temple," that is, the inner forecourt. Verse 11 continues: "While he clung to Peter and John, all the people ran together to them in the portico called Solomon's." This portico was situated on the temple square, but not within the forecourt. There should therefore have been a statement that the apostles, with the cured paralytic, had left the temple. As Dibelius observes (51, p 85), the Western text has removed the difficulty by supplying such a statement, with the words: "When Peter and John went out, he clung to them and went with them."

Another instructive example is Acts 19:13–16, a story which combines an anecdote about the sons of Sceva with traditions (mentioned in the gospels, for example, at Lk. 9:49) about the behavior of Jewish exorcists. That the Western text is secondary here can be seen from the way verse 14 is written in Codex Vaticanus on the one hand and Western witnesses on the other. Vaticanus has:

> 13. But some also of the strolling Jews, exorcists, attempted to name, over people having evil spirits, the name of the Lord Jesus, saying "I exorcise you by Jesus whom Paul proclaims."
> 14. And there were seven sons of one Sceva, a high priest, doing this.
> 15. And answering, the evil spirit said to them, "Jesus indeed I know and Paul I understand, but who are you?"
> 16. And the man in whom was the evil spirit, leaping on them and overmastering them both, was strong against them, so that they escaped out of that house naked and wounded.

In verse 16 a Greek word is used which normally means "both"; but Metzger notes (139, p 471) that "occasionally in sub-standard Greek" it can mean "all" (that is, more than two). The Western reviser took it in the former sense, in which it contradicts the statement of verse 14 that seven exorcists, not two, were involved. He avoided this contradiction by dropping the number seven from his verse 14. He knew too that there never had been a high priest named Sceva, and so he calls him merely a priest. His verse 14 reads accordingly (I quote it as given in Codex Bezae):

> In this connection, sons of a certain Sceva, a priest, wished to do the same. They had a custom of exorcising such persons; and coming in to [the abode of] the man who was demon-possessed, they began to invoke the name, saying "We command you by Jesus whom Paul to go out [sic] preaches."

The strange word order in the final clause is peculiar to Codex Bezae, and is explicable if we suppose that an earlier scribe had omitted "to go out" but had then put the relevant Greek word in the margin of his manuscript. The scribe who wrote Codex Bezae transferred the word from the margin to the text, but inserted it at the wrong place, before *preaches* instead of after it. This is one of the features which show that Codex Bezae is but a link in a long chain of copies.

Haenchen, from whom I have taken all these details, notes further that, by introducing "coming in" into verse 14, the reviser prepares the way for the mention of the house in verse 16, and also that he is careful to distinguish (as Vaticanus does not) between the Jewish exorcists of verse 13 and the sons of Sceva. He makes these latter into a different group of persons by beginning his verse 14 with "in this connection." His idea may well have been to make Sceva a pagan priest and his sons pagans. But these corrections mean that the narrative then implies that the Jews of verse 13 succeeded in driving out the demons, and that it was their success that encouraged the sons of Sceva to "wish to do the same" (verse 14 in Codex Bezae). Nevertheless, the reviser has retained in verse 13 the statement that the Jewish exorcists "attempted" to drive out the demons—a word which implies an unsuccessful attempt, and which makes good sense in Vaticanus, where the sons of Sceva are (or are among) the Jewish exorcists named in that verse.

Haenchen points to this detail as typical of the decisive evidence that the Western text is secondary to the Alexandrian, as the Western reviser can again and again be seen to create new problems in his attempts to eliminate unsatisfactory elements in the Alexandrian text (91, pp 178-9). Sometimes his corrections look harmless enough (or even like real improvements) in their immediate context, but in fact run counter to the theology that underlies Acts as a whole—as when he makes Peter preach the mission to Gentiles in Jerusalem shortly after the ascension (see p 3).

Of course, neither text is "original." But Haenchen thinks that, regarding Acts (he will not generalize about the New Testament as a whole) the perplexities and implausibilities of the Alexandrian text result from the original author working up his material into story form, that they are not due to corruption of an original text that gave the stories in more plausible form. On this view, then, the Alexandrian text gives in essence what the author of Acts actually wrote (91, p 205).

The examples so far considered suggest that the reviser did his work before Acts had come to be regarded as a sacred text which should not be altered. It would have taken longer for Acts than the gospels to achieve this high esteem, for the story of the spread of the church was surely less sacred than the story of its founder. Dibelius thinks that, unlike the gospels, Acts was used for regular readings in the churches only late in the second century, when all "apostolic" writings were carefully gathered together (51, p 89). It is never quoted earlier. Even books which were read at worship would have been changed in different ways in different localities, although each community would presumably have been concerned to preserve what was regarded, in that particular area, as the authentic text. But Acts would have been exposed to even greater hazards of redaction. It is, then, the more interesting that Haenchen (who after all did more than almost any other scholar to illuminate Acts) thinks that the Alexandrian text on which, in his view, the Western reviser worked is nevertheless close to the original, as the implausibilities in it can be seen to result from the author's own composition.

I turn now to the readings peculiar to Codex Bezae, a bilingual codex with Greek on each left-hand page facing Latin on the right. Each page contains a single column of text, which is divided into lines of varying length, each of which makes a complete unit of sense. Such codices were required where the original Greek was still read out at services, but where a line-by-line translation into the vernacular also needed to be read out, as Greek was hardly understood any longer in the area (see Metzger, 140, p 286). This requirement meant that the Greek and Latin texts needed to correspond closely.

Haenchen envisages a scribe who worked from an existing translation into his vernacular Latin and who sought out (in order to copy it) a Greek manuscript which already corresponded fairly closely to this Latin version. As, however, he was not very proficient in Greek, and as he was also trying to approximate the Greek to the Latin, he allowed the Latin syntax to influence the Greek he was writing in a quite untoward way. For instance, at Acts 13:28 the Western witnesses (differing here from the Alexandrian) have "they delivered him to Pilate for destruction." The Latin of Codex Bezae has, instead of the two last words: "in order that he might be destroyed." The Greek page of the Codex mixes these constructions and has: "They delivered him to Pilate in order that for destruction." The scribe has clearly taken "in order that" from the Latin page, but then — obviously following a Greek manuscript which lacked this conjunction — continued with the prepositional phrase in the Greek he was copying. Haenchen is able to give (91, pp 157–205) an impressive catalogue of such bad Greek resulting from the influence of the Latin part of the Codex, and also to show that some mistakes arose because the scribe was copying (and himself writing) an uncial hand, with no division between words and none of the accents on syllables used in cursive Greek writing.

I have said that at the beginning of this century Alexandrian readings were given preference over Western ones. Some scholars have, in recent years, tried to reverse this trend, since the Western text seems to have more Semitisms in its Greek, particularly in Acts. This, as Metzger says, may simply mean that "it was a Jewish Christian who prepared the Western text of Acts" (139, p 306). Others, however, see the Semitisms as of much greater significance. Christianity is of Jewish origin, and it is often supposed that the earliest Christian traditions would have been worded in a Semitic language (although all that has survived is in Greek or translation from Greek). In this view, a Greek text which shows traces of Semitic (particularly of Aramaic) idiom will have some claim to embody early, even authentic, tradition.

I shall reserve this question of Semitisms in the documents for more detailed discussion farther along in this book. Here I will note only that many who accord priority to the Western text naturally take their examples of Semitisms from Codex Bezae, as the principal Western witness, but they sometimes fail to distinguish between readings that are typically Western and those that are peculiar to this particular codex and explicable as scribal errors looking superficially like Aramaisms. A few examples will clarify my point.

At Acts 13:29 the Alexandrian text reads: "taking [him] down they laid [him] in a tomb." Codex Bezae has retained the participle "taking down" but follows it with an *and* as if, instead of this participle, there had been a finite verb (that is, as if the construction were: "they took him down and laid him in a tomb"). In Aramaic, a participle can in fact be followed by an *and,* which then in turn introduces a finite verb; and so the reading of Codex Bezae ("taking [him] and they laid [him] in a tomb") could be regarded as an Aramaism in the Greek. Haenchen's view, however, is that the *and* has simply been introduced from the Latin of the Codex, which has at this point two finite verbs linked by *and* (*deposuerunt et posuerunt in monumento*). We find the same at Acts 19:29 (an example which cannot possibly be understood as an Aramaism). The Alexandrian text reads: "they rushed . . . keeping a firm hold on." The Latin of Bezae has here: *impetum fecerunt* et *rapuerunt.* From this the scribe has formed, for his Greek text, the mixture: "they rushed *and* keeping a firm hold on. . . ."

Haenchen discusses and dismisses other examples of supposed Aramaisms in Acts, and concludes by noting that it is unlikely that the author of Acts (who is also, as is generally agreed, the author of *Luke*) would have tolerated Aramaisms unacceptable in good Greek when, in his *gospel,* he is concerned to improve the Greek of *Mark,* one of his sources (94, p 51). The peculiar stylistic features of the Greek text of Acts in Codex Bezae are, therefore in this view, not Aramaisms from the hand of Luke, but scribal idiosyncrasies of a late copyist.

As the Western text in general (not just the Western text of Acts) tends to be longer than other textual forms, high value was long attached to readings where this text (or at any rate some of its witnesses) is shorter. Such shorter readings occur, notably at the end of *Luke,* and have been called "Western non-interpolations," that is, they were regarded as passages where only the Western text had escaped interpolation.[3] However, now that the Bodmer papyri have shown that the longer form of these passages was already established in the second century, many scholars today regard the Western text as aberrant at these points.

A Reliable Text?

Apart from the omissions and additions of the Western text, the four textual families we possess do not differ very much, and (again apart from the Western aberrations) it would be difficult to base any doctrinal nicety on readings supported by one family against others. The ending of *Mark,* and *John*'s story of the woman taken in adultery, are among the rare instances of major deviation between manuscripts,[4] and these two passages cut across family frontiers; for the story in *John* is absent from many manuscripts which are both early and diverse, while the ending of *Mark* is not only absent from Vaticanus and Sinaiticus (the oldest Greek manuscripts of *Mark,* both witnesses of the Alexandrian text), but was also unknown to many of the Church Fathers (see Metzger, 139, pp 122-3). Both passages are also written in a style and vocabulary different from that of the gospel in which they occur.

However, although the four families are in broad agreement, none of them, not even the Alexandrian, can claim to represent the "original" text. Codex Vaticanus, for instance, is not without scribal errors and occasional attempts at harmonization (as when it introduces the wound in Jesus' side of Jn. 19:34 into Mt. 27:49). That the text we have has been manipulated is clear from such a passage as Lk. 16:16-8. Verse 16 affirms that the validity of "the law and the prophets" had lasted only until the time of John the Baptist, and verse 18 prohibits divorce, and so directly contradicts Deuteronomy 24:1-2. Between these two verses, which go consistently against Jewish religious law, verse 17 states that "it is easier for heaven and earth to pass away than for one dot of the law to become void." This was presumably interpolated by a Jewish copyist, or written originally as a marginal protest and later incorporated by an uninterested copyist. Caird, acknowledging the need for an "expedient" to overcome the contradiction, considers that the simplest one is "to regard the saying as . . . ironical" (34, p 190)! How are we to tell when Jesus is speaking ironically?

A number of the New Testament epistles were also not written as they now stand. Paul's letter to the Philippians is widely regarded as a fusion of three originally independent letters by him (see Vielhauer, 234, pp 160 ff). In 2 Corinthians, chapters 10-13 clearly belong to a different original letter from chapters 1-9, for the change in both subject matter and tone (from friendliness to hostility) at the beginning of chapter 10 is extremely abrupt (see Thrall, 201, p 5). An editor has here combined disparate material, even if he has not interfered with the original wording. 2 Cor. 6:14-7:1 may even be non-Pauline. Neither vocabulary nor style here are what one would expect of Paul, and the admonition to the faithful to avoid close contact with the corrupt pagan world—they are, for instance, not to marry unbelievers—does not fit its context (Thrall, 201, p 156). Lindemann notes (232, p 23) that this passage has been regarded as a typically Jewish piece of moralizing. And Vielhauer says that both its vocabulary and its ideas show closer affinities to Qumran texts than to Pauline letters (234, p 153).

There is some evidence that 1 Corinthians is also a fusion of originally independent Pauline letters; for here again different parts of it presuppose different situations, or different judgments of the situation on the part of Paul. Furthermore, the whole is addressed not merely to "the Church . . . at Corinth" but also to "all those who in every place call on the name of our Lord Jesus Christ" (1 Cor. 1:2). Some commentators ascribe this phrase to an editor who aimed to make all the Pauline material he has combined "ecumenically" valid (Vielhauer, 234, p 140).

From what Black and others have said (cf. p 2) about the ease with which drastic changes could have been made in the earliest period, one might expect the texts we possess to be very far from the originals. But Black himself insists that the "substance and content" of the gospels—and indeed of the New Testament books generally—did not suffer much in this way, and that the revisions were mainly minor changes of wording (18, p 280).

Surprisingly enough, there is something to justify this view. If the recent papyrus discoveries show that the big fourth-century codices are accurate copies of documents in existence by about AD 180, Justin Martyr enables us to reach a generation nearer the originals. He gives—about 150—such copious quotations from and summaries of the synoptic gospels as to allow the inference that they existed at that date in substantially their present form. (I illustrate this in JEC, pp 183-5; cf. Barnard, 6, pp 58-60). Although this still does not take us back to the earliest period of, in Black's words, a "fluid" text with different editions in different localities, the texts we do possess today can claim to be authentic in that each New Testament book can be shown to expound a distinctive theology which reflects the mind of a single writer. For instance, the nature and significance of Jesus and of his work is not the same in any two gospels. In particular, the authors of *Matthew* and *Luke* each adapt the *Gospel of Mark* differently from each other, yet in such a way as to testify to a consistent standpoint in each redactor.

There are admittedly unevennesses and contradictions within each gospel, as is inevitable in a work which draws on material of different provenance instead of making up its own story. Yet there is a clearly definable Christology in each, and this would certainly have been blurred if it had been subjected to wholesale rewriting by a number of hands. As for the New Testament letters, their substance often allows them to be assigned to different stages in the developing tradition. How, for instance, can the concern over circumcision in Paul's letter to the Galatians be anything but early, when the whole question had ceased to excite interest in the documents of the next generation? And what later Christian writer would have invented the quarrel between Peter and Paul (and even represented it as unresolved), which in this same epistle gives the occasion for Paul's statement of his theological position? (On both these matters, cf. pp 156 ff).

Nevertheless, not all theologians are willing to accept the modern printed text. O'Neill has recently argued that Paul's original letter to the Romans was much expanded to make it more suitable for general use and that the expanded text has become uniformly attested because "at various stages in the transmission powerful editors collected together as many manuscripts as possible and made a standard edition which became the one uniformly copied thereafter in that part of the Church" (152, p 14). O'Neill has similarly tried to strip Paul's letter to the Galatians of what he considers to be additions made at a later time when Christianity was more distinct from Judaism and engaged in different struggles (151).

Few will quarrel with O'Neill's statement that alterations to an original tend to be additions rather than deletions (for example, words and phrases written in the margin are later copied into the text). Such additions made in a later age will introduce the ideas of that age. But even if such changes have in fact been made in the New Testament, when one arranges its twenty-seven books in chronological sequence (admittedly a not uncontroversial undertaking!) one still finds a remarkable difference between the portrayal of Jesus in the earlier and in the later documents. On this difference the thesis of this present book is built. As later additions to the originals would tend to blur this difference, I need not fear that I am biasing the evidence in my favor by taking the critically edited text (which may include additions), as printed by, say, Westcott and Hort, Souter or Nestle, as basically reliable. In any case, we know of no earlier text. And I shall not set any passage aside as an interpolation unless I can give strong evidence for so doing. Writers denying the existence of a historical Jesus have been all too ready to remove in this way passages they find awkward. Trocmé complains, with some justice, of their "cavalier attitude to the texts" (202, p 7).

II   THE FACTUAL RELIABILITY OF THE GOSPELS

If we can accept the critically established New Testament text of today as more or less what the original authors wrote, the next question is whether they (and particularly the evangelists) give reliable facts about Jesus. To answer, we must know what type of documents the gospels are, how near in time they (or their sources, if these can be reconstructed) are to the events they purport to describe, and to what extent the statements in them are confirmed by documents written earlier or independently of them. Although such questions are, in the words of Hoskyns and Davey, "delicate and difficult," it is not reasonable to set them aside, as they do, as "ultimately irrelevant" on the ground that the New Testament "bears unmistakable witness to Jesus of Nazareth" and is "otherwise unintelligible" (103, p 204). It is the reliability of this witness to Jesus that is in question.[5]

Even today there is no universally accepted dating of the twenty-seven books of the New Testament and of other early Christian writings. Most scholars would, however, agree that the earliest of these documents are the Pauline letters and that they were written by AD 60. The gospels are usually put between 70 and 110, with *Mark* at about 70, *Matthew* and *Luke* a little later, and *John,* the latest, at about 100. Acts (written, as we shall see, by the author of *Luke*) and some of the pseudo-Pauline epistles are assigned to the turn of the century. I find all this convincing enough, except in the case of *Mark,* which I date at about 90 rather than 70, and I shall have to justify this view. But if it is correct, then all four gospels were written soon after 90 and drew some of their material from earlier documents which have not survived and from oral tradition, much of which must have been available, at any rate in some Christian communities, from about 80, although it would have taken time for them to have become generally disseminated.

What can be said about the relation between *Mark* and the other three gospels? Bruce notes that the gospels have been held to be unreliable because of what has been called their "inadmissible internal substantiation" of each other (27, p 13). He dismisses this objection to them by saying that we are not "dealing with four witnesses who had met together in advance and agreed on the story they were to tell." But what the objection really means is that *Matthew, Mark,* and *Luke* have substantial passages that are verbally identical. (For instance, 90 percent of the subject matter of *Mark* is represented in *Matthew,* largely in identical language.) The most commonly accepted explanation is that the authors of *Matthew* and *Luke* knew the *Gospel of Mark* and drew on it. Since they also completely contradict each other in some narratives they do not share with *Mark,* it is usual to suppose further that each wrote in ignorance of the other's work. In this book I shall accept both these suppositions (particularly the priority of *Mark*), although I am aware that a minority dissents from them.[6] If it is true that the *Gospels of Matthew* and *Luke* are *dependent* on *Mark,* then their accounts of events also narrated by Mark are not acceptable as *independent testimony.* Thus we have for these events not three witnesses but one. The real question then is: Did Mark obtain his information from reliable sources?

The fourth gospel has no long verbal parallels with the other three, but it nevertheless uses occasional phrases which suggest that, at certain points, it is dependent on sources strongly resembling theirs (cf. pp 125 ff).

Bruce adds that "it would be odd if anyone dismissed John Morley's *Life of Gladstone* as worthless for factual information because the author was Gladstone's friend." This comparison between Morley on Gladstone and the evangelists on Jesus would be relevant only if we could suppose that any of the evangelists had been personally acquainted with him. Such a supposition is today entertained only by the most conservative theologians. Even Dodd, whose 1971 book Bruce holds up as an example of exact scholarship which has vindicated traditional beliefs, admits to "serious difficulties" in this connection (56, p 22). If, for instance, it is asked whether *Matthew* is an eyewitness report, most theologians will at once reply (with Kümmel, 125, p 121) that its obvious use of *Mark,* a Greek gospel of a non-disciple, makes such a hypothesis "completely impossible." If critical theologians continue to use the names "Matthew," "Mark," "Luke" and "John," this is simply—as they expressly admit—because these ascriptions are well-known and therefore convenient.

The gospels are in fact anonymous. They contain no indication of authorship within their texts. (The chapter appended to *John* is, as we shall see, apparently an exception.) Their present titles ("according to Matthew," etc.) are not part of the originals; for written gospels were long alluded to and even quoted without any mention of titles, without being ascribed to named authors. Papias (bishop of Hierapolis in Asia Minor about 140) is the first to mention written gospels by name (he named *Matthew* and *Mark*); but even then these names do not seem to have been universally known or accepted, for Justin Martyr (about 150) was well acquainted with the gospels, but he does not say how many there are, nor does he name them.

Irenaeus (bishop of Lyons about 180) is the first to insist that the gospels are four in number and to name the authors of all four. Gospels and other writings used for reading in church would have been supplied with titles only when Christian communities acquired more than one gospel and needed some means of distinguishing them. For this purpose, they did not designate the documents "A" and "B," but hit upon the more homely ascriptions of "Matthew," "Mark," etc., which are now admitted to be "second-century guesses" (12, p 13). In some cases we can see that this guesswork was an attempt to harmonize dubious traditions (cf. p 146 f).

It is sometimes argued, in favor of the general reliability of the gospels, that they are full of contradictions and anomalies which no writer of fiction would have gratuitously invented. Mark, for instance, is anxious to blame the Jews for Jesus' death, yet does not make him die by sentence of a Jewish court — for example, by stoning — but at Roman hands. Why should he introduce the Romans (and so thwart his own purpose) if he were making the whole story up? The brief answer is that he was certainly not making it all up, but reworking an earlier tradition which blamed the Romans. Each Christian writer did not start with a completely clean slate, with freedom to say what he liked: he respected to some extent existing traditions. This can be seen from the way the authors of *Matthew* and *Luke* draw on *Mark*; they adapt without throwing Mark's text out completely. Mark's attitude to his sources was surely similar, so he did not drop Pilate from the Passion story but simply made him — however implausibly — do the bidding of the Jews.

Mark, then, was not an inventor but a redactor of traditions; these came to him, not in the form of an earlier gospel but as short, unconnected units from a great variety of sources, oral and written, after they had been used in the teaching and preaching of the very earliest church. The speeches of Jesus in *Mark* are sometimes simply a sequence of such independent units which the evangelist has strung together by means of what theologians call "catchword connections"; a word or phrase in one seems to have reminded the evangelist of a similar word or phrase in another independent saying. For instance, after "the fire is not quenched in hell," there follows: "For everyone will be salted with fire" (9:48–9). Having thus moved from fire to salt, the evangelist makes Jesus add two pronouncements on it: "Salt is good, but if the salt has lost its salt-ness, how will you season it? Have salt in yourselves, and be at peace with one another." It is, says Stanton, an "assured result" of New Testament studies that "the gospel traditions in *Mark* are like pearls on a string" (187, p 14).

Some of the sayings Mark ascribes to Jesus were obviously never spoken by a historical Jesus, but were concocted in a Christian community remote in place and time from the Palestine of AD 30. For instance, in Mk. 10:12 Jesus rules that if a woman divorces her husband and marries another, she commits adultery. Such an utterance would have been meaningless in Palestine, where only men could obtain divorce. It is a ruling for the Gentile Christian readers of *Mark,* which the evangelist put into Jesus' mouth in order to give it authority. This tendency to anchor later customs and institutions to Jesus' supposed lifetime played a considerable role in the building up of his biography.

Another instance where what Jesus allegedly says in *Mark* is obviously not authentic is the passage (7:1-23), where he bases an argument against the Pharisees on the Septuagint, the Greek translation of the Old Testament, where the Hebrew original says something different that would not have supported his case (see Nineham's admission, 148, p 189). That a Palestinian Jesus should floor orthodox Jews with an argument based on a mistranslation of their scriptures is very unlikely.

The whole incident is, however, perfectly intelligible if we suppose that it was drawn up in Mark's Gentile Christian community, which naturally read the Old Testament in the Greek version and ascribed to Jesus its own understanding of these scriptures. The Christians for whom Mark wrote were so remote from Jewish ideas that he has laboriously to explain Jewish practices, as when he states that "the Pharisees and all the Jews never eat without washing their hands . . . . And there are many other traditions which they observe" (7:3-4). Such a passage, incidentally, betrays that, in Mark's day, the freedom of Gentile Christian communities from the Jewish law was taken for granted, and therefore that he wrote considerably later than Paul, for whom this matter was still a burning issue.

Some who assert the reliability of the first-century oral tradition on which Mark drew point to the work of Riesenfeld (159) and Gerhardsson (77), who have contended that Jesus made his disciples memorize his teaching, as the rabbis did with their pupils. This view has, however, been severely criticized. Abel (1) says that it may be "dismissed outright" because a rigidly controlled school of oral transmission could not have produced the inconsistencies and contradictions which are so prominent in the gospels. And Anderson (one of the most recent commentators on *Mark*) asks: "if the words of Jesus were transmitted in such a closed and deterministic fashion, why should there be so many variant reports of single sayings of Jesus in the gospels?" He gives, as an example, Mk. 10:18 and its equivalent in Mt. 19:17. In *Mark* Jesus says: "Why do you call me good? No one is good but God alone. You know the commandments." In *Matthew* this is reformulated as: "Why do you ask me about what is good? One there is who is good. If you would enter life, keep the commandments." The earliest Christians believed that they were prompted by the spirit to state doctrines of Jesus (see p 30), and "the freedom they enjoyed under the promptings of the spirit would have tended less to the preservation of a static 'holy word' than to flexibility and the readiness to adapt the traditions in the face of ever-changing needs and challenges" (Anderson, 2, pp 18-9).

Diversity would also result from the early-Christian tendency to think of Jesus as having said and done what a great variety of Old Testament passages supposedly said the Messiah would do (see Davies' criticism of Riesenfeld and Gerhardsson, 50, p 477). There is also no indication in the texts that Jesus required his disciples to learn his teaching by heart. The gospels allege, on the contrary, that he did not follow traditional Jewish teaching methods. ("They were astonished at his teaching, for he taught them as one who had authority, and not as the scribes," Mk. 1:22.)

Mark, then, took units of tradition and made of them a connected story. Their historical authenticity is questionable not only for reasons already adumbrated but also because they are generally unmentioned by earlier Christian writers. I shall show in chapters 1 and 2 that extant Christian documents that can be dated plausibly before about 90 do not confirm the portrait of Jesus given in *Mark* and in the gospels generally, and that this portrait is current only from about that date. The earlier relevant literature is, as we shall see, substantial and does not consist only of the Pauline letters.

Almost everyone thinks that the gospels do at least establish that Jesus was crucified under Pilate, was probably arraigned by the Sanhedrin before being passed on to him and therefore lived in first-century Palestine. These are taken as irrefragable facts after criticism has done its worst with the remaining traditions. But the gospel accounts of Jesus' trial present serious historical difficulties. Reasons for doubting the historicity of what Mark says about his appearance before the Sanhedrin have been summarized by Nineham (148, pp 400 ff), and Catchpole has stated the objections made by Jewish scholars since the eighteenth century. He, however, thinks that few of these objections apply to the parallel account in Lk. 22:66-71, which he regards as independent of *Mark* and drawn from an ancient and reliable source (37, pp 153, 203). Many, however think that Luke's version avoids most of the Marcan implausibilities simply because it abbreviates and simplifies Mark's narrative.[7] One verse (Lk. 22:69) looks very much like a toning-down of Mark's implication that Jesus' second coming is imminent (a revision which, we shall see, would accord with Luke's overall theology). Catchpole agrees that this verse in *Luke* is secondary to *Mark*. To avoid accepting the whole narrative in which it occurs as likewise secondary, he has to regard the verse as an interpolation into the Lucan original (37, pp 154, 157).

Even so, all the difficulties do not disappear from *Luke,* and Catchpole concedes that Luke, no more than Mark, supplies an "eye-witness source" (p 155) to form a basis for a Christian record of the Sanhedrin trial (the only persons alleged to have been present being Jesus and his Jewish accusers). This surely means that what Christians came to believe on the matter was the product of their own reflections. Since they were convinced that Jesus was the Messiah, they readily imagined that the Jews, whom they knew did not accept him as such, had condemned him for Messianic claims; therefore they constructed an imaginary trial scene in which the Jews ask him about his Messianic status and condemn him for the claims he makes in reply (Mk. 14:61-4).

The gospel accounts of the trial before Pilate are likewise full of historical difficulties (see DJE, pp 63-5; JEC, pp 98-100). Evans' view is that "almost all the main factors" in the Passion story "have become problematical" (64, p 28). And Conzelmann finds that the Passion narratives altogether are shaped by the evangelists' own theological convictions; they are the result of "intense theological interpretation" which, he justly adds in a note, is apt to be overlooked by non-theological commentators, who take as historical fact what in fact owes its existence to theological motive (42, pp 37-8).[8]

Conservative theologians have recently written much in defense of the "reliability" of the gospels, but their more critical colleagues admit them to be, in many respects, purposeful fiction. Professor Enslin has argued that their accounts of Jesus' relations with John the Baptist are "Christian constructions," and that the two men in fact never met (60). Professor Conzelmann, whose criticism of the Passion narratives I have just recorded, thinks that they establish only the bare fact that Jesus was crucified: "Everything else about the sequence of events is contestible" (42, pp 37-8). Professor Evans finds that the undoubted contradictions between the resurrection narratives are not merely what is to be expected from genuine accounts of so bewildering an event but are there because each evangelist is grinding an axe of his own: "It is not natural confusion but rather the lack of it, and the influence of rational reflection and apologetic, which have given rise to the contradictions" (62, pp 128-9).

Some theologians have expressed fear lest critical study of this kind will dissolve the documents entirely into myth. The late Professor Werner, for instance, noted that, although Jesus' historicity is not now disputed to the extent that it was at the beginning of this century, anyone who wished to reopen that particular question could find from contemporary theologians plenty of material to support a negative view (211, p 237). And so there is.

III   PAGAN EVIDENCE ABOUT JESUS

No theory of Christian origins explains every item in the evidence; a residue of perplexities always remains. John Whale (reviewing DJE) thinks that, in denying Jesus' historicity, I have "more to explain away" than if I accepted it; that, for instance, my view does not account for "the silence of early anti-Christians who ought to have rumbled the fraud" (212). But I did deal with this matter, saying (DJE, p 15):

> Today Christianity has been so important for so long that one is apt to assume that it must have appeared important to educated pagans who lived AD 50-150;

and that if they fail to discuss Jesus' historicity or the pretensions of his worshippers, their silence must be attributed to their consciousness that they were unable to deny the truth of the Christian case. In fact, however, there is no reason why the pagan writers of this period should have thought Christianity any more important than other enthusiastic religions of the Empire. Dio Cassius, who wrote a history of the realm as late as about AD 229, makes no mention at all of Christians or of Christianity, and alludes but once to its then great rival, Mithraism. Because Christianity so long remained insignificant, except among the lower classes, its major pagan critics — Lucian (died about 200), Celsus, Porphyry (died 303), and the Emperor Julian (died 363) — all wrote long after the gospels had become established and gathered from these gospels that Jesus was a teacher and wonder-worker of a kind perfectly familiar to them. As they could thus assign him to a familiar category, they had no reason to doubt his historicity.

A more common complaint against my position is that I fail to "explain away" not pagan silence, but pagan reference to Christianity. Martin (135), for instance, mentions Pliny, Suetonius and Tacitus as "considerable hurdles" against the view that Jesus originated in legend. In fact Pliny's testimony has no bearing on Jesus' existence, and consists of a report to Trajan (AD 112) that Christians appear to be harmless people who meet at daybreak and sing hymns to the honor of the Messiah as to a god (*Christo quasi deo*). No one doubts that by 112 Christians worshipped Christ and that Pliny's statements reproduce Christian beliefs. Suetonius merely mentioned an agitator who caused disturbances in the ghetto at Rome by coming forward as the Messiah (see JEC, pp 185-6).

It is Tacitus to whom appeal is still most commonly made. He wrote (about 120) that "Christians derive their name and origin from Christ, who was executed by sentence of the procurator Pontius Pilate in the reign of Tiberius" (*Annals,* 15:44). Bouquet writes in this connection of an "undisputed record" of Jesus' execution under Pilate, and points for corroboration to the gospels, all of which made this execution their "culminating point." "No one," he adds, "can doubt when reading them that they contain vivid pictures of a real human being" (22, p 73). In fact he knows full well that many have doubted this; and the reality of the hero of the gospel story is not to be settled by aesthetic criteria such as vividness of portrayal, since much fiction is vivid.

I am surprised that appeal is still made so often to this passage in Tacitus, which everybody dates later than the gospels and which therefore was written at a time when Christians themselves had come to believe that Jesus had suffered under Pilate. There are three reasons for holding that Tacitus is here simply repeating what Christians had told him. First, he gives Pilate a title, procurator, which was current only from the *second* half of the first century. Had he consulted archives which recorded earlier events, he would surely have found Pilate there designated by his correct title, prefect. Second, Tacitus does not name the executed man as Jesus, but uses the title Christ (Messiah) as if it were a proper name. But he could hardly have found in archives a statement such as "the Messiah was executed this morning." Third, hostile to Christianity as he was, he was surely glad to accept from Christians their own view that Christianity was of recent origin, since the Roman authorities were prepared to tolerate only ancient cults (see Frend, 71, p 111). None of these facts is as much as mentioned by a recent conservative apologist, who confidently decides that, "from the contemptuous and hostile tone which Tacitus adopts towards the Christians, we may gather that he did not seek his information from them" (Bruce, 27, p 23).

Tacitus, as governor of the province of Asia (modern western Turkey) about AD 112, may well have had the same kind of trouble with Christianity that Pliny experienced as governor of nearby Bithynia at that very time. Hengel has recently noted that "Tacitus' precise knowledge of Christians and his contempt for them are probably to be derived from the trials of Christians which he carried out when he was governor in the province of Asia" (99, p 3). To decide from his "hostile tone" that his information does not derive from Christians, is entirely unwarranted.

The context of Tacitus' remarks itself suggests that he relied on Christian informants. He is writing about the burning of Rome in Nero's time and the belief that the fire had been started by order of the Emperor himself. "To scotch this rumor," says Tacitus, "Nero substituted as culprits, and punished with the utmost refinements of cruelty, a class of men loathed for their views, whom the crowd styled Christians." It is here that he adds that "Christus, the founder of the name," had been executed under Pilate. Already in the eighteenth century, Dupuis noted that it is probable from the context that Tacitus' interest in the matter went no further than the desire to give his readers some idea of who these Christians were, and that for this end it was sufficient to repeat what was being said by Christians (and others) in the Rome of his own day, nearly a hundred years after the supposed date of the crucifixion (57, pp 441–2). Supposing, Dupuis adds, a French historian had occasion to mention an Indian sect that had established itself in France, and had said that they were called Brahmins, after a certain Brahma who had lived in India. This would clearly not establish that any such person had in fact existed.

Theologians have repeatedly conceded all this. Johannes Weiss, who early in the twentieth century treated with derision the view that Jesus never existed, nevertheless agreed that Tacitus' account can convince only those who already believe, on independent evidence, that there was a historical Jesus (205, p 88). Schweitzer admitted that Tacitus' reference to the crucifixion under Pilate at best establishes that the church of the early second century believed in that event (see p 201). Nevertheless, many theologians of today will not have Tacitus' remarks set aside in this way. Robinson, for instance, says apropos of my views on the passage (as expressed in DJE): "By such methods any evidence can be dissolved" (165, p 449). Such a dismissive generalization hardly contributes to his aim of "exposing as bad history" my view that Jesus did not exist (166).

Thallus is also sometimes cited as a pagan witness to Jesus. Bruce describes him as writing "about AD 52," probably with knowledge of "the Christian narrative of the crucifixion." The note Bruce adds (p 30) gives the impression that it is only minor matters — for example, whether Thallus was a Samaritan and a freedman — and not this dating of AD 52 that are questionable inferences rather than established facts. I discussed Thallus in DJE and will not repeat myself, beyond saying that he probably wrote late in the first or early in the second century, and may not have mentioned Jesus at all. To use him as evidence that a Christian Passion narrative existed as early as AD 52 is fantastic.

In the following chapters I shall discuss only Christian evidence for the Jesus of history, since to my mind there is no worthwhile non-Christian evidence. This has repeatedly been conceded: by Schweitzer and, most recently, by Davies (49, p 36) in his comments on DJE, where I discuss the relevant pagan and Jewish material. Jewish traditions, though rich and detailed, contain — like the pagan ones — no independent reference to a historical Jesus, though Jews in the second century adopted uncritically the Christian assumption that he had really lived.

The two references to Jesus in *The Antiquities of the Jews* (AD 93) by the Jewish historian Josephus are, as has been widely admitted, interpolations. In fact no one can accept the longer of these two references (a glowing paragraph about Jesus) as being from the hand of this orthodox Jew, and it has to be regarded as at best a Christian reworking of a passage originally hostile to Jesus. But, as I have shown in DJE (p 10), the paragraph is intrusive in the context in which it has been placed, and, for this and other reasons, it must be an interpolation. Josephus' other, briefer reference to Jesus, although often impugned (see DJE, p 11) is still defended by some scholars (sometimes on obviously inadequate grounds, as I shall show, p 211). But it too is set aside as being interpolated, by L. Herrmann, whose *Chrestos. Témoignages païens et juifs sur le christianisme du premier siècle* (Brussels, 1970) is a thorough investigation.

1

Paul

I THE GENUINE PAULINES

Paul's letters are pastoral instruments of his mission to Christianize Gentiles in Asia Minor and further west. A considerable part of them consists in efforts to maintain the churches addressed, in what he considers to be the beliefs of the true faith. This, in barest outline, is that, when the time was ripe, God had sent his own son, Jesus, into the world to redeem mankind (Gal. 4:4–5) by atoning with his blood for man's sins. Sinful man has no claim on God's mercy and cannot earn salvation by pure living; man can only accept, as a gift of God's grace, the redemption which Jesus has wrought (Rom. 3:24–5). Hence, keeping the Jewish law is not a means to salvation and is no longer necessary to it. Faith in Jesus is the only requirement (Rom. 10:4). All with such faith live an entirely new existence (2 Cor. 5:17) and have been crucified with Christ to the world (Gal. 6:14). The day when Jesus will return to earth and when the dead will rise is near at hand, and believers have already received the gift of the spirit as a sign that this is so (Rom. 8:23; 2 Cor. 1:22; Gal. 4:6).

Obviously Paul's hostility to the Jewish law was controversial for a religion that accepted much from Judaism; and his view of the efficacy of the spirit in Christian living led some of his converts into all manner of spirit-inspired excesses. But, in the main, the kinds of deviation from the true faith that his letters controvert have to be inferred from such hints as they give, and "interpretation may depend upon the ability to identify his opponents, and to detect how far the controversy arose from their understanding of what he had previously said and from his belief that they had misunderstood it" (Evans, 63, p 239). When, for instance, we try to discover what he disapproved of in Christianity at Corinth, we find that "among the verses in 1 and 2 Corinthians of crucial importance, there is scarcely one of which the interpretation is not disputed" (Barrett, 7, p 270).

The modern European is familiar enough with the story (at any rate in outline) told in the gospels and in Acts. But he is bewildered when he turns from these to Paul's epistles and wonders how such turgid documents have come to constitute a quarter of the whole canon, even why they were admitted into it at all. One reason for their prominence is that they were not mere private correspondence but were meant to be read as doctrinal instruction at the assembly of a Christian community—as is clear from the exhortation (1 Thess. 5:27) to "have this letter read to all the brethren." At the end of the letter to the Colossians, the recipients are urged not only to have it read among them but also to see that it is read in a neighboring Christian church, which itself has a letter (presumably from Paul), which the Colossian church is to read. Conzelmann comments that such hints concerning the distribution of Paul's letters indicate on what basis they came to be collected (44, p 202).

The oldest extant manuscripts of these letters give them as a collection, but date only from the late second and early third centuries, when the Pauline corpus had long been established. Before Marcion issued his collection of ten Paulines in Rome about 140, smaller collections may well have been available in some of the areas where Paul had worked, though not in all of them, for some did not esteem his letters and had, as Bauer has shown (11, pp 213 ff), shaken off his influence. Polycarp and the author of 2 Peter (both writing in the first half of the second century) knew a number of Paulines (if not a comprehensive collection), as did also Ignatius, writing perhaps as early as 110. Clement of Rome knew (about 90) at least Romans and 1 Corinthians; and at about the same date the author of the letter to the Ephesians knew at least 1 Corinthians. It has been argued that he knew other Paulines too, but Lindemann, who has recently made a thorough study of Paul in the ancient church, thinks that this cannot be proved (232, p 129).

Earlier documents (Hebrews, 1 Peter) cannot be proved dependent on any Pauline letter, although Pauline theology was not completely forgotten until 90, and some elements of it had passed into the intellectual background against which both Hebrews and 1 Peter were written (see pp 59, 64). The canonical collection of letters ascribed to Paul arranges those addressed to churches, not chronologically (in what order they were written is very difficult to determine) but according to length, with the longest first. The four addressed to individuals are placed last.

The lay reader not only finds these epistles almost unintelligible; it comes as something of a shock to learn that they were written earlier than the gospels (and therefore provide more important clues as to how the earliest Christians regarded Jesus), even though they deal with a *later* period (after AD 30) than the gospels purport to portray and even though they are printed in Bibles after the gospels. External evidence confirms that they existed well before the gospels. Gospels were known and quoted by the middle of the second century, the Pauline letters much earlier.

The New Testament includes thirteen letters which name Paul as author, but some of these must be set aside as the work of later writers adopting his name and authority. However, the first four in the canon—the letter to the Romans, the two to the Corinthians and the one to the Galatians—are universally accepted as genuinely Pauline. The computer techniques tried on them by Morton and McLeman (145, pp 93–4) have confirmed that this substantial body of literature (longer than the remaining nine letters taken together) has a common author. Internal evidence indicates that this author wrote before 70, for his references to his contacts with a Christian community at Jerusalem show that the catastrophic destruction of that city in the Jewish War with Rome had not yet occurred. Indeed, he must have been a Christian before 40, for he tells that King Aretas of the Nabateans, who is known to have died in that year, had at one time sought to have him arrested because of his Christian activities (2 Cor. 11:32). He probably wrote nearer 60 than 40, for he tells the Galatians that he had been a Christian for at least fourteen years at the time of writing (cf. p 156) and the Roman Christians that he had already completed a very substantial missionary program (Rom. 15:19).

Of the remaining nine letters attributed to Paul in the canon, three are very probably by him: namely, that to the Philippians, the first of the two to the Thessalonians, and the brief note to Philemon, the master of a runaway slave. (Paul had become friendly with the slave, and urges the master to take him back without penalty). In the case of 1 Thessalonians one indication of genuineness is that the author writes of "we who are left alive" at Jesus' second coming (4:15) and thereby implies that he expects to be living when it occurs. A writer of a later age posing as Paul would surely have avoided committing himself to this position, which had proved to be false, and could easily have done so by putting "those who are left alive." But I need not argue the case for the Pauline authorship of these three letters. The reader will expect me rather to give reasons why I treat a canonical document ascribed to Paul as post-Pauline. This I shall do in the case of 2 Thessalonians, Ephesians, and the three Pastorals.

This leaves the letter to the Colossians. Recently an increasing number of scholars have argued that it was written by a pupil of Paul, not by the apostle himself (Bornkamm, 21, p 242 and Lindemann, 232, p 120). Conzelmann (44, pp 176–7) summarizes un-Pauline features in the style of the letter, and he and other commentators argue that its author has modified the ideas expressed in Rom. 6:3–5 so as to suggest that Christians have already entered upon a kind of resurrection life. Paul had said there that they *have been* buried with Christ in baptism and *will be* united with him in a resurrection like his. But in Coloss. 2:12 the past tense is used for both statements: "You *were* buried with him in baptism, in which you *were* also raised with him through faith in the working of God, who raised him from the dead." The writer does admittedly go on (in 3:3–4) to affirm the more Pauline view that "you have died and your life is hid with Christ in God," and that only at Christ's second coming "will you appear with him in glory." Commentators who take the epistle as being genuinely one of Paul's explain 2:12 as his accommodation to the gnostic views combatted there.

Colossians may well be pseudonymous, but it is nevertheless very close to Paul's thinking. (This, as we shall see, is not the case with 2 Thessalonians and the Pastorals.) Unlike Ephesians and the Pastorals it is a real letter (not a homily masquerading as a letter), composed to deal with theological problems that had arisen among the Christians at Colossae. It was presumably written, if not by Paul, then by a pupil very soon after his time. I shall therefore treat it as genuinely Pauline.

II PAUL'S FAILURE TO CORROBORATE THE GOSPELS

The eight Pauline letters I have accepted as genuine are so completely silent concerning the events that were later recorded in the gospels as to suggest that these events were not known to Paul, who, however, could not have been ignorant of them if they had really occurred.

These letters have no allusion to the parents of Jesus, let alone to the virgin birth. They never refer to a place of birth (for example, by calling him "of Nazareth"). They give no indication of the time or place of his earthly existence. They do not refer to his trial before a Roman official, nor to Jerusalem as the place of execution. They mention neither John the Baptist, nor Judas, nor Peter's denial of his master. (They do, of course, mention Peter, but do not imply that he, any more than Paul himself, had known Jesus while he had been alive.)

The failure to mention Peter's denial of Christ is highly significant. Paul's letter to the Galatians reveals that his position as leader of the Christian community at Antioch was threatened by Cephas, whom he also calls Peter (Gal. 2:7–8).[1] He calls him a hypocrite (Gal. 2:11–4), but does not allege against him anything as discreditable as his denial of his master (as recorded of Peter in Mk. 14:30 and parallels). Paul's silence is rightly taken by Enslin (59, p 130) as decisive evidence that this gospel story is a fiction, and its historicity has also recently been challenged on other grounds.[2]

These letters also fail to mention any miracles Jesus is supposed to have worked, a particularly striking omission, since, according to the gospels, he worked so many. Paul indicates that miracles may be expected wherever the Christian mission goes, for he includes the working of them among the "gifts of the spirit" and says God has appointed "miracle workers" within the community (1 Cor. 12:10 and 28). He claims to have himself won converts "by the power of signs and wonders" (Rom. 15:19), and among the "signs of the true apostle" he lists "signs and wonders and mighty works" (2 Cor. 12:12), which presumably include miraculous cures effected by casting out demons or unclean spirits. But he never suggests that Jesus effected such practices or worked miracles of any kind.

Like Paul, other early Christian writers also refer to the "power" of Christian preachers to effect "signs and wonders." The author of Hebrews declares (2:4) that God bore witness to these preachers "by signs and wonders and various miracles"; and the author of 2 Thessalonians speaks (2:9) of counter-demonstrations (inspired by Satan), with "all power and pretended signs and wonders." "Signs, wonders and powers" was obviously, as Käsemann notes (114, p 61), a standing phrase in these early days. It is the more significant that, only when we come to Acts, a later work, do we find this standing phrase applied to Jesus (not just to Christian missionaries), in Peter's description of him as "a man attested to you by God with mighty works [literally, 'with powers'] and wonders and signs" (Acts 2:22).

Another striking feature of Paul's letters is that one could never gather from them that Jesus had been an ethical teacher. Paul is not indifferent to ethical problems; on the contrary, his epistles abound in ethical admonition. But on only one occasion does he appeal to the authority of Jesus to support an ethical teaching which the gospels also represent Jesus as having delivered; and in this instance it is not necessary to suppose that Paul believed that the doctrine in question had been taught by the historical (as opposed to the risen) Jesus. The relevant passages are:

1 Cor. 7:10	*Mk. 10:11-2*
To the married I give charge, not I but the Lord, that the wife should not separate from the husband (but if she does, let her remain single or else be reconciled to her husband)—and that the husband should not divorce his wife.	Whoever divorces his wife and marries another commits adultery against her; and if she divorces her husband and marries another, she commits adultery.

We have seen (p 13) that Jesus could not, as Mark alleges, have told a Palestinian audience that a wife should not seek divorce, since in Palestine only men were allowed to do so. But Paul could appropriately urge such a ruling on the Gentile Christian communities to which he appealed; and if he told them it was Jesus' teaching, he would have meant (as many commentators admit) not a teaching of a Palestinian Jesus but a directive given by some Christian prophet speaking in the name of the risen one. (On the utterances of such prophets in the name of "the Lord," see p 30). This would have been the obvious way of supporting a ruling on divorce which the Christians of Paul's day were anxious to inculcate. At a later stage it would naturally have been supposed that Jesus must have said during his lifetime what it was believed the risen one had said through Christian prophets; and so the doctrine was, however inappropriately, put into his mouth as an address to a Palestinian audience by Mark.

Occasions when Paul appeals to a "word of the Lord" at all (whether on ethical or other matters) are rare, as I shall later show. I shall also show (p 33) how considerable is the quantity of ethical teaching that Paul gives in his own name, with no suggestion that Jesus had taught anything of the kind, even though the gospels put exactly the same doctrines into Jesus' mouth.

Most of the Pauline passages which theologians have adduced as implying that Paul did not know, of course, the gospels, but rather knew certain traditions about Jesus recorded in them, are obviously not to the point (as I showed in DJE, pp 22 f, 98-9). It is occasionally still alleged (for example, by Morton Smith, 184, p 3) that 2 Cor. 5:16 gives some basis for thinking that Paul knew Jesus during the latter's lifetime. What Paul there says is (in literal translation): "From now on we know no man according to flesh; if indeed we have known Christ according to flesh, we no longer know him (so)." If "knowing according to flesh" means personal acquaintance, then Paul is here saying that he now has no personal acquaintances at all ("We know no man according to flesh")! Commentators have pointed out that it is quite unnecessary to impute such an absurdity to him, and that "knowing Christ according to flesh" means having an "unspiritual" conception of him. (See, for instance, Robinson, 163, pp 23-4.)

Much more common is the claim that, precisely because Paul never met Jesus before the crucifixion, his references to those who were apostles before him (Gal. 1:17) and who claimed superiority over him are understandable only if we suppose that, unlike him, they had been personally acquainted with the historical Jesus (see, for example, O'Neill, 153). Paul himself, however, intimates that the very lateness of his own conversion, plus his black record as persecutor of the church, are the real reasons why others thought themselves superior; for he says: "I am the least of the apostles, unfit to be called an apostle, because I persecuted the Church of God" (1 Cor. 15:9). In spite of this remorse, he would not accept their claim to superiority, and insisted that as an apostle called by the Lord (1 Cor. 9:1) he is their equal.

Sometimes the statement of 1 Thess. 2:14-5, that Jesus was "killed by the Jews," is taken as implying that Paul knew more about the Passion than his other references to it might suggest. However, this passage was set aside, as an interpolation after AD 70, by a number of nineteenth-century scholars, and Pearson has said (154, pp 80-1) that most twentieth-century commentators refuse to follow them here only because they are overreacting to an earlier undue readiness to solve problems by resort to interpolation hypotheses. Let us study the evidence.

When Paul elsewhere refers to Jesus' death, he says repeatedly that he was "crucified" or "delivered up," never that he was "killed"; whereas the allegation that he was "killed by the Jews" is common in the gospels and Acts, which of course embody Christian traditions which developed later than Paul (see Friedrich, 72, pp 226-7, with references to gospels and Acts). Of more account is that the hostility to the Jews displayed at 1 Thess. 2:14-5 is very untypical of Paul. Grayston, who thinks the passage may be genuinely Pauline, never-theless notes (88, p 72) that other references to the Jews in the Pauline letters almost always contrast them with the Gentiles, and do not make them merely the opponents of Christians. (This latter attitude to the Jews typifies not the Pauline letters but the *Gospel of John,* where the term "the Jews," rare in the synoptics, is used some sixty times to designate Jesus' enemies.)

Furthermore, the passage in 1 Thessalonians also implies that, because the Jews killed Jesus and hinder the Christian mission to the Gentiles, God had finally and irrevocably rejected them. This conflicts with the genuine Pauline teaching of Rom. 9–11, according to which "God has not rejected the people which he acknowledged of old as his own" (Rom. 11:2 NEB), and will "save all Israel" (verses 25–6) in the fullness of time. The exact wording of 1 Thess. 2:16 is that "retribution" has overtaken the Jews "for good and all" (or "at last"). This statement, in a context where the writer betrays himself as concerned to win Gentiles to Christianity, surely alludes to some events that were of sufficient magnitude to be known internationally; and the obvious ones which would exemplify disaster to the Jews "for good and all" would be the desolation of their country by Roman forces in the war that began in AD 66 and culminated in the destruction of Jerusalem in 70. As the epistle is genuinely Pauline, and so of earlier date, this particular passage must then be a later interpolation.[3] There is ample evidence (given by Pearson, 154, p 84) that Christians after 70 interpreted the destruction of Jerusalem as a punishment inflicted by God upon the Jews for killing the Christ.

Let us next study the context of the passage. The whole letter begins (after initial greetings) with a thanksgiving ("we give thanks to God always for you all, constantly mentioning you in our prayers"), which is followed (up to 2:12) by Paul's reminiscences of his former relations with the Thessalonian church. The natural continuation after 2:12 comes only with 2:17, where Paul is again speak-ing of his dealings with that church, so that verses 13 through 16 are easily detachable from the context in which they have been placed. Moreover, verse 13 introduces a new thanksgiving (additional to that of chapter 1), in part with identical words and phrases as were used in the earlier one. Boers notes that verse 13 should be translated as: "And for the following (reason) we also give thanks to God unceasingly. . . ." This suggests that an interpolator is trying—by means of a thanksgiving parallel to Paul's own earlier in the letter—to introduce the anti-Jewish polemic that follows in verses 14–6 (Boers, 20, pp 151–2), where the Jews are charged not only with killing Jesus, but with "opposing all men." Pearson has noted that "it is somewhat surprising to find the characteristic Gen-tile charge of 'misanthropy' against the Jews reflected in the Pauline corre-spondence, although it is widespread in the Graeco-Roman world of the period" (154, p 83).

All this amounts to as strong a case as one can expect the evidence to pro-vide for regarding verses 13–6 as interpolated.

III   JESUS' EUCHARISTIC WORDS

There are three Pauline passages which seem to imply that Paul knew more of Jesus than I think is the case:

(1) Paul once mentions (1 Cor. 15:5) a Christian group called "the twelve" (contemporary with himself) and it is usually assumed that he is here referring to those who, according to the gospels, accompanied Jesus during his earthly ministry. This would make him and Jesus contemporaries. In DJE (ch. 5) I showed that this passage can be (and by some theologians is) understood quite differently.

(2) Paul refers to James, the leader of the Jerusalem Christians, in a way that seems to imply that Jesus and James were brothers and therefore that Paul and Jesus were contemporaries. I shall discuss this matter fully in ch. 8.

(3) Paul once reports, as a saying of Jesus, words similar to those which, in the synoptics, are represented as instituting the Lord's Supper or Eucharist. The RSV represents Paul as telling the Corinthians that Jesus spoke these words "on the night when he was betrayed." Before we study Jesus' eucharistic words (quoted in full on pp 27-8), let us consider the implications of this word *betrayed.*

The Greek does not have *betrayed* but *delivered up,* and there is no reference to an arrest or betrayal in a particular and known historical situation. Jesus is simply said to have been, like the suffering servant of Yahweh in Isaiah, delivered up for our sins. When at Rom. 4:25 Paul again states that he "was delivered to death for our misdeeds," he is surely alluding to this servant of Yahweh who "bore the sins of the many and was delivered because of their iniquities" (Isaiah 53:2, Septuagint). At Rom. 8:32 Jesus is again said to have been "delivered for us all," and at Gal. 2:20 we learn that he "delivered himself for me." (In all these cases I have given a literal rendering of the Greek). Cranfield notes (46, p 251) that Paul's words are "clearly based" on Isaiah and that not only is the word *delivered* significant in this connection but its use with other phrases occurring in the narrative of the suffering servant (Isaiah 52:13- 53:12, cf. DJE, pp 25-6) is also significant. Lindars suggests (128, p 240) that Paul's love of the Psalter led him to correlate Psalm 44:22 ("For thy sake . . . we were accounted as sheep for the slaughter," quoted at Rom. 8:36) with the depiction of the servant as a lamb led to the slaughter (Isaiah 53:7).

For the earliest Christians, Jesus was "delivered up" because this was part of God's plan to save mankind. Not until the gospels is the "delivering" given a historical context. Judas is said to have "delivered" him to the representatives of the chief priests; the latter "delivered" him to Pilate, who in turn "delivered" him to soldiers for execution. The gospels have made the "delivering up" into a series of precisely specified historical situations; and the RSV has allowed what the gospels say about Judas' betrayal to influence its rendering of Paul's statement.

The gospel story of Judas' betrayal is certainly fiction. Standard Christian works of reference admit that what he betrayed and why he betrayed are insoluble problems. Far from being too unedifying to be a Christian invention, the incident is typical of the type of fiction where a superlatively great hero is betrayed by a false friend, as with King Arthur, Roland, Siegfried, and many others. (On Judas, see DJE, pp 132–40).

Moreover, Paul gives his whole account of the origin of the Eucharist by way of criticizing the kind of Eucharist that was being practiced by Christians at Corinth, where, he says elsewhere (2 Cor. 11:4), Christian teachers were rivaling him by preaching "another Jesus" (cf. DJE, pp 99–101). In placing the origin of the Eucharist on the night when Jesus was delivered up, he clearly means to link it with his death, while the Corinthian Eucharist he is criticizing is likely to have linked it with his resurrection and to have celebrated not his death but his presence in all his power (see DJE, p 186). The Corinthian Christians would have believed that, through participation with the risen Christ in the sacrament, they were themselves made powerful and translated to a sphere higher than that of earthly things—to the realm of the redeemer.

Paul, however, acknowledged (as we shall see) only shame, humiliation, and pain in Jesus' earthly life and thought that these qualities ought to be reflected in the lives of Christians. His theology is in this sense a theology of the cross, and he goes on to say, in this same context where he gives Jesus' eucharistic words: "As often as you eat this bread and drink the cup, you proclaim the Lord's *death* until he comes." Bornkamm comments that "Paul's treatment of the Lord's Supper is a piece of actualised theology of the cross" (21, p 193). In sum, Paul's statement that the Eucharist originated on the night when Jesus was delivered up is not historical reminiscence but an attempt to discredit a rival interpretation of eucharistic efficacy.[4]

Let us now study the whole of what Paul says of Jesus' eucharistic words, and also the oldest synoptic account of them. I quote the RSV, and have italicized some of the words given by Paul but absent from *Mark*:

1 Cor. 11:23–6

23. For I received from the Lord what I also delivered to you, that the Lord Jesus on the night when he was betrayed took bread,

24. and when he had given thanks, he broke it, and said, "This is my body *which is for you. Do this in remembrance of me."*

25. In the same way also the cup, after supper, saying, "This cup is the *new* covenant in my blood. *Do this, as often as you drink it, in remembrance of me.*

Mk. 14:22–5

22. And as they were eating, he took bread, and blessed, and broke it, and gave it to them, and said, "Take; this is my body."

23. And he took a cup, and when he had given thanks he gave it to them, and they all drank of it.

24. And he said to them, "This is my blood of the covenant, which is poured out for many.

26. *For as often as you eat this*   25. Truly, I say to you, I shall not
bread and drink the cup, you proclaim   drink again of the fruit of the vine until
the Lord's death until he comes."   that day when I drink it new in the
                                        kingdom of God."

Mark has manipulated the whole of Jesus' eucharistic words, as given by
Paul, so as to bind them to a definite historical situation. (I am not saying that
Mark had read 1 Corinthians, but that he drew on a tradition similar to that
reproduced there by Paul.) Comparison of the two passages quoted above
shows that, while Paul's words represent Jesus as instituting a eucharistic practice (a cultic act which existed as a regular part of Christian worship in Paul's
time), no such implications are found in *Mark*, where the words are represented merely as spoken by Jesus in a particular situation the night before his
death and as pointing out what he will do after death.

The words I have italicized in Paul's account (absent from Mark's) bring out
the difference. Paul speaks of Jesus' "body which is for you," Mark only of his
"body"; Mark does not have the words "do this in remembrance of me," nor Paul's
interpretation (verse 26) of the religious significance of the act. Instead of this
interpretation, Mark has Jesus say that he is about to enter the kingdom of God.

Ruef summarizes all this by saying (169, p 97): Mark tells what Jesus did
"on the night when he was betrayed." (These *words* are not in *Mark*, but the
context of Jesus' eucharistic statement gives their substance, for it is immediately preceded by his prophecy that one of the twelve will betray him, and
followed, a little later that same night, by Judas' betrayal.) Ruef and other
commentators regard the historical narrative recorded in *Mark* (taken by the
evangelist from earlier tradition) as the original, and hold that Paul has adapted
such an original to explain the origin of the act of worship performed in his
own day. But there is general agreement that Paul was writing before Mark,
and so it is not intrinsically implausible to suggest that his version is the more
primitive one. Stories told to explain an existing religious practice (they are
known technically as "cult-legends") are notoriously unreliable. (A ritual tends
to persist after its original cause and significance have been lost from sight;
then among the worshippers legends arise which purport to explain it, although
it in fact explains them.) Once a eucharistic practice had been established
among Christians, it would be natural for them to suppose that Jesus had
ordained it. How it came to be established at all I have discussed elsewhere
(DJE, pp 185–9).

Another difference between Paul and Mark is that Paul makes Jesus speak
of a "new covenant," Mark merely of a "covenant." Ruef explains (169, p 119)
that Paul has in mind a covenant that supersedes that ratified between God
and Israel when blood was thrown first on the altar and then on the people
(Exodus 24:6–8). For Paul, it is no longer only the Jews who are God's people,
and the admission to the fold of such Gentiles as have faith in Jesus implies
that a new covenant has been made between God and his chosen ones.

The whole idea of a covenant with God is Jewish and was strange to a Greek. Mark, as the more Hellenistic of the two writers, stresses the covenant less and the atoning blood more. (Instead of Paul's "this is the new covenant in my blood," Mark has: "This is my blood of the covenant which is poured out for many.") By the time we reach the fourth gospel, there is no "covenant" at all in the eucharistic teaching in chapter 6, which centers on flesh and blood "given for the life of the world." Mark has obviously rephrased the words about the wine so as to make them exactly parallel to those about the bread; he makes Jesus say not only "this is my body" (as did Paul) but also "this is my blood." This change in phrasing shifts the emphasis away from the Jewish idea of a covenant; it has been seen as the beginning of a Hellenistic modification, whereby ideas of sacrifice came ultimately to replace all covenant ideas in the Christian Mass.

The idea of a covenant is no part of Jesus' teaching as given in the gospels, but it is very prominent in Paul's theology. God, he says (2 Cor. 3:6), "has qualified us to be ministers of a new covenant." At Gal. 4:24 he writes of the "two covenants" of the Old Testament, and his references to a new covenant clearly owe something to Jeremiah's prophecy (31:31 ff): "Behold the days are coming, says the Lord, when I will make a new covenant. . . ." The idea of a covenant is therefore Pauline, not Jesuine. Mark has retained the word *covenant*, which had been put into Jesus' mouth, but has contrived to place less emphasis on it.

Paul's version avoids equating the wine with Jesus' blood. Mark's narrative, where Jesus supposedly tells a Jewish audience to drink his blood, is not likely to be historical (see DJE, p 27). Hook agrees that "the very strong Hebrew objection to the idea of drinking blood" is "a particularly damaging objection" to the Marcan form of the eucharistic words (102, p 52).

Eucharist and baptism were the two most prominent rites in earliest Christianity, and so it is not surprising that Christians soon came to believe that Jesus had instituted them. We shall see (p 101) that in the case of baptism the sequence is the same as with the Eucharist: the earliest mention of Jesus' baptism does not specify time, place, or any attendant circumstances, but later writers say how and when they suppose the incident to have taken place. Once the event was believed to have occurred, later reflection would support this belief by supplying a historical setting.

IV WORDS OF THE RISEN JESUS

On several occasions, Paul claims to speak with the authority of "the Lord." For instance, having ruled that women are to keep silence in the church and that "it is a shocking thing that a woman should address the congregation," he adds that these instructions are not merely rulings of his own: "If anyone claims to be inspired or a prophet, let him recognize that what I write has the Lord's authority" (1 Cor. 14:34–7, NEB).

This formulation betrays that Paul is not here appealing to a statement made by Jesus during his lifetime but rather to an utterance of one of the early Christian "prophets," who were supposedly inspired by the spirit of the risen Jesus. Their characteristic ability was not to foretell the future, but, as Mitton expresses it, "to interpret the mind of Christ for their own time" (142, p 112). Just as Old Testament prophets introduced their directives with "thus saith the Lord," so the early Christian prophets — "appointed," Paul says, in the church by God (1 Cor. 12:28) — would have spoken in the name of the risen Lord. The seven letters of Christ to the seven churches in Asia Minor (Rev. 2–3) and other sayings of the risen Lord in this final book of the New Testament show, as Jeremias has noted, that early Christian prophets "addressed congregations in words of encouragement, admonition, censure and promise, using the name of Christ in the first person" (111, p 2).⁵ Paul himself tells that the "spiritual gifts" operative in early Christian communities included ability to prophesy and to make and interpret ecstatic utterances (1 Cor. 12:8–11): "He who prophesies speaks to men for their upbuilding and encouragement and consolation" (1 Cor. 14:3). As a result of possessing "the spirit," Christians "have the mind of Christ" (1 Cor. 2:9–16). Paul feels entitled to give ethical advice because he has "the spirit of God" (1 Cor. 7:40).

Such passages, says Nineham (148, p 21) show that early Christians "took it for granted that the heavenly Christ was continually revealing further truth about himself to his followers." The context of 2 Cor. 12:9 indicates that the saying of the Lord there recorded was given to Paul by revelation. And in 1 Thessalonians he repeats orders concerning sexual behavior which he had already given "through the Lord Jesus" (4:2). Commentators (for example, Whiteley, 213, p 59) say that the Greek implies rather "because of the inspiration of the Lord Jesus." The idea is that the instructions of the supernatural Jesus reached Paul or some other Christian seer through the spirit, not that Jesus gave them to companions in his lifetime. Hence Paul adds (4:8) that whoever disregards these orders "disregards not man but God, who gives his holy spirit to you."

Significantly the addressees are also told (5:19–21) not to "quench the spirit" nor to "despise prophesying," that is, not to ignore Christian seers who speak and prophesy allegedly under the influence of the spirit, but to "test everything," to scrutinize such utterances carefully. The same instruction is given in later Christian writings (1 John 4:1 and the non-canonical *Didache,* chapter 11). Without such scrutiny a community where the only authorities are those who happen to feel prompted by the spirit would be in continual danger of faction and anarchy. Paul tells that at Christian meetings anyone could stand up and promulgate a "revelation" he had received; that some were wont to make ecstatic utterances, not understanding what they were saying, while others supplied an interpretation (1 Cor. 14:26–32). The interpretation of unintelligible utterances could easily have proliferated incompatible doctrines.

Hill has protested that this view of early Christian prophets — which he agrees is "widespread" — does not "take with sufficient seriousness the part played by tradition in the early Christian community and the importance of the Twelve as witnesses of the tradition of Jesus' words" (231, p 264). But I question this premise that there ever was a Jesus who had been crucified a few years before Paul became a Christian and who had been accompanied by disciples who continued his teaching after his death.

V WHAT PAUL MIGHT BE EXPECTED TO SAY OF JESUS

I have been told that it is "an elementary error to suppose that because something is unmentioned it therefore did not exist or was not known about" (Stanton, 188). Of course silence on a topic does not prove ignorance of it; but a writer's silence is surely significant if it extends to matters obviously relevant to what he has chosen to discuss. And if we believe the gospels, there was much in Jesus' biography that would have been relevant to the disputes in which Paul was embroiled. These included, for instance, the following questions:

(1) Should Gentiles be admitted to the new faith at all, and if so, should they be required to keep the Jewish law?

Paul, who called himself "an apostle to Gentiles" (Rom. 11:13; cf. Gal. 2, passim) could not have believed that Jesus had charged his twelve disciples not to convert Gentiles ("Go nowhere among the Gentiles, and enter no town of the Samaritans, but go rather to the lost sheep of the house of Israel", Mt. 10: 5.) Nor could Paul, who fiercely criticizes the Jewish law and opposes circumcision of Gentile converts, have believed that Jesus had inculcated total acceptance of this law. ("Till heaven and earth pass away, not an iota, not a dot, will pass from the law until all is accomplished. Whoever then relaxes one of the least of these commandments and teaches men so, shall be called least in the kingdom of heaven," Mt. 5:18–9.)

Many theologians set these gospel passages aside as inauthentic, and accept only those which put the opposite view into Jesus' mouth: for example, that Christianity is to be preached to all nations (Mt. 24:14; cf. 28:19); and that the Jewish law is to be set aside and replaced by stipulations which Jesus lays down on his own authority (for example, Mt. 5:21–48). But Paul never suggests that Jesus taught these views either! At Mt. 12:41 Jesus declares that at the Last Judgment Gentiles will condemn "this generation" of Jews. (He is speaking to scribes and Pharisees.) Paul does not appeal to any such Jesuine teaching when he says (Rom. 2:27) that at the Judgment the uncircumcised will condemn those who have circumcision and the written code but break it. Again, Paul is "persuaded in the Lord Jesus" (the NEB renders this as "convinced as a Christian") that, contrary to what the Jewish law stipulates, all foods are permissible (Rom. 14:14). But he seems not to know that Jesus had taught such a doctrine (as, according to Mk. 7:19 he had).

As for the gospel passages where Jesus is explicitly made to base substantial amendments to the Mosaic law on his own authority, Käsemann finds that it is precisely the outrageous presumptuousness of such rulings which certify them as genuine; for no fabricator would have dared thus to put himself above Moses and attribute the resulting laws to Jesus (115, p 38). Apologists often apply exactly the opposite criterion—that statements Jesus makes in the gospels are genuine if they "ring true," that is, are what one might expect of a first-century Jewish teacher. The answer to Käsemann is that an early Christian community which held a reinterpreted version of the Jewish law would in time come to assume that their version had been ordained by Jesus.

Such a stage goes beyond anything suggested by Paul, who attacked the Jewish law ferociously but never suggested that the historical Jesus had done so.[6] To Paul, it was Jesus' crucifixion, not his teaching, that had abrogated the law (cf. Gal. 3:13). Paul is greatly concerned to protect Galatian Christians from Christian teachers who were pressing them to keep the Jewish law. Had he known that Jesus had criticized it, he could hardly have failed to say so in this context. Christian commentators are embarrassed not only by Paul's silence here but by the very existence of Judaizing Christian teachers (apparently from Jerusalem, one of the earliest Christian centers). Braun notes weakly in this connection: "The Torah-critical line in Jesus' thinking must have receded in Palestinian Christianity at the time when Paul had his controversies with the Judaists" (24, pp 249-50).

(2) Is Jesus second coming, which will end the world, imminent, and will it be preceded by obvious catastrophes or occur without warning?

On these points the second letter to the Thessalonians (probably not written by Paul) contradicts the doctrine of the (genuinely Pauline) first letter to them (see p 50); neither appeals to any teaching of Jesus, such as that detailed in Mk. 13. Paul might seem to possess knowledge of Jesus' teaching on the second coming when he declares "by word of the Lord" that Christians whose death happened to precede it will not forego its benefits; and that when "the Lord himself" descends from heaven with the sound of the trumpet of God, the Christian dead will rise first; "then we who are alive, who are left, shall be caught up together with them in the clouds to meet the Lord in the air" (1 Thess. 4:15-7). But Jesus gives no such assurances in the gospels, even though he there expatiates on his second coming.

By the "word of the Lord" on the matter, Paul means an utterance by one of the Christian prophets who believed that the risen Jesus was speaking through them. Convinced as they were that his second coming was imminent, they were particularly prone to make pronouncements concerning it. Grayston notes that the historical Jesus cannot have delivered the saying in the form given as "the word of the Lord" in 1 Thessalonians, since phrases such as "the Lord himself," "the Christian dead" and "we who are left alive" are written from the viewpoint of the early church. He adds that they "may have been a disclosure in vision or prayer," of the same kind that led Paul to specify details of the "mystery" of the general resurrection in 1 Cor. 15:51 (88, p 87).

(3) How shall Christians behave toward each other and toward outsiders?

Paul gives it as his own view (Rom. 13:8–10) that the law can be summed up in the one Old Testament injunction "You shall love your neighbor as yourself." According to Lk. 10:25–8, Jesus himself taught that love of neighbor (together with love of God) ensures salvation; but one could never gather from Paul that Jesus had expressed himself on the matter. In 1 Thess. 4:9 it is not Jesus but God who is said to have taught Christians to love one another. And the injunction not to repay evil for evil but always to do good to all is given in this same epistle (5:15) without any suggestion that Jesus had taught it (as according to the gospels he did in the Sermon on the Mount). In his letter to Christians at Rome Paul says "bless those that persecute you" (12:14 and 17) and "judge not" (14:13). Surely in such instances he might reasonably be expected to have invoked the authority of Jesus, *had he known* that Jesus had taught the very same doctrines. (The former doctrine is ascribed to him at Mt. 5:44 and Lk. 6:28, and the latter at Mt. 7:1 and Lk. 6:37.) In the same epistle he urges Christians to "pay taxes" (13:6), but does not suggest that Jesus had given such a ruling (Mk. 12:17). It is much more likely that certain precepts concerning forgiveness and civil obedience were originally urged independently of Jesus, and only later put into his mouth and thereby stamped with supreme authority, than that he gave such rulings and was not credited with having done so by Paul and (as we shall see) by other early Christian writers.

VI   THE SUFFERING JESUS OF PAUL

The manner in which Paul refers to Jesus is as instructive as what he fails to say about him. He calls him "the image of the invisible God, the first-born of all creation; for in him were all things created" (Coloss. 1:15). Such passages do not read like allusions to a near-contemporary human being. Paul believed in a Jesus who had existed as a supernatural personage before God "sent" him "in the likeness of sinful flesh" into the world to redeem it (Rom. 8:3) and who had "emptied" himself of his divine nature and humbly assumed human form (Phil. 2:6–11) by being born of a woman—not a virgin but a woman (Gal. 4:4).

This idea of Jesus' supernatural "pre-existence" before his birth on earth seems fantastic today, and to explain why Paul takes such a view, Schonfield has argued simply that he was a hypocrite—that he deliberately failed to mention what he knew to be Jesus' true teaching because it contradicted his own (175, p 54). This does not prevent Schonfield from arguing earlier (p 44) that the silence of Paul about a particular doctrine is evidence that it is *post*-Pauline.

Again, for Schonfield, Jesus was a descendant of David because Paul, among others, says so (p 22). But he was not originally regarded as a supernatural being wearing a human disguise, even though Paul, among other New Testament writers, alleged precisely this.[7]

Paul implies that Jesus' earthly life was lived in "bondage" to evil spirits, to "the elemental spirits of the universe," to whom all human life was subject, until his death liberated both him and mankind from them (Gal. 4:3–9; Coloss. 2:20). In his earthly life he humbly assumed "the form of a slave" (Phil. 2:7), and, according to Beare, the thought here is that "he was born into slavery to the Elemental Spirits, that he might redeem those who were subject to the same thraldom" (13, pp 82–3). In the next verse he is said to have been "obedient unto death," presumably to the power of these elemental spirits. Only at his death did he "disarm" them and "triumph over" them (Coloss. 2:15). All this implies that throughout his life he did not stand up to them by displaying supernatural powers, that he lived an obscure life of inconspicuous humiliation. Indeed, Paul expressly says that they caused him to be crucified because they were ignorant of his true identity: "Had they known God's wisdom, they would not have crucified the Lord of glory" (1 Cor. 2:8). Paul could not have represented the crucifixion as having resulted from such ignorance had he believed (what is asserted in Mk. 14:61–4 and parallels) that Jesus had been condemned to death for openly claiming Messianic, even supernatural status.

In this passage from 1 Corinthians, Paul calls the evil spirits responsible for the crucifixion "the rulers of this age." That angels or demons and not human rulers are meant is admitted by many commentators who explain that, by the beginning of our era, the Jews were so conscious of undeniable evil in the world that they could no longer accept that God ruled it. Therefore they repudiated the view, held in the Old Testament, that Satan and other angels were obedient instruments of God's will, and supposed instead that these demonic powers had rebelled and seized control of the world.[8] Paul's idea is presumably that these demonic governors had stirred men up to crucify Jesus, who by his death has broken the power of these angels, so that they could no longer bar man from God (cf. Coloss. 2:15). The keynote of Paul's theology is the reconciliation between man and God effected by their defeat.

It is not inappropriate to call these and other of Paul's religious ideas mystical. He repeatedly uses the phrase "in Christ" to express, as Mitton says, "identification with Christ, with his death and his risen life, as though Christ were a kind of corporate personality within which individual Christians and the Christian community as a whole may be included" (142, p 46). Mitton grants that this is akin to mysticism, although mysticism often implies that the human spirit is absorbed into the divine spirit, whereas for Paul sinful man is always to be distinguished from what is pure and holy. But whatever we term Paul's ideas, it is obvious that ideas of this kind did not need to be inspired by real knowledge of the career of a historical Jesus. It did matter to Paul that Jesus had a human history, that he did come to earth and was crucified there.

But when he mentions Jesus' death, he says nothing of Pilate or Jerusalem and may not have known or believed any more than he tells us, namely that Jesus was crucified some time in an unspecified past.

Paul's view is quite different from that of the gospels, where Jesus *is* recognized by evil spirits because he works prodigious miracles. Thus the "unclean spirit" he drives from a man says to him (Mk. 1:24): "I know who you are—the holy one of God." And when he "cast out many demons" he would not let them speak "because they knew him" (Mk. 1:34). Paul accepted no traditions of this kind. He is not merely silent about them but has a totally different view of Jesus. Indeed his express statements exclude them, and he comes very close to actually denying that Jesus was a wonder-worker. For he insists that he can preach only "Christ crucified"—a Christ who died a shameful death, not a Christ of signs and wonders (1 Cor. 1:22). The historical Jesus in whom Paul believed was thus someone whom he supposed to have lived such an obscure life that no details of it, apart from its termination on the cross and Jesus' eucharistic words when his Passion began, were known or were important.

Tannehill notes (197, p 125) that the ineffectualness (by ordinary standards) of Jesus' incarnate life is something that Paul repeatedly stresses. The Lord he says, told him: "my power is made perfect in weakness"; and for this reason Paul is "content with weaknesses, insults, hardships, persecutions and calamities" (2 Cor. 12:9-10). Having told the Corinthians that he "decided to know nothing among you except Jesus Christ and him crucified" (1 Cor. 2:2), Paul adds that he was with them "in weakness and in much fear and trembling," as if implying that weakness and suffering are appropriate to the Christian life because they characterized Christ's life. When he goes on to detail the humiliation and persecution he has suffered as a Christian, he tells them to "be imitators of me" (4:11-13 and 16). When he later repeats this injunction, he makes the claim that he himself is an "imitator of Christ" (11:1), as if implying that Christ lived a life of humiliation. (Cf. 1 Thess. 1:6: "You became imitators of us and of the Lord, for you received the word in much affliction.")

In another letter the recipients are likewise urged to imitate him rather than the "enemies of the cross of Christ" who "glory" in earthly things (Phil. 3:17-9). Again, at Rom. 1:3 Jesus is said to have become son of God "in power" at his resurrection. The implication is that he was "son of God in apparent weakness and poverty in the period of his earthly existence" (Cranfield, 46, p 62). At Rom. 8:17 Paul says that Christians appropriately "suffer with Christ," and Cranfield notes (46, p 408) that the *with* includes the idea of "in conformity with the pattern of His earthly life."

Christians did not, in Paul's day, have to reckon with being killed for being Christians (cf. p 108); and so to "suffer" with Jesus is not the same as to "die" with him (which Paul has discussed apropos of baptism in 6:3-12). Paul's statement, then, is that "we" Christians share his sufferings, but since this cannot mean his crucifixion, it refers to the fact that his life was one of suffering. At Rom. 15:3 Paul uses Psalm 69:9 ("The reproaches of those who reproached thee fell upon me") to characterize Jesus' life. According to the rendering of the NEB, Jesus "might have said" these words; that is, this citation from scripture is appropriate as a characterization of his life. Paul here, then, refers to the example of Jesus by means of an Old Testament quotation and shows no knowledge of what, according to the gospels, Jesus himself said on the subject (that is, Mk. 8:34, "If any man would come after me, let him deny himself and take up his cross and follow me").⁹

The few facts Paul does record about Jesus' incarnate life—his descent from David, the reproaches to which he was subjected, and his death (in unspecified circumstances)—are all said to be "according to the scriptures," that is, the Old Testament (1 Cor. 15:3-4, apropos of his death and resurrection). What Paul says here probably reproduces an existing Christian creed (for he calls it teaching he has "received"), so that this statement about Jesus' death may well represent one of the oldest pieces of written tradition in the New Testament. Even at this early stage, then, it is, as Evans has recently conceded, "apparent that already there was no immediate and direct access in the tradition to a bare historical event, but only to that event as apprehended and absorbed through the medium of the Old Testament" (64, p 6).

Paul has no difficulty finding Old Testament passages concerning a descendant of David who will rule the Gentiles (Rom. 15:12), but he does not say where Jesus' death is foretold. However, that Jesus "was delivered to death for our misdeeds" (Rom. 4:25) seems to be an allusion to Isaiah's account of the suffering servant of Yahweh (see p 26). Paul also refers to the Old Testament in connection with Jesus' pre-existence (saying that Christ had accompanied the Israelites at the time of their exodus from Egypt, 1 Cor. 10:4) and his subordination to God (1 Cor. 15:27-8). Nearly all New Testament authors twist and torture the most unhelpful Old Testament passages into prophecies concerning Christianity. Who, ignorant of Mt. 2:16-9, could suppose that Jeremiah 31:15 (Rachel weeping for her children) referred to Herod's slaughter of the Innocents?

But whereas the evangelists use the Old Testament extensively as foreshadowing many details of Jesus' incarnate life, Paul employs it rather for the purpose of supporting—from the Jews' own scriptures—items of Christian teaching which they most deplored: for example, that man is justified by faith in Jesus, not by keeping the Jewish law; and that salvation is not for the Jews as a nation, but only for those who turn Christian (as Paul hopes all of them eventually will). Paul quotes a great variety of Old Testament passages in connection with these two doctrines. He also supports his view on the wrath of God, on predestination, and on the nature of the resurrection body from the Old Testament, which provides him too with guidance on problems that had arisen within early Christian communities.

For instance, he uses it to show that women should have only a subordinate position in worship (1 Cor. 11:8); that Christian preachers have the right to be supported financially by their congregations (1 Cor. 9:9-12); that unintelligible ecstatic utterance has an unsettling effect on the congregation (1 Cor. 14:21); and that Christians should not marry unbelievers (2 Cor. 6:14–8).

Finally, he frequently appeals to the Old Testament when he gives ethical precepts: love your neighbor, leave retribution to God, give generously in a good cause, etc. Even on the few occasions when he does mention the Old Testament specifically in connection with Jesus' incarnate life, his purpose is to make a theological point rather than to find Old Testament sanction for Jesus' biography. Thus at Rom. 9:33 Isaiah is quoted to show Jesus as a "stumbling-stone" for the Jews, and at Gal. 3:13 Deuteronomy establishes that the crucifixion freed the world from the Jewish law and so opened salvation to Gentiles.

Paul, then, employs the Old Testament apropos of Jesus' life on earth very much less than do the evangelists, who, unlike him, do not regard Christ's life as having been lived exclusively in "bondage," in weakness, and in servility.

It is sometimes contended that Paul is silent concerning what the gospels record as Jesus' biography simply because he was writing to people who did not need to be reminded of such matters. But why, then, does he again and again mention his death by crucifixion, with which, in the terms of the case, they were equally familiar? And why do his many references to this event nevertheless give no indication of where, when, or under what circumstances it occurred? Although he says that the earthly Jesus was a descendant of David (Rom. 1:3), a Jew "according to the flesh" (9:5), he does not say in which of the many centuries since David he supposes Jesus to have lived. In the next section I shall try to show that he may well have assigned the crucifixion to one hundred or two hundred years before his own time and have been ignorant of the circumstances.

In sum, Paul has a different view of Jesus from that of the evangelists. In the gospels, Jesus' lifetime is not consigned to a vague past, but is firmly set in the first half of the first century in Palestine by linkage with such historical figures as John the Baptist and Pontius Pilate.[10] He does not live obscurely, but works prodigious miracles and impresses great crowds. And he delivers extensive teachings on ethics and on the circumstances which will attend his supernatural return to earth and the end of the world associated with it. How is it that these gospels, written only a generation later than Paul's letters, give such a different picture? And if Paul did not regard Jesus as a contemporary (or near contemporary) preacher and miracle-worker, on what was his view of Jesus based? I will discuss this latter question first.

VII   PAUL AND THE JEWISH WISDOM LITERATURE

Paul's letters, we saw, were written before AD 60. He himself says that he composed them late in his career as a Christian, and that there were already Christians before his own conversion. Christianity existed, then, by about AD 30.

These earliest Christians were Jews. Early Christian documents accept the God of Israel, the Old Testament, Jewish apocalyptic and angelology, and

Jewish ideas about the Messiah. A non-Jewish origin for a sect which embraced all this is out of the question. Hence the Jewish, rather than the pagan, religious background is likely to be of prime importance in explaining the conviction of the earliest Christians that, at some unspecified time past, a redeemer named Jesus had been obscurely crucified. This is not to say however that pagan ideas were unimportant for early Christianity.[11]

It is no longer in dispute that many religious ideas among Jews and early Christians originated as a result of musing on existing sacred and semi-sacred literature. The principle involved—of prime importance for religious development generally—can be briefly stated as follows. Written descriptions (in any respected document) of some person or event (historical or imaginary) may be read by those who know nothing of the real subject represented, and who may freshly interpret the document in accordance with their own knowledge. In this way they may take the writing to refer to people and events entirely unknown to the actual writers. In the Psalms, for instance, the term "the anointed," that is, "the Messiah," is used to designate the reigning king. Later generations, reading the Psalms when the historical kingship had ceased to exist, nevertheless assumed that the meaning of the Psalmist had some relevance to present times; and that, since there were no more kings in the old sense, his reference must be to another king or Messiah, perhaps in heaven, who would soon come down to earth. The Psalms played a particularly important role in developing ideas about Jesus' Passion.[12]

When Christianity originated, Jewish writings included a considerable body of "wisdom" literature, consisting in part of discussion of the fundamental principles of virtuous living, with advice on such matters as education and choice of friends. In some passages wisdom figures not just as an abstract idea, but is personified. Proverbs 3:19 and 8:22–36 represent Wisdom as a supernatural personage created by God before he created heaven or earth, and then mediating in this creation and leading man into the paths of truth. In the *Wisdom of Solomon* (from the Old Testament apocrypha) Wisdom figures as a hypostasis—separate from God yet of the same substance, "a breath of the power of God, a clear affluence of the Almighty" (7:25–7). She is the sustainer and governor of the universe who sits by the throne of God (8:1; 9:4). She comes to dwell among men and bestow her gifts on them, but most of them reject her. *1 Enoch* 42 tells that, after being humiliated on earth, Wisdom returned to heaven.

It is thus obvious that the humiliation on earth and exaltation to heaven of a supernatural personage, as preached by Paul and other early Christian writers, could have been derived from ideas well represented in the Jewish background. Paul was strongly influenced by the wisdom traditions, for statements made about Wisdom in Jewish literature are made of Jesus in the Pauline letters.[13] Paul's Jesus (like Wisdom) assists God in the creation of all things (1 Cor. 8:6)—a passage which has recently been said to be "unintelligible except against a 'wisdom' background" (101, p 21). At Gal. 4:4–6 Paul says that, in order to redeem us, God "sent forth his son" to earth "when the time had fully come," and then "sent the spirit of his son into our hearts."

Stanton (and others to whom he refers) think that the background to such views is the *Wisdom of Solomon* 9:10 and 9:17, where the sending of Wisdom from heaven and the sending of God's spirit from heaven are set alongside each other (83, p 154). Solomon prays to God: "Send her [Wisdom] forth from the holy heavens . . . so that she may labor at my side and I may learn what pleases thee . . . Whoever learnt to know thy purposes, unless thou hadst given him wisdom and sent thy holy spirit down from heaven on high?"

Paul also writes of "Christ in whom are hid all the treasures of wisdom and knowledge" (Coloss. 2:3. That they are hid conforms with his idea of Jesus' earthly obscurity.) Elsewhere he calls Christ "the power of God and the Wisdom of God," even though thus to venerate one who died by crucifixion may, he says, seem folly to those who know nothing of God's wisdom (1 Cor. 1:23-5).

In this passage from 1 Corinthians, Paul comes very close to expressly calling the supernatural personage that had become man in Jesus "Wisdom." The figure of the Messiah had of course not been equated by the Jews generally with that of Wisdom, but there were points of connection which made it easy for the early Christians to merge the two. And there was a large body of sacred and semi-sacred literature on which to muse. The latter was, for the earliest Christians, as important as the former; even Jews were divided at that time as to which books were to be included in the scriptures, and the Christians reverenced them indiscriminately (Vielhauer, 234, p 778). There was, further, no agreement, even among the Jews, as to which passages were to be interpreted Messianically, nor as to what the correct interpretation was. New interpretations were constantly being offered and new passages adduced, so that Jewish thinking about the Messiah varied greatly at different times and places.

At Phil. 2:6-11 Paul tells how Jesus as a supernatural personage humbled himself by taking human form, and was "obedient unto death," whereupon God exalted him to heaven. It is widely agreed that he is here quoting a Christian hymn based on a pre-Christian mythological scheme whereby a heavenly redeemer descends to earth and reascends to heaven "laden with the trophies of victory and opening the way for his followers" (Beare, 13, p 75). Vielhauer says that the *Ascension of Isaiah* (a Christian adaptation of a pre-Christian Jewish apocalypse) is of great importance as showing what kind of source these ideas had (234, p 526). I discussed it in this connection in JEC (pp 291-6).

The wisdom literature is also relevant as a source. Fuller thinks that it is the myth of the descent and ascent of Wisdom that underlies this hymn quoted by Paul (74, p 212). Admittedly, the Jewish wisdom literature does not state that Wisdom lived on earth as a historical personage and assumed human flesh in order to do so. The statement is that she was available as man's counsellor, but was rejected, even humiliated, and then returned to heaven. However, Haenchen (228, p 129) shows how easy it would have been for readers to suppose that, when the texts spoke of Wisdom "setting up its tent" on earth, the meaning was that Wisdom had assumed human flesh—since "house of the tent" or, simply, "tent" is used (even in the New Testament at 2 Cor. 5:1 and 4) in the sense of man's earthly existence. Furthermore, in the *Wisdom of Solomon* there is mention of "the just man," Wisdom's ideal representative ("age after age she enters into holy souls and makes them God's friends and prophets," 7:27). He is not only persecuted but even condemned to a "shameful death" (2:20). God tests him with such chastisements, and then, finding him worthy, confers great blessings on him, in the form of immortality (3:5). He will be "counted one of the sons of God" (5:5) and receive "a fair diadem from the Lord himself" (5:16). This just man is said by his enemies to style himself "the servant of the Lord" (2:13).

Georgi (52, p 271) has argued that the whole depiction of this just man is influenced by the account of the servant of Yahweh in Isaiah 52:13–53:12. This servant was "exalted and lifted up," even though he was despised and rejected of men and persecuted unto death, humbly bearing their iniquities. What Isaiah says about the shameful but atoning death of this servant could well have suggested that he had been crucified (cf. JEC, p 229), and the reference in Zechariah 12:10 to mourning for an innocent and pious man who had been "pierced" would also have put readers in mind of crucifixion. (In the gospels, the use of chapters 9–14 of Zechariah in connection with the Passion is explicit and extensive: see Evans, 64, pp 11–2). In sum, musing on the wisdom and other Jewish literature could have prompted the earliest Christians to suppose that a pre-existent redeemer had suffered crucifixion, the most shameful death of all, before being exalted to God's right hand.

Of great importance, however, is that any hints of this kind from sacred literature that Jesus was crucified would have been confirmation of traditions concerning actual historical crucifixions of holy men in Palestine, which must have been known to the earliest Christians. The Jewish historian Josephus tells that Antiochus Epiphanes, king of Syria in the second century BC, and the Hasmonean ruler Alexander Jannaeus, of the first century BC, both caused living Jews to be crucified in Jerusalem (113, 12:5, 4, and 13:14, 2. Josephus expressly notes that in these cases the punishment of crucifixion was not inflicted *after* execution, as it often was.)

Both periods of persecution are alluded to in Jewish religious literature (in such works as *The Assumption of Moses,* the Dead Sea Scrolls, and the *Similitudes of Enoch*), and Jannaeus' crucifixion of 800 Pharisees left a particularly strong impression on the Jewish world. Paul's environment would, then, have included the knowledge that pious Jews had been crucified long ago, although dates and circumstances would probably have been only vaguely known. And Jewish traditions on which the Talmud drew persistently place Jesus among these ancient victims by dating him somewhere in the second century BC (see DJE, pp 198–9).

Historical tradition about crucifixions long ago may well have confirmed in Paul's mind the suggestions of the wisdom literature. Wilcox has complained that this is mere "groping around for any theory, however speculative, to avoid the alternative of taking Jesus' existence as a possibility" and to avoid taking his crucifixion as "an actual event which would well fit the stormy early years of Pilate's administration" (215).

I would reply by making a distinction between taking his existence as a possibility and taking it for granted. If we do not begin by assuming that Jesus died about AD 30 under Pilate, then there is little in Paul that would suggest it, and this little can be otherwise explained. When we further find that there is equally little in other extant early Christian writers that would suggest it, then it is surely not inappropriate to ask whether the idea of Christ crucified might have originated in another way. And the way I have suggested is hardly to be set aside as grossly "speculative," for in Paul's day the wisdom literature *did* exist, and he *was* indebted to it. Furthermore, the habit of *musing on* such literature and extracting hidden meanings from it *was* well-developed; and knowledge of crucifixions of long ago—since they had made a strong enough impression on the Jewish world to be repeatedly alluded to—*was* available.

I think that these factors also answer one of the objections which Ziesler (in very courteously worded comments) has made to my views: namely, "assuming Wells is right, Paul, if he did know that the Christian faith had only lately appeared, ought to have known also that it was based on a myth of dying and rising, not on an historical occurrence" (235, p 7). I agree that Paul knew quite well that *faith* in Jesus had only recently appeared, even though (on my view) he supposed Jesus to have lived long ago. That there is no contradiction here will be shown in the next section of this chapter. The point I would reiterate here is that Paul (and his contemporaries) would have been more readily persuaded by a new interpretation of familiar scriptures and prophecies, an interpretation which seemed to elucidate remote historical events of which he had some (albeit sketchy) knowledge, than by the kind of historical evidence that might impress a modern skeptic.

What is particularly difficult to understand is that Paul should refer to Jesus as a pre-existent supernatural personage if in fact this Jesus had been a contemporary with whose friends, relatives, and followers Paul himself was personally acquainted. Instead of abandoning this assumption that Paul and Jesus were human contemporaries, some apologists have dealt with the problem by arguing not merely that the historical Jesus was no more than a man, a Galilean preacher, but even that Paul originally regarded him as a mere man who had been elevated to more exalted status only after death. For instance, Frances Young (contributing to a book which has the professed aim of representing Christianity as "something which can be believed by honest and thoughtful people") argues that the wisdom literature did indeed influence Paul, but that its effect was to distort his original modest idea of a Jesus who was, in origin, human (101, pp 20–1).

As evidence that Paul originally thought Jesus a man Goulder points (in the same volume) to 1 Thessalonians (widely accepted as the earliest of Paul's extant letters and dated about 50); it lacks any reference to Christ's pre-existence. But, as Goulder is well aware, this short epistle (a mere five pages in the NEB) was addressed to those who feared that Christians who had died (or would die) before Jesus' second coming would not partake of its benefits, and Paul's purpose was to reassure them. Being concerned only with the second coming, he had no occasion in this epistle to refer to Jesus' status before he visited earth. His references to Jesus' present powers in no way conflict with the presupposition that the person described in such terms had always been, for him, supernatural. And this would be in accordance with the explicit affirmation of pre-existence in his other epistles.

Goulder confidently rules that "pre-existence" is absent from Paul's earliest thinking about Jesus because it is "inconceivable to a Jew" (101, p 77). He seems to mean inconceivable as an attribute of the Messiah. "Jewish sources never think of the Messiah as divine or pre-existent," although rabbinic traditions maintain that "the *name* of Messiah is created before the world" (83, pp 143, 146). He attributes Paul's references to "wisdom" to somewhat unwilling assimilation of a Christology formulated by rival Christian teachers, which they in turn had taken from Samaritan theology.

His evidence that Samaritan ideas greatly influenced earliest Christianity, and that they included a Gnostic-type supernatural redeemer, is far from strong. Nevertheless, he believes that prior to exposure to them, Paul taught "the straight Galilean" doctrine (101, p 77) that Jesus, born a man, had been raised from the dead and would soon return to earth to effect the final judgment. At the same time, Goulder concedes (p 81) that Paul says next to nothing about Jesus' life on earth, and that "the Galilean tradition" comes through to us only in *Mark*. (He himself finds the "Galilean" view, with its implication of a second coming, as unacceptable as the Samaritan-inspired one, and calls upon "our generation . . . to formulate its Christology anew," p 85.)

Frances Young finds it significant that Paul remained monotheist enough to avoid actually calling Jesus "God," whereas some later New Testament writers speak of "our great God and Savior Jesus Christ" (Titus 2:13, cf. 2 Peter 1:1). Again, whereas Paul characteristically says "God raised" Jesus from the dead, many second-century Christians insisted that he rose by his own power. But the fact that more exalted status and wider powers came in time to be ascribed to him does not alter the fact that, for Paul, he is certainly a supernatural, if not a divine personage. Dr. Young seems to think that, since he was given supernatural status earlier than divine status, we can infer by extrapolation an even earlier period when his status was held to be merely human. But none of the very early documents support this suggestion, and his supernatural status is affirmed not merely by Paul but also in other documents (for example, the epistle to the Hebrews) which, as we shall see, are arguably of earlier date than any gospel, or if contemporaneous with some of the gospels, then at any rate independent of them.

VIII PAUL AND THE RESURRECTION

Apart from the crucifixion, Paul repeatedly mentions one other Jesus-event: the resurrection three days later. The idea that a return to life would follow quickly, if at all, is a natural one. And Christians would also naturally suppose that death had had but brief power over their Lord. Pagan divinities whom no one now believes to have existed were also resurrected on the third day (see DJE, p 31). Although Paul and other early Christians supposed (in my view) that Jesus' death and resurrection had occurred long ago, they thought he would return soon, in their own lifetime, to bring the world to an end and effect a universal judgment.

It was in this atmosphere of intense Messianic expectation (derived from the Jewish background) that they began to be sure that he was already near, that he was actually appearing from time to time to some of them, so that his final coming could not be long delayed. Paul, for instance, tells that the risen Jesus appeared to him after having already appeared to a number of persons who had been Christians before his own conversion: "He appeared to Cephas, then to the twelve, then . . . to more than five hundred brethren at one time" (most of whom, Paul says, are, at the time of writing, still alive); "then to James, then to all the apostles" and "last of all . . . to me" (1 Cor. 15:5-8).

In these early days of Christianity, leaders of Christian groups based their authority on the fact that they had been vouchsafed such appearances. Thus Paul, on this basis, claims that he is as much an apostle as the other recipients (1 Cor. 9:1).[14] All these resurrection appearances were recent, in that they were experienced (albeit perhaps over a period of years) by persons who were Paul's contemporaries.

But Paul does not say that the crucifixion and resurrection were also recent. He simply lists the appearances, beginning with that to Peter and ending with that to himself. This latter, even in the orthodox view, took place some time, perhaps even years, after Jesus' death. In sum, Paul's belief that Jesus' ghost had repeatedly been seen in recent times does not tell us anything about Paul's idea of the date of Jesus' death. It is our familiarity with the gospels—later documents representing later developments in the tradition—that leads us to assume that Paul supposed the appearances to have followed rapidly after the crucifixion and resurrection, and to have been vouchsafed to men who had been companions of a historical Jesus.

If (as I believe) Paul did not regard the crucifixion and resurrection as recent events, then the significance of the appearances would have been to convince him that the general resurrection of the dead, and the final judgment of both living and dead, were to occur very soon. Christ was risen: that, for Paul, meant that all would rise. (In this sense, Christ raised from the dead is "the first fruits of those who have fallen asleep," 1 Cor. 15:20.) But now that he was not only risen, but had also begun to appear to men, the final events which would bring the world to an end could not be long delayed.

O'Neill urged against this theory, as stated in DJE, that, if Paul had really regarded Jesus' death and resurrection as events of long ago, then he would surely have invented apostles of bygone ages who preached the risen Jesus (153). I would answer that, in Paul's view, Jesus lived and died in obscurity and attracted no followers until he began in Paul's own days to make resurrection appearances, thus informing men of the fact of his resurrection and convincing them that the end of the world was at hand.

As, then, appearances of the resurrected Lord were of importance in the early church in establishing apostolic authenticity, it is at first surprising that those recorded in the gospels correlate poorly with those posited by Paul. The canonical gospels know nothing of an appearance to James, or to five hundred. And although Cephas was, according to Paul, the first to see the risen one, Peter plays but a very minor part in the gospel resurrection stories (see DJE, p 32 and note). In *Matthew* and *John,* appearances to women (unmentioned by Paul) are given pride of place. This suggests that the gospels were written at a time when establishing one's apostolic authority by reference to appearances had ceased to be important. Mark, whose Christology led him to represent Jesus as dying deserted by his disciples, introduced women instead of them as witnesses of the crucifixion and burial, and naturally represented these women as going to the tomb on Easter morning, where they receive the resurrection news from an angel in the empty sepulcher. Matthew initiated a tradition of actual appearances of the risen one to these women by supplementing Mark's story.

It is also noteworthy that, while Paul has nothing to say of the locality where the appearances occurred, later Christian documents which are explicit on this matter contradict each other. Matthew locates the appearances to the disciples exclusively in Galilee, whereas Luke confines them to Jerusalem, seventy miles away. Such major discrepancies concerning a matter of the greatest importance to early Christianity suggests that stories of the appearances are legends. Initially Christians would simply have believed that Christ was risen; later, various stories about his appearances entered the tradition as attempts to substantiate this claim.

That Christ rose from the dead does not of itself give him any share in God's sovereignty. To achieve this he must be exalted to heaven, to sit at God's right hand. Resurrection, then, and exaltation or heavenly session are not identical, although it was natural for the earliest Christians to assume that the latter followed the former immediately. Paul does not suggest any discontinuity when he writes of "Christ Jesus . . . who was raised from the dead and is at the right hand of God" (Rom. 8:34). And in Phil. 2:8-9 the sequence of events is said to be: Jesus dies and God exalts him to heaven. In Paul's view, the postresurrection appearances were made from heaven.

The evangelists, however, writing a generation later, were anxious to establish the reality of the resurrection by making the risen one return—even if only for a few hours—to the company of disciples who had known him before his death. It was natural to represent him as doing this before his exaltation, and so the possibility was given of terminating his resurrection appearances with a distinct act of ascension. This possibility was not taken up by Mark and Matthew, but fully exploited by Luke. (In the appendix to *Mark* the ascension is stated in phrases clearly drawn from *Luke*.) In *Luke* and Acts the physical reality of Jesus' post-resurrection body is brought out by making him eat and drink with his disciples (Acts 10:41) as he had done before his death. Paul would surely have rejected as blasphemous any claim to have eaten and drunk with the exalted one, and his claim that this person had appeared to him is intelligible, as we have seen, as religious experience. Luke's story of the risen Jesus consuming broiled fish (Lk. 24:41-3) represents later apologetic, relevant to a situation where Christians were replying to Jewish and Gentile incredulity with a narrative which established the physical reality of his resurrection.

2

Non-Pauline Epistles Earlier Than About AD 90

I INTRODUCTION

If Paul were the only early Christian writer to be silent about, or in conflict with the gospel picture of Jesus, one might plausibly attribute his silence to some personal tendency, such as predilection to mysticism and correlative indifference to history. It has in fact often been argued that the reason why he mentions neither the time (Pilate's prefecture) nor the place (Jerusalem), nor any of the attendant circumstances of the crucifixion is that he was preoccupied with the significance of the cross as a cosmic saving event. But we find that all those of the extant post-Pauline epistles of the New Testament which are likely to have been written before the end of the first century (and probably before 90) refer to Jesus in essentially the same manner as Paul does. They stress one or more of his supernatural aspects — his existence before his life on earth, his resurrection and second coming — but say nothing of the teachings or miracles ascribed to him in the gospels, and give no historical setting to the crucifixion, which remains the one episode in his incarnate life unambiguously mentioned, at least in some of them.

These early post-Pauline epistles constitute a considerable body of literature: the second letter to the Thessalonians, the letters to the Ephesians and the Hebrews, the first letter of Peter, and possibly also the letter of James and the three of John (although these may be slightly later, and John 1 alludes to a baptism). Surely these writers, independent of each other as they mainly are, cannot all be supposed to have believed that Jesus lived the kind of life portrayed in the gospels and yet to have been silent even about the where and

47

when of this life. The first Christian epistles to depict him in a way which shows significant resemblances to the gospels' portrait of him are some of those which are widely agreed to have been written about the end of the first century, say between 90 and 110: the three-so-called Pastoral epistles (the two to Timothy and the one to Titus), the second letter ascribed to Peter, and — outside the canon — the anonymous letter (known as 1 Clement) ascribed to Clement of Rome and the seven letters of Ignatius.

Since these later epistles (after 90) do give biographical references to Jesus, it cannot be argued that epistle-writers generally were disinterested in his biography, and it becomes necessary to explain why only the earlier ones (and not only Paul) give the historical Jesus such short shrift. The change in the manner of referring to him after 90 becomes intelligible if we accept that his earthly life in first-century Palestine was invented later in the first century, but it remains a riddle (so far unexplained by theologians) if we take his life for historical fact.

In this chapter I shall discuss the early post-Pauline letters. It will be necessary to give detailed arguments concerning dates and authorship, as these matters are far more controversial than was the case with the eight Paulines we have already considered.

A number of the letters to be studied in this chapter are widely, and to my mind rightly, regarded as pseudonymous. The educated man of today is apt to be shocked by the suggestion that a writer might pretend to be someone not himself. But the Christians of the first two centuries regarded authorship differently. As Kelly says (118, pp 5–6): they "had little or no interest in the personality of the human agent who wrote their sacred books. The Spirit who had spoken through the apostles was still active in prophetic men, and when they put pen to paper it was he who was the real author of their productions. It was therefore legitimate to attribute all such writings (apart, of course, from compositions which were by their very nature personal) to one or other of the apostles, who had been the mouthpieces of the Spirit and whose disciples the actual authors, humanly speaking, were."

II THE EARLIEST PSEUDO-PAULINES

The Second Letter to the Thessalonians

The second letter to the Christians at Thessalonica (the modern Salonica) is ascribed to Paul in the canon and claims to have been written by him. There are, however, good grounds for regarding it as from a later hand.

Of the two Thessalonian epistles, one is dependent on the other, as can be illustrated from their opening sentences. These (differing in this respect from the admittedly genuine Paulines) are very similar in their wording, which is also distinctive in that Paul does not call himself an "apostle" (as he does at the beginning of all but one of his letters to other churches).

1 Thess. 1:1–2	*2 Thess. 1:1–3*
1. Paul, Silvanus and Timothy, to the Church of the Thessalonians in God the Father and the Lord Jesus Christ: Grace to you and peace. 2. We give thanks to God always for you all . . .	1. Paul, Silvanus and Timothy, to the Church of the Thessalonians in God our Father and the Lord Jesus Christ: 2. Grace to you and peace from God the Father and the Lord Jesus Christ. 3. We are bound to give thanks to God always for you, brethren . . .

Most commentators regard the second letter (half the length of the first) as the derivative one. This view is supported by 1 Thess. 2:17–3:6, a passage which strongly suggests that Paul is here writing for the very first time to the Thessalonians,[1] and also by 2 Thess. 2:15, which correlatively implies that he had previously written to them. In the second instance he tells them to "hold fast to the traditions you were taught by us, either by word of mouth or by letter." Whiteley notes that the (aorist) tense of the Greek rendered here as "were taught" means that the letter with the relevant teaching cannot be 2 Thessalonians itself (as some have maintained) but must be a previous letter.

If 2 Thessalonians is derivative, was it culled from 1 Thessalonians by Paul himself? A single author, writing two brief letters of this kind, would not normally use so many of the same phrases in both—particularly as the tone of the two letters is so different. 1 Thessalonians is "the least doctrinal and most personal" of all Paul's letters to the churches (Knox, 84, p 995). It expresses his affection for and grateful remembrance of the pagans he had recently caused to "turn from idols to serve the true God" (1:9). 2 Thessalonians, however, is entirely lacking in this personal warmth. If we assume that Paul is its author, then, although his mood had changed so much since the writing of 1 Thessalonians, he nevertheless was content to use a great deal of that earlier letter. This seems unlikely.

Another piece of evidence against Pauline authorship is the affirmation of 2 Thess. 3:17: "I, Paul, write this greeting with my own hand. This is the mark in every letter of mine. It is the way I write." The real Paul does indeed twice state (Gal. 6:11 and 1 Cor. 16:21) that he wrote the conclusion of a letter in his own hand instead of dictating it. But, as Bailey notes (3, p 138), in neither of these two passages is there any suggestion that the purpose of the signature is to authenticate the letter. Its purpose there is rather "to bring the apostle with a few especially strongly felt concluding words close to the Church in question." And so 2 Thess. 3:17 "makes most sense as the product of the pseudonymous author who wished to allay any suspicions of inauthenticity which his letter might arouse." He certainly reckoned with letters falsely ascribed to Paul, for (writing, of course, as "Paul") he warns his readers (2:2) against pernicious teaching contained in "some letter purporting to be from us." In his admittedly genuine writings Paul never reckons with letters forged in his name, and if it is the real Paul who is speaking here in 2 Thess. 2:2, it is strange that he should allude to this matter of great seriousness only with this brief remark (cf. Linde-mann, 131, pp 37–8).

The second Thessalonian letter is, then, non-Pauline. The author is most emphatic that the addressees must accept the doctrines he puts to them. They are to hold aloof from any Christians who do not do so (3:6). Such persons, it is implied, will be frightfully punished at the second coming (1:8–10). His motive in pretending to be Paul is clearly to claim Paul's authority for doc-trines which he feels are not merely correct but essential to salvation. His prin-cipal concern is to correct, in Paul's name, what he regarded as misconceptions about the second coming.[2] In order to do so, he flatly contradicts what 1 Thessa-lonians says on this subject. Let us compare the doctrines of the two letters.

In the genuinely Pauline first letter, Jesus' return is expected soon. Chris-tians are "waiting" for God's son, "whom he raised from the dead," to come from heaven and "deliver us from the wrath to come" (NEB "from the terrors of the judgment to come," 1 Thess. 1:10). The addressees are urged to live faultlessly so as to be "unblamable in holiness before our God and Father at the coming of our Lord Jesus Christ with all his saints" (3:13). Although some of the faithful have already died, they will not forego the benefits of his com-ing (cf. p 32). Furthermore, this destructive "day of the Lord" will come unher-alded, "like a thief in the night," at a time of apparent peace and security (5:1–11). It seems from this that 1 Thessalonians was written to reassure those who had begun to feel uneasy because the world seemed quite stable and there was no sign of its coming to an end.

2 Thessalonians, however, stresses that the second coming is not to be ex-pected soon. It posits, in the manner of Jewish apocalyptic writing, a series of upheavals that must precede the end: first a rebellion, then the revelation of the "man of lawlessness" who is presently being restrained by someone (2:6) or something (2:7). (Perhaps the Emperor is meant, or the imperial authorities generally, as those responsible for law and order.) Only when this restraining influence is "out of the way" will he "take his seat in the temple of God, pro-claiming himself to be God." His "coming by the activity of Satan will be with all power and pretended signs and wonders." But "the Lord Jesus will slay him with the breath of his mouth and destroy him by his appearing and his coming." Some of these details about the end-events are paralleled in the Dead Sea Scrolls (see Grayston, 88, p 101) and hence could have been part of the author's intellectual background.

The contradiction here with the teaching of 1 Thessalonians is sharp. If the end will be preceded by obvious catastrophes, then it will not come when all is peace and security. Some have argued that both letters were written by Paul and that he changed his mind about the end-events in the interval between writing them. But the teaching of the second letter cannot represent a change in the mind of the real Paul; for when the author gives this teaching, he asks the addressees: "Do you not remember that I was still with you when I told you this?" (2:5).

The purpose of 2 Thessalonians' teaching about the end-events is to controvert Christians who took a different view. According to the translation of the old Authorized Version, what these Christians erroneously supposed was that "the day of the Lord is at hand" (2 Thess. 2:2). This translation makes good sense in the context where, as we have seen, the author goes on to explain that the end is by no means yet at hand. However, the Greek verb in the original can sometimes mean "to be present" (rather than "to be at hand"). And as it bears this meaning in other New Testament passages, in the Septuagint, in Josephus and Philo, and in a number of papyri, more recent translators have supposed that this is what it means here, and have rendered the doctrine which the author of 2 Thess. is indicting as "the day of the Lord is now present" (RV), "the day of the Lord has come" (RSV), or "the day of the Lord is already here" (NEB; see the discussion by Stephenson, 189).

The author complains that the erroneous view (whether that the day is imminent or that it has already come) is being supported by a letter or letters "purporting" to be from Paul. If those who held the erroneous view really supposed that the day of the Lord had already come, then they had presumably misunderstood Paul's teaching and taken "the day" to mean not Jesus' second coming, but the outpouring of spiritual gifts (such as ability to prophesy and speak in tongues) which had already occurred in Christian communities. Certain statements which Paul had made in 1 Thessalonians (at 5:4–8, where he speaks of Christians as sons of light and of the day, no longer in the darkness) could have been misinterpreted and taken to mean that "the day of the Lord" had already come in this sense. Since, however, the Christian community addressed in 2 Thessalonians is enduring "persecutions and afflictions" (1:4), it is more likely to have been in danger of believing that the day of the Lord was coming soon, rather than that it was in any sense already there. But whatever the dangerous teaching was, the author argues against it by explaining that the end will not come soon; he thereby contradicts the teaching of 1 Thessalonians.

The one sustained ethical maxim of 2 Thessalonians, namely "keep away from any brother who is living in idleness" (3:6) is probably meant as criticism of Christians who had given up work because they thought the second coming imminent, who had (in Stephenson's phrase) "put down their tools and started star-gazing" (189, p 445). This criticism, coupled with the author's own view of the second coming, marks him as "a man of the second or third Christian generation, when the church saw its hope of a speedy end to history receding and was preparing itself for a witness in history of indefinitely long duration" (Bailey, 3, p 143).

It is difficult to assign a more precise date to 2 Thessalonians. The community addressed is said to be under persecution (1:4), but there is no indication that persecution was the official policy of the Eastern Empire, nor that the penalty for profession of Christianity was death. The suggestion in 2:4 that the man of lawlessness has yet to take his seat in the temple of God has often been held to indicate a date earlier than 70, when the Jerusalem temple was destroyed.

But Dibelius has shown that the profanation of the temple was such a standing theme that it was repeated even in apocalypses known to have been written after 70 (see refs. in Vielhauer, 234, p 100).[3] Friedrich thinks that the reference to "the temple of God" is not to the Jerusalem temple at all, but that the author is simply using traditional ideas and formulations ("I am a God, I sit in the seat of God," Ezekiel 28:2; "I will sit upon the mount of congregation," Isaiah 14:13) in order to express the idea that the lawless one is showing the whole world that he is displacing God and setting himself up in his place (72, p 264). Thus a date of composition later in the first century is not excluded. It is favored by Lindemann (131, p 44) and Bailey (3, p 143); Vielhauer (234, p 100) suggests the mid-80s. The fact that the author assumes Paul's name means that his authority was highly regarded by the author and recipients.

The non-canonical letter known as *1 Clement* indicates that Paul was esteemed in Rome and in Corinth by 95 (see p 79 ff), but he may not have been widely esteemed much earlier and was not esteemed everywhere even then (cf. p 20). We saw that the author of 2 Thessalonians does not claim the title "apostle" in the prescript of the letter. The real Paul, as a latecomer to the faith, had on occasions to affirm with some vehemence that he was as much an apostle as those who had been apostles before him. If 2 Thessalonians had been written before Paul's status had been fairly established, the author might perhaps have stressed his claim to the title (cf. Lindemann, 232, p 43). On the other hand, the letter is unlikely to have been written later than the turn of the century, since Polycarp (who, as we shall see, could have written as early as 120) seems to have known the work (and accepted it as Pauline).[4]

Neither Thessalonian letter bases its eschatological teaching on what Jesus is supposed to have taught. But in due course both of the two incompatible doctrines were put in his mouth, and Mark and Matthew, each drawing at this point of his gospel on disparate sources, ascribe both views to him within one and the same speech. Mk. 13:5–31 specifies unmistakable antecedents of the second coming, while verses 33–7 urge watchfulness in case it comes unexpectedly. Mt. 24:6–14 likewise specifies catastrophes which will precede the end; but in verses 42–4 warning is given that it will be upon us unexpectedly "like a thief in the night" (the very phrase that had been used — without appeal to any teaching of Jesus — in 1 Thess. 5:2).

2 Thessalonians makes no mention at all of Jesus' incarnate life, not even of his death. His resurrection is also unmentioned. But we need not suppose the author ignorant of the crucifixion and resurrection; for this letter is even shorter than 1 Thessalonians (itself a mere five pages in the NEB) and seems to have been compiled largely from material in that letter in order to put the author's different view of the second coming. The warning against idleness in 3:6 is given "in the name of our Lord Jesus Christ." The author here represents Paul as inspired by the spirit of Jesus (cf. p 30), not as appealing to a teaching delivered by the historical Jesus. (No such teaching is ascribed to him in the gospels. Indeed, the Sermon on the Mount encourages idleness.[5])

The Epistle to the Ephesians

The canonical letter to the Ephesians purports to be the work of "Paul, an apostle of Christ" (1:1), but there are clear signs that it is not. Paul is represented in it as having "heard" of the faith of the Ephesian Christians (1:15; cf. 3:2), but the real Paul had been in Ephesus and had experienced this faith at first hand (1 Cor. 15:32). The letter seems to be a summary of his teaching written by a Paulinist about 90, and an adaptation of some of his ideas to the needs at that time of the Christian churches as a whole. It cannot have been written much later, as Ignatius borrowed phrases from it about 110 (see Mitton, 141, pp 132–5). Another indication of date is that Ephesians draws on Paul's letter to the Colossians (and is therefore later), and is very probably itself drawn on by (and therefore earlier than) the first epistle ascribed to Peter (written probably about 90, see p 64 ff).

Mitton has compared passages from Colossians that are used in Ephesians with similar passages in 1 Peter, which, however, diverge somewhat from the wording of Colossians but follow the slightly different wording in Ephesians. This seems to establish that the author of 1 Peter knew Ephesians directly. However, this argument has not been universally accepted as decisive, and some scholars (for example, Kelly, 119, p 14) still prefer to hold that 1 Peter and Ephesians are independent of each other and drew on a common source, perhaps a liturgical tradition. Such a view naturally attracts the more conservative, for, as Mitton notes, "it makes possible the retention of the Petrine authorship of 1 Peter and the Pauline authorship of Ephesians" (142, p 18).

If it is instructive to see what the author of Ephesians took from Colossians, it is no less so to note what he refrained from borrowing. He makes no mention of the "heresy" against which Paul had there protested (which included worship of angels, Coloss. 2:18). That conflict concerned a specific past situation, which was no longer of interest. He also drops the reference in Coloss. 3:4 to Jesus' second coming, a topic prominent in Paul's thinking and mentioned in every one of his genuine letters (except the brief personal note to Philemon). Unlike the real Paul, the author of Ephesians does not expect the second coming in the foreseeable future and writes about "the coming ages" (2:7), meaning coming generations of Christians (cf. 3:21, 4:13). Like the author of 2 Thessalonians, he was writing when initial hopes of the speedy return of the risen one had faded.

This is one reason why he does not share Paul's reservation about marriage. Paul had advised the unmarried to remain so and even "those who have wives" to "live as though they had none," for "the appointed time has grown very short" (1 Cor. 7:25–9). There is none of this in Ephesians, even though the author does write about marriage and compares the ideal marriage relationship with the intimate link between Christ and the church (5:22–33). Again, he tells the Ephesians to bring up children "in the discipline and instruction of the Lord" (6:4). Only when the end of all things had ceased to appear imminent could provision appropriately be made for a future generation.

Some of the words drawn from Colossians are used in a new sense, foreign to Paul's genuine letters. In Colossians "the mystery hidden for ages and now made manifest" is Christ himself (1:26–7; 2:2), but in Ephesians the mystery is God's purpose to "unite all things" in Christ (1:9–10), particularly Jews and Gentiles in one church (3:3–6). Coloss. 1:20 speaks of God "reconciling all things to himself" through Jesus, but the estrangement thus overcome is that between God and man, whereas in Ephesians divisions between men are also annulled. For the real Paul, the terms for admitting Gentiles into the church at all had been the subject of protracted and painful controversy. Ephesians, however, is addressed to Gentiles (2:11) in a situation where all such problems are over and done with; and in this epistle "the Church" always means the one universal church (never the local congregation, as often in Paul's letters) and is revered as the "bride" of Christ (5:32–3) in a manner foreign to Paul.

Again, the church is also said to be "built upon the foundation of the apostles and prophets, Christ Jesus himself being the cornerstone" (2:20). The real Paul had insisted that there can be no other foundation to the Church than Christ himself (1 Cor. 3:11). Ephesians was, then, written when apostles and Christian prophets provided the link between the period of Jesus' resurrection appearances and the Christians of the late first century.

In his own letters Paul repeatedly criticizes Jews who boast that they perform all the works required by the stringent Jewish religious law and are therefore justified before God. His view is that no one can be justified by works, but only by faith. Ephesians expresses these same ideas, but in words more likely to be intelligible to Gentiles unacquainted with Jewish thinking, a concession which the real Paul never made, even though his appeal was to Gentiles. Thus we read at Ephes. 2: 8–9: "By grace you have been *saved* through faith; and *this is not your doing,* it is the gift of God—not because of *works,* lest any man should boast." (Italics mine)

Mitton notes that Paul would have written "justified" rather than "saved" (as in Gal. 3:8 where he writes of the Gentiles being "justified by faith"). He would also have said that being justified is not the result of keeping the law (rather than "not of your own doing"); and he would have written "works of the law," not simply "works."

The author of Ephesians has dropped the reference in Coloss. 1:16–7 to Jesus' pre-existence as an agent in the creation of all things. If he is less interested than was Paul in Jesus' supernatural past, he might be expected to show more concern with the flesh-and-blood Jesus of history. He does indeed aver that "in his flesh" and by his crucifixion he broke down the wall dividing Jews from Gentiles (2:15). But he shows no tendency to stress his historical existence in the manner soon to be adopted by Ignatius against Christians who regarded it as unimportant and who were concerned only with the eternal Christ and the spiritual truths he had revealed. On the contrary, the author of Ephesians himself accepts that Christians have already entered upon a kind of resurrection life that raises them above the world and its history: God "raised us up with him and made us sit with him in the heavenly places in Christ Jesus" (2:6).

The enemies with whom the author contends are likewise not of this world, not "flesh and blood" but supernatural spirits, "the principalities, the powers, the world rulers of this present darkness, . . . the spiritual hosts in the heavenly places" (6:12), and "the prince of the power of the air, the spirit that is now at work in the sons of disobedience" (2:2). The author clearly accepts Paul's view that the region between earth and heaven is peopled with hosts of evil spirits, whose function is to foment strife and discord on earth. And the church, which contends against them, is spoken of in metaphysical rather than historical terms. It is admittedly founded on apostles and prophets, but is essentially a "glorious" church, "without spot or wrinkle," "cherished" by Christ its supernatural head (5:23-9). The supernatural forces of evil were already checked when God "raised Jesus from the dead, exalted him to his right hand" and put them "under his feet" (1:20-2). Nonetheless, they became aware of God's plan to save mankind only "through the Church" (3:10). The meaning is that only when the church had produced a united fellowship of Jews and Gentiles did these hostile supernatural powers realize how God was frustrating their attempts to produce discord.

It thus seems that the author retains much of the Pauline view that Jesus lived on earth obscurely, without attracting the attention of hostile spirits. He does, however, say that Jesus "came and preached peace to you who were far off and peace to those who were near" (2:17). "You who were far off" could mean the Gentiles; and, as Mitton notes (142, p 110), the passage may well reflect a form of the tradition represented in the gospels that Jesus' appeal was to those whom pious Jews treated as outcasts.

But the author seems to know no details of this preaching of peace. The ethical precepts in the epistle include injunctions to speak the truth, to control anger, to do honest work, to refrain from evil talk, and to be mutually kind and forgiving (4:25-31). In none of these instances is there any appeal to the teaching or example of Jesus, and in the next verse (5:1) the addressees are instructed to "imitate God," not Jesus. Christ is merely said to have loved us; and (as in Gal. 2:20) he "gave himself up for us, a fragrant offering and sacrifice to God" (5:2). In true Pauline fashion, the author declares that the "mystery" of how "the Gentiles are fellow heirs" with the Jews was revealed to him and to other apostles and Christian prophets "by revelation" (3:3-6), not by anybody's preaching.

III   THE LETTER TO THE HEBREWS

The titles of the letters in the canon which claim Paul as their author indicate the addressees ("to the Romans," etc.). The letter to the Hebrews is also identifiable in this way (unlike the remaining New Testament epistles, which go by the name of the author: James, Peter, John, or Jude). For this reason it has always been associated with the Paulines and in many Bibles is actually ascribed to Paul, although it does not in fact purport to come from him and is not written in his style.[6] The oldest manuscripts bear the title "to the Hebrews," and the NEB follows them in calling the work simply "A Letter to the Hebrews." But these manuscripts themselves date only from the third century, and it may well be that even the title they bear is not original, but was added in the second century by a reader who assumed that the author was concerned to prove Jewish ritual obsolete, with the reader having no knowledge of who the author was or whom he was addressing.

There is no indication within the letter itself that it was addressed originally to a Jewish-Christian community. Converts from Judaism would hardly have needed the warning not to "fall away from the living God" (3:12). The author never uses the words *Jew* and *Gentile* and draws no distinction between the two types of Christians. The document may have originated not as a letter, but as some kind of discourse, perhaps a sermon sent from one Christian community to another. For unlike the Pauline letters, which begin by introducing their author and identifying the recipients (for example, "Paul, a servant of Jesus Christ . . . to all God's beloved in Rome"), it lacks any epistolary introduction and plunges straight into theological assertion. An epistolary conclusion has been added—information about events in the sender's community and greetings to certain persons in the other. But even these references are only apparently concrete and specific, and may therefore be a fiction of the author, who intended thereby to supply a quite general sermon with the conventional Pauline ending to a letter. In this view, the document was not addressed to a particular community at all, but had in mind the situation of the church in general (so Vielhauer, 234, pp 240–1, with refs. to earlier work by Dibelius).

The opening verses (1:1–4) adumbrate the argument that Christianity, as the successor of Judaism, is the final revelation:

1. In many and various ways God spoke of old to our fathers by the prophets;
2. but in these last days he has spoken to us by a Son, whom he appointed the heir of all things, through whom also he created the world.
3. He reflects the glory of God and bears the very stamp of his nature, upholding the universe by his word of power. When he had made purification for sins, he sat down at the right hand of the Majesty on high,
4. having become as much superior to angels as the name he has obtained is more excellent than theirs.

We see from this that the author, like Paul, thought he was living in the "last days" (1:2) of the world; and he later (10:37) implies that he expects Jesus' second coming soon. We see that, as in the Paulines, the description of the Son is based on Jewish ideas of Wisdom. Thus the Son existed before the world, which God "created through him" (1:2); and he "reflects the glory of God," etc. (1:3). The obvious parallels in the wisdom literature are given by Montefiore (143, p 36). Again like Paul (and unlike Matthew, Luke, and John) the author makes Jesus ascend to heaven immediately at his resurrection: "When he had made purification for sins [as we shall see, by his suffering and crucifixion] he sat down at the right hand of the Majesty on high" (1:3). This is reiterated at 10:12: "When Christ had offered for all time a single sacrifice for sins, he sat down at the right hand of God." And finally, my quotation of the author's opening verses shows (1:4) that, like Paul, he found it necessary to attack Christians who worshipped angels and to argue that Jesus is superior to them.

Chapter 1 continues with an exegesis of seven Old Testament passages in order to establish Jesus' superiority to angels. Neither the early Christians nor the Jews contemporary with them understood the *historical* allusions in the Jewish scriptures; many statements in these scriptures which refer to a specific historical situation were interpreted by the Jews as pertaining to the coming Messiah, and hence by the Christians as references to Jesus (cf. p 38).

For instance, our author asks (1:5): "To what angel did God ever say . . . 'I will be to him a Father and he shall be to me a son'?" The quotation is from 2 Samuel 7:14, where Yahweh is speaking of David. The rabbis, however, had supposed God to be making a promise concerning the Messiah, and so for the author of Hebrews the reference is to Jesus, who is thereby shown to be the son of God and superior to any angel. The next quotation in Hebrews (1:6) is from the Septuagint, or Greek, version of the song of Moses (Deuteronomy 32:43): "Let all God's angels worship him." Our author makes the "him" refer to Jesus instead of to God by alleging that God spoke these words "when he brings the first-born into the world," that is, at the birth of Jesus. (This idea appears at a later stage of the developing tradition in Lk. 2:13 as a story of the heavenly host singing praises to God at the time of Jesus' birth.)

A major concern of the author of Hebrews is to argue that God has set aside as outmoded the sacrificial system of the old covenant, and here again exegesis of the Old Testament is important to the argument. He claims that Jesus "made purification for sins" (1:3) "for all time" (10:12) by his sacrificial death, and so has rendered unnecessary the daily ministrations of priests "offering repeatedly the same sacrifices which can never take away sins" (10:11). In particular, the day-of-atonement ritual conducted by the Jewish high priest is criticized, by representing Jesus as a more effective high priest, even though, for the author of Hebrews as for Paul, Jesus in his incarnate life supposedly was not of the priestly tribe of Levi, but in the line of David (7:13-4). This objection to his priesthood is solved by arguing that he has been given a special priesthood of unique order, surpassing that of the old Aaronic line, and patterned after the priest-king Melchizedek, who had no genealogical affinity with Aaron's tribe of Levi, yet was superior to him (7:4-10). Psalm 110:4 says: "Thou art a priest forever after the order of Melchizedek." The author of the Psalm was, as Montefiore has noted (143, p 97), "probably thinking of some Hasmonean prince who would combine in his person both royal and priestly office." But for the author of Hebrews (7:17) such statements were taken as prophecies spoken by God that referred to Jesus.

This reliance on the Old Testament has been held to have some bearing on the date of writing. To prove the superiority of Jesus' high priesthood, the author alludes to the account of the portable tent or tabernacle which Yahweh instructed Moses to build during the wilderness wanderings. It was divided into two by a veil which separated off the sanctuary (Exodus 26:33), and only on the annual day of atonement could the high priest pass through this veil, taking with him the blood of sacrificed animals (Leviticus 16). Our author accepts that "without the shedding of blood there is no forgiveness of sins" (9:22), but he holds that Christ has made the Levitical ritual obsolete by entering heaven, "the greater and more perfect tent," and by offering his own blood, "thus securing an eternal redemption" (9:11–2), whereas that secured by the Levitical high priest endures only for a year.

Now a writer who wished to discredit Jewish sacrificial ritual might reasonably be expected to point to the destruction of the Herodian temple in Jerusalem in 70, had he been writing after this date. But a striking feature of the argument of Hebrews' author is that it makes no mention of the temple, and is concerned only with the mobile desert sanctuary as described in the Old Testament. His silence about the temple is admittedly in line with his general silence about Jewish history of the first century, even where the facts of that history would have supported his argument. When, for instance, he writes of the inadequacies of high priests (5:1–4), he takes all his information from the Old Testament without alluding to the disgraceful abuses of the office in the first century, or to rabbinic discussions about that office. Perhaps he was remote from Palestine (he does write excellent Greek) and ignorant of its recent history in any detail. He obviously was not familiar with the ritual of the Herodian temple; otherwise he would not have said that the high priest makes daily sacrifice for sin (7:27), nor that the altar of incense stands in the Holy of Holies (9:3 f). (Both these statements, although not true, are quite intelligible as inferences from what is said in the Old Testament).

But if he wrote after 70 he could hardly have been unaware of the destruction of Jerusalem and of its temple, which was known internationally; that he chooses to rely on the Old Testament and does not turn the ruin of the temple to account has suggested to some that he wrote earlier. The fact that sacrifices continued to be made (on a reduced scale) at the temple after 70 (if indeed it is a fact and if it had been known to him) would not have deterred a writer, who is quite generally utterly arbitrary in his exegesis, from making capital of the temple's destruction.

This whole argument would be very strong if the author of Hebrews were in fact arguing against Jewish sacrificial ritual as practiced in his own day. But as we have seen, he does not reckon with Judaism as a theological opponent. His concern is to show that "Jesus is the surety of a better covenant" (7:22) than that described in the Old Testament, that he is the realization of the new covenant promised there (8:8). The author divides Christians, according to their state of enlightenment, into "children" and "the mature." The former need "milk," in the form of instruction in Christian fundamentals; the latter need "solid food" (5:11–6:1), and by this is obviously meant the author's own doctrine of the high priesthood of Christ, presented as a cultic mystery enacted in heaven with no cultic counterpart on earth. Vielhauer thinks that the author worked out this doctrine by reflection on the basic idea of Christ making intercession in heaven (234, p 246).

A date of composition later than 70, then, is not required, although it is not excluded. Hebrews may well have been written later than the Paulines, although overlap between its ideas and theirs is insufficient to prove it dependent on them. Most commentators think it must have been written before the anonymous epistle ascribed to Clement of Rome (which I shall give reason to date at the end of the first century), and argue that it is quoted (though not ascribed to any author) there. However, Theissen has recently given grounds for questioning the dependence of this epistle on Hebrews.[7] Nevertheless, Hebrews shows internal indications of a first-century date. (Vielhauer suggests the 80s or 90s). The Christians addressed in it have not been persecuted to the point of martyrdom (12:4), and so the conflict between church and state, which was quite marked from about 90, had not yet become a general phenomenon in the Eastern Empire. The church addressed also shows only rudimentary organization, in that its leaders are referred to simply as leaders (13:7 and 17), not as bishops or elders. Like Paul, the author still believes that Jesus' second coming is imminent (10:37), whereas writers who lived when this expectation had been disappointed for some time tend to defer the event. And the failure to mention any Christian heroes also suggests an early date; the long list of persons who have been distinguished by their faith is drawn exclusively from Jewish history as recorded in the Greek Bible, which includes the fourteen books of the Apocrypha.

Let us now see what the author has to say about Jesus' incarnate life. He repeats the Pauline idea of Jesus as the pre-existent son of God, who participated in the world's creation, and, as an act of obedience, came to earth in human form and experienced human suffering. Like the Jesus of Phil. 2:8, who was "obedient unto death," he "learned obedience through what he suffered" (Hebrews 5:8). For Paul, Jesus' suffering resulted from his submission in his human form to supernatural forces of evil, and his death broke their power (see p 34); and for the author of Hebrews he likewise assumed human form "that through death he might destroy him who has the power of death—that is, the devil—and deliver all those who through fear of death were subject to lifelong bondage" (2:14-5). For both, God responded to Jesus' obedience by raising him to his right hand, whereupon he is acclaimed (Phil. 2:10-1; Hebrews 1:13 and 2:9) and effects the salvation of all who obey him. This three-stage schema of pre-existence, suffering, and exaltation is explicitly set out in Hebrews 5:5-10:

Pre-existence	vss. 5–6	[God said to Christ] "Thou art my Son, today I have begotten thee" . . .
Suffering on Earth	vss. 7–8	In the days of his flesh, Jesus offered up prayers and supplications, with loud cries and tears, to him who was able to

		save him from death, and he was heard for his godly fear although he was a Son. He learned obedience through what he suffered.
Exaltation	vss. 9–10	And being made perfect he became the source of eternal salvation to all who obey him, being designated by God a high priest after the order of Melchizedek.

I have punctuated verses 7–8 as Roloff has suggested (168, p 152), not beginning a new sentence with "although he was a Son," but making this refer to what has preceded instead of what follows. The idea, then, is that, although he was God's pre-existent son, the prayers he spoke on earth were heard not because of that, but because of his "godly fear": that is, as a man on earth he could find a hearing with God only on the same basis as any other man, namely through fear of God and submission to his will. But whereas other men had been alienated from God by "fear of death," which had kept them in "lifelong bondage" to the devil (2:14–5), Jesus retained his "godly fear" when suffering and so was able, even then, to turn in prayer to God and be heard.

Some commentators have taken the statement of 5:8 that Jesus *"learned* obedience through what he suffered" as implying a progressive process of learning and a moral development during his incarnate life, details of which must therefore have been known to the author. But the sinlessness of Jesus (posited in 4:15) precludes any such suggestion of a moral schooling. Roloff justly takes "obedience" here to mean "the conscious and willed acceptance of the will of God while living the earthly life. Jesus did not, like other men, allow the conditions of earthly existence to lead him into contradicting God and hence into sin; but he 'learned as he suffered,' that is, he retained his obedience under those conditions in that he turned to God and sought communion with him" (168, pp 156–7).

The statement of 5:7 (quoted above) about the earthly Jesus' prayers to God "who was able to save him from death" – prayers which were heard because of his humble submission – is an application of the words of Psalm 22. It is not a reference to the gospel Gethsemane story, but conflicts with it. The Jesus of the gospel prayed in Gethsemane to be spared death and his prayer was not granted. The context in Hebrews shows that the author interprets Jesus' prayer not as a plea to be spared death, but to be delivered from the grave, and that this was granted (when God resurrected him). Roloff is able to say (168, p 146) that recent studies of this passage have shown conclusively enough that the material was not taken from traditions underlying the synoptic gospels, let alone direct from them.[8]

Other passages in the epistle that look superficially like corroboration of the gospels turn out not to be so. The statement that Jesus was "tempted" simply refers to his suffering and death. (A literal rendering of the Greek of 2:18 gives "being tempted in as much as he suffered.") He "learned obedience through what he suffered," and by his faithfulness under temptation was "made perfect" and thus competent to save men (5:8–9). The "hostility he endured from sinners" (12:3) designates not altercations with scribes and Pharisees, but again submission to a shameful death on the cross, after which he took his seat at the right hand of God (12:2).

The failure of the author of the epistle to refer to gospel material germane to his arguments is certainly striking. The "new covenant" mediated by Jesus is said to have been ratified by his blood, without reference to any words of his on the subject (such as those recorded by Paul or Mark). Again without reference to any teaching of Jesus, the author recommends brotherly love, hospitality to strangers, and the honoring of marriage (13:1–4). The injunction to "avoid love of money and be content with what you have" (13:5) is supported by quoting the Old Testament, not Jesus. Had the author known the substance of the gospel discourses, he could hardly have accepted as normal (6:16) the swearing of oaths (forbidden in the Sermon on the Mount). Had he known that Jesus had worked miracles, he would surely have said that Jesus had authenticated his teaching with their evidence, not merely that those who "heard" him had done so. Such silence about any miracles of Jesus, coupled with emphasis on the importance of miracles in authenticating Christian teachers, is exactly what we found in Paul (see p 22).[9]

The author of Hebrews quotes (2:6) the phrase "Son of Man" from Psalm 8 in a context where he is applying the passage that follows in the Psalm to Jesus. But he does not attempt to do this with the phrase "Son of Man." Had he known it as designation for Jesus, as it is used in the gospels, he could hardly have failed to do so. Again, he takes the stern view (unknown to Paul) that there can be no second repentance, that apostates can never be forgiven (6:4–6), and supports it with citations from the Old Testament and by mentioning Esau, who, after his crime, "found no chance to repent," even though he sought "with tears" to "inherit the blessing" (12:17). The author can hardly have been acquainted with the story of Peter's denial of his master. Finally, the author devotes chapter 11 to a eulogy of faith, and many Old Testament characters and their deeds are mentioned as signal examples, but none of the instances familiar from the gospels. (For details, see JEC, p 158.)

There is, however, one passage in the epistle which has been taken to mean that, in the author's view, Jesus not only suffered and died, but also preached on earth. (We saw something similar in Ephesians; cf. p 55). The author is concerned to show that the Christian message is authenticated by a chain of historical tradition going back to Jesus himself. (To anchor in this way what he considers to be correct doctrine would be an obvious way of repudiating the "strange and diverse teachings" then leading Christians astray.) In this context he says: "Salvation was declared at first by the Lord [literally, received a beginning when spoken by the Lord] and was attested to us by those who heard him, while God also bore witness by signs and wonders and various miracles and by gifts of the holy spirit (2:3–4)."

We saw that already, at 1:2, it was said that "in these last days" God "has spoken to us by a Son." Did the Son speak during his incarnate life? Was the initial message of 2:3 "declared" by the earthly or by the risen Jesus? Commentators are divided on this issue. Grässer, who thinks the reference is to Jesus' preaching on earth, nevertheless notes (86, p 265 and note) that the question *what* Jesus proclaimed as the "beginning of salvation" is not put by the author, unless perhaps he answers it in 2:12 with Psalm 22:22, which is there interpreted as Jesus saying to God: "I will proclaim thy name to my brethren [that is, to those whom Jesus redeems], in the midst of the congregation I will praise thee." (Montefiore notes [143, p 63] that it is possible that this verse of the Psalm "was used in the early Church as a *testimonium* of the presence of the risen Lord at its worship.")

The first link in the chain of historical tradition was, in any case, the words of Jesus. The second link is constituted by those who "heard" him and attested his message "to us." Grässer says that the author and his contemporaries may well have received the message not from those who heard Jesus directly, but second- or third-hand, from hearers of hearers, who are not excluded by the wording of 2:3 (86, pp 267–8). Even if, then, the writer supposed that the original auditors heard the historical, rather than the risen Jesus, the latter's lifetime is not necessarily thereby made a matter of the immediate past. Grässer thinks that the alternative—either words of the earthly Jesus or of the risen one—would not have seemed significant to the author, for whom Jesus was always the supernatural son of God, "the same yesterday and today and forever" (13:8). For such a Christology, words of the earthly Jesus would be as acceptable as words spoken to Christians in the spirit by the living Christ. Nevertheless, if the author did allow the possibility that Christians of his own day were linked by unbroken historical tradition with the historical (not merely with the risen) Jesus, then he probably regarded the incarnate life as less remote than Paul seems to have done.

This difference between our author and Paul is borne out by a further statement in the epistle. Paul, we recall, believed that God had sent his Son to earth "when the time had fully come" (Gal. 4:4) and that the Christian lives in a new era. "If anyone is in Christ, he is a new creation; the old has passed away, behold the new has come" (2 Cor. 5:17). Such ideas would allow an easy transition to the view that Jesus' life and death on earth inaugurated the final epoch (however long) of human history—however long, that is, this epoch had already lasted since his death and resurrection.

Even if, say, one or two hundred years had elapsed since those events, the final epoch had nevertheless, on this premise, begun, and it would soon culminate in his return to end the world and to judge mankind. This idea that his life and death on earth inaugurated the final epoch could be expressed by saying that he lived and died "in these last days," "at the end of the age," or "at the completion of the ages." Such a statement is lacking in Paul, but is explicit at Hebrews 9:26: "He has appeared once for all at the end of the age to put away

sin by the sacrifice of himself." This doctrine suits the author's theological purpose, which, as we have seen, was to show that, whereas the sacrifices offered
by the high priest need to be repeated once every year, Jesus' sacrifice is single
and unique. If he had intended to offer himself as a sacrifice more than once,
he would have had to make (so our author here suggests) a beginning earlier;
but by waiting until "the end of the age" he has deprived himself of any opportunity of repetition. Jesus' death, then, ushers in the world's final epoch.

It would be a natural further transition in thought to suppose that Jesus
died in the quite recent past. Whether the author of Hebrews had made this
transition in thought, it is not possible to say. The idea is not found in any
other of the early (before 90) epistles we are at present considering. On the
other hand, the less radical development which is certainly evidenced in
Hebrews (that he lived and died in the "last days") is found also in the first of
the two letters ascribed to Peter, which falls within the early period, and to
which we now turn.

IV   THE FIRST EPISTLE OF PETER

This letter is addressed to Christians in certain localities in Asia Minor, and the
author introduces himself as "Peter an apostle of Jesus Christ." Commentators take for granted that this can only mean the Galilean fisherman who
according to the gospels was a personal disciple of Jesus. But if the epistle was
written when the gospels, and even most of the traditions underlying them,
were still unknown (and I shall give evidence that this is in fact the case) then
"Peter" in the introductory verse means simply the apostle who (as we know
from Paul's letters) was prominent in the early Jerusalem church. This Peter
may have had no preresurrection acquaintance with Jesus any more than had
Paul, and personal acquaintance with a historical Jesus was imputed to him
only at a later stage of the developing tradition.

The question of the letter's authenticity would then become: Was it written
by this person, some time between, say, AD 50 and 70, or by a later writer posing as he? We cannot hope to establish the first of these two alternatives.
When it is asked whether an epistle ascribed to Paul is really his work, we can
compare its doctrine with those of the genuine Pauline letters. But we know
next to nothing of the opinions of the Peter with whom Paul contended in
Jerusalem.

1 Peter purports to be by the apostle Peter obviously because he was
regarded at the time of writing as a person of some authority — but not necessarily on the ground that he had been a companion of the historical Jesus.
"Apostle" in the earliest Christian literature does not mean "companion of
Jesus," but someone who has had supernatural experience of the risen Jesus
and has been called to his service by such a vision. This is the sense in which
Paul uses the word, and he says that Peter was an apostle in this sense. The
first author who uses "apostle" fairly consistently in the sense of "companion

of Jesus" is Luke (both in his gospel and in Acts, also from his hand); his purpose was to resist the heresy rife in his day by limiting the true doctrine to what has allegedly been proclaimed by men who had kept Jesus' company from his baptism to his ascension.[10] It is quite possible that 1 Peter is ascribed to the "apostle" Peter, in the older sense of the word.

A Galilean fisherman could hardly have been capable of the "scholarly correct Greek" and the, albeit limited, "range of rhetorical conventions" employed in the epistle. Such features, says Kelly (119, p 32), show the author to have had "a technical training" which we could not plausibly attribute to the Peter of the gospels. Those who nevertheless take him for the author suppose—on the basis of 5:12, "by Silvanus, a faithful brother as I regard him, I have written . . . to you"—that he had the letter drafted by a colleague, as statesmen do with their speeches today. On the other hand, if the letter is pseudonymous, written perhaps even when Peter was known to be no longer alive but at a time when Silvanus was known to the recipients, then this reference to him would have the purpose of certificating him as a trustworthy interpreter of the apostle's mind.

The author describes himself (5:1) as a "fellow elder" (like the "elders" of the Christian communities he is addressing) "and a witness of Christ's suffering." *Witness* (*martus*) does not imply an eyewitness (for which different words are used in the New Testament; see 2 Peter 1:16 and Lk. 1:2). Not even the gospels make Peter an eyewitness of the crucifixion but represent him as deserting and denying his master well beforehand. *Martures* means "those who give testimony" (for example, the two witnesses of Rev. 11:3). Commentators have noted that the Greek connects the author's claim to be a "witness" closely with his statement that he is a fellow elder. Hence it has been understood to mean that both Peter and the elders bore witness by their preaching to the sufferings of Christ. Perhaps, as Kelly suggests (119, p 199), it is implied not only that he has preached Christ crucified and has constantly dwelt on his suffering, but also that, like the Christians he is addressing, he has suffered for doing so. From such hints traditions to the effect that Peter was martyred could well have arisen.

The author reiterates (5:10 and 14) that Christians are "in Christ," meaning, as Kelly notes (119, p 221), that baptism has enabled them to share the life of the risen Christ. The formula "in Christ" is typically Pauline, occurring some 160 times in Paul's letters to express the conviction that Christians are mystically united with Christ. Not that the author of 1 Peter had read Paul (of many of whose major doctrines he shows no knowledge), but that some Pauline ideas had entered into the Christian thinking which constituted his background.

1 Peter seems to have been written after 70, since it is very probably dependent on Ephesians.[11] The author professes to be writing "in Babylon,"[12] probably meaning Rome. Hunzinger (108) has given evidence that in Jewish literature Rome is called Babylon (responsible for the destruction of the first temple)

only after Roman forces destroyed the second temple in 70. It is more likely that the Christians borrowed the usage from the Jews than vice versa. On the other hand there are reasons for not putting 1 Peter later than about 90. Its Christology is still relatively primitive, in that Jesus is represented as subordinate to God. For instance, "God raised him from the dead," whereas later tradition credits him with power to effect his own resurrection. The conviction that "the end of all things is at hand" (4:7) has not yet waned, as in some writers at the turn of the century. The Asian Christians addressed are not without some organization; their "elders" are not senior citizens but leaders with financial and other responsibilities (5:1-5). Nevertheless, there is no articulated hierarchy of church officers—neither deacons nor bishops are mentioned—such as Ignatius posits for Asia Minor very early in the second century. And there is no hint of the doctrine that the elders are custodians of the sound tradition of doctrine (cf. Kelly, 119, pp 30, 197).

The persecuted Christians addressed in this epistle are told to rejoice that they are enabled to "share Christ's sufferings" (4:13). They must expect to be "reproached for the name of Christ" (4:14) and vilified as wrongdoers (2:12), but there is no suggestion that they are facing the death penalty. (The "fiery ordeal" which comes upon them to "prove" them (4:12) is a metaphor describing any trial which has the refining effect of fire, a metaphor familiar from the Old Testament, and one which the author has already used at 1:7: "You . . . suffer various trials, so that the genuineness of your faith, more precious than gold which though perishable is tested by fire, may redound . . . to praise and glory.") It is implied (4:15-6) that, like thieves, they may be sentenced by pagan courts; the reference here seems to be not to provincial governors but to local magistrates, before whom Christians might well be brought on a charge of fomenting disorder.

Christians were disliked because they withdrew from contact with others and because they confidently proclaimed that the world was coming to a prompt and catastrophic end. If their fellow-citizens brought charges against them, the authorities would have to investigate these and would likewise have been biased against Christians, even though they did not at that time systematically persecute them simply for being Christians (cf. Goppelt, 81, pp 58-9). Not only is there no suggestion in the epistle that the death penalty was inflicted, but also the author actually urges the Christians addressed to obey the imperial authorities: "Be subject for the Lord's sake to every human institution, whether it be to the emperor as supreme, or to governors as sent by him to punish those who do wrong and to praise those who do right" (2:13-4).

It is difficult to believe that a Christian author would write like that at a time when the imperial authorities as such (not merely local magistrates) were actually carrying out anti-Christian policies, as they are known to have done from about 90 (cf. p 108). The author's suggestion that persecution of Christians is worldwide (5:9) merely reflects his beliefs that the end of the world is near and that persecution is one of its signs (4:17). Goppelt thinks that the epistle presupposes the kind of relationship between Christianity and the authorities which could have existed any time after Nero's pogrom in 65 but before the deterioration which began about 90 (81, pp 63-4). Best, however, thinks that all but the final years of this period must be excluded to allow sufficient time for Christianity to have established itself in the numerous areas in Asia Minor mentioned in the first verse of the letter (223, p 540).

This is the first pseudonymous epistle we have studied which is ascribed to someone other than Paul. Lindemann has made the interesting suggestion that non-Pauline Christianity would have been aware of its lack of "apostolic" tradition and would have tried to remedy this by creating letters allegedly written by other apostles. He thinks that 1 Peter represents such an attempt, written perhaps in Asia Minor (the destination of the letter according to 1:1) by a Christian who had moved there from a locality where the Pauline tradition was not known in the first century. (Syria, for instance, would be a possibility. Paul was well known in Asia Minor and Greece, where he had taught, and also in Rome, as is clear from 1 Clement, but the first evidence of acquaintance with him in Syria comes from the second-century letters of Ignatius of Antioch.)

On this view, the author of 1 Peter would not have felt quite at home in the Pauline communities of Asia Minor, and therefore tried to express his own theology in the form of a letter he ascribed to an apostle other than Paul, although inevitably the Pauline ideas current in Asia Minor influenced him to some extent. His statement in 5:13 that he wrote in "Babylon" is part of the fiction. The persecution suffered by the Christians he is addressing derives from the Roman authorities, and his statement in 5:13 means to say that Peter wrote this letter from a situation of persecution in Rome (Lindemann, 232, pp 253, 259, 397). That the letter was really written in Rome is unlikely, as later documents which were certainly composed there do not refer to it, although it would have been relevant to their purposes.

The author of 1 Clement, for instance, writing in Rome at the end of the first century (see p 79) had a high regard for Peter and Paul, and quotes 1 Corinthians as authoritative but knows nothing of any letter by Peter. Nor does the Muratorian Canon, the oldest extant list of Christian sacred books, written about 180. The pseudonymous letters of the New Testament, says Vielhauer, were generally written in the areas to which they purport to be addressed — Asia Minor in the case of 1 Peter, where it was known to Polycarp early in the second century (234, p 588). As to 1 Peter's final references to Silvanus and to "my son Mark" (5:12-3), these two men would have been known as companions of Paul. That the author here represents them as in his (not Paul's) company means that "the author is aiming at establishing the authority of Peter in areas of Pauline mission" (234, pp 586, 589).

The language of 1 Peter is that of a single writer, but the body of the work (1:3 to 4:11) stands as a unity within the whole. The reader is almost surprised to find that the letter goes on after the solemn doxology and amen at 4:11. Furthermore, some passages within the main section could imply that those addressed have just been baptized. They are said, for instance, to be "born anew" (1:3 and 23) and "like new-born babes" (2:2); their pagan neighbors are surprised and offended that they no longer join them in drinking and other excesses (4:4). We can hardly suppose that all Christians in these localities of Asia Minor (which included some areas where Paul had preached) were recent converts who had suddenly alienated the neighboring pagans. The passage is better understood as addressed to those who were in the process of adding themselves to an already existing Christian community.

Again, within this main section persecution is said to be in store for them, not something they are already experiencing; whereas in the concluding section (from 4:12 on) it is already upon them. This discrepancy would be intelligible if the main section were composed as an address to candidates for baptism, who would become objects of persecution only on joining the community at baptism. This was the hypothesis of Perdelwitz in 1911, and Vielhauer has recently endorsed it (234, p 585). On this view, the author has supplemented a baptismal sermon with an appeal to those already baptized to be steadfast, and then given the whole out as a letter of Peter by adding the opening and closing verses (1:1–2 and 5:12–4).

Had the author known the doctrine of the gospel Jesus that discipleship means suffering and persecution (for example, Mk. 8:34–8 and parallels), he would surely have appealed to it as relevant to his purpose. He tells those he is addressing to be ready with their defense when called to account (3:15), and is thereby in conflict with Mk. 13:11, where Jesus rules that Christians brought to trial should not be anxious beforehand what to say but should rely on the promptings of the holy spirit when arraigned. But more often the author of 1 Peter gives the same instructions as Jesus is reported in the gospels to have given, yet fails to invoke his authority or to give any kind of quotation from his teaching. Here are a few examples, with the gospel parallels to which no appeal is made:

1 Peter	*Gospels*
Christians are to maintain good conduct so that pagan neighbors "may see your good works and glorify God" (2:12)	Be a light for the world "so that they may see your good works and glorify your father who is in heaven" (Mt. 5:16)
"If you suffer for righteousness sake, you will be blessed" (3:14)	"Blessed are those who are persecuted for righteousness' sake." (Mt. 5:10)
Keep sober and watchful because the end of all things is at hand (4:7).	"Watch, therefore, for you do not know on what day your Lord is coming" (Mt. 24:42).

The author of 1 Peter tells his readers to love their fellow Christians (2:17 etc.), to practice hospitality ungrudgingly to one another (4:9), to have unswerving faith (2:7–8), and to bless instead of returning evil for evil. They are to avoid dissension and to be humble (3:8), to abstain from all passions of the flesh (2:11), to put away all malice, guile, insincerity, envy and slander (2:1). The author seems never to have heard of the Sermon on the Mount, and when he quotes authorities, these are passages from the Old Testament, not words of Jesus. Thus the injunction to bless the evil-doer and not to return his evil is supported (3:10-3) by quoting Psalm 34:12-6 ("Let him turn away from evil"), not by reference to Jesus' words as reported in Mt. 5:38-48 (against an eye for an eye) or Lk. 6:27-8 ("Bless those who curse you"). Proverbs 3:34 ("God opposes the proud but gives grace to the humble") is quoted at 5:5 to support the injunction to humility, and one would never suspect that Jesus had told his followers to "learn from me, for I am meek and lowly in heart" (Mt. 11:29).

The author of 1 Peter does not know of Jesus' manner of life but only of his death as exemplary behavior, and even what he says about that is based on the Old Testament (on the story of the suffering servant of Yahweh in Isaiah 53), not on historical reminiscence (for details, see JEC, pp 153-4). As in the Pauline letters, Jesus here, in 1 Peter, figures only as a pre-existent supernatural personage (that is, he existed before he was born on earth),[13] who came down and died for us. In the early Christian epistles generally, any ethical inferences made apropos of his behavior are drawn from these bare facts of his coming to earth and dying, as when Paul argues (Phil. 2:8) that he showed exemplary humility in condescending to take human form. What Jesus did or taught between birth and death remains, at this stage of Christian tradition, utterly unknown. In 1 Peter the moral uprightness of Christians is not said to depend on their following any Jesuine teachings, but on their relation to the risen Christ.[14]

The list of vices given in the epistle (for example, malice, guile, insincerity, envy, and slander, 2:1) is taken not from Jesus but probably from catalogues of misconduct in common use in Hellenistic popular diatribe and in the ethical propaganda of later Judaism (including the Qumran sect). Such lists frequently occur in other early Christian epistles (for example, Romans, 2 Corinthians, Ephesians, etc.), again with no appeal to the teachings of Jesus. Commentators, noting the marked similarities between these precepts and those of the Sermon on the Mount, say that the former are "echoes of," or "recall" the latter. But it is entirely possible that the opposite is true, namely, that after certain ethical and religious precepts had become established in early Christianity, it came to be believed that Jesus had taught them while on earth.

The interpretation of the Old Testament in 1 Peter is as arbitrary as that in other early Christian writings. Leaney writes in this connection of the "bold use of scripture" in the epistle (127, pp 29-30). For instance, the author urges his readers to come to the Lord, "to that living stone, rejected by men, but in God's sight chosen and precious" (2:4). The "stone which the builders rejected" (Psalm 118:22) was, in the meaning of the psalmist, Israel oppressed by her powerful neighbors; but Christian circles took the reference to be to Jesus, the rejected Messiah. (The next stage—documented in Mk. 12:10—was to represent Jesus himself as having understood it in this sense.)

The author of the epistle argues that God accepted Jesus' voluntary death as an offering which once and for all (3:18) makes full atonement for human sin. His redeeming blood "was like that of a lamb without blemish or spot" (1:19). The author is here thinking of the Passover lamb, which must be "without blemish" (Exodus 12:5), and this idea of Jesus as the Passover lamb may have been responsible for the later tradition that he actually died at Passover. It is obviously important for the author to believe that he spent time on earth as a man. His suffering and death was vicarious in that he endured the penalties which "our sins merited." And he could represent us in this way only by becoming fully human, by having a "body" in which he "bore our sins" (2:24).

Although Jesus' earthly existence is of importance to the author, he does not assign it to a definite historical period, but merely—like the author of Hebrews—to the last times. Jesus, he says, was "destined before the foundation of the world, but was made manifest at the end of the times for your sake" (1:20). Kelly notes (119, p 75) that this verse "bears all the marks (balanced antithesis, solemn tone, etc.) of being an excerpt from either a credal text or, more probably, a Christological hymn." And he shows that it is characteristic of the author of this epistle to draw on liturgical and other pre-existing material. If he is doing so in this verse, then the idea it expresses (that Jesus' life on earth marks the final epoch, however long, in world history) was already current in his day and may be presumed to have entered Christian tradition very soon after Paul. (I have shown on what basis when I discussed Hebrews.)

The next stage in the developing tradition would be to interpret "the end of the times" to mean the recent past, and then to specify exactly when in the recent past Jesus had lived and died. Such a stage goes beyond the position of the author of 1 Peter, who is not merely silent about the precise period when Jesus lived but actually writes in such a way as to show that he cannot have believed that he had been executed under Pilate. His insistence that imperial governors "punish those who do wrong and praise those who do right" (cf. p 65) surely means that he could not have accepted any tradition that Jesus, whom he expressly describes as without blemish, had been condemned to death by Pilate.

In this connection it is highly significant that the pastoral epistle 1 Timothy (written, as we shall see, *after* 90), which does link Jesus with Pilate, does not state that governors punish evil-doers, and urges rather that intercession "be made . . . for . . . all in high positions, that we may lead a quiet and peaceable life" (2:1-2); whereas Paul (writing shortly before 60 and silent concerning Pilate) had anticipated the standpoint taken in 1 Peter and had declared that the governing authorities punish only wrongdoers (Rom. 13:1-7). All this constitutes strong evidence that Pilate entered Christian thinking about Jesus only late in the first century.

V THE EPISTLE OF JAMES

This epistle is one of the most enigmatic documents in the New Testament. It is silent not only about Jesus' teachings, but also about his life, death, and resurrection. Nothing is said of a Davidic descent, nothing of a crucifixion, no hint of an atonement. When the author exhorts the brethren to be "patient until the coming of the Lord," he mentions, as a shining example of patience in suffering, not Jesus but "the prophets who spoke in the name of the Lord" (5: 7–11). This "coming of the Lord," he says, is near, and the author therefore lives "in the last days." But nothing in his epistle suggests that this will be Jesus' *second* coming. In the only explicit mention of him after the opening verse, he is simply said to be "the Lord of glory" (2:1).

This lack of reference to what even Paul records as basic Christian events is remarkable and bewildering. On the other hand, however, the epistle is full of teachings that very closely parallel the Sermon on the Mount, although the author does not in any way suggest that Jesus had delivered them.

The author introduces himself as "James a servant of God and of the Lord Jesus Christ" (1:1). It is obvious from Paul and from Acts that a person of this name was an influential leader of the Jerusalem church in the middle of the first century, and the author seems to be posing as this person. It is but a pose, for although he insists that "the whole law" must be kept, he refers (2:10–2) only to the ethical demands of the Decalogue and seems to have no interest in the law's ceremonial and dietary regulations. This is certainly not the attitude of the James whom Paul mentions, whose representatives persuaded all the Jewish Christians at Antioch to withdraw from table fellowship with Gentile Christians (Gal. 2:12). The author of the epistle of James also keeps what Guthrie (90, p 74) admits to be a "curious silence" concerning the "burning question" of circumcision with which the James whom Paul mentions was so deeply involved. And the author's silence concerning the resurrection would be very perplexing if he were the Jerusalem James, whom Paul includes in his list of those to whom the risen Jesus had actually appeared (1 Cor. 15:7).

The James of whom Paul writes is identified by most commentators as Jesus' brother. I shall give detailed justification for not accepting this view (see chapter 8 below). The James of the epistle does not claim to be any more than a "servant" of Jesus.

Dr. Robinson tries to turn the absence of references to Jesus' life, death, and resurrection to account by arguing that, if the epistle of James were not genuinely the work of James the opponent of Paul (whom Robinson, with most commentators, regards as Jesus' brother), such references would have been inserted later to add credence and verisimilitude (164, p 129). The answer to this is that the epistle was long ignored (for details see Kümmel, 125, p 405) and was accepted into the canon very late. Even Eusebius, writing about 325, classed it among the "disputed books." No doubt it was ignored because regarded as useless — "not of much value for doctrinal polemics" as Sidebottom puts it (182, p 20). But it would hardly have been ignored if it had been thought to be the work of Jesus' brother.

To explain the author's strange silences, it has sometimes been argued that his epistle is really a Jewish tract adapted for Christian use (as is known to have occurred in other cases; for example, *2 Esdras* and the *Didache*). But, as Seitz remarks (84, p 457), surely "no editor would have been satisfied with so slight a revision." And the epistle is not even strongly Jewish in orientation. It mentions neither the Jews nor Israel by name nor any of Judaism's characteristic institutions. And we have seen already that, when the author appeals to the Jewish law, he has in mind only a very limited area of it. For all its lack of interest in the person of Jesus, the work is decidedly Christian, for, as we shall see, it includes a discussion about the efficacy of faith and works which, while clearly a protest against Paulinism (or rather against what some Christians were taking for Paulinism), cannot be understood as a *Jewish* protest. For it was Paul's doctrine about the Jewish law that gave offense to Jews; and yet James is quite unaware that Paul's discussion of faith and works involves this law at all. This point is well brought out in Sophie Laws' recent commentary (see p 74).

The epistle is not a real letter dispatched to a specific community of Christians but a literary composition for Christian readers in general. It is addressed "to the twelve tribes in the Dispersion" (1:1). Jews living outside their Palestinian homeland and hoping to return to it were known as the Dispersion or Diaspora. But since the epistle is Christian and shows no sign of missionary writing, this address can scarcely mean the Jews. Jewish Christians of the Dispersion might be meant, although it is strange to designate them as the twelve tribes. It is much more likely that the author means to address Christians in general as "the true, Israel that lives on earth in a foreign country and has its home in heaven" (Kümmel, 125, p 408).

1 Peter is similarly addressed "to the exiles of the Dispersion," a metaphor for Christians hoping not for Palestine but for heaven as their homeland (1 Peter 1:4), and with no abiding home on earth, where they face persecution. The idea that the church is the true Israel, the appointed heir of both the revelation and the promises made to the Jews, is frequent in the New Testament. Paul calls Christians "the Israel of God" (Gal. 6:16) and declares that "we are the true circumcision" (Phil. 3:3).

The epistle of James is, then, not a letter but a homily or sermon of general applicability, with admonitions which are mostly ethical and which are loosely strung together, one idea suggesting another often by the mere association of a single word. In these respects the work follows the tradition of the Jewish wisdom literature. Indeed the author probably knew the *Wisdom of Jesus the Son of Sirach* (the apocryphal book *Ecclesiasticus*) in its Greek version; for "many of his ideas, for example, endurance under trial or humiliation; wisdom as a gift to be sought from God; the need for faith and avoidance of a divided heart in approaching God; God's mercy toward those who love Him, etc., are found in similarly close association in Ecclesiasticus" (Seitz, 84, p 458).

Halson gives evidence that the "vocabulary, style, form and theme" of the epistle are dependent on the wisdom literature of the Septuagint (228a, p 311). It was not the representation of Wisdom as a supernatural personage in this literature that appealed to James, as it had done to Paul and the author of the letter to the Hebrews. James shows how Christians could draw on a quite different aspect of the wisdom literature and defines wisdom in purely ethical terms, saying: "The wisdom from above is first pure, then peaceable, gentle, open to reason, full of mercy and good fruits, without uncertainty or insincerity" (3:17). Paul and James together thus show how wide and diverse the influence of this wisdom literature was on early Christianity.

Parallels with teachings ascribed in the gospels to Jesus are equally close in James to parallels with the teaching of the wisdom literature. Williams has noted that "as we read James, we are reminded again and again of the Sermon on the Mount" (216, p 84). It is all the more striking that James never refers to the gospels nor to Jesus as the source of the moral precepts in which his epistle abounds. He never repeats the exact wording of the gospels and so is not quoting them. The following passages in the epistle that are paralleled in Matthew's version of the Sermon on the Mount show how numerous and close the parallels are.

1:2	Count yourselves happy when you have to face trials (cf. Mt. 5:10-2).
1:4	Be perfect (cf. Mt. 5:48).
1:19–20	Avoid anger (cf. Mt. 5:22).
1:22	Do not merely listen, but act on the message you hear (cf. Mt. 7:24 ff).
2:10	To break one stipulation of the law is to break the whole (cf. Mt. 5:19).
2:13	Only those who show mercy will obtain it (cf. Mt. 5:7).
3:18	"The harvest of righteousness is sown in peace by those who make peace" (cf. Mt. 5:9).
4:4	Friendship with the world is enmity with God (cf. Mt. 6:24).
4:10	"Humble yourselves before the Lord and he will exalt you" (cf. Mt. 5:5).
4:11–12	Do not judge others (cf. Mt. 7:1-5).
5:2 ff	Riches become rotten, fine clothes become moth-eaten (cf. Mt. 6:19).
5:10	The prophets are examples of suffering and patience (cf. Mt. 5:12).
5:12	Do not use oaths, do not swear by heaven or by earth, but say simply "yes" or "no" (cf. Mt. 5:33-7).

Guthrie (90, p 68) supplements these with four more from other parts of *Matthew*:

1:6	Have faith without doubting (cf. Mt. 21:21).
2:8	Love of neighbor is a royal law (cf. Mt. 22:39).
3:2-3	Guard against hasty speech (Mt. 12:36-7).
5:9	The divine judge is standing at the doors (cf. Mt. 24:33).

Sidebottom thinks that James and Matthew are independent of each other and draw on traditions that had something in common. Sophie Laws likewise notes that "the parallels which exist between Matthew and James are in sayings which could readily be absorbed into the general stock of Christian ethical teaching" (231a, p 14). Sidebottom thinks that James knew these traditions as they existed at an earlier stage of their development, for his letter lacks the references to persecution and the controversy with the rabbis which characterize the traditions in the form in which they are given in Matthew's account of the Sermon on the Mount (182, p 15).

In the Sermon on the Mount, Jesus, in the course of instructing his disciples how to pray, recites the Lord's prayer to them and its request to God not to "lead us into temptation" (Mt. 6:13). Why should God wish to lead us into temptation, unless it suits his larger purpose? Then what would be the use of praying? Commentators rightly say that such questions may be beside the point, since the Greek for *temptation* can mean not only what the English word implies but, alternatively, "trial" or "test," in the sense of persecution, even martyrdom.

It is, however, of interest that such questions seem to have troubled James, for he says: "Let no one say when he is tempted, 'I am tempted by God'; for God cannot be tempted with evil and he himself tempts no one" (1:13. The Greek verb here for "to tempt" corresponds to the noun used for "temptation" in the gospel.). It seems, then, that James knew of Christians who supposed that "temptation"—in one or other of the senses which the Greek can carry—comes from God, and that, whatever they took this to mean, James understood it as implying that God tempts man. It may well be that the Christians he is here criticizing actually used a prayer or liturgical formula which included the words "lead us not into temptation." But it is very unlikely that such a prayer had, at that time, been attributed to Jesus. At any rate, James, in repudiating it, does not suggest that this was so.

The reasonable inference from the evidence is that James was writing in a situation where Christian writers were familiar with the wisdom literature but had not yet ascribed its teachings to Jesus. The parallels between James' ethical doctrines and those of the gospel Jesus are too close and too numerous to allow the hypothesis that James, although he does not appeal to Jesus' authority, was nevertheless aware that he had taught them.

The letter of James is, then, a piece of moralizing modelled on wisdom literature. It treats only one strictly theological doctrine, namely the issue of justification by faith, and thus raises the question of its relation to the Pauline letters. Paul argues (cf. p 19) that when a man comes before God the judge, he cannot justify himself by claiming that he has achieved righteousness by keeping the Jewish law. For Paul, man is so sinful that any claim to acquittal based on such righteous works is out of the question, and salvation can come only from faith in Christ's redeeming sacrifice. Paul, then, says that a man is justified by faith in Christ, apart from the works of the law (Rom. 3:28; Gal. 2:16), and he gives Abraham as an example.

James, however, says that a man is justified by works and not by faith only (2:14) and also goes on to give Abraham as an example. If James is replying to

Paul, he has either misunderstood or caricatured Paul's argument, for Paul never contended for faith without works, and held that works are the fruit of faith, as is clear from the ethical section (5:13–6:10) of his letter to the Galatians. Rather than impute to James obtuseness or worse, some commentators have made him the earlier writer (of about 48). However, as Sophie Laws points out in her recent valuable commentary on James, this cannot be squared with the polemical tone which he adopts on this matter. For instance, he asks: "Do you want to be shown, you foolish fellow, that faith apart from works is barren?" (2:20). This tone implies that James was attacking a doctrine which he supposed some Christians were disposed to accept; and what was in question was presumably some form of the Pauline doctrine.

James need not have known any of Paul's actual letters, as Paul's dictum concerning justification by faith had very likely become a standing phrase which, although still attributed to Paul, was used and understood independently of the meaning he had given it in his letters. There is evidence enough that, by the end of the first century, Christian writers were well aware that Paul had preached a doctrine of justification by faith—however little else they knew of him. The letter to the Ephesians (see p 54) puts it into his mouth, as do the pastoral 2 Timothy (at 1:9) and Acts (at 13:39; see pp 164–5). That James did not in fact have in mind the precise passages in which Paul expounds his complicated argument is suggested when we find him using the word *works* in a sense different from Paul. As Dr. Laws observes:

> When Paul speaks of "works" in relation to justification, he speaks consistently and explicitly of works of obedience to the Jewish Law . . . . The Law plays, however, no part in James' argument at this point, and his understanding of *works* is most naturally seen in terms of the deeds of charity demanded in 2:15–16 (231a, p 129).

In these verses 15–6, which introduce James' discussion of faith and works, he is saying that if a well-fed and well-clad Christian comes across a fellow-Christian who is hungry or without proper clothing, it is not sufficient for the former to suppose that God will provide for the latter's bodily needs and to do nothing in this direction himself. For James, such deplorable behavior would be an example of faith without works (verse 17). Paul himself knew that his teaching about salvation through faith alone was being twisted so as to license antinomianism or libertinism. Nevertheless, "it does not seem likely that James . . . met it in this connection: his concern here is not with immorality but with quietism, the argument that confession of God is all, that expressions of trust in God obviate the necessity for taking any action about human need" (Laws, 231a, pp 131 f).

In sum, the original context of Paul's argument, namely "the rejection of Judaising tendencies in the Churches and so of the Law as the means of justification, has been left behind, and 'works' are clearly not understood [by James] as works of obedience to the Law, but as 'good works' in terms of general charitable activity" (*Ibid.,* p 16). This kind of reinterpretation of Paul is evidenced also in the pastoral epistles (see p 91). From a critic of the Jewish law he was made into a straightforward moralist, as the conflicts of his own day were over and forgotten.

It follows that it is unlikely that James is trying to refute the slogan "faith without works" as the spokesman of a Jewish Christianity that accepted the Jewish law. Rather he attacks this slogan (in Lindemann's phrase) "in the name of a Christianity orientated towards Wisdom." And, for Lindemann, he chose the pseudonym James because this was a name which carried anti-Pauline implications (232, pp 249–50). Paul had written of his dispute with James of Jerusalem in his letter to the Galatians, and this serious quarrel would have passed into Christian tradition and have been known even to those who had not read Paul.

If, then, the epistle is pseudonymous, it will surely have been written after the lifetime of James of Jerusalem, perhaps at about the turn of the century. Dr. Laws gives evidence that it was known to the author of *The Shepherd of Hermas,* a Christian work which she and others date in the early decades of the second century (231a, pp 22–5, 42 n).

The epistle of James evidences a Christianity which, while indebted, like early Christianity generally, to Judaism (accepting, for instance, the authority of the Jewish scriptures and the belief in one God and in his laws as moral commandments), is nevertheless highly distinctive in its lack of emphasis on the person or example of Jesus. The epistle is—I again quote Dr. Laws—"the most consistently ethical document in the New Testament, but its various warnings, precepts and words of encouragement are not based on a theological principle in any way remotely comparable to, for instance, Paul's drawing of ethical conclusions from his proclamation of the death and resurrection of Christ" (p 27).

James, then, shows the existence of a Christianity which was primarily an ethical way of life, with a minimum of Yahweh and an absolute minimum of Jesus. It is unlikely that any such Christianity could have arisen in the first or early second centuries if Jesus had had the importance ascribed to him in the gospels. If, however, Jesus never existed, and the earliest Christians had but vague ideas about his supposed life, and conflicting estimates of its importance, then a group breaking away from the synagogue could have formulated the kind of ideas we find in James.

3

Epistles of the Late First and Early Second Centuries

I INTRODUCTION

The letter of Jude was probably written a little after 90, and the three Johan-nine letters may, but need not be, dated that late. The first of the three implies that both the writer and the Christians he is addressing believed that Jesus had been baptized while on earth. I have noted (p 29) that it is not surprising that such important rites as Eucharist and baptism should early be attributed to the historical Jesus. But apart from this reference to Jesus' baptism in 1 John, the epistles of Jude and John do not give a portrait of Jesus significantly fuller than that of the epistles already discussed.

It seems, then, that some epistles which may be later than 90 go on portray-ing Jesus in much the same manner as the earlier documents. This is to be ex-pected. For a group of opinions is not dropped by everyone everywhere as soon as a later set of opinions, which is finally to supplant the first, has arisen.

Early Christianity consisted of communities largely independent of each other, each with some doctrinal ideas of its own. Evidence for this is the fre-quency in the literature of complaints about other Christians with unacceptable ideas about Jesus.[1] Some communities will have retained older views while others were advancing. But from about 90 we do find that here one and there another Christian body begins to ascribe to Jesus one or more of the aspects of his life and work that were, about that very time, being synthesized in gospels which would have circulated in yet other communities. *1 Clement,* for instance (written about 95) ascribes ethical teachings to him in words reminiscent enough of gospel formulations to have been derived from sources on which the gospels themselves drew. The Pastoral epistles (of about 100) and 2 Peter (probably written a little later) are still unaware that Jesus gave such teachings, for they make no appeal to him when discussing the same subjects. Nevertheless these documents do advance on earlier ones in other significant respects. 2 Peter alludes to the miracle of the transfiguration, and the Pastoral 1 Timothy suggests (3:16) that Jesus' life on earth was far from obscure.

1 Timothy also puts Jesus' life in the early first century by mentioning Pilate, a point that is reiterated by Ignatius (writing about 110). Both authors are concerned to criticize Christians with other views of Jesus. The author of the Pastorals does not argue with his Christian opponents, but simply refers them to what he calls the traditional teaching, giving little indication of what that consists of. Scholars think that most of his references to doctrine are merely quotations, for example, from early Christian hymns, creeds, or prayers, and that his one reference to Pilate is quoted from a creed recited at baptism. Ignatius, however, states fairly fully, against other-minded Christians, what correct Christian doctrine is, and mentions Pilate repeatedly in this connection, in such a way as to suggest that other Christians did not agree with this dating. He says, for instance, that the faithful are "not to yield to the bait of false doctrine, but to believe most steadfastly in the birth, the Passion and the resurrection, which took place during the governorship of Pontius Pilate."

My argument, then, is that the traditions collected in the gospels were beginning to be available when this later (after 90) group of epistles was written. The distinction I have drawn between the early group of epistles (those prior to 90) on the one hand, and the later epistles (of 90–110) and the gospels on the other, is not to be set aside with the (albeit true) observation that earlier documents are not always more reliable than later ones.[2] My point is that, in the case in question, if the later documents give historical facts, the truth, about Jesus, the earlier writers could not have written as they did.

We have already seen how the Pauline view that Jesus died in an unspecified past ("when the time had fully come," Gal. 4:4) soon developed into the statement that he died "at the end of the times" (Hebrews and 1 Peter). Such an interpretation did not immediately find general acceptance. It is not asserted in the Johannine letters, nor in *1 Clement*. Originally it may have meant no more than that his first coming inaugurated the final epoch (however long) of history, the epoch which would culminate in his return. But it could easily have been taken to mean that he had been on earth in the recent past; and then it would be natural to reflect on this recent past, to pinpoint the period in which he had allegedly lived and thus give it a precise historical context.

Such reflection, which in my view began only after 70, led to linking him with Pontius Pilate. One factor which facilitated such a radical change in ideas was the Jewish War with Rome from 66, culminating in the capture and destruction of Jerusalem in 70 and involving the dispersal and reduction to insignificance of the Palestinian Christianity known to Paul. These events represented a break in continuity which would have made it very difficult indeed for Christian writers at the end of the century to have reliable ideas about Palestinian Christianity before 60. (A suggestive parallel could be the Thirty Years' War in Germany (1618–48), after which Germany's medieval past was long lost from sight and laboriously recovered from archives only in the eighteenth century.)

All the earliest extant writings that linked Jesus with Pilate (1 Timothy, *Mark,* and the work of Ignatius) were written by men active 90–110 in Gentile communities[3] which, if Mark is anything to go by, had but hazy ideas about Palestine.[4] If Christians were beginning about 90 to think that Jesus had lived recently, they could not plausibly have supposed that he had been active in their own time or immediately before; otherwise there would be many who could offer first-hand reminiscences of him, and it was clear this was not the case. An earlier date would therefore be sought; Pilate would then naturally come to mind as the person who could appropriately be considered as his murderer; for he was particularly detested by the Jews, and is indeed the only one of the prefects who governed Judea between AD 6 and 41 who attracted sufficient attention to be discussed by the two principal Jewish writers of the first century, Philo and Josephus.

Some of the epistles considered in this chapter are not printed in modern Bibles. The New Testament canon of today comprises only those books which the whole church finally accepted as inspired. The four gospels and the thirteen letters ascribed to Paul were accepted as such in the second century, but doubts long persisted about such epistles as Hebrews, Jude, and 2 Peter, while on the other hand works now excluded were long accepted by individual churches. *1 Clement,* for instance, was for a time included in the canon of the Egyptian and Syrian churches, and three of the six extant manuscripts of this epistle are Bible manuscripts (Vielhauer, 234, p 530). For the purpose of investigating the development of the Christians' view of Jesus, an early document may be helpful whether or not it was accepted at any stage as authoritative.

I must now give my reasons for dating as I do the epistles I put after 90. If I also outline their contents, this will illustrate the kinds of pressure which led Christians of the late first and early second centuries to define what they considered to be the historical basis of their faith.

II   THE FIRST EPISTLE OF CLEMENT AND THE NERONIAN PERSECUTION

The letter known as *1 Clement* is not included in the New Testament. It is anonymous and is addressed by the church of Rome to that of Corinth. Christian tradition from about 170 ascribes it to the Clement who is supposed (on dubious evidence) to have headed the Roman church from 88 to 97. I shall call the author Clement. The purpose of his letter is to censure Corinthian Christians for deposing some of their leaders. For him, it is a "moral duty to bow the head" and "take one's seat on the stool of submission" before church leaders (ch. 63). Study of first-century Christian epistles shows that their authors were very much concerned with correct doctrine (with what constitutes the proper faith) and with church order (the machinery for the conservation and propagation of the faith).

Clement does not accuse the Corinthians of any doctrinal error and seems to suppose that correct doctrine will follow from adequate church order (obedience to the leaders). We shall see that, only slightly later, Ignatius of Antioch actually urges obedience to bishops as a safeguard against heresy. Clement's letter thus testifies to what Elaine Pagels has called "a dramatic moment in the history of Christianity," in that this document is the first to argue for dividing the Christian community between clergy and laity, supervisors and subordinates (233, pp 34–5).

Nearly all commentators agree that Clement was writing about 95. Something that could indicate an earlier date is his allusion to the Old Testament commands that sacrifices are to be offered at the proper times and places; for in this context he notes, using the present tense, that certain rites "are performed" only in the Jerusalem temple (chaps. 40–1). Had he written after its destruction in 70, he might perhaps have used the past tense, although there is some evidence that temple sacrifices did continue on a reduced scale after the temple was gone (see Clark, 225). Josephus, who certainly knew of the temple's destruction and was writing near the end of the century, also used the present tense in referring to the temple sacrifices in the context of Old Testament commands concerning offerings (113, 3, 224–57). Commentators think that Clement was likewise quoting the Jewish regulations as they existed while they were still in force.

Clement mentions (ch. 5) the persecution unto death of "the greatest and most righteous pillars" of the church, which took place "in the recent past," in "our generation." These examples of suffering are recent, in comparison with the Old Testament ones just cited. And "our generation" could surely cover events of thirty years back. Lindemann notes that the expression is often used simply in the sense of "Christendom" (232, p 74 n). The author then mentions the sufferings of Peter and Paul, and may well wish to suggest that these too are recent; but the way he writes of them is so vague that they cannot be very recent events that were really known to him.

Peter, he says, "endured many labors and, having borne his testimony, went to his due place of glory." This does not specify martyrdom, but may imply it. He adds that Paul came "to the limit of the west" and "bearing his testimony before kings and rulers, passed out of this world." Paul himself recorded (Rom. 15:24 and 28) that he intended to travel to Rome and Spain. Clement, who knew Paul's letter to the Romans (he paraphrases a passage from it) obviously inferred from it that he had carried out these travel plans and that, since nothing more was heard of him, he had died in Spain. As Merrill has observed (137, p 292), Clement seems to have no knowledge of the manner or place in which Peter or Paul died, but "thought it eminently proper for them to die as martyrs, and therefore ventured to intimate rather than confidently affirm it."

All this suggests that he was writing at least twenty or thirty years after they had passed from the scene.

Clement next alludes to the "torture" of a "great multitude" of Christians "in our midst." Since he is writing from Rome, this seems to refer to Nero's persecution there in 64 or 65, evidenced by Tacitus. Perhaps this is also to be understood as recent. But again, would this necessarily mean more recent than thirty years ago? He does indeed begin his letter by saying that all manner of "bothering things" have prevented him from writing earlier. But it is arbitrary to assume that he is here referring to the Neronian (or any other) persecution.

Tacitus (writing about 120) accuses Nero of having executed in savage fashion a "great multitude" of Christians at Rome as scapegoats for arson, for which Nero himself was rumored responsible. It would be surprising if a great multitude of them had lived at Rome as early as 65, and Merrill has plausibly argued (137, p 101) that Tacitus is here exaggerating for rhetorical effect, since his purpose was to paint the emperor as black as possible and to show that his behavior toward these admittedly contemptible persons (from Tacitus' standpoint) had been unreasonably severe and had brought him just opprobrium. (Hence, Tacitus adds that "there arose a sentiment of pity due to the impression that they were being sacrificed not for the welfare of the state, but to the ferocity of a single man.")

Apart from Clement, no Christian writer mentions Nero's persecution until Melito, bishop of Sardis about 170. The silence of earlier Christian writers suggests that the persecution was local (confined to Rome and not extending to the provinces) and was quickly terminated. Melito writes as though persecution in his own area in Asia was rare in his lifetime, and Tertullian records that there was no persecution in North Africa before 180.

Conservative Christian scholarship has long exaggerated the effects of Nero's persecution, alleging that it resulted in the prohibition of Christianity by law. However, Frend concedes that there is no evidence that Nero's Senate ever enacted such a law; and that, even if it had, "Nero's suicide and his subsequent *dammatio memoria* by the Senate would have voided his legislative acts." Furthermore, "an edict presupposes a certain degree of importance for its subject, which it is doubtful whether the Christians at this stage could claim" (71, p 166). Frend, like Merrill, sees the difficulty of supposing that there was a "great multitude" of them at Rome as early as the 60s. No doubt the Christian community in Rome from the 70s exaggerated the extent of Nero's persecution, and Clement's reference to a great multitude of sufferers is what one might expect a Roman Christian to say within a generation of the event.

Clement shows no sign of living in a situation of tension between church and state. His remark (ch. 7) that "we are in the same lists and the same contest awaits us" is a metaphor which takes up that of the Christian "athletes" in ch. 5. As Robinson notes (164, p 330), this "need have no reference to . . . persecution . . . but, as in the New Testament generally, . . . may be a summons to the common Christian struggle." Clement does not merely pray for obedience to "our governors and rulers on earth" (ch. 60). He even says that it is God who has given them "glory and honor" and authority to rule (ch. 61). He prays for their "health, peace, harmony and security" that they may exercise their authority "without offence." There is certainly no suggestion that they made his own life difficult. Some New Testament writers who did live under persecution regarded it as presaging the end of the world (see, for instance, on 1 Peter, p 65). Clement, however does not expect the end to come soon. In ch. 20 he contemplates the majestic course of nature in a way which presupposes its permanence, if not its eternity (Clarke, 39, p 28); and he makes provision for a future generation of Christians when he urges that "our young people" be trained up in the fear of God (ch. 21).

In ch. 44 there is mention of presbyters, who were appointed when *successors* of the apostles had died and who have already been in office for *a long time*. This would seem to take us into the 90s. Clement does not claim to have been acquainted with men who themselves had known apostles personally. The author of Hebrews could be understood as making this claim (cf. p 61). Clement thus seems more remote from Christian origins.

In ch. 42 Clement says that the apostles "received the gospel . . . from the Lord Jesus Christ" who was sent from God. This statement reproduces the Pauline view that Jesus is a supernatural personage sent into the world. Clement then adds: "When they had received their orders and had been filled with confidence by the resurrection of our Lord Jesus Christ, they went out . . . preaching the gospel." It is not clear from this (nor from the Greek original) whether or not they received their orders before the resurrection, during Jesus' incarnate life. We have seen that what the author of Hebrews said on this matter was equally ambiguous. Clement nowhere mentions the twelve and may well not have believed the apostles to have been companions of the historical Jesus. He regarded Paul as an apostle, but surely not as a companion of Jesus. As Lindemann has observed (232, p 80), all that Clement is here alleging is that the commissioning of the apostles goes back to Christ himself.

After the resurrection the apostles "went out in the confidence of the holy spirit." Clement himself speaks "through the holy spirit" with Jesus' voice, and must therefore be obeyed (chaps. 59 and 63). He thus retains the early Christian emphasis on the prompting of the spirit.

Clement does not refer to any written gospel, and I have shown elsewhere (JEC, pp 165–7) that he fails to allude to a good deal of gospel material which would have suited his argument very well. He does, however, quote certain teachings which "the Lord said," and he regards them, with the Old Testament, as authoritative. The purpose of his letter (to censure a rebellion against church leaders) gives him occasion to moralize, and it is clear that, by the time he wrote, moral teachings of Jesus were available and could be drawn on for this purpose. The words of Jesus which he quotes are not taken from the gospels (see JEC, pp 167–9) and in Köster's view (124, p 23) are drawn from an earlier layer of tradition. These quotations are, as Goodspeed notes, "highly stylized and seem more naturally explained as being derived from catechetical teaching" than from any written gospel (79, p 9 f).

A story of the Passion would also have served Clement's purpose well—he several times mentions Jesus' redeeming blood—but it does not seem to have been available. As evidence of Jesus' self-abasement he quotes (ch. 16) the story of the suffering servant of Yahweh from Isaiah 53. He never mentions Pilate, although one detail recorded of Pilate in the gospels would have suited his argument particularly well. Clement devotes chapters 3 to 6 to showing that jealousy and envy bring no good, and illustrates this thesis with copious references to events narrated in the Old Testament and to events of the more recent past. What he does not mention is the example one would expect to come to the mind of a Christian writer acquainted with the gospels: namely, the tradition that the death of Jesus was caused by the envy of the multitude. Mk. 15:10 and Mt. 27:18 record that Pilate tried to persuade the people to let him release Jesus; "for he knew that for envy they had delivered him up." Clement, then, knew that Jesus "taught us" (ch. 59) and gave his blood for us (chaps. 21 and 49), but there is no indication that he had precise ideas about the circumstances of his death.

III   THE EPISTLE OF JUDE AND THE SECOND EPISTLE OF PETER

The author of Jude calls himself "Jude, a servant of Jesus Christ and brother of James." He does not say which James, but he may have in mind the author of the epistle of that name who introduces himself as "James a servant of God and of the Lord Jesus Christ" (also without saying which James). Christian tradition has identified these authors, Jude and James, with the brothers of Jesus included in the list given in Mk. 6:3 ("Is this not the son of Mary and brother of James and Joses and Judas and Simon, and are not his sisters here with us"). However, neither author shows any knowledge of the teachings of Jesus given in the gospels.

Jude, for instance, urges his readers (verse 17) to "remember the predictions of the apostles of our Lord Jesus Christ" that false teachers will mislead the faithful in the last times. In one of Jesus' gospel discourses about the last times, he warns that "false Christs and false prophets will arise and show signs and wonders, to lead astray, if possible, the elect" (Mk. 13:22). Had the author of Jude known this or any similar Jesuine teaching, surely he would have appealed to it rather than to the teaching of apostles. And this injunction to "remember" what they had predicted for the last times suggests that he—living as he supposed (verses 18, 21) in these last times—regarded these apostles as belonging to a past generation. He does not, either here or elsewhere, include himself among their number. They are the authorities of the past on whose work and prestige the church has been founded (Leaney, 127, p 100).

The epistles of both Jude and James took a very long time to achieve general recognition;[5] this in itself suggests that they were not originally accepted as works by Jesus' brothers. Commentators concede that it would be "extraordinary if, while Jesus left no written works behind him, *two* of his brothers had written considerable tracts in the Greek language, and that these had been preserved, had come into general use about two hundred years after they were written, and had been treated as canonical ever since" (Williams, 216, p 95; endorsed by Leaney, 127, p 81). Williams adds: "When one knows the immense popularity in those times of attaching a new work to an old name (possibly because the old hero was thought to have inspired with his spirit a contemporary prophet) one cannot help hesitating long before accepting the traditional view."

The author of Jude may have been a Jewish Christian, for he is familiar not only with the apocryphal *Book of Enoch*—he is the only New Testament writer to quote from an apocryphal work and this may not have endeared him to the Church Fathers—but also with a story about the archangel Michael (verse 9), which derives from another apocryphal work, *The Assumption of Moses*. (This has not survived and is known only from a fragment of a Latin translation and from quotations in later writers.) He claims to be addressing Christians in general (verse 1), but he is clearly concerned to criticize a "heresy" that must have been restricted to a particular locality. As Guthrie says, he "has in mind a concrete situation, however much he may have supposed that the Church generally needed the same message" (90, p 237).

The heretics he attacks are Christian. They have "gained admission" (verse 4) and still participate in the community's Eucharist (verse 12), although he cannot bring himself to refer to them as "brothers" and designates them "certain people." He describes them as thoroughly licentious—in theological polemic opponents are often represented as morally debased—and says that they "revile the glorious ones" (verse 8), probably meaning angels, who in late Jewish tradition figure as guardians of the world, with the function of seeing that God's laws are obeyed in it. While Paul and the author of Hebrews had to contend with Christians who evaluated angels too highly, Jude is faced with believers who took the opposite view. All this argument about angels does not suggest that early Christianity had a strong basis in historical fact.

In controverting these heretics, Jude makes it obvious that he was writing at a time when "the faith" had come to mean fixed and settled formulas from which any deviation was reprehensible. Thus he speaks of "the most holy faith" (verse 20), which "was once for all delivered" (verse 3). In the earliest Christian documents *faith* often means an attitude of belief in Jesus which will ensure salvation and does not often denote the content of belief. That it here (as in 2 Peter 1:1) means a set of inflexible propositions which constitute Christian doctrine points to a later stage of development (evidenced in, for instance, 1 Tim. 4:1 and 6: "Some will depart from the faith by giving heed to deceitful . . . doctrines"; "the words of the faith and of the good doctrine which you have followed").[6]

Jude's conception of the faith and his reference to the apostles as persons of the past whose predictions must be "remembered" make it impossible to date his epistle before 70; most commentators assign it to the end of the first century.

Much of the epistle of Jude is found also in 2 Peter (particularly in its middle chapter); and the evidence is that Jude was written first and then adapted and expanded by the author of 2 Peter. Both writers, in castigating contemporary heretics, say they will be punished as were the malefactors of the past, and then give a list of Old Testament examples. Jude does not give them in their order of occurrence in the Old Testament, but 2 Peter does. It is easier to suppose that the latter writer put a random list into proper order than that the former disrupted a chronological sequence.

Another telling comparison is between Jude 9 and 2 Peter 2:11. Jude (following *The Assumption of Moses*) has it that, whereas the heretics presume to revile angels, the archangel Michael did not take it upon himself to rebuke even a fallen supernatural personage (the Devil, when the two contended over the body of Moses). 2 Peter has made this incident into a generalization: "Bold and willful," the heretics "are not afraid to revile the glorious ones; whereas angels, though greater in might and power, do not pronounce a reviling judgment on them before the Lord." 2 Peter has also dropped the quotation from *Enoch* in Jude 14–5. It seems, then, that 2 Peter was written "when these apocryphal works were going out of favor, so that he saw fit to generalize the statement about the angels in such a way as to obscure the apocryphal origin of the tradition" (Sidebottom, 182, p 99). Alternatively (or additionally) he may have been trying to make the material he found in Jude more intelligible to a Gentile audience ignorant of Jewish apocryphal literature.

Sidebottom characterizes 2 Peter as "a reissue of Jude expanded to deal with the question of the end of the world" (p 69). Jude does not suggest that the false teachers he attacks denied Jesus' second coming. He merely calls them "scoffers following their own passions" (verse 18). 2 Peter, however, is faced with scoffers who say: "Where is the promise of his coming? For ever since the fathers fell asleep, all things have continued as they were from the beginning of creation" (3:3–4). The fathers who have died are clearly an earlier generation of Christians to whom the expectation of a speedy end to the world had been extended; this detail shows that the writer himself belonged to a later generation. His counsel is that Christians should live lives of holiness and thus not merely await but actually "hasten" the end (3:12) — the only New Testament passage which clearly states that man can influence God's decision to inaugurate the final judgment.

When the writer of 2 Peter first mentions his Christian opponents, he uses the future tense ("there will be false teachers among you who will secretly bring in destructive heresies," 2:1). But this attempt to speak from the standpoint of the historical Peter breaks down, and he soon lapses into the present tense ("they are not afraid to revile the glorious ones," 2:10; "they revel in the daytime" and "have eyes full of adultery," 2:13–4). At 2:15 the activities of these offending persons are even reported in the past ("they have gone astray and

followed the way of Balaam"). The events which "Peter" is supposed to be prophesying have, then, already begun to occur in the author's own day.
Förster sums up the relation between Jude and 2 Peter as follows:

> There is no reason why a letter by Peter should be reissued in a shortened form under the name of Jude whose authority was so much less significant than that of Peter. But it is immediately comprehensible that the letter of Jude should be expanded by entering in upon the question of the delay of the Second Coming and should be reissued under the name of Peter to assure it of greater influence (84, p 758).

The dependence of 2 Peter on Jude is in itself strong evidence that the author is not in fact the man he purports to be, namely "Simeon Peter, a servant and apostle of Jesus Christ" (1:1). *Simeon* is the correct Hebrew and Aramaic form of *Simon* and aims at stamping the writer as the Jewish-Christian apostle. The author attempts further to authenticate himself by alluding to 1 Peter, saying (3:1) that "this is now the second letter that I have written to you." The opening sentence of his letter is obviously based on the initial words of 1 Peter (and to some extent of Jude), but there is little in common in the substance of the two Petrine epistles, and 2 Peter was in fact written in a completely different situation that presented different problems. That the author did nevertheless know and refer to 1 Peter shows that, at the time of writing, "1 Peter carried authority and had a certain distribution" (Fornberg, 67, pp 12, 14). 2 Peter's approach to the question of the second coming shows that he is much the later writer; for 1 Peter simply affirms that "the end of all things is at hand" (4:7), whereas 2 Peter is at pains to explain why it has not yet come. It is not that the Lord is slow in fulfilling his promise, but because he is patient and wants to give everyone a chance to repent (3:9).

The writer also places himself on a level with Paul, whom he designates as his "beloved brother" (3:15). This indicates a time when Peter and Paul were regarded, from a later date, as the chief apostles of the church — as in Acts or in the letters of Ignatius — a time when the church had become aware of its distance from the first Christian generation and had no idea of how sharp the conflicts between the leading personalities of that generation had been. That the author of 2 Peter was in fact no contemporary of Paul is revealed from his knowledge of a collection of Pauline epistles which he designates as "scripture" (3:15-6), a word writers of the first century had reserved for the Old Testament and its Apocrypha, and which they never used for the books of the New Testament.

The writer finds that "there are some things hard to understand" in Paul's letters and he shows no knowledge of Pauline theology (in contrast to 1 Peter; this is further evidence that the two writers are not identical). It is the Pastorals, not the genuine Paulines, to which 2 Peter shows affinities (for example, in the conception of faith and in the abuse of heretics and their "myths" and the complaint that they are motivated by gain: 2:3, cf. Titus 1:10–1). This in itself places the work in a second-century milieu. Furthermore, the author's Christology is much more advanced than that of the Pauline epistles, where Jesus is subordinate to the Father, will finally deliver up the kingdom to him (1 Cor. 15:24 and 28) and himself then be merely the first-born among many brothers (Rom. 8:29). In 2 Peter, however, the eternal kingdom is Jesus' own (1:11), and the concluding doxology (3:18) is addressed not to God but to Jesus, something which occurs only in the later books of the New Testament. (The only unambiguous parallel is in the Pastoral 2 Timothy, at 4:18.) For all these reasons, the majority of scholars regard 2 Peter as a second-century work. Kelly (119, p 237) puts it at 100–110, others at as late as 130.

What does this relatively late work know of Jesus? It presupposes his atoning death when it describes him (2:1) as the master who "bought" Christians. Like other canonical epistles, it shows no knowledge of his teachings. Faith, knowledge, self-control, steadfastness, godliness, brotherly affection, and love are listed at 1:5 without mentioning him. When the author urges his readers to be "without spot or blemish" and to be "at peace" (3:14), the authority to whom he refers for support is not Jesus but Paul. This, however, shows not ignorance of Jesus—the writer must have known from Christian tradition, as represented for instance in 1 Peter 1:19, that Jesus was without blemish—but high evaluation of Paul's writings as "scripture." At 3:2 the addressees are told to "remember the predictions of the holy prophets [of the Old Testament] and the commandment of the Lord and Savior through your apostles."

This is a reworking of Jude 17 ("remember the predictions of the apostles of our Lord Jesus Christ"); its emphasis on apostles as mediators of the teaching derives from that verse, where the apostles, rather than Jesus, are the authorities appealed to. The apostles presumably received the teaching from the risen Jesus or from his spirit, and it is unnecessary to suppose that the author is implying that they were his companions during his incarnate life.

Like Jude and the authors of 2 Thessalonians (2:3) and of the Pastorals (1 Tim. 4:1–3; 2 Tim. 3:1–5), our author believes that the end of the world will be heralded by perverse teaching, blasphemy, immorality, and apostasy (see 2:1–3); but he, no more than they, suggests that Jesus had prophesied such things. The reasonable inference is that such ideas were commonplace in early Christianity, and were only later put into Jesus mouth (for example, at Mk. 13:22). Again, like Paul (1 Thess. 5:2), our author thinks that the Day of Judgment (when in his view the earth will be destroyed by fire) will come suddenly "like a thief" (3:9–10). This is another early Christian commonplace (cf. Rev. 16:15 and 3:3, where the risen Jesus tells John: "I will come like a thief") and only later was Jesus made to say this during his supposed incarnate life (Mt. 24:42–3).

The author of 2 Peter also claims that "the Lord Jesus Christ" had "revealed" to him that he was soon to die. This in itself places the epistle within the genre of pseudepigraphical valedictories, such as *The Testaments of the Twelve*

Patriarchs, where each Patriarch on his impending death gives his descendants spiritual instruction to keep and follow and after he is gone.[7] Our author likewise writes his message so that "after my departure you may be able at any time to recall these things" (1:15). He is probably presupposing that Peter was martyred, an idea current from the end of the first century. (It is suggested in *1 Clement* 5 and stated by the risen Jesus in the chapter added to the fourth gospel, Jn. 21:18 f). Again, he is not necessarily claiming that it was the historical Jesus who revealed to Peter, in whose name he writes, his impending death. The idea may be that the risen Jesus or the spirit effected the revelation.

Something which looks much more like an echo of an incident in the gospels is the author's claim that:

> . . . we did not follow cleverly devised myths when we made known to you the power and *coming* of our Lord Jesus Christ, but we were eyewitnesses of his majesty. For when he received honor and glory from God the Father and the voice was borne to him by the Majestic Glory, "This is my beloved Son, with whom I am well pleased," we heard this voice borne from heaven, for we were with him on the holy mountain (2 Peter 1:16-8). [Italics added.]

This clearly has some relationship to the transfiguration story as related in Mk. 9:2-8 and parallels, and the words of the divine voice are almost identical with Mt. 17:5. The purpose of the author of 2 Peter is to convince his readers that Christ has a heavenly form which can be manifested and which therefore guarantees (against the scoffers) his second *coming,* when he will appear in majesty. One would naturally expect a writer with such a purpose to refer to one of Jesus' post-resurrection appearances rather than to an incident in his incarnate life, and it may well be that he did suppose that this "transfiguration" was in fact a post-resurrection event. Bultmann thinks (30, p 278 n) that the phrase "receiving honor and glory" can refer only to Jesus' resurrection or exaltation to heaven (which, in the earliest traditions, are simultaneous; cf. p 44). And Kelly observes (119, p 320) that *The Apocalypse of Peter* (an apocryphal work written about 135), which drew some of its material from 2 Peter (p 236), understood the transfiguration as a post-resurrection story.

Mark's transfiguration story tells that Jesus took Peter, James, and John up a high mountain. In what follows only Peter plays an active role, and the other two are mere extras. They all see Moses and Elijah in conversation with the transfigured Jesus, and Peter then suggests making three shelters, one for each of these three. Mark does not impute any plausible motive for this suggestion, and implies that Peter was talking nonsense because he was terrified. Then a cloud appeared and out of it came a voice saying: "This is my beloved Son; listen to him." In the Ethiopic version of *The Apocalypse of Peter* (discovered in 1910) the details of the story are more intelligible. There is a reason for the presence of Moses and Elijah: they have come to fetch Jesus into heaven. Peter's motive in wishing to build the three shelters seems to be to retain

Jesus on earth; for Jesus angrily replies to him that only a shelter made by his heavenly Father will suit him and the elect.[8] The cloud too has a function: it has come to bear the three away to heaven (see Hennecke, 100, 680-2).

Goetz argued in 1927 that both the synoptic gospels and the apocryphal *Apocalypse* drew the incident from an older story, that this older story is better preserved in the *Apocalypse* than in the synoptics, and that it may well have been a story of an appearance of the risen Jesus to Peter (78, pp 77-81). One would expect such a story to have been current early in Christian tradition, for Paul tells that Peter was privileged to receive the first resurrection appearance (1 Cor. 15:5). In this view, the gospel transfiguration narrative (although unlike any other Easter story that has survived) is a resurrection story which Mark (or his immediate source) has put back in time into the earthly ministry of Jesus.

Because, then, the author of 2 Peter probably regarded the "transfiguration" as a post-resurrection event, he is unlikely to have taken it from the gospels, but both he and they would have drawn it from earlier tradition. He knew that the incident was believed to have taken place in the presence of Peter and other apostles, and hence he tries to authenticate himself as Peter by classing himself among these privileged eyewitnesses. To this end he no longer speaks as *I* (as he had done in the verses immediately before, when reporting that Jesus had revealed to him that he was soon to die) but as *we*. If he is really Peter the apostle, as he claims, then we must suppose that this privileged eyewitness of the transfiguration wrote a letter which is a mere rehash (without acknowledgment) of that of the non-apostle Jude (a letter which in any case belongs to post-apostolic times).

Another feature of this reference to the transfiguration is that it constitutes an appeal to what the readers would accept as fact, in contrast to the "myths" which, presumably, were prominent in the religious teaching of which the writer disapproved. Later he likewise controverts those who scoff at the doctrine of Jesus' second coming by appealing to (what he and his readers took for) historical fact, namely the Flood (3:5 ff): God had—as a matter of undisputed fact—destroyed all life on the world on that occasion, and this gives the necessary assurance that he will do so again at the final Judgment. Rejection of "myths" is equally conspicuous in the Pastoral epistles. 1 Tim. 4:7 deplores "godless and silly myths" (cf. 1 Tim. 1:4 and Titus 1:14), and emphasizes instead a historical fact from Jesus' life on earth (his "testimony before Pontius Pilate").

It seems, then, that about the turn of the first century, controversy with opponents with fantastic ideas led Christian writers to underline what they considered to be the historical basis of their faith. It may have been pressures of this kind which made the transfiguration into a historical incident in Jesus' life, instead of a resurrection appearance.

IV   THE PASTORAL EPISTLES

Timothy is named as a companion of Paul in six of the undoubtedly genuine Paulines, and Titus in two of them. The three New Testament letters addressed to these men (two to Timothy and one to Titus) are called "pastorals" because Timothy and Titus are given instructions on running the church. These letters are, then, concerned with the organization and structure of the church as an institution, as the means of safeguarding true doctrine.

All three letters are from the same hand. Houlden writes of their "overwhelming stylistic homogeneity" (105, p 23). All three begin by naming Paul as their author. However Vielhauer notes (234, p 216) that today they are almost universally regarded as not by Paul, even by conservative and Catholic scholars. In the first place, the author treats Timothy and Titus as subordinates, calling the former, for instance, "my child in the faith" (1 Tim. 1:2). In the undoubtedly genuine Paulines, Timothy figures as a colleague of Paul; as his "fellow-worker" (Rom. 16:21), "brother" (Coloss. 1:1, 2 Cor. 1:1 and Philemon 1), and fellow "servant" of Christ (Phil. 1:1). His relegation to a subordinate position in the Pastorals is one indication that their author is someone anxious to represent Paul as a figure of authority and Timothy as a trustworthy bearer of his inheritance (Houlden, 105, p 48).

2 Tim. 1:5 points in the same direction. The author here says that Timothy's sincere faith "dwelt first in your grandmother Lois and your mother Eunice." That it dwelt *first* in them means that he has taken it from them, not merely that he shares it with them. The real Paul could hardly have referred in this way to three generations in the faith with no hint of conversion from either paganism or Judaism of any of the persons mentioned, and with no suggestion of the inadequacy of pre-Christian beliefs. But a writer of fifty or sixty years later, when Christianity had been established for several generations, might attribute such a statement to him.

The Pastorals name many persons (twenty in 2 Timothy alone) as helpers or opponents of Paul, and these personal references have often been adduced as evidence of authenticity. Most of the names are otherwise unknown—only seven of them are mentioned in the undoubtedly genuine Paulines. Fictitious personal references are common as a stylistic device in ancient pseudepigraphical writings (see Brox, 224, p 275), and Lindemann holds that the names in the Pastorals fulfill a literary function, namely to stamp Paul as an intensely active and well-connected missionary (232, p 48).

That the author is a post-Pauline writer is sometimes betrayed by the very way he handles these names. At 2 Tim. 4:10-1 and 16, for instance, Paul is made to complain that all his companions other than Luke have deserted him. Yet a few verses later, at the end of the letter, the author has sufficiently forgotten this alleged isolation to write greetings that constitute the conventional conclusion to a letter; here Paul, far from being alone, sends greetings from "all the brethren" and even specifically names four of them. This suggests that the earlier reference to his isolation is part of the writer's portrait of him as "a moving example from an already heroic past," as "an example to discouraged Christian leaders" of the writer's own day, who are to learn that it is the lot of those who serve the gospel to endure isolation (Houlden, pp 34, 131, 134).

In the same context Paul is made to tell Timothy: "When you come, bring the cloak that I left with Carpus at Troas, and also the books, and above all the parchments" (2 Tim. 4:13). This is sometimes adduced as a detail too trivial for a pseudonymous writer to have invented. But evidence has been given (see Brox, 224, pp 292-3) that to ask for items of clothing that had been left behind is an epistolary commonplace which therefore could easily have been included as an appropriate touch in a fictitious letter. Moreover, the request does not fit Paul's situation as represented in the epistle. He has stated (verse 6) that he is awaiting execution, and so what use has he for his cloak and his books, particularly as they will take months to reach him.

Paul's theology is very imperfectly represented in the Pastorals. They lack many of his major themes, and where the author does use Pauline words, the doctrine is often lost — "transposed into a new key" or "deprived of its cutting edge," as Houlden says (p 28). An example is the reference to "the law" in 1 Tim. 1:8. In the undoubtedly genuine Paulines this expression means the Jewish law, but here it means the moral teaching accepted by Christians. Clearly, whether the Jewish law was to be kept was no longer an issue by the time the Pastorals were written. The transformation of Paul into a pure moralist reaches its climax three verses later, where "the ethical commonplaces which have just been listed are identified as the substance of 'the glorious gospel'" (Houlden, p 53).

There are further grounds for regarding the Pastorals as pseudonymous, written between 100 and 140 by someone familiar with some of Paul's letters but with a poor grasp of his theology. The obviously genuine Paulines begin to be quoted by later writers (1 Clement, Ignatius, etc.) from about 95, but there is no certain attestation of the Pastorals until about eighty years later.[9] Furthermore, although like each other in language and diction they differ very much in these respects from the undoubtedly genuine letters of Paul.[10] More specifically, certain important religious ideas are denoted, not with the terms employed consistently by the real Paul for these ideas, but with terms common in philosophical and religious discussion in the Greek world.[11]

Kelly, who regards the Pastorals as Pauline, argues (118, p 50) that an imitator is not likely to have so repeatedly attributed to Paul an idiom which is found in none of his acknowledged letters, and he thinks that Paul changed his vocabulary in his later years. But it can be equally argued that an imitator is quite likely to have put an idiom into Paul's mouth if that idiom formed part of his own intellectual milieu.

Since there is evidence that Paul dictated his letters (at Rom. 16:22 the scribe introduces himself and conveys his own greetings to the addressees), attempts have been made to account for the unusual language of the Pastorals by supposing that he entrusted not only their writing but also their drafting to a secretary. As they are linguistically alike, we should have to suppose that the same secretary was employed on all three occasions. But in fact the Pastorals show no signs (as there clearly are in Romans, 1 Cor. 16:21, and Gal. 6:11) that Paul used a secretary at all.

Another reason for regarding the Pastorals as pseudonymous is that the situations presupposed in them cannot be fitted into Paul's life as known from the undoubtedly genuine Paulines, nor even into the account of his travels given in Acts. Scholars who nevertheless take the Pastorals as Pauline have to argue that he was released from his imprisonment at Rome reported at the end of Acts, and that he then missionized both in Ephesus (where according to 1 Tim. 1:3 he left Timothy and himself moved on to Macedonia) and in Crete, where (according to Titus 1:5) he left Titus behind him. As 2 Timothy represents Paul as a prisoner in Rome (1:8 and 16–7) expecting execution (4:6), the argument is that this refers to a second and final Roman imprisonment after these missionary journeys, supplementary to what we know of his travels from other canonical sources.

I shall argue later (p 151 ff) that it is most unlikely that he was ever released from the captivity reported at the end of Acts, and that, even if he had been, the author of Acts did not believe that he had ever returned to Asia. And this, as Vielhauer notes (234, p 222) was not merely the private opinion of the author of Acts, for the Eastern church generally knows nothing of a return by Paul to the eastern Mediterranean. Kelly thinks that, if the life-situations presupposed in the Pastorals are fictitious, the author would have been careful to have drawn them from readily recognizable incidents in Paul's life (118, pp 8–9). But there is no reason to believe that Acts was available to him, and to construct plausible itineraries was not an easy task and one which he really had no motive to undertake. Why should he bother to try to make clear to himself and his readers in which of the periods of Paul's activities (known to him or assumed by him to have occurred) each of his three letters was supposed to be placed?

The situation presupposed in the Pastorals is in itself implausible. Paul's undoubtedly genuine letters (apart from the brief Philemon) are addressed to Christian communities, but these three address two individuals who are not simply his disciples but his official representatives (Timothy in the church of Ephesus, Titus in that of Crete), who are to give effect there to the instructions set out in the letters. These instructions are not emergency measures, but rulings which are to govern the routine behavior of the Christian community over a considerable length of time, and which therefore could not be unfamiliar to a Timothy who had really been Paul's companion in an Ephesus mission.

Indeed, the author says (1 Tim. 1:3) that he has already instructed Timothy by word of mouth and even that he hopes soon to be back in his company ("I hope to come to you soon, but I am writing these instructions to you so that, if I am delayed, you may know how one ought to behave in the household of God," 3:14–5). The possibility of delay is hardly a sufficient motive for the penning of instructions which Timothy has already received verbally.[12] The statement that Paul intends to visit Timothy soon is sometimes adduced as one of the letter's little touches of authenticity. But it could easily have been included because it was known to be typically Pauline. Paul had "longed" and "hoped" to see the Roman Christians (Rom. 1:11 and 15:24) and had told the Corinthians: "I am ready to come to you" (2 Cor. 12:14).

The instructions are not meant for Timothy alone. They include prayers for kings and for all in high office, rules about the behavior of women and slaves in the community, and specification of moral qualifications for those appointed to posts of authority in the church. There is also mention of a Christian order of widows, with strict rules of membership, whose essential task is continual prayer (1 Tim. 5:9 ff). Such an order is never mentioned in the undoubtedly genuine Paulines but is documented for the early second century by both Ignatius and Polycarp.

If the Pastorals were written early in the second century, the point of representing these instructions as orders which Timothy must carry out would be to stamp them with the authority of Paul the apostle and thus ensure that they are observed in the churches of the author's own time. This applies particularly to the stipulations about deacons, elders, and bishops. In this view, then, the Pastorals represent "a time when the Church is setting a high value on stable and peaceful congregational life and therefore values highly the leadership which will perpetuate it. To this end, its officers are beginning to acquire proper status" (Houlden, 105, p 74). They are even being paid. At 1 Tim. 5:17-8 the author recommends that "elders who rule well" should be given double pay, and in support he quotes, as scripture, the Septuagint of Deuteronomy 25:4: "You shall not muzzle an ox when it is treading out the grain" (that is, the animal must be allowed an occasional bite).

The real Paul, arguing in what Kelly calls "characteristically rabbinical fashion" (118, p 126), had already quoted this passage as evidence of God's will that Christian ministers should be supported by their congregations (1 Cor. 9:9). But the real Paul says little about church officers (apart, of course, from apostles, the Lord's personally chosen ambassadors). In his churches members were moved by the spirit to perform various tasks; different men had received different spiritual gifts (1 Cor. 12:4 ff and 28 ff) and so the spirit was the organizing principle of the Christian congregation. There was "no need for any fixed system with its rules, regulations and prohibitions" (von Campenhausen, 36, p 58). Paul never suggests that "elders" are persons holding a particular office. He does once mention "bishops and deacons" (Phil. 1:1) but normally refers to leaders only in general terms, for example, "those who labor among you and are over you in the Lord and admonish you" (1 Thess. 5:12); "persons who lend assistance and exercise rule" (1 Cor. 12:28). One thus gets the impression that such leaders in Paul's churches were not appointed to their office but acquired the lead because of their zeal and ability.

In the Pastorals the situation is very different. The spirit-moved prophets so much stressed in the genuine Paulines have moved into the background. They are mentioned only in passing when we are told that the elders lay their hands on the man who has been marked out by the word of the prophet (1 Tim. 1:18 and 4:14). On the other hand elders hold an office (as in other post-Pauline writings—Acts, James, 1 Peter, 2 John and Rev.). They are appointed (Titus 1:5), ordained through the laying on of hands, and are supported by the community (1 Tim. 5:17 ff and 22). The bishop "must not be a recent convert" (1 Tim. 3:6), a statement which shows that, at the time of writing, the church addressed had been in existence for quite some time. The author is careful not to fit Timothy and Titus themselves into this (really post-Pauline) scheme of church officers. They are not said to be bishops or elders, but the personal disciples of Paul. But with this item of church management, which would have been feasible in Paul's day, the author has combined the more developed hierarchy of his own time.

This hierarchy, although advanced compared with that of the Pauline churches, is less developed than that advocated by Ignatius about 110. He suggests that each of the churches of Asia Minor then had its own monarchical bishop, its senate of presbyters, and a group of deacons closely attached to the bishop's person. 1 and 2 Timothy are also addressed to an Asian church, but there the bishop is still a member of the body of elders and not necessarily its leader. He simply has certain ministerial and pastoral functions which other elders do not necessarily have.[13] His privileges and powers are not, then, very clearly demarcated from those of the elders as a body, and this, says von Campenhausen, "corresponds to the actual situation at the beginning of the monarchical episcopate" (36, p 108). This is often taken as evidence that the Pastorals, although post-Pauline, must be dated before the letters of Ignatius. But in fact the monarchical authority of the single bishop may simply represent what Ignatius regarded as desirable, not what actually prevailed when he wrote (cf. p 102).

Another reason often advanced for dating the Pastorals not much later than 100 is that they include no developed theory of apostolic succession like that enunciated in *1 Clement* 42 and 44, where we are told that the original apostles received their instructions from Christ, appointed their first converts to be bishops and deacons, and arranged that these should be succeeded in office by other accredited persons. It is admitted that Timothy is instructed to "entrust what you have heard from me . . . to faithful men who will be able to teach others also" (2 Tim. 2:2). But it is held that, in the Pastorals, the disciple of Paul is not the representative of a certain type of office (that of bishop), but the guarantor of the genuine tradition (Conzelmann, 43, p 57); and that it is not the chain of succession that is stressed, but rather the chain of tradition.[14] I doubt whether this argument can really be used to date the Pastorals, since the idea of apostolic succession is certainly present in them, even if it is not stressed. Timothy is said to have received the spirit of God through the laying on of Paul's hands (2 Tim. 1:6) and of those of the elders (1 Tim. 4:14), and he passes it on to others in the same way (1 Tim. 5:22). Titus is also directed by Paul the apostle to appoint elders (Titus 1:5).

That the Pastorals are entirely free from the legends about Paul that proliferated later in the second century is also no argument against dating them as late as 140. Vielhauer (234, pp 236–7) is impressed by von Campenhausen's arguments that the Pastorals show strong affinities in content and structure to the epistle of Polycarp, and this would allow such a dating. One can really say no more than that they could have been written any time after 100 and that the evidence does not actually require a later date.

When the Pastorals were written the traditional teaching was being endangered by "false teachers"; the author uses Paul and his faithful pupils to counter such heresy. It was vital for him, says Houlden, "in an uncertain present, when heresy was hard to grapple with, and when it was not easy to find criteria on which to base oneself, that there should be a past to appeal to" (105, p 34). The false teachers advocated renunciation of marriage and abstinence from certain foods (1 Tim. 4:3) and held that "the resurrection is past already" (2 Tim. 2:18). Commentators explain that "they chose to identify the resurrection not with the raising of the body on the last day, but with the mystical dying and rising again which the Christian experiences in his baptismal initiation" (Kelly, 118, p 185).

Some of their ideas are comparable to those combated in Colossians, and so the nature of the heresy is not in itself a reason for dating these letters after Paul's time. What is, however, so different from Paul's manner is that the author does not *argue with* his opponents, but simply rejects other views as incorrect, often in an abusive fashion. (Hanson comments on Titus 1:16 that "it looks as though he is simply piling up abusive epithets indiscriminately.") Nor does he give much indication of what the traditional teaching, which must be held fast, consists. There is one reference to "the sound words of our Lord Jesus Christ" (1 Tim. 6:3), but the author does not quote any words of Jesus; it seems likely that he uncritically believes that Christian teaching as a whole originates with him.[15]

In some passages in the Pastorals Paul is made to refer to the false teachers as active in the present, as when he instructs Timothy to discipline them (1 Tim. 1:3) or to avoid them (2 Tim. 3:5). In others the author is conscious that they did not exist in Paul's day, and that he must therefore be made to prophesy their coming. 2 Tim. 4:3 makes him say that "there will be a time" when many will abandon the sound teaching, and 1 Tim. 4:1 that, according to the spirit (that is, information from some spirit-moved Christian prophet), this abandonment will occur "in later times" (at 2 Tim. 3:1 in "the last times"). The idea that "the last times" will be characterized by heresy and apostasy is represented in the Habbakuk commentary (2:5 f) of the Dead Sea sectaries and in Christian thought of the late first century (for example, 2 Thess. 2:3 and 1 John 2:18), and was in due course put into Jesus' mouth (Mk. 13:22). But in the Pastorals the "last times" can imply no more than a final epoch which may nonetheless endure for long. The author shows no signs of believing that the second coming is imminent, and thinks rather that God will bring it to pass "at the proper time" (1 Tim. 6:15).

Whereas the real Paul expected the end in his lifetime, the pseudo-Paul of 2 Tim. 2:2 tells Timothy to pass on Paul's teaching to "faithful men" who in turn "will be able to teach others." Again, while the real Paul had taken a somewhat negative view of marriage because he believed the end to be very near (cf. p 53), the author of the Pastorals opposes Christian teachers who forbid marriage. An expectation that the world will continue without prompt catastrophe is also implied in his injunction to Timothy to see that prayers be made for kings and others in authority "that we may lead a quiet and peaceable life" (1 Tim. 2:1-2).

Houlden observes (105, p 27) that "the air we breathe here is that of Luke-Acts and Ephesians, where too the settled position of the Church seems to be presupposed, rather than that of Paul's undoubted works." And so the Pastorals recommend behavior suitable for the consolidation of the church in an enduring world, and formulate a conception of good citizenship which has led some commentators to label these letters as "bourgeois." This is certainly not the impression made by the undoubtedly genuine Paulines. Houlden asks: "Is it really conceivable that Paul should drop so many of his central ideas and take on so many of the flatly conventional concepts of the period?" (105, pp 31-2)

Any embarrassment at the delay of the second coming is avoided in the Pastorals by stressing the benefits of the first, "the appearing of our Savior Christ Jesus, who abolished death and brought life and immortality to light through the gospel" (2 Tim. 1:10). Here the bright "now" is contrasted with the gloomy pre-incarnation past. Conzelmann observes that this whole passage, with its terminology of "appearing" (epiphany) and "salvation"—ideas hitherto associated with the second coming—"is intended to transfer to Christ's first epiphany all those effects which were originally expected from the glorious epiphany in the last days" (43, pp 104-5). This was an important factor in the invention of details of Jesus' alleged life on earth. In Paul's genuine letters his earthly life had been utterly obscure. But the more it came to be regarded as a glorious epiphany, the more pressure there would have been to construct details that represented his life as such.

If our author had known the gospels or their sources, surely he would have made some appeal to Jesus' ethical teachings when discussing the same subjects. In fact, without any such reference, he advocates love, faith, steadfastness, kindliness, patience, peace, a pure heart, and clean speech. Slaves must respect their masters (whether or not the latter are Christians) and relatives must be financially supported. Riches are not to be coveted. (In the Sermon on the Mount Jesus' instruction is to be unconcerned about them: Mt. 6:25-33 = Lk. 12:22-31). Against those who enjoin abstinence from certain foods, the author declares that "everything created by God is good" (a view ascribed to Jesus in Mk. 7:19 in a context of discussion of Jewish ritual regulations). Men should pray "without anger or quarrelling" (1 Tim. 2:8; Jesus' teaching is that genuine prayer is impossible for those who are unforgiving or who nourish grudges: Mk. 11:25, Mt. 5:23-4, 6:12). Women should distinguish themselves not by finery of apparel but by good deeds (1 Tim. 2:10; cf. Jesus' prophecy that at the judgment the sheep shall be separated from the goats on the basis of good deeds: Mt. 25:31–46). In none of these cases does our author appeal to any teaching of Jesus.

When the author quotes Deuteronomy as scripture which proves the entitlement of ministers to financial support, he adds: "The laborer is worthy of his hire." It is not clear whether he means to designate this also as "scripture." It is ascribed to Jesus at Lk. 10:7, but the author of the Pastorals surely did not know *Luke,* let alone regard it (or its sources) as "scripture," a term long restricted to the Old Testament and its Apocrypha. The maxim may derive from some lost apocryphal writing which the author regarded as scripture, or it may merely be a common proverb (and cited as such by Jesus in *Luke*).

What, then, does he know about Jesus? He regards him as pre-existent (God gave us "his grace in Christ Jesus ages ago," 2 Tim. 1:9), as having "come into the world to save sinners" (1 Tim. 1:15), given himself "as a ransom for all," as "the mediator" between God and men. He was truly man (1 Tim. 2:5-6), that is, he really assumed human flesh (cf. 1 Tim. 3:16). He "abolished death and brought life and immortality" (2 Tim. 1:10)—this last word being that used by the real Paul in 1 Cor. 15 for the resurrection of the body. He will "judge the living and the dead" (2 Tim. 4:1) and "if we deny him, he also will deny us" (2 Tim. 2:12, stated without reference to Mt. 10:33, "whoever denies me before men, I also will deny before my Father who is in heaven").

It is generally agreed that many of the author's references to Jesus are quotations from existing creeds, hymns, or liturgies. The injunction to "remember Jesus Christ, risen from the dead, descended from David" (2 Tim. 2:8) is "probably a fragment of semi-stereotyped credal material" (Kelly, p 177), for the "Jesus Christ" (instead of "Christ Jesus") is unique in this epistle, and the reference to the descent from David is irrelevant in the context. More obviously, 1 Tim. 3:16 is an excerpt from a primitive hymn. It consists of three couplets, each containing one line referring to Jesus' activity in heaven (marked A below) and one line referring to his life on earth (B):

> B. He was manifest in the flesh
> A. Vindicated in the spirit.
>
> A. Seen by angels
> B. Preached among the nations.
>
> B. Believed on in the world
> A. Taken up in glory.

"Vindicated [the Greek means "declared righteous" or "justified"] in the spirit" means: shown to be a truly spiritual being at his resurrection. "Seen by angels" refers to their worship of him as he was exalted to God's right hand. (The idea is expressed in Phil. 2:9-10 and Coloss. 2:15.)

1 Tim. 6:12 instructs Timothy to "take hold of the eternal life to which you were called when you made the good confession in the presence of many

witnesses." The reference is to baptism, which in early Christianity was administered before the assembled congregation, with the candidate making a solemn affirmation of his faith. What follows is regarded as deriving from a primitive baptismal creed: "I charge you in the presence of God who gave life to all things, and of Jesus Christ who in his testimony before Pontius Pilate made the good confession. . . ."

Second-century evidence shows that, as the candidate stood in the water, he was asked whether he believed in God the Father and in Jesus Christ who had suffered and risen again (see Kelly, p 143). In another passage, which is also regarded as quoted from a liturgical or catechetical formula, our author affirms that Jesus gave himself as a ransom "at the proper time" (1 Tim. 2:6). This goes no further than Paul's statements that he died "at the right time" (Rom. 5:6), that his incarnate life occurred "when the time had fully come" (Gal. 4:4); whereas the passage I have just quoted, with its reference to Pilate, gives Jesus' time on earth a precise historical setting. This is no invention of our author's. Not only does the reference occur in a passage which scholars agree is based on a pre-existing creed but also in a work which deplores all originality in theology. The author is a purveyor of other men's ideas and tries (not altogether successfully) to make a consistent whole of what he collected from disparate sources. It is, for instance, typical of his failure to work out a coherent Christology when he says in one verse that God is our savior, and then assigns that same function to Jesus in the next (Titus 1:3–4). If the Pastorals were written as early as the turn of the century, and drew from existing tradition the idea that Jesus was executed under Pilate, this tradition must have existed by about 90.

As we shall see, Ignatius differs from the Pastorals by stating fairly fully against heretics what correct Christian doctrine is. And so it is not surprising that he mentions Pilate repeatedly, whereas there is but this one mention of him in the Pastorals.

V   THE LETTERS OF JOHN, IGNATIUS, AND POLYCARP

Five New Testament books have titles ascribing them to someone named "John": a gospel, three epistles, and an apocalypse. The only one of these in which the author's name is said within the book itself to be John is the apocalypse, and there is wide agreement that this work was not written by the author of the other four. (For the evidence, see JEC, p 279). Of these four, the gospel and the first epistle are anonymous, and the second and third epistles purport to be written by a person who calls himself "the elder," a term which, in these two letters, seems to mean the leader of a Christian community who speaks with some authority.

That the author was "John" is not asserted in either the gospel or the three epistles, and their attribution to an apostle or elder of that name is evidenced only from late in the second century. (The fourth-century ecclesiastical historian Eusebius does indeed say that Papias (AD 140) "used quotations from the first epistle of John." But this need not imply that Papias ascribed it to John any more than did Polycarp, who quoted it even earlier; cf. p 105). 1 John differs from 2 and 3 John not only in being completely anonymous, but also in lacking the most obvious characteristics of a letter. As the author neither discloses his name nor greets, or even names, addressees, he did not seem to wish his work to be regarded as a letter.

2 and 3 John each consists of but a single chapter. The author of the former rejoices that some Christians in the community he is addressing "are following the truth." It soon becomes apparent that the author means that they are untainted by a certain heresy, known today as Docetism, which as we shall see is also fiercely opposed in 1 John. In 2 John the addressees are instructed that any preacher who brings such perverse doctrine is not to be allowed in, or even greeted.[16] The effect of this would be to force him to move on elsewhere and so to safeguard the community from him. The writer could hardly have known of Jesus' injunction to greet and even to love one's enemies (Mt. 5:44–8).

The third letter (3 John) is by the leader of a Christian community who praises voluntary missionary work undertaken by its members. There is reference to another Christian community, led by one Diotrephes, which is not unnaturally unenthusiastic about the influx of preachers from the writer's community. Nowhere is there any mention of false doctrine. The quarrel between the writer and Diotrephes is not doctrinal, but a petty issue of authority between two leaders.

The only substantial document among the three Johannine letters is the first of them, and its anonymous author may not be the same person as the elder who has written the second and third.

In DJE (p 44) I uncritically accepted the consensus of opinion that 1 John was written as late as 90–110. But this dating has become established only because all three Johannine letters have been linked with the fourth gospel, which is generally admitted to be late. Recent scholarship, however, suggests that 1 John is so different in doctrine from that gospel that it may well be independent of it (see, for instance, Moody Smith's summary of recent discussion, 144, p 234). For instance, 1 John still maintains the early Christian doctrine (dropped in the fourth gospel) that the world is about to end. Its Christology is also less advanced than that of the fourth gospel. It treats Jesus as a supernatural and pre-existent person (sent into the world by the Father), whose blood cleanses us from all sin (1:7) and who now speaks on our behalf to the Father (2:1). But although Messiah, advocate, and Son, Jesus is still firmly subordinated to God (for whom the more abstract titles used in the epistle are reserved), not one with him as in the fourth gospel (cf. Houlden, 104, p 60). And (again unlike the gospel) this John never appeals to Old Testament scripture. Nor does the writer ever appeal to "any authority that he possesses by virtue of his position" (*Ibid.*, p 17) — in contrast with the Pastoral and Ignatian letters, which are agreed to be post-90, when an ecclesiastical hierarchy was well developed.

1 John begins in a prophetic style, grammatically incoherent and quite different from the style of what follows. In these opening verses the writer proclaims a message which he represents (verse 3) as new to the persons addressed:

> 1. That which was from the beginning, which we have heard, which we have seen with our eyes, which we have looked upon and touched with our hands, concerning the word of life—
> 2. the life was made manifest, and we saw it, and testify to it, and proclaim to you the eternal life which was with the Father and was made manifest to us—
> 3. that which we have seen and heard we proclaim also to you, so that you may have fellowship with us; and our fellowship is with the Father and with his Son Jesus Christ.

Houlden notes (104, p 52) that most modern critics agree that this passage is not evidence that the author was an eyewitness of Jesus' life. By "that which" (neuter, not masculine in the Greek), the author seems to mean not the Son but the truth concerning the nature and work of the Son. This interpretation seems required by *concerning* (near the end of verse 1). "Concerning the word of life" probably means "concerning the message that gives life," that is, the Christian message. Important is the distinction between the *we* who know this message and the *you* to whom it is now being newly imparted.

In Houlden's view, *we* means responsible Christian teachers, authoritative Christian opinion, and the writer "speaks for and is at one with all who have thought rightly about Jesus 'from the beginning,'" including, of course, the first eyewitnesses, with whom he feels at one (104, p 53). In the sequel, he drops the pretense that the addressees are only now being informed of the true doctrine, and says that they have known it from the beginning (for example, 2:24. "Let what you heard from the beginning abide in you"). Perhaps, then, the opening words of the epistle are couched in the style of a prophetic revelation merely in order to give weight to the author's overall purpose.

This purpose was to combat gnosticizing Christians, who had formed a separate group (2:19) and who were denying that Jesus had "come in the flesh" (4:2). Here again the epistle differs from the fourth gospel, which attacks not Christians but the Jews, who there represent "the world," which refuses to believe in Jesus. The opponents of the epistle writer were clearly not prepared to accept the Pauline view (2 Cor. 5:21) that the heavenly Jesus had assumed a body of flesh—and had thus placed himself open to sinfulness—in order to redeem us by his suffering. They were Docetists (that is, "seemers"), who insisted that Jesus only *seemed* to have a real body of flesh but in fact had lived on earth as a phantom.

The Docetists attacked in 1 John (and also in 2) regarded flesh as sinful, and suffering and pain as incompatible with the divine nature. The obvious way of controverting such views—for a writer who had real familiarity with Jesus' biography—would have been to point out that he was born from a human mother (and had thus acquired real flesh) and to cite those of his activities that involved this flesh in real pain and suffering. But the author or authors of 1 and 2 John make no attempt to do this, whereas Ignatius of Antioch, writing probably a little later, and combating exactly the same Docetic teachings, insists repeatedly that Jesus was the child of Mary, was persecuted by Pilate, and nailed to the cross in the flesh. This does suggest that Ignatius was able to draw on information about Jesus that had not been available earlier.

1 John is the earliest document that indicates that Jesus was believed to have been baptized. This detail of doctrine was apparently accepted both by the writer and by the heretics he criticizes; for he implies that they accept that Jesus "came with the water" and deny only that he "came also with the blood" (5:6). The meaning seems to be that, while both parties agreed that he had been baptized, the heretics thought he could not have experienced genuine suffering and pain.

As Eucharist and baptism were important early Christian rites, it is natural that both should be early affirmed as instituted in some way or other by Jesus, whether he really existed or not. And with both Eucharist and baptism the sequence is the same. The earliest mention of a connection with the historical Jesus is couched in quite general terms, and only a later writer alleges a definite historical situation. This, we saw (p 27–8) is the most striking difference between Paul's account of Jesus' eucharistic words and that of Mark. The author of 1 John likewise does not indicate time or place when he alludes to Jesus' baptism. It was left to Ignatius to affirm that it was John the Baptist who baptized Jesus.

Since I published DJE in 1975, the question of the date and authenticity of the letters attributed to Ignatius of Antioch has become completely open. The consensus of opinion in 1975 was that, of these letters, seven are genuine, namely those he addressed to the churches of Ephesus, Magnesia, Tralles, Rome, Philadelphia, and Smyrna, and the one to Polycarp, bishop of Smyrna. [I shall use obvious abbreviations in referring to these seven.]

Lightfoot's arguments (summarized in JEC, pp 164–5) were very influential in establishing this consensus after centuries of debate. In this view, these seven are the oldest extant Christian documents after the Paulines that are neither anonymous nor pseudonymous, and Ignatius wrote them some time between 110 and 120 while he journeyed under guard from Antioch to Rome to be martyred there. (The fourth-century ecclesiastical historian Eusebius put Ignatius' martyrdom shortly before Trajan's death in 117, but it is not clear what his grounds were. Harrison [98, p 315], and more recently Corwin [45, p 3] think that the early years of Trajan's successor Hadrian are a possibility.)

In 1979, however, R. Joly argued that none of these seven letters could have been written before the martyrdom of Polycarp in 161 (*Le dossier d'Ignace d'Antioche,* Brussels, 1979). In the same year J. Rius-Camps offered the less drastic hypothesis that, while the letters to Ephesus, Magnesia, Tralles, Rome, and Smyrna are genuine (although the one to Smyrna originally formed part of the one to Ephesus, and all except the one to Rome include some interpolations), those to Philadelphia and to Polycarp are third-century forgeries; and further that, since Ignatius did not in fact know Polycarp, this reason for dating the genuine material as late as the second-century—instead of near the end of the first century—vanishes (*The Four Authentic Letters of Ignatius*, Rome, 1979).

The clearest indications of a date later than the first century are the references to three tiers of clergy: the bishop is above a presbyterate, and below them both stand deacons (see von Campenhausen, 36, p 97 and refs.). But these references all occur in passages which Rius-Camps puts aside. If, however, they are genuine, and Ignatius did advocate the monarchical authority of the single bishop, this would still not in itself necessitate a date later than about 100; for (as Bauer notes, 11, p 70) the bishop's authority may well have been what Ignatius regarded as desirable, rather than what actually prevailed. Even so it would represent a considerable sophistication, and therefore a later stage, in comparison with the loose organization of the Pauline communities.

C. Munier (writing in the *Revue des Sciences Religieuses*, 54 [1980], 55–73) has challenged the findings of both Joly and Rius-Camps, noting (against the latter's interpolation hypothesis) the unity of vocabulary and style that pervades all seven letters. He thinks that we know nothing for certain of the place, date, or circumstances of Ignatius' death, and that the seven letters, as they now stand, are the work of a redactor from the mid-second century.

The whole question is therefore wide open. And so I propose—while bearing in mind the possibility that all seven letters *may* be forgeries of the mid-second century or even later—to proceed by accepting as genuine the minimum which Rius-Camps allows to stand as such (without however necessarily accepting his early dating of this material); and I shall draw only on it, except when I expressly indicate the contrary.

We can see clearly enough that Ignatius wrote considerably later than Paul, for he refers to both Peter and Paul as persons of authority of a past period, and he is acquainted with several of Paul's letters (Ephes. 12; Rom. 4). Although he once states the older doctrine that the Father raised Jesus from the dead, he also records, in the very same letter, the more advanced view that Jesus "raised himself" (Smy. 2 and 7). In accordance with this attribution of divine power to him is the statement that he was "God in flesh," whereas writers who are undoubtedly within the first century represent him as subordinate to God.

Ignatius describes himself as "a prisoner for the name's sake" (Ephes. 3). His crime, then, was the fact that he was a Christian, and this suggests a second-century situation, or at least one later than 90 (see pp 108–10). He expresses the idea, common from about then, that Jesus was a supernatural being who "in these last days" "came down from the Father" and returned to him (Mag. 6–7). But his claim "to comprehend celestial secrets and angelic hierarchies and the dispositions of the heavenly powers, and much else, both seen and unseen" (Trall. 5) is the kind of pneumatic religion common from Christianity's earliest days; and he also still believes that "the end of all things is near" (Ephes. 11).

In spite of the fact that Ignatius' letters together are only as long as *1 Clement,* he mentions in them more details of Jesus' incarnate life than any epistle writer we have so far studied. He asserts, for instance, that Jesus was baptized by John (Smy. 1), that he submitted to baptism in order to "purify the water" (Ephes. 18), that is, to make efficacious the means of baptism. Clearly, the desire to certificate as effective the baptismal practices of the early church could in itself have given rise, without historical basis, to the belief that Jesus had himself been baptized. That he submitted to baptism by John the Baptist is often regarded as a biographical detail which no Christian would have invented. (To this I shall return, p 211.)

The principal purpose of these letters is to preserve the unity of the church in the face of heretics, characterized as "a pack of savage animals" (Ephes. 7), as "beasts of prey in human form" (Smy. 4). The faithful must not merely "keep away" from them, but "avoid all mention" of them (Smy. 7). Those who even give them a hearing are bound, with them, for "the unquenchable fire" (Ephes. 16). This is the fiercely sectarian attitude we have met already in 2 John; and indeed the heresy attacked is the same as the one combatted there, namely that Jesus never had a real human body (Smy. 5), so that his sufferings were "not genuine" (Trall. 10) but an "unreal illusion" (Smy. 2).

Ignatius confutes the Docetists' view that Jesus had lived as a fleshless phantom by pointing in the first instance to the circumstances of his birth: he was of the royal line (descended from David); he was "truly born" from a human mother, the Virgin Mary. (He clearly regards Jesus as descended from David through Mary, since he never mentions Joseph nor suggests that Jesus had a human father. This idea that Mary was of Davidic descent was common in the second century, in spite of the contrary affirmation of Lk. 1:36.) He also holds that Jesus was dependent on food and drink like any other man (Trall. 9).

But it is the reality of the Passion that he stresses most. Against the heretics he insists that "suffer he did, verily and truly" (Smy. 2). He was "truly nailed to the cross" (Smy. 1) in known historical circumstances, namely "in the days of Pontius Pilate's governorship" (Mag. 11; Trall. 9). In one letter he is even more precise in dating the event "in the days of Pontius Pilate and Herod the Tetrarch" (Smy. 1). As Corwin notes (45, p 114), he was clearly anxious to offer as much evidence as he could of the inescapable reality of the fact. The same motive underlies his claim that Jesus' death occurred "in the sight of all heaven and earth" (Trall. 9).

Ignatius further agrees with the gospels in regarding Jesus as a teacher (Ephes. 15). The one passage where he calls Jesus "the Son of man" (Ephes. 20) — a very striking agreement with them — is set aside as an interpolation by Rius-Camps. There are good reasons for thinking that Ignatius did not know *Luke* (see JEC, pp 171-2) but may have known *Matthew,* although he may have known only some of the traditions on which Matthew drew (DJE, pp 92 and 93 n 9). Neither Ignatius nor Polycarp make any reference to the *Gospel of John*.

We turn finally to Polycarp's letter to the Philippians, written at Smyrna. The form of church organization there was much the same that we find in the Pastoral epistles. Polycarp alludes to a college of presbyters, supported by a body of deacons, with an order of Christian widows (Harrison, 98, p 283).

Harrison argued in 1936 that this letter is a fusion of two originally independent documents from Polycarp's hand. In ch. 13 the author inquires whether the recipients have any news of "Ignatius and those with him," who were therefore still alive at the time of writing, or so recently dead that the news had not reached Polycarp. Ch. 9, however, was written when Ignatius was known to be no longer alive; for it is there said that "the blessed Ignatius" and others "are gone to their appointed place in the presence of the Lord, with whom they also suffered." According to Harrison, the earlier document (ch. 13 and the brief concluding ch. 14) was written as Polycarp's covering note to a collection of Ignatian letters which, he says in ch. 13, he was forwarding to the Philippians at their request. The later document (chaps. 1–12) embodies advice he gave them, also at their request (as he says in ch. 3). The two documents were fused perhaps when a copyist overlooked the space between them left by a predecessor who had written them both out.

These arguments were well received until the reopening of the Ignatian question in the late 1970s and early 1980s implicated the authenticity of ch. 13 in Polycarp's letter. Rius-Camps, for instance, thinks that this chapter is not by Polycarp at all, but was forged to give credence to the idea that he had collected Ignatius' letters and thus to validate them with his authority. But even on this view, the main body of Polycarp's letter is both genuine and post-Ignatian.

Polycarp does not merely quote doctrines worded very similarly to those in the Sermon on the Mount. He actually gives them *as sayings of Jesus*. There is good reason to believe that he knew both *Matthew* and *Luke* (see JEC, p 173).

Like Ignatius, Polycarp speaks out against those who deny that Jesus had "come in the flesh": yet he does not follow Ignatius and deal with them by alluding to incontrovertible facts in Jesus' biography which establish his humanity, even though he must have known — if he knew either Ignatius' letters or gospels — that Jesus had a human mother and was crucified in a specific historical situation. His silence is intelligible by virtue of the principal reason he gives for writing, namely, not to controvert heretical teaching but to dilate on "righteousness," at the request of the Philippians (ch. 3).

One of the presbyters at Philippi had brought disrepute on his church by some act of fraud (ch. 11), and Polycarp is reacting primarily to this ethical problem. He constantly warns against avarice and specifies (ch. 6) the duties of presbyters, stressing that they must be merciful, compassionate, and forgiving. Only in chapter 7 of this, in any case short, epistle does he attack those who deny that Jesus had a body of flesh and who assert (presumably by interpreting the terms in a spiritual, non-literal sense) that there is no resurrection or judgment. (Ignatius had said that, according to the Docetists, the resurrection, as well as the Passion, only "seemed" to take place.)

Almost the whole of Polycarp's letter consists of phrases taken from various New Testament books, from *1 Clement*, and from the Ignatian letters. He has, as Vielhauer puts it (234, p 564) not a single idea of his own, and rarely formulates in his own words what he has to say. And the one sentence where he speaks against those who deny Jesus' flesh is in large part a loose quotation from 1 John 4:2-3. Polycarp says (ch. 7): "For everyone who shall not confess that Jesus Christ is come in the flesh is antichrist; and whoever shall not confess the testimony of the cross is of the devil."

The corresponding passage in 1 John is: "Every spirit which confesses that Jesus Christ has come in the flesh is of God, and every spirit which does not confess Jesus is not of God. This is the spirit of antichrist." Polycarp's phrase "is of the devil" is also derivative, from 1 John 3:8. That he does not reproduce the exact wording of the epistle accords with his usual manner of being "inexact in his borrowings from books which he certainly knew quite well" (Harrison, 98, p 286).

In ch. 12 Polycarp quotes as "scripture" two phrases: "be ye angry and sin not" and "let not the sun go down on your wrath." These, combined together, can only derive from the canonical letter to the Ephesians (4:26), where the first phrase is quoted from the Septuagint of Psalm 4:4, but the second is not from the Old Testament nor from any known work which Polycarp might have regarded as scripture. That he refers to this Christian document as "scripture" shows that his respect for some early Christian literature is as great as for the Old Testament. So it is understandable also from this that he refutes Docetism, not by rehearsing the details of Jesus' incarnate life but by quoting an earlier Christian writer's indictment. His recipe against heresy is in any case not argument but exhortation to protect oneself from its temptations by prayer and fasting (ch. 7). Vielhauer has noted that, if we can believe Irenaeus, who had known him personally, Polycarp's habitual method of coping with heresy was to shut his ears, not to reason with it (234, p 565).

I have now given enough evidence of the discrepancy between Christian epistles prior to 90 and those of later date, when traditions had become available which made Jesus a teacher and/or miracle worker and placed his life in the early first century. Second-century literature of later date than the letter of Polycarp in no way militates against my thesis. I showed in JEC (pp 174-7) that the *Epistle of Barnabas* (about 130) clearly states that Jesus was a teacher and miracle worker who appointed twelve to preach the gospel. The so-called second epistle of Clement (about 150) frequently quotes words of Jesus in support of its doctrines, and refers to "what the Lord said in the gospel." Aristides and Justin Martyr also write (about this same time) of Jesus in the way one would expect of those acquainted with the gospels, or at least with the traditions underlying them (see JEC, pp 180-3). But chapters 1 and 2 have shown that these traditions are not confirmed by the very earliest Christian literature. It is not just that Paul and other early writers are silent about this or that historical detail but that what they do say about Jesus does not suggest that they had in mind the supposedly historical situation portrayed in the gospels.

4

The Synoptic Gospels as Post-AD 70 Documents

I MARK'S APOCALYPSE AND THE ROMAN PERSECUTION OF CHRISTIANITY

Jesus is definitely linked with Pilate in the Pastoral epistle 1 Timothy, in the Ignatian letters, and in *Mark* and later gospels. I have argued that the author of 1 Timothy was drawing on an earlier tradition of, say, about 90. If Mark can plausibly be held to have written as late as this, then it becomes intelligible why both Paul and other epistle writers up to about 90 know nothing of the traditions embodied in the gospels and why only post-90 Christian literature is able to draw on them. What, then, are my reasons for putting *Mark* at 90 instead of, with most theologians, at about 70?

I find no substance in the conservative position that Mark obtained his information from a Peter who had been a companion of the historical Jesus. The second-century Church Fathers based this view on the affectionate reference in 1 Peter (taken as from the hand of the apostle) to "my son Mark" (see DJE, p 77, and Anderson, 2, p 17). Haenchen rightly notes (92, p 131) that, whatever the Fathers thought, the freedom with which evangelists later than Mark adapt his work shows that in the first century it was not regarded as based on authoritative pronouncements by Peter or any other apostle.[1]

Many commentators (e.g. Vielhauer, 234, p 347) believe that Mk. 12:9 (where Jesus is made to predict that God will "destroy the tenants" of his vineyard because they have murdered his "beloved son") presupposes knowledge of the destruction of Jerusalem in 70. Mark, then, was writing at *some* time later than that; I propose to try to date his gospel from what it says about persecution and from other references in its little apocalypse, chapter 13.

We have seen (p 81) that Nero's persecution of Christians in 65 was an isolated incident confined to Rome. After Nero, there is no specific documentation of imperial persecution until the time of Trajan, who is known, from the younger Pliny's letter to him (AD 112), to have persecuted Christians in the province of Pontus Bithynia (along the southern coast of the Black Sea). What Pliny says shows that persecution of Christians was at the time not a complete novelty nor established imperial policy, but had occurred locally and sporadically (see DJE, p 42). Every Roman subject who was not a Jew was bound to at least nominal conformity to the state religion as much as to its political system; and every Christian, however politically loyal, was likely to refuse if required to show his loyalty by making sacrifice to the state gods. Hence persecution of Christians was bound to occur from time to time, almost anywhere in the Empire, once the practices of taking an oath by the emperor's genius, of offering libation and incense before his statue, and addressing him as *Dominus* (Lord) had become prevalent.

There is general agreement that these practices first grew up in the reign of Domitian (AD 89–96) and were retained by Trajan and later emperors. Robinson, who interprets much of the evidence very differently from the way I do, does not dispute that "Domitian ordered himself to be called 'our Lord and our God'" and that "it is possible that the demand for some act of worship of the emperor was introduced in Domitian's reign for the detection of Christians" (164, pp 236–7). In other words, from about 90 practices to which no convinced Christian could submit were increasingly demanded of Roman subjects; refusal to comply meant death.

Christians had had to suffer for their faith earlier. Paul was whipped by order of synagogues; and he—or an interpolator (see p 24 ff)—states that Thessalonian Christians were harried by Thessalonian unbelievers just as Judaean Christians were by orthodox Jews (1 Thess. 2:14–6). But he says nothing that would suggest that, in his day, persecution was an official policy of the Roman state. It is true that Acts 16:11 ff shows Paul, at Philippi, in trouble with the local (Roman) authorities; this report is confirmed by Paul's own reference (1 Thess. 2:2) to "injury and outrage" which he had suffered there. This probably occurred because he was taken for a Jewish missionary, and propaganda on behalf of Judaism was forbidden among citizens of a Roman colony (see refs. in Haenchen, 94, p 435 n 2. Acts 16:20–1 does in fact describe Paul and his fellow missionary as "Jews" who "advocate customs which it is not lawful for us Romans to accept"—although the author of Acts represents this as mere pretext covering the real reason for hostility, namely the financial interests of a pagan cult.).

In Acts 19 the religious and civil authorities of Ephesus are represented as protecting Paul from a mob, which is criticized for failing to bring specific charges against him. This is an indirect admission that, at the time referred to by the author of Acts, the mere fact of being a Christian did not constitute an offense (cf. Haenchen, 94, p 513; Frend, 71, p 159); whereas from about 90, Christians who refused to show loyalty to Rome by submitting to the required religious tests could be condemned to death for the mere "name" of being a Christian. Throughout Acts, when Paul is harried in one place (usually by resentful Jews), he transfers his missionary activity to another, until he is disturbed there by the arrival of Jews from the first locality, who stir up the people against him. This local harrying of individual Christian *missionaries* at the instigation of religious rivals is quite different from persecution of Christian *communities* by the imperial authorities.

Robinson would not agree that imperial persecution of Christianity became common only from about 90. He seems to think that any Christian writing, composed anywhere in the Empire and dispatched to any part of it, which suggests that the mere profession of Christianity is a capital offense, could as well have been written under Nero as under Domitian or Trajan. He admits that the Neronian persecution is documented only for Rome, but he insists that the silence of our informants in the provinces does not allow us to infer that there was "nothing of the sort" going on there. He takes Tacitus' statement that Nero persecuted a "great multitude" of Christians at Rome as quite accurate (not as rhetorical exaggeration, as I have suggested, p 81) and regards this persecution as an event which left its mark on the whole Christian world. He tries to show that mere profession of Christianity was a crime in 65, by referring to Tacitus' statement that the first persons whom Nero had arrested in Rome for the fire (for which he himself was rumored responsible) were "those who confessed."

Robinson argues that this cannot mean "confessed to arson, of which it is made clear that they were innocent, but to their faith" (164, p 157). But this is disputed by some commentators. Merrill, for instance, thinks that once the first people arrested (persons popularly known to be Christians) had pleaded guilty to arson, their "confession" in open court "would convince the populace that the generally detested sect was as a body guilty of the fire that had stripped so many thousands of home and possessions, and made them vagabonds and beggars. From this point on in the investigation it would be legally necessary only to convict a man of being a Christian. Condemnation to death for conspiracy to commit the arson would immediately follow" (137, p 129).

Mark envisages persecution of Christian communities in the last days of the world, that is, in his own times. He makes Jesus say, apropos of these last days: "They shall deliver you up to councils, and in synagogues shall ye be beaten; and before governors and kings shall ye stand for my sake" (13:9, RV). Mark reckons with a situation where merely being a Christian involves the death penalty from the Roman state: "Brother shall deliver up brother to death and the father his child: and children shall rise against parents and cause them to be put to death" (13:12). One member of a family will, then, denounce another to the authorities for the capital offense of being a Christian.

Haenchen notes that the phrase "cause them to be put to death" (here, in the context of "delivering them up to death") only makes sense if the "name" ("ye shall be hated of all men for my name's sake") of the next verse is a capital crime. Winter has correlated this statement that the faithful will "be hated of all men for my name's sake" with the mention by Tacitus and Pliny of the *nomen Christianum,* which, he says (220, p 33), "was the technical designation of an offence against Roman law, the offence of professing to be a Christian. To profess Christian beliefs was of itself illegal even if not accompanied by criminal behavior." We recall (see p 102) that Ignatius, on his way to martyrdom in Rome, described himself as "a prisoner for the name's sake."

Next in Mk. 13 Jesus says enigmatically:

> But when ye see the abomination of desolation standing where he ought not (let him that readeth understand), then let them that are in Judaea flee unto the mountains: and let him that is on the housetop not go down, nor enter in, to take anything out of his house: and let him that is in the field not return back to take his cloak (RV).

The phrase "abomination of desolation" is taken from the book of Daniel, where it is used to allude to the heathen altar which the Syrian Seleucid ruler Antiochus Epiphanes erected in the temple at Jerusalem in 168 BC. The author of Daniel was alive when this happened but pretends to have lived centuries earlier and to prophesy it. He refers to it in such a veiled manner that the Christian evangelists supposed that the "abomination" had not yet arrived, and that Daniel's "prophecies" in fact referred to events which would come to pass in their own day and age — events which were to presage the end of the world. For, according to Daniel (and to Mark), the sacrilege is to inaugurate a period of unprecedented distress, after which the end will come.

Mark, then, is telling his readers that some event will occur — perhaps as a culmination of the persecution of Christians mentioned in the immediately preceding verses — which will fulfill Daniel's prophecy, and that people in Judaea are to "flee to the mountains." Now Mark was not writing for Judaean Christians; he laboriously explains Jewish customs for the benefit of his readers, who were obviously Gentiles ignorant of them (see p 13). Commentators have repeatedly noted that he also betrays an ignorance of Palestinian geography hardly compatible with the assumption that he lived anywhere near that country.[2] But if he was not writing for Jews, why should he wish to tell Judaeans what to do at a particular moment?[3]

The only convincing explanation of Mark's enigmatic instructions that I have seen is that given by Haenchen (93, pp 444-8). He first rules out the interpretation of many commentators, that "the abomination of desolation standing where he ought not" refers to the desecration of the temple by Romans in AD 70. For, he asks, why should the Judaeans flee when the Roman armies have already passed through Judaea and reached Jerusalem? And why are they told to flee immediately when they see the abomination? The implication is that by flight they will escape from it. Furthermore, why does Mark hint ("let him that readeth understand") that he is communicating an important instruction in enigmatic wording?

Haenchen answers these questions by pointing to *1 Maccabees,* which gives a historical account of the reign of the Seleucid Antiochus Epiphanes. This apocryphal work tells (1:54) that "the abomination of desolation was set up on the altar," that pagan altars were built throughout the towns of Judaea, and that death was the penalty for refusal to comply with the king's decree to offer sacrifice at them. Evasion was possible only by "fleeing to the mountains" (2:28). Christians of the first century would not have suspected that the events reported in *1 Maccabees* were the same as those prophesied in veiled manner in the book of Daniel. Nevertheless, the narrative of *1 Maccabees* could have served to show Mark how state persecution—which he was expecting—might be implemented. And Mark's reference to the necessity of "fleeing to the mountains" (as, according to *1 Maccabees,* the priest Mattathias and his sons had done after slaying the royal commissar) when the "abomination" appears, suggests that he had the incidents of *1 Maccabees* in mind.

Haenchen argues, then, that what Mark envisaged was an attempt by a Roman emperor to force pagan worship on Christians, as Antiochus had done on his subjects. The Book of Revelation reckons with such a possibility. The point was not baldly stated, since open criticism of imperial power would have been dangerous not only for the author but also for the community in which his book was used. For this reason, Revelation's author sometimes writes "Babylon" when he means "Rome," and disparages an emperor without mentioning his name. But to make sure that he will nevertheless be understood, he several times insists that his readers should seek out the secret sense of his words ("If any man hath an ear, let him hear"; "Here is wisdom" for him "that hath understanding" etc.).

Haenchen argues that Mark had to be equally cautious of Rome, and for that reason adopted the same method of warning his readers that his message was in coded form ("let him that readeth understand"). And he decodes Mark's message to read: As soon as preparations (that is, the setting up of an image or altar) are seen being made for a compulsory sacrifice to a pagan god or to the emperor himself—as soon, then, as the sacrilege is seen standing "where he ought not to be"—then those in Judea (that is, Christians) are to flee to the mountains. Judea is named because Mark regards the coming Roman persecutions as fulfilling the prophecy of Daniel; he reproduces Daniel's phrasing so as to be unintelligible except to his Christian readers, who will understand that, although only those in Judea are mentioned, Christians anywhere in the Empire are meant. But it did not suit Mark's purpose to reproduce Daniel's statement that the abomination would be erected in "the sanctuary" (the temple), and so he writes of the abomination (a noun of neuter gender) standing where *he* (masculine gender) ought not to be.

The lack of grammatical agreement between pronoun and noun seems deliberate, due to Mark's envisaging the abomination as a picture of the emperor. According to Rev. 13:15 the picture will even speak, that is, behave as a person. The writer had presumably come across the speaking images of pagan temples, made to speak by the skill of the priests (see Sweet's comment on this verse, 194, p 216). Mark insists that immediate flight is necessary when the abomination appears, for, if Christians wait until they are brought before this heathen image or altar, they will be left with a choice only between compliance or death.

If Haenchen is right, then Mark is not necessarily writing *before* Roman armies had passed through Judaea; nor is a pre-70 date for his gospel established by his failure to mention the cessation of the daily offering in the temple, which Daniel links with the abomination and which also occurred in August of 70. For, in Mark's interpretation, the abomination no longer refers to events connected with the temple. (Mark's Jesus does—at 13:1-2—foretell the destruction of the temple, but does not place it among the events presaging the end of the world; his discourse on these events begins only at 13:6. On the discontinuity between 13:1-2 and what follows, see DJE, pp 79-80.)

Haenchen does not infer from his own interpretation that Mark was writing as late as 90. He thinks that he may have written at Rome about 70 and that he looked back on the Neronian persecution of the 60s as a situation that could recur in the form of a more general persecution with which Christians would have to reckon (92, p 116). However, Haenchen admits (on the same page) that the intense anxiety expressed in Mk. 13 is not entirely explicable in terms of memories of Nero's behavior.

My suggestion is that this anxiety fits a situation of about 90 very well. Mk. 8:34-5 also shows how appropriate this later date is. The passage says: "And he called to him the multitude with his disciples, and said to them 'If any man would come after me, let him deny himself and take up his cross and follow me. For whoever would save his life will lose it; and whoever loses his life for my sake and the gospel's will save it.'"

A man who loses his earthly life for the gospel's sake will, then, thereby save his heavenly life. Haenchen comments: "Here the sort of persecution depicted later in many Acts of Martyrs is presupposed. The individual is asked: are you a Christian? If he replies 'Christianus sum' he is executed" (92, p 117).

Perrin agrees that these verses in *Mark* imply "formal persecution of Christians as Christians." We cannot, he adds, name the emperor concerned, but we can say that preparation of the readers for the possibility of persecution "is a very real part of the Marcan purpose" (156, p 52).

The situation to which Mark refers in chapter 8 thus belongs not to the lifetime of Jesus, but to a later period. Indeed, the whole setting in which Mark gives these words shows that they are not authentic. They are spoken as Jesus and his disciples make their way to the villages of Caesarea Philippi, about thirty miles north of the Sea of Galilee. In this thinly populated area, where Jesus is going for the first time, there could be no "multitude" for him to summon suddenly as an audience. That Mark nevertheless represents the teaching as addressed to a crowd means that he is concerned to underline its relevance for Christians everywhere. His motive in making Jesus go so far north at all was probably to provide a setting for the next incident in his gospel—the transfiguration. This, like other important revelations, had to be sited "on a high mountain" (9:2), available only in the north.

Returning now to Mk. 13, Jesus goes on to say (verse 30) that "this generation" will live to see the end of the world. This saying was probably put into his mouth to reassure Christians at a time when many had begun to feel uneasy because the end (represented as imminent in the earliest Christian writings) had failed to occur. It has been asked how Mark could possibly have invented, or even assimilated such a saying from his sources, if he had been writing a generation or more later than the period he assigns to Jesus' life. Now at Mk. 9:1 Jesus says that only *some* of his contemporaries will experience the end. This saying has been regarded as originally a remark of an early Christian preacher, which was later credited with the authority of Jesus. Mark assimilated it, and that he did so suggests that he wished the saying of 13:30, which he surely also took from earlier tradition, to be interpreted in a like sense.[4]

It was not impossible for some who had been alive in AD 30 to be still alive near the end of the century. In 13:29, Jesus, who is represented as addressing four intimate disciples (Peter, James, John and Andrew), concludes his account of the events leading up to the end by telling them: 'When ye see these things coming to pass, know ye that he [the Son of man] is nigh." If we took this literally, we should have to infer that, in the view of the writer, these four disciples would still be alive at the end of the world. But Mark did not think with such historical precision. He regarded both the saying of 9:1 and the statements in chapter 13 (which he himself put together from various sources to form a continuous speech) as addressed to the Christians of his own day. As Haenchen notes (93, p 451), every reader would feel that he belonged to "this generation" of 13:30.

II LUKE'S REWRITING OF MARK'S APOCALYPSE

Mark may well have drawn on Christian material that associated the destruction of Jerusalem with the end; but if so, he reworded it, divorcing (as we have seen) the "abomination of desolation" from the connection with Jerusalem and its temple that it had in Daniel and, quite possibly, in his own immediate source. He has retained from that source the reference to the end, but not the one to Jerusalem. When Luke rewrote this section of *Mark,* he interpreted it as an allusion to the destruction of Jerusalem and made this reference more detailed and specific, but he was very careful *not* to link it with the end. The reasonable inference is that, when Luke wrote, years had passed since the destruction of the city in 70.

If we take Mark's apocalyptic discourse in chapter 13 as a whole, we see that his Jesus foretells the following sequence of events as leading up to the end of the world:

(1) false proclamations of the end (v. 6)
(2) wars and rumors of wars (v. 7)
(3) conflict of nations, earthquakes, and famines (v. 8)
(4) persecution of Christians (vss. 9–13)
(5) "abomination of desolation" and flight of "those in Judea" to the mountains (vss. 14 ff)
(6) signs of the end in the heavens (vss. 24–5)
(7) arrival of the Son of Man, who will come down from the clouds to effect a final judgment (vss. 26–7).

Luke understood item 5 as Jesus' prophecy of the destruction of Jerusalem, and from a knowledge of how this had been accomplished by Titus' armies he changed Mark's wording so as to make the reference clear. Instead, then, of writing of the abomination of desolation, Luke says: "When you see Jerusalem surrounded by armies, then know that its desolation has come near" (21:20). Luke also interpreted the sack of the city as a judgment on the Jews for their rejection of Christianity. This is clear from the way he modifies the verses about the flight to the mountains which follow Mark's reference to the abomination of desolation. [In quoting the relevant passages from the RV that follow, I have italicized, in the Marcan extract, a phrase dropped by Luke, and in the Lucan extract the phrases with no equivalent in *Mark,* which serve to bring out Luke's idea that the sack of the city was a judgment.]

> *Mk. 13:14–9*: Then let them that are in Judaea flee unto the mountains; and let him that is on the housetop not go down, nor enter in, to take anything out of his house; and let him that is in the field not return back to take his cloak. But woe unto them that are with child and to them that give suck in those days! *And pray ye that it be not in the winter.* For those days shall be tribulation such as there hath not been the like. . . .

> *Lk. 21:21–4*: Then let them that are in Judaea flee unto the mountains; and let them that are in the midst of her [Jerusalem] depart out; and let not them that are in the country enter therein. *For these are days of vengeance,* that all things which are written may be fulfilled. Woe unto them that are with child and to them that give suck in those days! For there shall be great distress upon the land, *and wrath unto this people.* And they shall fall by the edge of the sword and *shall be led captive into all the nations.*

The final Lucan phrase here quoted correlates well with Josephus' statement that the youths of Jerusalem were sold into slavery. And the italicized Marcan phrase dropped by Luke makes good sense in *Mark,* where a future calamity is imagined. But it would make no sense at all for Luke's readers to be asked to pray that God's judgment on the Jews—for Luke already a thing of the past—be mitigated.

Robinson, quoting the conservative Swedish theologian Bo Reicke, objects that if Luke wrote his gospel after the historical siege of Jerusalem in 70, he "must be accused of incredible confusion when he spoke of flight during that siege." It is in fact true that, as Kümmel says in his standard handbook, Luke had "no accurate conception of the geography of Palestine,"[5] nor of the topography of Jerusalem.[6] Having changed Mark's "abomination" to "armies encircling Jerusalem," he did not see any need to change Mark's next verse (about Judeans fleeing to the mountains). He did, however, somewhat clumsily reword Mark's next statements (about the man on the housetop or in the field not delaying his flight) so as to make them refer to the topic *he* has introduced to replace Mark's: namely, Jerusalem. Men are to leave, not their houses or fields, but Jerusalem. That flight from a city surrounded by armies might well have been difficult did not deter him from thus bringing the Marcan wording into line with his own scheme.

Although Luke thus interpreted item 5 of Mark's discourse (the abomination) as an event of the past, he knew that Mark's items 6 and 7 (celestial signs of the end and arrival of the Son of Man) had not yet materialized. So he makes clear that 5 (as interpreted by him) is not to be followed immediately by 6, saying that Jerusalem will be occupied by aliens for a considerable time ("trodden down by the Gentiles, until their times are fulfilled"). Only then will Mark's items 6 and 7 occur. The detail about the armies surrounding the city, followed by insistence that its desolation is not a prelude to the end, strongly suggests that Luke is looking back to the Jewish War as an event no longer of the immediate past.

Robinson thinks that Luke's references to Jerusalem's destruction in verses 20–4 are far too brief and inexplicit to have been written after the event. But Luke's brevity is due to the fact that he is restricted to an insertion he is making in the Marcan apocalyptic text he is adapting, while trying at the same time to retain the enigmatic character of the Marcan original. Robinson takes some trouble to show that the events of 70 are alluded to in some detail in Jewish literature of later date. He thinks it "incredible that if parts of the New Testament came from the same [later] period, nothing of the kind is reflected in it." But is it surprising that Jewish literature should be much more exercised by the Jewish catastrophe than is post-70 Christian literature, which was written primarily for Gentile Christians with little interest in Jerusalem?

Luke made further changes in Mark's sequence of events, probably because the persecution of Christians (Mark's item 4) was occurring in his own time, and so he could not place it before Mark's item 5 (since he interpreted this latter as referring to an event of the past).[7] To avoid completely recasting the speech as given in *Mark,* he made Jesus begin a new speech after Mark's first two items by introducing Mark's item 3 with the words: "Then said he unto them." He also supplements this third item with a reference to signs of the end in the heavens. By means of the interpolated introductory words a clear break or caesura is placed between Mark's items 2 and 3 – that is, between false proclamations and wars on the one hand, and the conflict of nations, earthquakes, famines, and signs of the end in the heavens on the other. (Luke supplemented Mark's item 3 with signs in the heavens.) The importance of this caesura emerges from the sequel; for, like Mark, Luke next mentions persecutions; but instead of placing them (as does Mark) as the next event in the eschatological drama, he says they will occur "before all these things." The fact that Luke's Jesus has begun an entirely new speech at item 3 means that the persecutions are to precede, not all of the events hitherto mentioned but only all those specified in this new speech – that is, the persecutions are to come before the signs of the end in the heavens. This can be made clear by quoting Lk. 21 (RV) and italicizing the significant material added to *Mark*:

1 False proclamations	8: And he said, Take heed that ye be not led astray: for many shall come in my name, saying I am he; and, the time is at hand: go ye not after them.
2 Reports of wars	9: And when ye shall hear of wars and tumults, be not terrified: for these things must needs come to pass first; but the end is not immediately.
caesura	
3 Conflict of nations, earthquakes, etc., *and* *signs in the* *heavens*	10: *Then said he unto them,* Nation shall rise against nation, and kingdom against kingdom. 11: and there shall be great earthquakes, and in divers places famines and pestilences; *and there shall be terrors and great signs from heaven.*
4 Persecutions (*but at an* *earlier date*)	12: *But before all these things,* they shall lay their hands on you and shall persecute you . . .

The account of the persecutions continues until verse 19, and is followed by the details of Jerusalem's destruction (vss. 20–4). Then Luke proceeds (vss. 25–6) to Mark's items 6 and 7 (signs of the end in the heavens and arrival of the Son of Man). Luke gives, then, two references to the signs of the end – the one in verse 11 (significantly added to the Marcan account) is taken up again in verses 25–6; and the latter follows the assurance that the Gentile occupation of the desolated Jerusalem will endure for a considerable time. The order of events, as envisaged by Luke, is therefore (as Haenchen has argued):

(1) false proclamations of the end (v. 8)

(2) reports of wars (v. 9)

(3) siege and destruction of Jerusalem (as a judgment of Israel) and occupation of the city by Gentiles for a considerable time (vss. 20–4)

(4) persecution of Christians (vss. 12–9)

(5) conflict of nations, earthquakes, etc. and terrifying signs in the heavens (vss. 10–1, resumed at vss. 25–6)

(6) appearance of the Son of Man (v. 27)

Further evidence normally regarded as demonstrating that Luke knew what had happened in 70 is the speech (unique to *Luke*) which Jesus is represented as making as he drew near Jerusalem (19:41–4 *RV*):

> He saw the city and wept over it, saying . . . The days shall come upon thee, when thine enemies shall cast up a bank about thee, and compass thee round, and keep thee in on every side, and shall dash thee to the ground, and thy children within thee: and they shall not leave in thee one stone upon another; because thou knewest not the time of thy visitation.

The Greek word here translated as *bank* means "stake, palisade or rampart." Josephus, who wrote as an eyewitness of the events of 70, tells that the Romans under Titus erected siegeworks round Jerusalem. Robinson, however, quotes Dodd's comment that there are features in Josephus' account of the Roman capture of Jerusalem that are more distinctive than these siegeworks — features which "caught the imagination of Josephus and, we may suppose, of any other witness of these events. Nothing is said of them here [in *Luke*]." But this is intelligible enough if Luke was not a witness of the events, but wrote about 90 without firsthand knowledge of the siege and without a copy of Josephus at his elbow.

Dodd also notes that, although Josephus mentions many atrocities, "he does not say that the conquerors dashed children to the ground." The argument seems to be that Luke alleges this and was therefore ignorant of what really happened because he wrote before the event. But the phrase "will dash thee to the ground, thee and thy children within thee," may well mean only to destroy the city and all its inhabitants. Dodd also thinks it significant that Luke's language here is "soaked in the Septuagint." Of course Luke writes in a solemn, deliberately archaic Old Testament style, befitting—to his mind—his holy subject matter. This does not mean that he has only Old Testament events, and not recent ones, in mind.

III   CHRISTOLOGY AND CHRONOLOGY IN LUKE

Luke has entirely dropped the early-Christian expectation of a speedy end to the world. A man who believed that the world would end almost at once might write a gospel (since knowledge of Jesus and his teaching could be considered essential to salvation at the coming Judgment), but he would hardly go on to compose an account of the spread of the faith, as Luke did in Acts. And the way he rewrote Jesus' words (as given in *Mark*) to the high priest makes it quite clear that he did not expect Jesus to return to earth soon. According to Mk. 14:62, these words were: "*You will see* the Son of Man seated at the right hand of Power, and coming with the clouds of heaven."

Luke rewrote this so as to exclude the suggestion that some contemporaries would witness his second coming; he also wanted (as Franklin brings out, 70, pp 28, 174) to show that, although invisible, Jesus is no mere hero of the past, but—by virtue of his exaltation on God's right hand—Lord of the present. Luke's version reads: "*From now on* the Son of Man *shall be seated* at the right hand of the power of God" (Lk. 22:69). Stephen, at an ecstatic moment before his martyrdom, was said to have looked into heaven and discerned Jesus in position at God's right hand (Acts 7:56).

Luke's doctrine of the spirit is likewise adapted to the purpose of stressing Jesus' *present* power. From the first, Christians believed that his exaltation at his resurrection made possible the gift of the spirit, the mode in which, after his death, he remains present with believers. Acts represents him as giving the spirit from heaven (where he himself receives it from God, Acts 2:33), after promising it (1:8) to his disciples at his ascension. As Acts postpones the ascension until forty days after the resurrection,[8] the author naturally made the giving of the spirit occur at the next available festival, Pentecost, fifty days after the sabbath that follows Passover. Luke could not accept the older view that the gift of the spirit presaged the end of the world and enabled Christians to make ecstatic utterances. He says nothing of the Pauline "tongues of ecstasy" (1 Cor. 14:5) but instead makes his Pentecost miracle into an ability of the apostles to speak foreign languages (Acts 2:5-11), which enables them to preach throughout the whole world. The resulting universal witness to Jesus serves as proof of his present and continuing power, as well as a fulfillment of the promise he made to the apostles at his ascension: "You shall receive power when the Holy Spirit has come upon you; and you shall be my witnesses . . . to the end of the earth" (Acts 1:8).

Another aspect of Luke's Christology also reveals him to be a relatively late writer. We have seen that many early Christian documents assert that Jesus existed before the world's creation. However, the Jesus of *Luke*-Acts does not figure as a supernatural personage before his birth, but as "a man attested to you by God with mighty works" (Acts 2:22), who achieved supernatural status only when he was exalted to God's right hand at his ascension.

Finally, Luke is in such complete confusion over the chronology of events that occurred in the first half of the first century as to suggest that he was not close in time to them. In Acts 5, where the scene is Jerusalem about the mid-30s, Gamaliel reviews bygone Messianic risings and mentions that of Theudas. But we know from Josephus that Theudas' Messianic promises were made when Fadus was procurator (AD 44–46) and so could not have been known to Gamaliel at the time when he is represented as speaking. It is mere evasion of the difficulty to suppose (as does Bruce, 26, p 147) that there was another Theudas, who did much the same as the one in Josephus, but a few decades earlier.

Gamaliel continues by saying that, *after* Theudas, there was a Messianic uprising under Judas the Galilean at the time of the census. Luke knows of only one census, that under Quirinius (Lk. 2:1-2) of AD 6 — forty years *before* Theudas. In his gospel Luke compounds the muddle by dating this census of AD 6 under Herod, who died in 4 BC.[9] Could Luke have been writing about 60, as Robinson argues, when he is so wrong about some events which had occurred within twenty years of that date? Is it not much more likely that he wrote after the break in continuity of tradition occasioned by the Jewish War of AD 66-73?

IV MATTHEW AND THE END OF THE WORLD

During his ministry Jesus chose twelve disciples and sent them out with instructions on what they should preach, which are recorded in Matthew's tenth chapter. They are to "heal the sick, raise the dead, cleanse lepers and cast out demons" (Mt. 10:8). Jesus warns them (vss. 16–22) that they will be persecuted during this mission, and adds (v. 23): "You will not have gone through all the towns of Israel before the Son of Man comes." Matthew, then, makes Jesus predict that the end will come during the lifetime of the twelve. Robinson thinks that this militates against the view of most scholars that Matthew was writing well after AD 70; for if, he says, the evangelist had really written some fifty to sixty years after Jesus' death, "it is surely incredible that there are no traces of attempts to explain away or cover up such obviously by then unfulfillable predictions" (164, pp 24–5).

Scholars have shown that Mt. 10:5 ff does not represent an authentic speech by Jesus but is an artificial composition by Matthew, for it includes sayings that are set in quite different contexts by Mark and by Luke. For instance, the warnings of persecutions (Mt. 10:16–22) are taken from Mk. 13:9 ff, from Jesus' apocalyptic discourse, which Matthew reproduces in his chapter 24 but without these Marcan references to Christians being brought before tribunals of all kinds. Matthew's reason for transferring these references to his chapter 10 is to make them an integral part of what Jesus says Christian missionaries generally (including those of Matthew's own time) are to do and to suffer.

Jesus is made to tell the disciples to take neither money nor provisions with them; they are to be dependent on the sustenance offered by those who receive their preaching (Mt. 10:9–10). The purpose of this injunction is clearly to ensure that missionaries are seen to act from the purest of motives, not in order to enrich themselves. When they enter a city or village, they are to take accommodation from a "worthy" resident (that is, they are to lodge with the pious, not with persons of ill-repute, or who are ill-disposed towards Christianity), and they are to stay in these same lodgings for the whole period of their missionary activity in the area (10:11), presumably to avoid rivalry and jealousy between families competing for their favor. As Haenchen has observed, the evangelist obviously has in mind not missionaries who rush from one place to another from fear that the end of the world will come quickly, but rather missionaries who stay in an area long enough to found a Christian community there.

All these instructions, then, concern the founding of Christian communities through activity spread over a long period; they are not intelligible as directives given to disciples who soon return to the speaker (as the twelve are represented as doing). Matthew has set the instructions in an artificial context in order to claim Jesuine authority for rulings on missionary behavior generally. It is, for instance, stipulated (10:23) that when the missionaries are persecuted in one city, they are to leave and preach elsewhere. Here again, we see that the persecution envisaged was not universal, not part of the Messianic woes of the world's last days, but local and sporadic. It is presupposed that, by transferring to another place, the preachers will be free to carry on their work. The need for a ruling in Matthew's day on such a practical problem as whether to court martyrdom or to flee and work elsewhere naturally led to the conviction that the Lord had laid down what was to be done, and hence to the formulation of this Jesuine utterance.

But what of the second half of this verse (10:23), where the disciples are told that "you will not have gone through all the towns of Israel before the Son of Man comes"? Matthew, whenever he wrote, knew quite well that, at his time of writing, the Son of Man had not yet come. It would be absurd to suppose that he regarded Jesus' statement as a delusion, but nevertheless faithfully recorded it. Evangelists who manipulate their material so freely would not ascribe to Jesus doctrines they regarded as mistaken. Matthew, then, does not mean us to understand, by the "you," merely the twelve. He is thinking of Christian missionaries in general, in his own time in particular, as we have seen from the fact that he makes Jesus give instructions about the founding of Christian communities over a considerable period, even though (according to the gospels themselves) this was not effected by the twelve in Jesus' lifetime.

What he is saying is that the Christian mission in Israel — the conversion of the Jews — will not have been completed when the end comes. Paul had held that the Jews, jealous at the success of the Gentile mission, would eventually turn Christian, and then, he had implied, the end would come (see p 121). Matthew's opinion, however, is that the Jews will still be largely unconverted at the end. It is not here suggested that it will come quickly, but rather that the missionaries have a long and arduous task before them, a task of such magnitude that it will remain uncompleted at the end.

Matthew has not, however, given up hope that the end will come soon, although many of the Christians he is addressing obviously had. The evidence for this is that, when he later reproduced Jesus' apocalyptic discourse as given in Mark 13, he does not rewrite it substantially as Luke did, but adds to it a second part (twice as long as the part he has taken from *Mark*) in which, in a series of parables and injunctions, Christians are urged to be watchful and ready for the end (Mt. 24:37–25:46). Such long and detailed emphasis of this single point can only mean that the non-appearance of the end had caused the Christians to whom Matthew was appealing to waver in their expectancy. In the part of the discourse which he shares with *Mark,* the "abomination of desolation" is expressly said to have been "spoken of by the prophet Daniel" as "standing in the holy place" (Mt. 24:15). This probably means the temple.

Nevertheless, Matthew does not here include specific allusions to the fall of Jerusalem (as does Luke). We shall see in the next section of this chapter that Matthew chooses to allude to it elsewhere in his gospel. Garland has recently noted that the "major concern" of chapter 24 of *Matthew* is "to make absolutely clear that the fall of the Temple and the end of time were distinct events. The church must continue on for some time to come" (76, pp 29–30). Mt. 23: 38–9 (see DJE, p 87) also aims at interposing an interval between 70 and Jesus' second coming.

V THE REJECTION OF THE JEWS IN MATTHEW AND LUKE

Further evidence that Matthew was writing considerably later than Paul can be found in the strongly negative attitude to the Jews expressed in places in his gospel.

The earliest Christian communities were within Judaism (see p 37–8) and shared the fundamental tenet of the Jewish faith that Israel is the chosen people. It was, of course, perplexing for these early Christians that most Jews nevertheless refused to accept Jesus as Messiah. Paul accounts for this by distinguishing (Rom. 9:6 ff) Israel "after the flesh" from Israel "after the spirit" (the small group that has turned Christian) and holds that only the latter constitutes the true Israel for whom the Old Testament promises were meant.

He also, and alternatively, argues that God has temporarily hardened the Jews' hearts so as to make Christian missionaries turn to Gentiles, with the result that the Jews, jealous of the success of the Christian mission, will eventually themselves accept Christianity. Thus he says (Rom. 11:2): "God has not rejected his chosen people," and (vss. 25–6): "a hardening has come upon part of Israel, until the full number of the Gentiles come in, and so all Israel will be saved." He has to press these views with considerable emphasis on the Gentiles in the Christian community at Rome, who had obviously given up all hope of converting Jews and regarded them as irrevocably damned.

Such gospel passages as Mt. 8:10–2 and Lk. 13:28–30 (expressing the conviction that the sons of the kingdom will be cast into outer darkness at the Judgment) represent the triumph of this negative attitude. The fourth gospel is consistently anti-Jewish throughout. We see then that the anti-Jewish tendencies of the New Testament become more pronounced in the documents which scholars have regarded on other grounds as the later ones. And this is exactly what one would expect if these documents really are later and reflect the growing hostility of a new religion toward its parent.

Let us now turn to the parable of the great supper (Mt. 22:2–14 and Lk. 14: 15–24), a good illustration of evangelists putting rejection of the Jews into Jesus' mouth. Matthew tells that:

> The kingdom of heaven is likened unto a certain king, which made a marriage feast for his son, and sent forth his servants to call them that were bidden to the marriage feast: and they would not come. Again he sent forth other servants, saying, Tell them that are bidden. . . . Come to the marriage feast. But they made light of it, and sent their ways, one to his own farm, another to his merchandise: and *the rest laid hold on his servants, and entreated them shamefully, and killed them. But the king was wroth; and he sent his armies and destroyed those murderers and burned their city.* Then saith he to his servants, The wedding is ready, but they that were bidden were not worthy. Go ye therefore unto the partings of the highways, and as many as ye shall find, bid to the marriage feast. And those servants went out into the highways, and gathered together all as many as they found, both bad and good: and the wedding was filled with guests. (RV)

Commentators agree that "they that were bidden" to the feast are the Jews as the chosen people. They refuse the summons of the king of heaven's first servants (the Old Testament prophets) and then likewise a second summons from "other servants" (Christian missionaries), whom they even kill; whereupon the king punishes them with the destruction of their city, after which the Christian mission switches to Gentiles, "both bad and good." The italicized passage (where the evangelist makes his point that the destruction of the city was a punishment) is clearly alien; it is absent from Luke's version of the story, and Matthew's text runs on naturally if it is deleted, for after the military expedition the preparations for the supper remain exactly as they had been. Furthermore, "the rest," with which the emphasized passage begins, connects but clumsily with the preceding statement that "they went their ways."

The words I have italicized are, then (as Robinson agrees, 164, p 20), "an addition probably by the evangelist." The remainder of the parable reached him as a tradition which both he and Luke adapted in slightly different ways,[10] with the result that Luke tells a rather different story, namely that "the poor, the maimed, the blind and the lame" (the despised classes among the Jews) were brought to the supper when the invited guests (the respectable classes of Jews) refused to come. Luke is here clearly boosting the poor and weak in his usual manner. To accommodate the Gentiles, he has it that there were still some empty places, and so other people were "compelled" to come in from the highways and hedges. In Luke there is no king (the host is merely "a certain man") and no burning of any city. It is thus clear that Matthew has adapted a story, in a source document used also by Luke, to introduce a reference to the military destruction of Jerusalem by fire, which occurred in 70. The question is: Was the evangelist writing before 70, and forecasting that the Jews would be thus punished, or at a later date, with knowledge of what had happened in the Jewish War? Robinson is among the minority of commentators who take the former view. Let us look at his grounds.

First, following Rengstorf, Robinson notes that the "burning of the city" was a literary cliché common in parables concerning kings and in historical narratives that relate the capture and destruction of a town in the briefest possible way. Had the passage been written after 70, he argues, one would expect it to bring out the salient events of that date in much greater detail. He contrasts Matthew's brevity with the "visions" of apocalyptic seers who pose as men who lived long ago, and predict in considerable detail events which had in fact already occurred and were known both to the writer and to his audience. The obvious answer to this is that Matthew is not writing an apocalyptic vision but making an insertion, necessarily brief, into a pre-existing parable; and that despite its brevity, the insertion has the effect intended; namely, to bring up to date the history of God's dealings with the Jews.[11]

Robinson thinks (164, p 25) that if Luke and Matthew had been writing as late as 90, they would not have been interested in Jesus' predictions concerning 70 (if the historical Jesus had actually made any) and certainly would not have invented speeches that endowed him with such historical foresight. Only if the evangelists were writing about 60, when relations between Jews and Romans in Palestine were becoming tense, would his views (real or imagined) on the matter have been, as Robinson sees it, of interest.[12]

The way the two evangelists tell the story of the great supper in fact reveals motives: they are concerned to put into Jesus' mouth an epitome of Christian history up to the decisive moment when Christianity had turned away from Jews and addressed only Gentiles, and to represent the destruction of Jerusalem as a punishment for the Jews' rejection of him. In the story of the supper as told in both gospels, Israel not only is punished but also loses its position as the chosen people. "None of those men which were bidden shall taste of my supper" (Lk. 14:24).

Robinson also stresses that the fall of Jerusalem is never once in the New Testament mentioned "as a past fact." But it is hardly surprising that the gospels — which purport to describe events up to AD 30 — should fail to mention those of 70 as past. Epistles written before 70 were necessarily ignorant of its events; and epistles of later date were concerned with other matters.

Christians, as well as Jews, are fiercely criticized by Matthew, who must have been writing for a somewhat demoralized Christian community. The Jesus of Matthew, says Garland, is "threatening and judgmental," and delivers "vivid and stark warnings of ultimate destruction for the disobedient." Thus:

Salt that has lost its savor will be thrown out and trodden under foot (5:13). Many will enter the wide gate that leads to destruction (7:13). Trees which do not bear good fruit will be cut down and thrown into the fire (7:19, cf. 3:10). Those who cause stumbling in others will be thrown into the eternal fire (18:5-9, cf. 5:29-30).

Garland adds (76, p 82) that many of these sayings are either unique to Matthew or more severe there, if paralleled in other synoptics. Moreover, "what is remarkable is that nearly all are ostensibly addressed to the disciples and implicitly to Matthew's community." It thus seems that his church was "a mixture of weeds and wheat, good and rotten fish, good and evil wedding guests, faithful and evil servants, and . . . has its share of false prophets and hypocrites" (p 214). Probably the persecution to which it was subjected had demoralized it; for Matthew makes Jesus prophesy that under the impact of persecution "many will fall away and betray one another and hate one another. . . . And because wickedness is multiplied most men's love will grow cold" (Mt. 24: 10–2).

5

The Fourth Gospel

I ITS RELATION TO THE SYNOPTICS

The fourth gospel is a major piece of evidence in Robinson's recent attempts to vindicate the trustworthiness of the New Testament. He is not the only theologian who still believes that it contains primitive and reliable historical traditions. Its relation to the other gospels is therefore of some importance.

The *Gospel of John* cannot be harmonized with the synoptics. Whereas they have long passages in common, no passage of any length in *John* is verbally identical with anything in them. *John* shares a number of incidents with them (for example, the call of the disciples and the cleansing of the temple), but "in every case the time or location is changed and the whole scene differently imagined" (Lindars, 130, p 27). John records relatively few incidents in Jesus' life and makes them the basis of extended discourses that have no counterpart in the synoptics and which are not about the kingdom of God, of which Jesus speaks repeatedly there, but about his own dignity as the spokesman for and ambassador of the Father.

Nevertheless, John does from time to time use a word or phrase in a story identical with what is found in the story told very differently in the synoptics. Either the author knew one or more of them and willfully deviated from them, or else he depended on source material in part identical with theirs and rewrote it in the light of his own theological purposes. Commentators used to take the former of these two views, but there is now some agreement that the latter view makes better sense of the evidence (particularly since there are no passages in *John* of any length which are verbally identical with passages in other gospels).[1]

If, then, John did not know the synoptics, this may be due to the purely local distribution of any one gospel within a single Christian community in the earliest days. However, since gospels did circulate more widely before long, his ignorance of them probably means that *John* was written at about the same time as the others.

John is inimical to the early Christian view that the world would soon come to a catastrophic end and the living and the dead be brought to judgment as a new era is inaugurated. His idea is, rather, that the blessings of the coming age are available here and now to those who have faith in Jesus. For instance, although he allows Jesus to declare that there will be a future judgment, at the same time he makes him correct this doctrine by saying that the reference is not really to the future at all: "The hour is coming, *and now is,* when the dead will hear the voice of the son of God . . ." (5:25-9; cf. 4:23). In the story of the raising of Lazarus from the dead (recorded only in *John*), Jesus assures the sister of the deceased that "your brother will rise again" (11:23). She takes this to mean that "he will rise again in the resurrection at the last day."

To make Jesus' audience misunderstand his words (by construing them as meaning what they obviously seem to suggest) is what Lindars calls (130, p 53) one of John's "favorite tricks." It is not documented in the other gospels, and its function is to enable Jesus, by correcting the misunderstanding, to enunciate the theology of the fourth gospel. Hence, in the Lazarus story Jesus counters the woman's reference to a general resurrection at the end of time by declaring: "I am the resurrection and the life; he who believes in me, though he shall die, yet shall he live, and whoever lives and believes in me shall never die" (11:25-6).[2] Dodd agrees that here "the evangelist appears to be explicitly contrasting the popular eschatology of Judaism with the doctrine which he wishes to propound" (55, p 147). All this makes it obvious that we cannot expect any allusion in *John* to the eschatological discourses that are prominent in the synoptics and therefore that we must look elsewhere for indications of its date.

John makes no mention of Sadducees or Zealots (prominent in the first half of the first century) but names only the Pharisees as the Jewish leaders. This, says Lindars (130, p 37) reflects the situation after the elimination of Sadducees and Zealots in the Jewish War with Rome, 66-73. Furthermore, at Jn. 9:22 a couple are represented as refusing to admit that their son had been cured by Jesus "because they feared the Jews" who "had already agreed that if anyone should confess him to be the Christ, he was to be put out of the synagogue." This is supposed to refer to conditions obtaining in Jesus' lifetime, but it seems more likely that the evangelist wrote in knowledge of the synagogue's official cursing of heretical Jews by means of an insertion into its chief prayer authorized by Rabbi Gamaliel II, about 85. (This prayer expressly curses "the Nazarenes and the minim," and the latter included Jewish Christians. See Barrett, 8, pp 166-7.)

John's phrase about followers of Jesus being "put out of the synagogue" is repeated at two other points in his gospel (12:42 and 16:2), and Robinson (who thinks it implies no more than the type of harassment Paul had suffered) nevertheless concedes that it is "unparalleled anywhere else" (164, p 273). Moreover, at 16:2 Jesus is made to prophesy the exclusion from the synagogue, whereas the other two references to it represent it as actually obtaining in his day. We have seen examples in the New Testament epistles of similar confusion between prophecy and actuality arising from the attempt to make a figure of the past (Peter or Paul) "prophesy" elements in the author's own situation (see pp 85, 95).

John gives numerous topographical details of Jerusalem and its environs, and these are sometimes cited as evidence that he was writing in Palestine well before the end of the first century. Barrett, however, thinks that he was probably drawing on material where "names and events were already tied together." This material could have been written about 80 by someone well acquainted with Jerusalem. That would not make it authentic. John himself was probably less well informed. Barrett says in this connection that "the reconstruction of a biography, or of a biographical itinerary, is so difficult, that one may doubt whether the evangelist, the last editor of the gospel in its present form, was interested in topography at all" (10, p 38). His statement that Caiaphas was high priest "that year" (Jn. 11:49) – the year when Jesus aroused Jewish hostility by raising Lazarus from the dead – implies (wrongly) that the high priest changed annually, and some commentators regard this as a reason for placing John at a distance from first-century Palestine. Others avoid this inference by understanding "that year" as the memorable year of Jesus' Passion – "that fateful year of judgment and salvation," as Evans puts it (64, p 54).

John himself was, of course, not writing for Palestinians, for, like Mark, he often explains Jewish terms ("Messiah means Christ," and "Cephas means Peter," 1:41-2) and attitudes ("The Jews have no dealings with Samaritans," 4:9). Moody Smith sums all this up, saying that although *John* "doubtless contains chronological and topographical material worthy of historical scrutiny, it presents a picture of Jesus which, when placed alongside that of the synoptics, can be regarded as historical only in the most rarified sense of the word" (144, p 236).

Evidence external to the gospel also points to an origin at the end of the first or beginning of the second century. The lack of any references to it in the letters of Ignatius and Polycarp means that, if it existed about 115, it was not yet widely diffused or generally accepted. But it almost certainly existed by 140, for a papyrus fragment of it (unlikely to be part of the autograph copy) has been dated about 150; this may have been written twenty or thirty years earlier.[3] Patristic evidence (to which Lindars refers, 130, p 28) suggests that about this time Gnostic Christians (heretics from the standpoint of what later became established as orthodoxy) knew and used the fourth gospel, with the result that extant Christian writers (whom we have come to regard as "orthodox") long hesitated to quote it.

John, like Paul and the author of Hebrews, stresses Jesus' pre-existence and uses Jewish wisdom categories in order to do so. The *word* in John's prologue (the word "through whom all things were made," and who "was in the world" yet rejected there) corresponds with the idea of wisdom and its functions (cf. p 38). That virtually everything said of this *word* in John's prologue had already been predicated of Wisdom in Judaism is, as Moody Smith observes (144, p 242) a widely acknowledged fact. Lindars thinks that all the "I am" sayings in *John,* where Jesus affirms his own exalted status, are also "best understood in terms of a Wisdom Christology" (129, p 46). Mark had merely implied rather than stated Jesus' pre-existence (cf. DJE, pp 103-4) and Luke had denied it (see p 118). But John, drawing on presynoptic sources, assimilated the association of Jesus with wisdom, which we saw so strongly developed in Paul. Jesus' pre-existence is quite blatantly stressed in *John,* for at 17:5 he is made to remind God of the splendor they had experienced together before the world was created—a passage which drew from Strauss the comment that, if it is an authentic utterance, then Jesus must have been mad (191, p 50).

II THE AUTHOR

We have seen already that all four gospels were originally anonymous, as the earliest writers who quoted them did not assign them to a named author. Apart from the title "according to John" (which, like all the gospel titles, was not part of the original manuscripts, but was added by unknown hands before the end of the second century), the fourth gospel is anonymous from its prologue to the words which terminate chapter 20 and which are clearly meant as a solemn conclusion to the whole gospel. Chapter 21 however (an appendix added later) identifies the author as "the beloved disciple." Only the fourth gospel mentions such a person, and makes him figure in three incidents in earlier chapters: the last supper, the crucifixion, and the discovery of the empty tomb. The intention of chapter 21, in ascribing the whole gospel to this allegedly close friend of Jesus, is to represent it as the writing of an eyewitness. But this suggestion carries no weight, not only because it occurs only in an appended chapter but also because (as Lindars says, 130, p 32) all three incidents where the beloved disciple figures in the fourth gospel have parallels in the other three gospels *where he plays no part.* The inference is that, at these points, the fourth gospel drew on source material similar to that which underlies the other three but reworked it so as to introduce the beloved disciple. This is particularly clear in the case of the story of his visit to the empty tomb (Jn. 20:2-10), a story which—as Bultmann has shown—the evangelist has clumsily inserted at this point. Let us briefly review the details.

Chapter 20 begins with Mary Magdalene arriving at the tomb on Easter morning and finding the stone rolled away. There was no mention of any stone in the burial narrative of this gospel, and so here, in 20:1, John seems to be following a tradition independent of the one on which he had drawn there. Furthermore, the natural continuation of this verse comes only with verse 11, where Mary, still standing outside the tomb weeping, looks into it and sees two angels inside. The intervening verses (2-10), however, tell how she ran from the tomb—she is not said to have looked into it before doing so—and told Peter and the beloved disciple that the body had been removed and that "we know not where they have laid him." That she knows the body to be missing suggests that this unit of tradition (vss. 2-10) assumes that she has already inspected the tomb; but the unit has here been inserted into a story (verses 1 and 11 ff) which makes her only subsequently inspect it.

It is also strange that she reports (v. 2) that *we* do not know what has become of the body. This suggests that the evangelist is here adapting (so as to make it refer to her only) a tradition similar to Luke's story that a number of women found the stone rolled away on Easter morning. This suspicion is confirmed when we find that, just as Luke follows this incident by making Peter go to the tomb, so the fourth evangelist likewise continues: "Peter therefore went forth." The verb here is singular in the Greek, but the evangelist nevertheless adds: "and the other disciple, and they went toward the tomb."

Clearly, a story concerning Peter has been clumsily expanded so as to include the beloved disciple. On arrival they both entered the tomb, and the beloved disciple "saw and believed." It is not said that Peter believed. On the other hand, it is implied that belief was no obvious matter, for they did not then realize that the Old Testament had predicted Christ's resurrection (v. 9). The two men are then said to return home (v. 10), after which the narrative returns to Mary Magdalene at the mouth of the tomb, as in verse 1, as if the intervening incidents had not happened. As Haenchen has noted (93, p 556) the whole intervening story can serve only the purpose of increasing our respect for the beloved disciple.

Who, then, is this beloved disciple? The fourth gospel does not say, but the second-century church naturally assumed that he must be one of the inner group of three who, according to the first three gospels, were Jesus' most privileged companions, namely Peter and James and John, the sons of Zebedee. These three alone were present at the raising of Jairus' daughter (as related by Mark), at the transfiguration (as related by all three synoptics) and at Gethsemane (as related by Mark and Matthew). Furthermore it was obvious that, of these three intimates, Peter cannot be the beloved disciple as the two are mentioned as different persons in the fourth gospel; and since James was, according to Acts, martyred early, it seemed clear to the Church Fathers that the beloved one could only be John.

Unfortunately for this theory, the incidents which represent Peter, James, and John as particularly close to Jesus occur only in the first three gospels. In the fourth (where alone the beloved disciple figures) there is no raising of Jairus' daughter, no transfiguration, no Gethsemane agony—in fact no mention of the sons of Zebedee until the appendix (ch. 21). Indeed, Peter, James, and John, although prominent in the synoptics play but a minor role (or none at all) in *John,* where prominence is assigned to disciples unknown to the synoptics (Nathaniel, Nicodemus, and, of course, the beloved disciple). The fourth gospel, then, leaves the beloved one anonymous. The author of the appendix decided to represent this anonymous person as the author of the gospel, and the identification of him with John is the work of second-century harmonists.

That John neglects the twelve disciples—as a group they play practically no part in *John*—in favor of characters unknown to the synoptics in itself shows that the material on which he drew was in some ways specialized and independent of them. One of the disciples mentioned only in *John* is Philip; Haenchen notes (93, p 257) that such a discovery as the Gnostic *Gospel of Philip*, found at Nag Hammadi, shows that Philip is important in relatively late traditions.

III   JOHN'S REWORKING OF TRADITIONAL MATERIAL

Examples of John's reworking of source traditions will illuminate both his methods and his unreliability as a historian. He tells (5:1-9) how Jesus healed a cripple at a sheep-pool called Bethesda at Jerusalem—a story not found in the other gospels—but fuses it with the story (represented in Mk. 2:1-12) of the man let down through the roof of the house at Capernaum in Galilee. The fusion is betrayed by the fact that Jesus' final instructions "take up your bed and walk" are verbally identical in the two gospels (Jn. 5:8 = Mk. 2:9). This identity is particularly striking because the word for bed (*krabbatos*) is a colloquial one which Matthew and Luke have taken pains to avoid in their adaptation of the Marcan story.

Jn. 8:12—"he who follows me will not walk in darkness, but will have the light of life"—is a saying absent from the other gospels, but formed by adapting a well-known Old Testament quotation about people who "walked in darkness" but have seen a "light" (Isaiah 9:2) and combining it with traditional sayings on discipleship, typified in Peter's statement (Mk. 10:28) that he and others have left everything and "followed" Jesus. Such examples, says Lindars (129, pp 24, 61), show the fourth evangelist using only fragments of his source material—a phrase or even a mere word—and working them into narratives and discourses which are his own compositions. Starting with a small kernel from a source, he surrounds it with a whole chapter of his own theology.

Reworking is also apparent in John's story of Jesus raising Lazarus from the dead. It is without synoptic parallel, but Morton Smith (183) has recently given good grounds for holding that a version of *Mark* which existed by 120 contained a story similar enough to allow the inference that both derive from a common source. In John's story, when Jesus arrives on the scene Lazarus is already dead and buried; one of his two sisters says, somewhat reproachfully: "Lord, if you had been here, my brother would not have died" (11:21). These words seem to have been in John's source, for they are followed by a passage of typically Johannine theology (to which I referred, p 126); the evangelist succeeds in getting back to the story (and to his source) only by making the other sister of the deceased speak exactly the same words to Jesus (v. 32b, identical with v. 21b).

John next represents Jesus as "deeply moved in spirit and troubled" (v. 33), and as asking where the dead man has been laid. The Greek word for "deeply moved" surely belonged to the source, for it implies anger rather than grief, and John has been able to use it with the latter implication only by adding, as a gloss on it, a parallel phrase ("troubled") from his normal vocabulary. Verse 33 is followed by obviously Johannine material: Jews (who appear as Jesus' enemies throughout *John*) pointing out that Jesus, although able to cure blindness (as he did in ch. 9) was apparently powerless to prevent Lazarus' death. After this the evangelist's return to his source is betrayed when he again makes Jesus be "deeply moved" (v. 38, which repeats the same, inappropriate, Greek word) before proceeding with the miracle.

If, then, John used sources, we naturally ask whether reliable traditions were embodied in them and whether they can be sifted from his reworking. At Jn. 6:15 we are told that Jesus, perceiving that the people "were about to come and take him by force to make him king, withdrew . . . into the mountain . . . alone." Conservative scholarship has interpreted this as a truly ancient tradition which the synoptics were afraid to include because of its dangerous (anti-Roman and therefore subversive) political implications (see, for instance Dodd, 54, and Hunter, 107, p 44). Robinson has recently taken the same view, and thinks that the Jews' attempt to make Jesus a king fits the situation that obtained in pre-70 Palestine (164, pp 264 ff). Robinson has been sharply criticized on this by Nineham, who noted (in a radio discussion between the two) that the Palestinian Jews never attempted to make anyone king, not even during their war with Rome from AD 66.

John's story of Jesus' flight to avoid being made king comes at the end of a narrative about the miraculous feeding of 5000 people, an incident which occurs also in *Mark*. The study of such stories has shown that they do not represent an accurate record of a real event but rather one layer of a developing tradition; other layers (earlier or later in the development of the same story) are represented in other gospels, or even in the same gospel. Mark tells that Jesus fed 5000 (6:35–44) and later 4000 (8:2–9). The two accounts contain striking verbal similarities. Most commentators agree that both reproduce the same underlying tradition in different stages of development and that, because the numbers (of loaves, persons, etc.) differ, Mark wrongly supposed that two different traditions (each representing a separate incident in Jesus' life) were involved.

If we can assume that a miracle story is likely to become exaggerated by being told again and again, then, as far as the numbers are concerned, Mk. 8 gives a relatively early version; for here seven loaves are required to satisfy 4000 people and what is left over fills only seven small baskets. But in Mk. 6 five loaves are sufficient for 5000 and the leftovers fill twelve large baskets. (The difference in size of baskets is clear in the Greek, but is not often indicated in translations. How baskets of any kind came to be available at the remote locality where the miracle is sited neither Mark — nor any other evangelist who includes a similar story—deems necessary to explain.) Matthew further expands this by alleging that women and children, in addition to 5000 men, were fed. On the other hand, the statement in Mk. 6:37 that 200 *denarii* (200 pennyworth in the translation of the RV) would be needed to provide bread for the multitude points to a stage (earlier than the version of the story given by Mark) when fewer than 1000 people were involved.

All this shows that numerous versions of this feeding story were circulating. John could have drawn his account from any one of them, not necessarily from the ones extant in the synoptics. That he did draw on a tradition similar to those represented there is clear from the fact that he too has five loaves feeding 5000 people, with twelve large baskets of leftovers. He also used the phrase "200 *denarii*" (even though in his account this sum is said to be *insufficient* to provide enough bread for the crowd present). Also, John writes of "five *barley* loaves," and this suggests that all these feeding stories are to some extent inspired by the story of Elisha's lesser miracle in having twenty barley loaves and a little fresh grain distributed among one hundred men so that "all ate and had some left" (2 Kings 4:42–4). As Nineham has observed, Jesus' behavior in feeding the crowd represents him as "fulfilment of the Law and the prophets," as "the one sent by God to usher in the ultimate salvation to which Law and prophets had pointed forward" (148, p 178).

John's version of the feeding miracle differs from the other extant ones by its greater emphasis on Jesus' enormous power. We are told that, followed by a great crowd, he went "up on the mountain" and "there sat down with his disciples" (Jn. 6:3). He is not said (as in the account of Mk. 6) to have taught the people, nor (as in Mt. 14) to have healed them. John's account of the story simply sets the scene which gives occasion for Jesus to display his miraculous powers. Furthermore, in *John* the miracle is not as it were forced on him by an emergency. In Mk. 6 his disciples point out to him that he has detained the people with his teaching in a "lonely" or "desert" place, and that, at near nightfall, they are far from home, shelter, and food. Jesus thus has some obligation for relieving distress which his own behavior has occasioned. (That one meal would not really put everything right did not occur to the author of this story.)

In *John,* however, there is no teaching that detains the people, they are not in a lonely place, and it is not evening. (Evening comes only in John's next incident, after Jesus had fed and dismissed the crowd and withdrawn in solitude.) Jesus asks Philip—who as we saw is a disciple mentioned only in *John*—how to feed the multitude. He does not have to have his attention drawn to their needs, as in Mk. 6. But he is only pretending to seek advice, and in fact knows from the first that he intends to work a miracle (Jn. 6:6).

In John's version, then, the miracle is not really called for by the situation, but is, as Strathmann says (190, p 108), introduced as a voluntary demonstration of Jesus' power. And it is in line with this that the conclusion of the story is expanded so as to underline the great effect the miracle had on the crowd: "When therefore the people saw the sign which he did, they said, This is of a truth the prophet that cometh into the world. Jesus therefore perceiving that they were about to come and take him by force to make him king, withdrew again into the mountain himself alone" (Jn. 6:14-5, RV).

The implication is clear: how easily Jesus could have become an earthly king, had he not insisted that his kingship is "not of this world" (Jn. 18:36), and how impressed the people must have been to have wished to make him their Messianic king. As this detail fits both John's Christology and the tendency of his version of Jesus' life—to emphasize his power—there is no need to take it as a record of historical fact.

Nevertheless, the feeding miracle at this stage of development—where it has become truly prodigious and where Jesus acts without any constraint from earthly pressures—probably existed before John and was one of the traditions he drew from some source; for his own understanding of the miracle is a little different, and is given later when he makes Jesus declare that the people miraculously fed had nevertheless failed to discern the truth of which the physical feeding had been a mere sign, namely that he himself is the bread of life (6:26 and 35-6).

Other episodes in *John* show likewise that the author has assimilated an existing story but added some comment of his own that corrects its implications or gives them a new direction. This technique shows that he, like the other evangelists, did not invent all his account of Jesus but was to some extent bound by pre-existing traditions, which he reworked. Haenchen well illustrates the process in his analysis (91, p 82 ff) of the story of how the official's son was healed. John's version of this event is based on a tradition in some respects similar to what underlies the parallel stories in Mt. 8 and Lk. 7, where a Gentile puts Jews to shame by his exemplary faith, believing that Jesus has only to speak the word to cure a sick person miles away.

In John's source, the emphasis was not on faith, but—as so often—on the greatness of Jesus' miracle. (The miracles recorded in *John* are, quite generally, more impressive than those found in the synoptics, and John seems to have taken them from a source in which they served simply as demonstrations of Jesus' power.) The suppliant is no longer specified as a Gentile, since his background is of no importance for the purpose of illuminating Jesus' power; and he achieves true faith only *after* the cure has been effected (Jn. 4:52-3). These details can confidently be ascribed to John's source, because his own standpoint is stated in what is obviously an insertion he has made into this pre-existing story, namely Jesus' statement (v. 48): "Unless you see signs and wonders you will not believe." After this, verse 49 works back to the situation reached in verse 47 and thus resumes the story:

46. At Capernaum there was an official whose son was ill.

47. When he heard that Jesus had come from Judea to Galilee, he went and begged him to come down and heal his son, for he was at the point of death.

48. Jesus therefore said to him, "Unless you see signs and wonders you will not believe."

49. The official said to him, "Sir, come down before my child dies."

The inserted words (v. 48) are inappropriate in the context of this story: the father was not asking for a sign in order to achieve faith in Jesus, but was concerned solely with saving his child's life. But they well express the evangelist's own theology that proper faith in Jesus should be independent of signs and wonders, and that those who witness miracles often fail to discern their true significance as pointers to Jesus' unique relationship to the Father. For John, then, the miracles are "signs" in the sense that, rightly understood, they point to something beyond themselves to something intangible and metaphysical. The signs are drawn from a source, but their metaphysical interpretation is the evangelist's own.[4]

If different stages of developing tradition are discernible in the feeding stories and in those about the cure of the official's son, the same is true of the stories of Jesus walking on the water that follow the feeding stories in Mk. 6, Mt. 14, and Jn. 6. This incident was surely inspired by Job 9:8, where (in the Septuagint version) it is said of God that he "walks on the sea as on firm ground." Matthew supplemented *Mark* by making Peter too walk on the water. And in *John,* Jesus does not step from the water into the disciples' boat (as he does in *Matthew* and *Mark*) but, as they were about to take him aboard, "the boat was immediately at the land to which they were going," a further miracle. "It is hardly possible to doubt," notes Haenchen (91, p 91), "that this enables one to see into the process of the tradition's growth." Such stories served to show that Jesus does not leave the faithful in the lurch, but is miraculously present in their hour of need. Matthew's addition inculcates the moral that the believer is safe so long as his mind is exclusively on Jesus and not on earthly pitfalls.

If, as I have suggested, John is independent of the synoptics, then the walking on the water directly follows the feeding miracle in two independent gospels (*Mark* and *John*). This implies that the two incidents were linked in the traditions underlying both. But the linkage is artificial, in the sense that the two incidents were originally independent stories, not successive events in the life of a historical Jesus. Their original independence is betrayed by the clumsiness of the linkage even in the versions extant in the gospels.

In Mk. 6, for instance, Jesus, having fed the crowd, "immediately made his disciples get into the boat and go before him to the other side [of the lake] . . . while he dismissed the crowd." His desire to pray (6:46) is hardly an adequate motive for thus sending the disciples ahead at this time of night—it had already "grown late" (6:35) before the feeding—and, as Nineham says (148, p 180), "when we read in verse 47 that the disciples were already well out on the lake by the time *evening came,* we realize that it is futile to try to fit these chronological indications into a single coherent whole. . . . The purpose of these verses seems to have been to set a scene in which the disciples were *out on the sea,* while Jesus was *alone on the land* (v. 47)," and thus to make it possible to tell the story of the walking on the water at this point.

In *John* the transition between the two incidents is equally artificial. Having dismissed the crowd, Jesus withdraws "to the mountain again" (Jn. 6:15). But he has never left the mountain of verse 3, where he effected the feeding. His motive for withdrawal is not, in this gospel, for prayer but rather from a desire to avoid being made king by the multitude. The disciples, left to themselves, cross the lake of their own initiative.

Why should such incidents be linked if successive events in Jesus' life do not underlie them? The answer seems to be that what were originally independent stories were early (before the gospels were written) strung together if they had some common theme, such as teachings all in parables (as in the motley sequence of Mk. 4), or miraculous demonstrations. We have seen (p 12) that sayings of Jesus were linked (by means of catchwords) in a similarly arbitrary way.

John used the stories of feeding the multitude and walking on the water as a lead into a discourse where Jesus is made to state the evangelist's own theology, namely that Jesus is "the bread of life" (6:35). We saw that the transition is effected by making Jesus declare that the people miraculously fed had nevertheless failed to discern this truth of which the physical feeding had been a mere sign. (Later in the discussion John calls these people "the Jews"; that is, he slips into his normal way of designating Jesus' opponents in these discourses.) These people object that they cannot accept him unless he gives a sign comparable to the manna miracle, and they quote to him, as a text of scripture: "He gave them bread from heaven to eat." In rabbinical teaching, the manna was understood as a kind of precursor of the Mosaic Law.

Jesus is made to cap this Jewish argument by saying that he himself is the true heavenly food, the true teaching. And to put his point he quotes Isaiah 54: 13: "and they shall all be taught by God." Thus "the manna tradition, the feeding of God's people, is interpreted in terms of the provision of the true teaching" (Lindars, 130, pp 74–5). Jesus supersedes the Law just as the Law superseded the manna. We see from this example how ancient documents were interpreted and reinterpreted, events alleged in them being taken to mean or symbolize something that mattered to a later day and age. Lindars points to the significance of the fact that this whole Johannine discourse is prefaced by Jesus' claim that in fact "Moses wrote of me" (5:46).

Much of the teaching which John puts into Jesus' mouth is concerned with this major point of dispute between Christians and Jews: namely, whether Jesus has the qualifications of the Messiah. It is very important to note that such passages do not reflect the biography of a historical Jesus, but rather *scenes imagined on the basis of disputes in progress when John wrote.* (We have seen that his gospel shows evidence of tension between church and synagogue). Much in this gospel, says Lindars, is "a sermon addressed to Christians in order to deepen and strengthen their faith in a situation where Jewish objections to Christianity are a matter of vital concern." To us it may seem dishonest that John composed speeches and put them into Jesus' mouth. But doubtless he felt that the spirit of Christ was upon him, and that he could therefore speak with the mind of Christ—as we know from 1 Cor. 2:16 that early Christian preachers did (cf. p 48). If we accept Lindars' contention that John's gospel is essentially an adaptation of homilies he delivered originally to a Christian assembly, possibly at the Eucharist (the discourse on the bread of life obviously suits this setting), then we can suppose that his function was to supply the assembly with revelation, knowledge, prophesying or teaching, as in the early church, alluded to in 1 Cor. 14:6.

6

Semitisms in Greek Gospels and in Acts

Many apologists point to Semitisms in the gospels, both of form (grammar, syntax, and vocabulary that seem to be influenced by Semitic patterns of speech) and of content (knowledge of Jewish customs). It has been argued that these features characterize material derived from early and authentic tradition.

Against this inference, Sanders has noted that a tradition reflecting Jewish customs does not necessarily have either an early or a Palestinian basis, for "certain segments of the Church, up to about the year 135, were in as close contact with Jewish communities as other segments were with Hellenistic communities," so that reference to Jewish customs may well tell us "more about environment than date." He notes that Christianity moved north (into Syria) and east, as well as into the Hellenized west, and that many second- and third-generation Christians were Semites (170, pp 195-6, 231).

In sum, the idea that the Judaic period of Christianity as a whole preceded the period in which Hellenistic influences came to be felt is false; there was a continuing relationship between Christianity and Judaism that paralleled the Hellenizing influence in the West. Goppelt (80) shows that at Antioch in Syria, Jews and Christians remained in close contact much later than 135. Paul of Samosata (heretical bishop of Antioch in the third century) and Lucian of Antioch (who died in 312) were fructified by Jewish theology, and as late as the fourth century Chrysostom (educated at Antioch) had to warn the faithful against adopting Jewish customs and attending Jewish religious services.

Sanders gives some interesting examples of the way Matthew introduced Jewish elements lacking in the equivalent narrative in *Mark*. Mt. 23:5, for instance, mentions that the scribes and Pharisees "make their phylacteries

137

broad and their fringes long." Phylacteries are small cases of parchment or leather containing a piece of vellum on which were inscribed texts of the Law, and fringes are tassels which the Jew was obliged to wear on the corners of his outer garment. The corresponding passage in Mk. 12:38 makes no mention of these specifically Jewish features, and says merely that the scribes "like to go about in long robes." It looks, then, as if Matthew had knowledge of Jewish customs which has influenced his interpretation of *Mark* at this point. Whereas Mk. 5:27 merely says that the woman with the issue of blood touched Jesus' garment, Mt. 9:20 says that she touched "the fringe of his garment," that is, its sacred part.

Sanders argues that Matthew would not have introduced these Semitisms for his own benefit, but for that of his readers; and many commentators have taken the view that he was writing in Syria, where, we have noted, Christians and Jews long remained in close contact. Entirely consistent with Sanders' findings is Goulder's demonstration that a substantial number of the Aramaisms of form in Matthew's Greek (which Black and others have claimed as evidence of early and authentic tradition) have been imposed by Matthew on Marcan material which lacked them. This, says Goulder, suggests that Matthew was a Greek speaker who thought in Aramaic, not that he drew on primitive material rich in Aramaisms (82, pp 117, 121).

Sanders has made a very wide study of Aramaisms in Greek New Testament manuscripts and in patristic and apocryphal writings, and has found that there was "no tendency to do away with Semitisms in the later material" (170, p 230). "Although some of them are fairly frequently avoided in the post-canonical tradition, they are also fairly frequently added." It follows that, although Semitisms may be present in early traditions, their presence cannot be alleged as proof of antiquity. Mark's Greek includes elements regarded as Aramaisms, but it is no longer reasonable to hold, with Taylor, that they indicate that his gospel "must, in the main, bear a high historical value" (198, p 65).

The best-known scholar of New Testament Semitisms is Matthew Black. His discussion of them is not free from a priori assumptions. "Jesus," he says, "must have conversed in the Galilean dialect of Aramaic" and so "at the basis of the Greek gospels there must lie a Palestinian Aramaic tradition, at any rate of [his] sayings and teachings" (18, p 16). On the next page he admits that Syrian Aramaic may have influenced the evangelists' work: "Palestinian Jewish Aramaic was a dialect little known outside of Palestine; much of the Palestinian Aramaic Gospel tradition may have passed through the more familiar medium of Syriac before it was finally written down in Greek."

Unless, then, we can distinguish Syriac elements from Palestinian ones in the gospels' Greek, their "Aramaisms" may simply represent Christian tradition as it existed, say, at Antioch, which Black calls "the first great Christian centre" (p 17), where Syriac was spoken along with Greek in the first century. Klijn has pressed this objection, saying, "We cannot always be sure whether we are dealing with Aramaisms or the influence of the Syriac language" (123, p 17).

Black himself admits as much when he says that although Syriac and West Aramaic can be distinguished as two different dialects, they have so much in common that, in Greek texts, differences between them are hard to detect (18, p 33).

Many of the constructions which Black instances as Aramaisms are not actually wrong in Greek, nor even unusual in the Koine or Hellenistic Greek in everyday use when the gospels were written, but are simply, as he points out, more frequent in Aramaic. A weakness in his evidence is that so many of his Aramaisms occur only in Codex Bezae. He infers from this that Bezae has preserved the primitive text more faithfully. But we have seen grounds for doubting this (cf. pp 6 ff). The relevant constructions may be more frequent in Bezae partly because the author's style is more popular and less literary than that of the Lucan original.

Black insists that Aramaisms are particularly frequent in the speeches Jesus makes, and he regards it as certain that "an Aramaic sayings-source or tradition" lies behind them (p 271). One of his examples is the construction where a subject or object noun is later picked up by a pronoun. (An instance in a speech occurs at Acts 7:35 ff: "This Moses, whom they denied . . . this [man] led them forth.") This construction is not inappropriate in Koine Greek, but is more frequent in Hebrew or Aramaic (p 51). But Norden has shown (see refs. in 91, pp 193–4) that it is a stylistic feature of Hellenistic rhetoric generally, and is evidenced in Philo, who certainly does not write substandard Greek. It is therefore not surprising to find it used for speeches of Jesus in the gospels and for speeches of Peter and Stephen in Acts.

Another construction which Black regards as "highly characteristic of Aramaic" (p 56) is *asyndeton* (one clause following another with no linking conjunction). He concedes that his examples include instances where even Greek would have asyndeta, "as at the opening of a continuous passage or speech" (p 58). This natural Greek usage is surely one reason for its occurrence in New Testament speeches. In Acts, for instance, there is no linking conjunction where a preacher, after briefly greeting his audience with such words as "brethren, hear me," is made to state the essence of the Christian message, which in this way stands out the more clearly. In other instances too asyndeton serves to emphasize an idea. Black notes that, in the synoptics, asyndeton is common only in *Mark,* the rough style of which is smoothed by Matthew and Luke. He concedes that Mark may have written in this way merely because such constructions were usual in Jewish or Syrian Greek, and that they are found also in *The Shepherd of Hermas,* a Christian work usually dated about 140 and which no one supposes to reproduce early and authentic tradition (pp 56–60).

Parataxis (linking two clauses with *and*) is very frequent in Aramaic and also in the gospel sayings of Jesus. Black admits that it is, however, not uncommon in unliterary Greek and in the papyri, that its occurrence in Jesus' speeches may have something to do with the fact that these are made up largely of individual dicta (from various strands of tradition) which the evangelists have strung together, and that "the prophetic utterance attributed to our Lord falls naturally into short graphic sentences" (p 63).

Black also sees Aramaic influence underlying textual variants. There is, for instance, an all-purpose particle *dᵉ*, which is used in Aramaic as a relative pronoun (who, which), as the sign of the genitive case, and as a conjunction (equivalent of *because, in order that,* etc.). When a speech of Jesus has a relative pronoun in one manuscript and a conjunction in its place in another, Black infers that both readings go back to an Aramaic *dᵉ*, which could have been understood by a Greek writer in either way. Thus Mt. 6:5 has: "When you pray, be not like the hypocrites, for (*hoti*) they love to . . . ." The Vulgate has not "for they love" but "who love." Goulder, however, offers what he calls a "simpler explanation" of this variant; namely that "Matthew wrote his favorite causal *hoti,* which was misread as *hoi*" (82, p 119).

Black does not claim to be able to infer the actual words of Jesus from Aramaisms in his sayings and holds that our Greek gospels give us interpretations, rather than translations, of what he said. "The end-product in Greek is often less the mind of Jesus than the ideas . . . of the Greek evangelists" (p 275). But as Calvert has noted, an Aramaism (which may not even be a sign of antiquity) in one of the sayings in Greek attributed to Jesus may be merely "a sign that the material went back to the Aramaic Church" (35, p 218). The Hellenistic churches certainly invented "words of the Lord," and there is no reason why Aramaic-speaking ones should not have done so too.

The whole problem of Aramaisms is complicated by the question of how the Western Greek texts are related to early translations into Old Syriac and Old Latin. It is not known whether the Greek influenced the language of these translations or the translation languages, the Greek. Klijn notes that entirely different theories have been proposed (122, p 22). For instance, it has been supposed that the Greek was first translated into Latin by a Jew (hence the Syriac features of the Old Latin versions), and that Syriac features came into the Greek when a Greek manuscript was copied and assimilated to the Latin of a bilingual codex. Chase argued at the end of the last century that assimilation to Old Syriac texts was a predominant factor in the formation of the Greek and Latin of the Western text of the gospels. Black recognizes the complexity of the problem when he discusses textual variants in our Greek gospels which, he thinks, may be due to an Aramaic source. They remind us, he says, that our canonical four are "four only of a large number of early Greek forms of the Gospel tradition." He adds:

All these Greek Gospels in so far as they transmitted the sayings of Jesus, must have embodied translations of Aramaic which often differed from the translations used or made by the four Evangelists. The most probable explanation of the few remaining Greek variants from Aramaic is that, in the earliest period of textual transmission, the writings of the Evangelists have been variously influenced by or assimilated to other well-known extra-canonical Greek versions of the Words of the Lord. Such variations . . . could be multiplied from the ancient versions [i.e. translations], the Old Latin and the Old Syriac, and from patristic quotations. And it seemed [from evidence adduced earlier in Black's book] very probable that the Old Syriac had been influenced at its source by an extra-canonical and apocryphal Gospel tradition of the sayings of Jesus (p 279).

So on the one hand, variant readings which show Semitic idiom have a serious claim to be considered original; yet on the other, Semitic idiom can point to a secondary text influenced by an outside source. "Who," Klijn pertinently asks, "is able to decide . . . whether we are dealing with a 'primitive' Aramaized Greek text or with a reading that 'has been influenced by an extra-canonical . . . Gospel tradition'?" (123, pp 16–7) This ambiguity, he says elsewhere, "taken in conjunction with possible Syriac influence on some of the witnesses, seems to make it a hopeless task to look for any results on these lines, so long as we are in the dark about the textual history of the earliest period" (122, p 150).

Many New Testament Semitisms are no more than "Septuagintalisms," that is, imitations of the Hebraic Greek of the Septuagint (the Greek translation of the Jewish scriptures). Christians felt that it was appropriate to use this Biblical Greek when writing of holy matters, much as the language of the King James Bible used to be felt appropriate for occasions of solemnity. (It has been noted as a relevant parallel that the language of *The Pilgrim's Progress* is largely derived from the English Bible). Sanders mentions, as a noncanonical example, the apocryphal *Protevangelium* or *Book of James,* the many Semitisms of which are, he says, "purely literary" and "borrowed from the Greek Bible." This work is neither early — it is later than the canonical gospels because dependent on them — nor Palestinian, as the author makes gross errors in his geographical references. It shows "the ease with which a person far removed from Palestine and Syria and without knowledge of any Semitic tongue could duplicate the style of Semitically influenced Greek by reading the Septuagint and other Greek literature which depended on Hebrew or Aramaic" (170, pp 298–9).

Luke certainly imitates the Greek of the Septuagint. Black discusses the phrase "at that very hour" which Luke uses repeatedly. He calls it "a Lucan Aramaism," but admits that "it may be due to Syriac influence, or it may have come from the Septuagint version of Daniel" (p 109). In Acts Luke makes the apostles speak a "holy language," modelled on the Jewish-Greek of the Septuagint, above all for their missionary work in Palestine (which is the substance of the first half of Acts). After chapter 15 Luke turns his attention to the spread of the gospel in the wider Roman world, and appropriately lets Paul make speeches in a style that is more Hellenistic. Haenchen notes how deliberate Luke's style is, in that when Paul addresses a mixed audience of Jews and educated Gentiles (Acts 26:14–8), he gives (as words of the risen Jesus) a Greek proverb as well as Old Testament phrases. Thus the first half of Acts sounds more "Semitic" than the second because it employs Biblical language more extensively (94, pp 66, 72, 73 n 2).

Wilcox has claimed that Acts contains a small number of "hardcore" Semitisms, not derivative from the Septuagint. Some of his examples of these do occur in the Septuagint, although they are not particularly common there. Others could, according to Black (17, p 22), be derived from Greek versions of the Old Testament which diverge to some extent from the Septuagint. Yet others — what Wilcox calls a "not inconsiderable number" of them (214, p 185) — are found only in Codex Bezae and its allies. For instance, this codex does not call the pseudo-prophet of Acts 13:6 simply Bar-Jesus, but gives a rendering of the name which presupposes a more exact translation of the Semitic Bar Jeshua. Wilcox would fain regard this reading as "an element of primitive tradition left unrevised" in this codex (214, p 89). But we have seen that the revisor of the Western text of Acts was better informed than Luke himself about Jewish matters (cf. p 4), and he may here simply be displaying his learning. Wilcox himself concedes that this reading (and others of his hardcore Semitisms) may merely evidence "the activity of a Semitic-thinking scribe" (pp 89, 185).

The hardcore Semitisms are, Wilcox says, mere words or phrases in a speech or narrative characterized in style and content as typically Lucan. He admits that some of them "probably serve only to indicate that the stories in which they occur sprang from an Aramaic milieu" (p 110). He thinks that these Aramaisms already existed only as residual traces in Greek stories before Luke came across them and that Luke himself has "thoroughly rewritten" the material "for his own purposes" (p 181). As Wilcox thus concedes so much, it is somewhat surprising that he repeatedly claims that a residual Semitism is a sign of the "antiquity and authenticity" of the story in which it occurs (for example, pp 89, 177, 184). He even suggests that, when Peter, Paul, and Stephen are made in Acts to quote the Old Testament in words which do not exactly reflect any standard text (Hebrew or Greek), Luke is in fact recording the words these speakers actually used at the time (p 54). A different view of the nature of the speeches in Acts will be argued below.

A recent article by Horton claims that the evidence of the papyri reveals that Jews who wrote Greek did not introduce Hebraisms when they were writing contracts or personal letters. For ordinary discourse they employed the standard Greek of the day (the Koine); only in religious writings did they try to introduce Hebrew elements into their Greek. Thus the Semitisms in the Septuagint are intentional and do not reflect incompetence in the translators. Horton thinks that, if Jewish Greek is confined entirely to religious texts, it was probably used in religious contexts generally (196, p 14); taking up a suggestion made by Black, he says that this Jewish Greek may have had its home in the spoken language of Diaspora synagogues. In other words, Hellenistic Jews at their religious services used a Koine larded with Semitisms, as an appropriately solemn language, just as extemporaneous prayer today tends to be based on Biblical language. This theory of a "synagogue Greek" in the Greek-speaking Diaspora would account for Semitisms of all kinds in religious writings (not only for direct imitations of the language of the Septuagint). It would, as Black says, "provide the early Church with a matrix from which the varieties of New Testament Greek are derived" (17, p 23).

Horton supports this view that a Semitic Greek is likely to have been spoken in Greek-speaking synagogues with evidence that, when Hebrew was spoken instead of Greek, a special liturgical Hebrew was employed which mixed classical Biblical Hebrew with the vernacular Mishnaic Hebrew (used in the first centuries BC and AD as a spoken language in addition to Aramaic or Greek: see the revised Schürer, 178, pp 27–8). The idea was to employ for cultic purposes a language felt to be appropriately holy. Horton thinks that Aramaisms, as well as Hebraisms, may well have crept into synagogue Greek just as into the mixed Hebrew, and he holds that this is the best basis for explaining most of the Semitisms of *Luke* and Acts (196, p 21).

Finally, Jesus speaks a few Aramaic words in the gospels. Goulder (101, p 50) says: "Matthew usually, Luke always translates these: they cannot have been created by the Greek-speaking Churches, and are likely to be remembered from Jesus himself." They in fact could have been created by an Aramaic-speaking or bilingual church: early or late (for the generation which flourished about AD 30 was not the last to speak Aramaic), in or outside Palestine (for Judea did not have a monopoly on the Aramaic language). In fact, however, it is more likely that the Aramaic words which Jesus speaks in two of Mark's miracle stories were actually created in a Greek-speaking church. At Mk. 5:41 he cures a little girl: "Taking her by the hand he said to her, 'Talitha cumi,' which means, 'Little girl, I say to you, arise.'" And at 7:34–5 he treats a deaf man with a speech impediment, saying to him "'Ephphatha,' that is, 'Be opened.' And his ears were opened, his tongue was released." Hull makes the following comment on these incidents:

> Foreign words are a very familiar feature of magic spells and the papyri are full of examples. What counted as foreign names and strange sounds naturally depended on the situation of the magician. In the Coptic magical papyri Greek appears as the strange and forbiddingly authentic sound, while in the Greek magical world Jewish names and words had special prestige. The general practice was to summon a god or demon by the tongue he was believed to understand or which stood in some relation of sympathy to that god. So it is only to be expected that Jesus, a Jewish wonder-worker operating on Palestinian demons with the power of the great Hebrew God, should utter his commands in a Jewish language. Aramaic is used rather than Hebrew, perhaps since Aramaic, being the spoken tongue, would tend to creep into the stories as they were repeatedly told. The magicians would be little concerned about distinctions between the two languages; both had the flavor of authentic Palestinian power (106, p 85).

In this chapter I have dealt only with the synoptics and Acts with good reason. Barrett says that it is extremely difficult to weigh the evidence on Aramaisms in the fourth gospel, and that it is "not likely that any two students would agree in their judgment" (10, p 10).

7

The Lucan Documents in Relation to the Pauline Letters

I   INTRODUCTION

Whether the Paul of the Pauline letters is compatible with the Paul of the Acts of the Apostles is a problem that has exercised theologians for generations. Harnack tried to show (in three volumes published between 1906 and 1911) that Acts' account of Paul's relation to the Jews, to their religious law, and to Jewish Christians, is fundamentally accurate. However, Harnack's contemporaries Overbeck and Wellhausen took, in works of 1870 and 1914 respectively, a very different view.

Today theologians are equally divided on this matter, with Dodd, Bruce, Bo Reicke, and Robinson taking Harnack's view, while Haenchen, Conzelmann and Vielhauer argue for the more radical position. Vielhauer wrote in 1950 that the "crass contradictions between Acts and the Pauline letters, concerning both historical fact and theological doctrine, have not been explained by Harnack and his successors" (203, p 246). In this chapter I shall set out the arguments of some of these radical scholars (notably Haenchen), and Robinson's 1976 defense of the more orthodox position. At many points I shall follow Haenchen's commentary on Acts without giving references to it, as this valuable work is available in English translation (Oxford 1971).

II   THE AUTHOR OF THE GOSPEL ACCORDING TO LUKE AND THE ACTS OF THE APOSTLES

The earliest writer who is known to have speculated about the authorship of Acts is Irenaeus, bishop of Lyons. Writing about 180, he realized that Acts and *Luke* were by the same author. Both, for instance, begin with a dedication to the same person, Theophilus, whom the author of Acts refers to "the previous book" in which, he says, he has "dealt with all that Jesus began to do and to teach." This is clearly the gospel dedicated to Theophilus, and modern scholars have removed any doubts that *Luke* and Acts are from the same author by demonstrating that Acts follows *Luke* in details where *Luke* deviates from the other canonical gospels.

All four gospels were, we saw (p 11), originally anonymous. Irenaeus, however, thought that the author of *Luke*-Acts must have been someone who travelled as a fellow-missionary with Paul. For in Acts the author, without saying who he is, nevertheless sometimes writes about we or us, referring to Paul and his companions. At 16:10, for instance, Acts' narrative of Paul's second missionary journey changes abruptly from the third person ("they went through the region of Phrygia and Galatia") to the first person ("we sought to go forth into Macedonia"). There are later passages with a similar change, and each of the "we" sections begins a sea voyage with Paul and in part reads like a diary kept by one of the voyagers. Thus 16:11–2 reads: "Setting sail therefore from Troas, we made a straight course to Samothrace, and the day following to Neapolis and from thence to Philippi."[1]

Irenaeus thought that the companion who wrote these "we" passages, indeed the whole of Acts, is the man who Paul himself names as Luke in his own epistles. At Coloss. 4:14 Paul mentions "Luke the beloved physician," and at the end of the epistle to Philemon he includes greetings from "Luke my fellow worker." According to 2 Timothy (the author of which poses as Paul, and was certainly accepted as Paul before the rise of critical theology in the nineteenth century) Paul, when a prisoner in Rome, had only Luke as his sole remaining faithful companion: "Only Luke is with me" (4:11). Since the "we" passages in Acts end with Paul's voyage to Rome, Irenaeus fixed on Luke as the companion who wrote Acts and therefore also the third gospel. The reader who knows only Acts could never infer who wrote it, as it does not indicate whose is the voice speaking in the "we" passages. It seems clear that Irenaeus' views are attempts to harmonize various statements within the canonical books. There is no evidence that he had any independent knowledge of who the author was.

Robinson says that Acts is ascribed to Luke by "unanimous external tradition" (164, p 86). But unanimity here means merely that later Christian writers uncritically repeated what Irenaeus said. When fifty repeat the statement of one, the number of significant witnesses is one, not fifty-one. And this unanimous tradition does not begin until the final quarter of the second century.

Robinson also thinks that the ascription to Luke cannot be guesswork, because, he says, guesswork would have fastened the third gospel, if not Acts, on someone who had been a personal follower of Jesus and not merely of Paul. Now admittedly, by the late second century, there was a disposition to believe that a canonical gospel must have been written by an apostle—understood, as in Acts, as someone who had witnessed Jesus' whole public ministry and his resurrection. But the author of the third gospel had clearly implied in his prologue that he was not a companion of Jesus. He there says:

> Many have undertaken to draw up a narrative of the things which have been accomplished among us [that is, among Christians], just as they [the events] were delivered to us by those who from the beginning were eyewitnesses and ministers of the word. It seems good to me also, having followed [investigated][2] all things accurately from the beginning [that is, beginning with Jesus' birth], to write an orderly account [too].

Thus the eyewitnesses delivered their testimony orally, and only then did many (not alleged to have been eyewitnesses) draw up a narrative. The author is writing even later, after these "many" and thus knew nothing of gospels written by apostles.

Another reason why Irenaeus was not able to suppose that the author of *Luke*-Acts was a companion of Jesus is that the "we" passages occur only in Acts and not in the gospel. "We" is used in Acts in the sense of "Paul and his companions" (including, according to Irenaeus, the author). But there are no "we" passages in the gospel which, in similar manner, could be interpreted as "Jesus and his companions, including the author." An author who used "we" in order to stress an intimacy with Paul can hardly be supposed to have refrained from using it in order to disguise an intimacy with Jesus.

The "we" passages in Acts have led many interpreters to suppose that the author must have participated in the voyages so described, or must at least have drawn his account from the diary of a participant. Since these passages are in the same style as the rest of the book, Robinson (164, p 87) and others believe that Luke drew them from his own travel diary, which he had kept on journeys with Paul. But, if he used sources for these sections of his narrative, the stylistic uniformity of the whole book may merely mean that he adapted all source material that he had in the same way. There is evidence that he did collect available traditions as a basis for some of his narratives in Acts,[3] and it is possible, if unlikely, that these included either a travel diary or travel reminiscences written by some companion of Paul. That Luke had the habit of imposing his own style and vocabulary on his sources is obvious from the way in which he rewrote passages from *Mark* in his own gospel.

It has, however, been argued that—whether or not he is drawing on some source at these points—in using "we" for accounts of Paul's sea voyages, Luke is merely following a convention of Greek literature. Robbins, for instance, gives considerable evidence that sea voyage narratives "would be expected to contain first-person narration whether or not the author was an actual participant in the voyage. . . . By the first century AD a sea voyage recounted in the third person would be considered out of vogue in Hellenistic literature" (196, p 228).

Luke certainly uses "we" consciously and carefully, for while it usually means "Paul and his companions," its meaning is (obviously deliberately) changed to "his companions only" immediately preceding a scene where Paul plays the leading role and where the "we" is dropped; thus after six verses of "we" in its primary sense of "Paul and his companions," it is said at 16:17 that Lydia "followed Paul and us." Here, then, Paul is distinguished from "us," which includes only his companions. There follows a story (with no "we" at all) about how Paul was maltreated by opponents. Exactly the same sequence occurs when the "we" reappears in 20:5 and 21:1: first in the sense of "Paul and his companions," then in the sense of "his companions only" (20:13 f and 21:12–4), and finally a story about Paul with no pronoun. In sum, the "we," which occurs only in narratives about Paul's sea journeys, enters abruptly and without explanation, but is carefully phased out repeatedly so as to leave the stage to Paul. It seems, then, that the "we" conflicts with the author's desire to let the limelight fall on Paul and is therefore dropped whenever Paul is the center of attention.

Luke has also sometimes inserted "we" into passages where—but for the literary convention Robbins mentions—it seems inappropriate. 27:1, for instance (which begins the fourth and last of the "we" sections in Acts), depicts the voyage of prisoners, including Paul, to Italy under the command of a centurion from Caesarea: "And when it was decided that *we* should sail for Italy, they delivered Paul and some other prisoners to a centurion." The "we" is, as a statement of fact, out of place, since what has been decided was to send the prisoners—not a friend of Paul who travelled on the same ship. A few verses later the centurion is said—equally inappropriately—to "put *us* on board."

Haenchen, who has drawn attention to all of the preceding, thinks that the accounts may have been present in some travel diary (not Luke's own) from which he drew, and that he retained the "we" and even inserted it into some passages that lacked it or which he composed entirely himself, in order to suggest to the reader that these parts of his narrative derive from eyewitness reports, from a notebook written by someone who had been with Paul on the relevant voyages (91, pp 260, 264).

On the other hand—and here I go beyond what Haenchen suggests—Luke's purpose could have been to suggest, not that some authority had travelled with Paul but that he himself had done so. Thereby certain crucial events—such as the divine prompting to carry the Christian mission into Europe, apropos of which "we" makes its first appearance (16:10)—are authenticated not merely by some witness who had been with Paul but by Luke's own witness. If he wrote about AD 100, Luke might have pretended to have known Paul to give strength to his testimony, whereas he could not have pretended to have known Jesus, even though at the beginning of his gospel he stressed the importance of eyewitness testimony.

On balance, however, I am inclined to regard "we" merely as a literary device, as suggested by Robbins. It makes its final appearance in the account of Paul's voyage to Rome (Acts 27:1–28:16), and in this long narrative Paul appears only in a few fictitious little incidents (without "we") which glorify him and which are easily detachable from the rest. For instance at 27:9–11, although he is supposed to be a prisoner on board, he advises the centurion, the ship-owner, and the captain on whether to proceed with the voyage. The centurion in charge of prisoners (who in verse 11 alone decides the question by accepting the advice of the captain and owner and discounting that of Paul) would in reality have had no jurisdiction concerning maritime problems. Certainly Paul, charged with sedition, would not have been accepted by the captain and owner as a partner in nautical discussion, for he speaks as Christian prophet, not on the basis of maritime experience. He has never even travelled this route before (see Haenchen, 52, pp 250–1).

Equally artificial is the situation in verses 21–6, where he delivers a speech bidding all take heart, as though he were preaching in a synagogue rather than on a ship during a violent storm. Bornkamm thinks that, for his account of this whole voyage, Luke drew on an existing piece of writing that had nothing to do with Paul and inserted such episodes into it (21, p 103).

III ACTS' KNOWLEDGE OF PAUL

Luke's source material for Acts amounted to considerably less than was available for his gospel. The disparity is particularly obvious if one compares Jesus' speeches in the gospel with the speeches of the apostles in Acts. The alleged words of Jesus were treasured by Christian communities as shreds and patches of tradition which the evangelists have put together to form continuous discourses. But what apostles had said by way of promoting the faith was less important for salvation and was not treasured in the same way. Thus Luke himself had to compose the speeches which he thought they must have made at what he regarded as important junctures.

At Acts 1:19–20 for instance, Peter, addressing 120 Aramaic-speaking Jewish Christians in Jerusalem, refers to Aramaic as "the language of the inhabitants," and goes on to elucidate in Greek, for their benefit, one word. He then presents them with a proof from prophecy taken from the Septuagint, a proof which the Hebrew text does not permit (for details see Haenchen, 91, pp 208–9). This alone suffices to show that what Peter says in Acts cannot be taken as a true reflection of the ideas of the Jerusalem Christians he is supposed to have led, but must have been drawn up in a Hellenistic community.

Again, in Acts 15:13 James likewise appeals to the Christian Jews of Jerusalem by quoting a passage from the Septuagint which distorts the Hebrew original. And his purpose is, by such means and in front of such an audience, to justify the mission to the Gentiles. Conservative theologians (anxious to regard the speeches of various apostles in Acts as "echoes" of genuine and early apostolic preaching which survived as oral tradition from which Luke drew) have resorted to desperate expedients to explain away the difficulties. For instance, Bruce supposes (26, p 298) that James knew the Septuagint and quoted it out of courtesy to Paul and his companions who were present on the occasion.

Luke composed not only the speeches but also the so-called narrative summaries in Acts, the passages which generalize about the way the church developed (for example, Acts 2:42–5; 4:32–5). These generalizations can sometimes be seen to be based on one single instance which conflicts with others.[4]

Acts ends with Paul a prisoner in Rome, yet living in relative freedom there and preaching Christianity "unhindered"—the very last word in the whole book. The progress of Christianity from Jerusalem to Rome represents a neatly rounded period of church history and an appropriate point at which to stop. To achieve such an effective finale, Luke disguises the fact that the Christian mission had reached Rome long before Paul,[5] and he is thus writing with a certain dramatic sense, not exclusively from concern to report historical fact accurately. Nevertheless, Robinson asks why Luke did not tell us at least the outcome of Paul's trial in Rome. He cannot believe that he knew the outcome and yet failed to report it, and so he infers that Luke wrote before Paul's case was decided. But before we accept this dating, another possibility must be considered: that Luke knew that Paul had been condemned and executed, but, for good reason, preferred to allude to these events rather than describe them explicitly.

Commentators have long noted that one purpose in Acts is to represent Christianity as entirely innocuous politically, as contravening no Roman laws.[6] To this end, the author represents it as within the Jewish religion (which was tolerated by the Romans). Indeed, for the author of Acts, Christianity is the true religion of the Jews, based on proper interpretation of the Old Testament prophecies in which the benighted non-Christian Jews have failed to discern references to Jesus. Hence Acts repeatedly makes Roman officials behave with tolerance toward Christians—and this means, in effect, toward Paul, for it is he who carries Christianity westward from Jerusalem into the Roman Empire. Let us study some examples.

Sergius Paulus, proconsul of Cyprus, "believed" (Acts 13:12). Luke does not allege outright that he was converted, but invites us to think it in a context where, however, it could be conceded that only belief in Paul's power to work miracles was implied. Gallio, proconsul of Achaia, rejects the Jews' complaints about Paul as of no concern to Roman authorities and as pertaining to mere Jewish doctrinal niceties (18:14–5); in other words, he discerns, as in Luke's view a Roman official should, that this new religion remains within the framework of Jewish theological ideas.

At Ephesus, the Asiarchs, men concerned to promote the cult of the emperor, appear as Paul's friends (Acts 19:31), and the town clerk declares the Christians there to be innocent of sacrilege and blasphemy (19:37). Claudius Lysias, tribune at Jerusalem, and the governors Felix and Festus refuse all Jewish requests for Paul's condemnation. Festus apparently regarded the disputes between Christians and Jews much as Russian authorities today would view differences between Methodists and Baptists. Thus he says that Paul's Jewish accusers "had certain points of dispute with him about their own superstition and about one Jesus, who was dead, but whom Paul asserted to be alive" (25:19). The poor pagan is naturally represented as finding the Christian doctrine of the resurrection unintelligible. Luke's main point, however, is that as a Roman official he is not competent to decide theological issues; so he is represented as calling the Jewish King Agrippa[7] for advice in a scene purely of Luke's imagination.[8] Paul explains to Agrippa that, according to Moses and the Prophets, "the Christ must suffer," and rise from the dead to bring light to both Jews and Gentiles (26:22–3). He is sure that "none of these things" has escaped Agrippa's notice, "for all this was not done in a corner" (26:26).

Thus the death and resurrection of Jesus and the miracles of the earliest church are alleged to be public events which have claimed the attention of the highest authorities. Christianity is, then, no side-show, but has its place in the history of the Roman Empire. Furthermore, if Christianity is the true Judaism, the theologically competent Jewish king cannot be allowed to go on record as rejecting it. And so Luke hints—with an ambiguous phrase reminiscent of his manner with Sergius Paulus—that Agrippa came near to conversion (26:28). Agrippa and Festus finally agree that Paul "is doing nothing to deserve death or imprisonment" (26:31). If he had not appealed to Caesar, adds Festus, he could go free; therefore, he is sent to Rome, but even though awaiting trial, he is allowed to preach freely there.

The author who tells all this would have been glad indeed to report Paul's acquittal. The evidence of the text suggests that he fails to do so not because he wrote before the case had been decided but because he *knew* that it did not lead to an acquittal. The final verses of Acts state that Paul lived in Rome in relative freedom, in lodgings at his own expense, "for two whole years" (28:30). Haenchen is surely right to say (94, p 647) that the man who wrote this surely knew that, after these two years, a change occurred, and what it was that happened. Luke is aware that Paul stood before Nero's court in Rome; for during his voyage as a prisoner to Rome an angel tells him (Acts 27:24) not to fear shipwreck since God has decreed that he must survive to "stand before Caesar."

Furthermore, Luke has earlier made Paul say, in a farewell speech to Christian clergy as he leaves Asia for Jerusalem (where he is arrested by the Romans to save him from the fury of a Jewish mob), not only that imprisonment and affliction await him but that he will never subsequently return to the areas where he has labored as a missionary: "And now, behold, I know that all you among whom I have gone about preaching the kingdom will see my face no more" (20:25). This sorrowful pronouncement is repeated a little later (v. 38), a sure sign that the author attached great significance to it. The implication is that he knew Paul was never released from prison but died a martyr.

It has sometimes been argued that Luke could not sensibly have pleaded for tolerance had he been writing after Nero's persecution of Christians at Rome in the 60s. But the contrary is the case. Nero's insane actions were condemned after his suicide and were not binding on his successors. Luke could rationally urge the post-Neronian Roman authorities to revert to the old policy of tolerance, and he tries to impress on his readers the extent of this former tolerance with his stories of the kindly attitude of Roman officials to Paul. It would indeed have somewhat spoilt this apologetic endeavor had he gone on to tell that Paul was finally executed in Rome.

Robinson protests that Luke would not have "glossed over in silence the common knowledge that he [Paul] and Peter and 'a vast multitude' of other Christians in the city had . . . been mercilessly butchered" by Nero soon after AD 64 (164, p 89). I have tried to show (pp 81, 109) that Robinson greatly exaggerates the importance and extent of Nero's persecution of Christians, and that Tacitus' reference to a "vast multitude" of them who were killed at Rome in 64 or 65 is rhetorical exaggeration. The Neronian persecution certainly did not quickly become common knowledge throughout the empire and neither Tacitus nor any reliable authority makes Peter a victim of Nero. I have shown elsewhere (JEC, pp 216-7) that there is no real evidence that Peter was ever in Rome at all. Robinson's statement that, by the end of the 60s, it was "common knowledge" throughout Christendom that Peter and Paul had been "mercilessly butchered" there is fantastic.

For further indications of the date of composition of Acts and of the author's knowledge of the real Paul, let us look more closely at the farewell speech to the clergy put into Paul's mouth as he leaves Asia, the speech which hints at his martyrdom. The situation is that he is returning by ship to Judea, having completed what will be his final missionary journey. His own letters show that his motive in going to Judea was to present to the Jerusalem Christians the large sum of money collected for their benefit during his missionary work (cf. p 157). Of this collection Luke says nothing, but represents him as in a hurry to reach Jerusalem in order — pious Jew that he was — to celebrate Pentecost there. He did not break his voyage at Ephesus because time was short.

Luke's sources may have informed him correctly that Paul did not stop at Ephesus on the occasion of his return from the west. But the real reason for this would have been that he feared for his life in this city where he had suffered serious persecution earlier (1 Cor. 15:30-2; 2 Cor. 1:8-10). Luke seems to know nothing of this or at any rate presents an idealized picture (Acts 19) of Paul's sojourn in Ephesus. Luke proceeds to contradict the motive of haste by making Paul land at Miletus (50 kilometers from Ephesus) and summon the elders of the Ephesian church to listen to him there.

From this we can gather that, in Luke's day, Christian communities were led by "elders" — a church organization more advanced than that known to the real Paul of 1 and 2 Corinthians (cf. JEC, p 164). Furthermore, it is taken for granted that Paul, as a hero of the bygone heroic age of the church, was so influential that he had only to summon elders and they would come at once. A swift-footed messenger would have needed two days to convey his summons to Ephesus, and they would have required at least a further three to reach Miletus. And yet we are told that Paul did not call at Ephesus "so that he might not have to spend time in Asia" (Acts 20:16).

The point of making Paul land at Miletus, thus contradicting his alleged haste, is to supply an occasion and an appropriate audience for a summary, in a farewell speech, of the exemplary nature of his missionary work; he also issues a warning that the church will not keep the purity which has hitherto characterized it and its leaders. This speech, like all the speeches in Acts, did not reach the author as source material, but is his own composition.[9] Having said that he will be imprisoned and will not return, Paul warns that the future church will be rent by dire heresies: "I know that after my departure fierce wolves will come in among you, not sparing the flock; and from among your own selves will arise men speaking perverse things, to draw away the disciples after them" (20:29-30). Surely the writer who put this into his mouth knew of heresies after Paul's time which divided the church, and it is widely admitted that the reference is to Gnostic heresies.

The book of Revelation (which most commentators date in the 90s) shows how strong Gnosticism was in the Christian churches of Asia Minor, and there is other evidence to the same effect for the early second century (see Bauer, 11, pp 233 ff). The author of Acts is, then, alluding to such developments which must have been in existence when he wrote. This argument is not nullified by supposing, as Robinson does, that the book of Revelation was written in the 60s. Paul is expressly referring to heresies which will arise *after* his time. The author of Acts was therefore writing, at the earliest, late in the first century.

But since he wanted to tell a story of a pure, undivided church, he stopped before reaching his own times. The period he depicts is what one might call the apostolic age—the age of pristine missionary fervor, when (from a respectable distance in time) the church could be represented as still free from all the weaknesses that characterized it in the author's own day. In reality, however, it was even in Paul's day by no means free from doctrinal struggles. His own letters show him embroiled in fierce controversy with other Christians; and the more we study what these letters tell us about Paul's life and views, the clearer it becomes that the author of Acts belonged to a later generation, with little real knowledge of these early conflicts.

IV ACTS AND PAUL'S LETTERS CONFRONTED

Let us, then, look at what Paul tells in his own letters about his Christian life, and compare it with the version we find in Acts. Paul himself, writing to the Galatian church, recalls his conversion, the occasion when the risen Jesus appeared with a summons to "preach him among the Gentiles" (Gal. 1:16). This revelation seems to have occurred at Damascus, for Paul adds that he *returned* there after spending the first period of his Christian life in Arabia. Pious commentators have taken this statement to mean that he made a pilgrimage to the Sinai peninsula in order to put aside his past as persecutor of Christianity (a past to which he repeatedly confesses in his letters) by meditation at Israel's holy places. But by Arabia he probably meant the kingdom of the Nabataean Arabs (which stretched almost as far north as Damascus). Since he supposed that Jesus had been revealed to him in order that he might "preach" Jesus, he went there surely as a missionary. It is hardly surprising that he left Damascus, if that was where he had persecuted Christians, and if, by his conversion, he had severed his links with the Jewish community of the city.

Paul never suggests that his preaching in Nabataea was successful. It did, however, arouse the hostility of the ruler of the kingdom, Aretas IV; and so Paul returned to Damascus, although even there Aretas' commissioner watched for him in order to seize him (2 Cor. 11:32-3) and he had to flee the city. He then went, so he tells us, to Jerusalem, where he spent a fortnight with Cephas and also met "James the Lord's brother" (Gal. 1:18-9). This first visit occurred "three years" after his conversion (or escape from Damascus; it is not clear which).

What could he have achieved in conversation with Peter? Certainly not recognition as the apostle of the Gentiles with freedom to preach to them a Christianity that did not involve keeping the Jewish religious law; for this would have made his later negotiations with Jerusalem superfluous. He had, as yet, no missionary successes to back any theological claims, and he could at best have been accepted on his first visit as one of the many persons to whom, according to his own account (1 Cor. 15:5 ff), the risen Lord had in fact appeared.[10] Nevertheless his next move was to preach "in the regions of Syria and Cilicia" (Gal. 1:21) successfully, for his fame now reached the Christians in Judea (to whom he was still unknown personally), who glorified God when they heard that the former persecutor of Christians was now a Christian (vss. 22-4). Thus, according to Paul, the sequence of events in the first three years of his life as a Christian was:

(1) conversion in Damascus
(2) unsuccessful missionary work in Nabataea, and return to Damascus
(3) flight to Jerusalem, where he spent only a fortnight
(4) successful missionary work outside Palestine

Paul's motive for summarizing these facts was to deny that he is subordinate to the Jerusalem Christian leaders. The suggestion had obviously been made that he had no authority to deviate from their doctrine; hence it is in reply to such charges that he declares that he was a Christian for three whole years before going near Jerusalem and that even then he spent but a fortnight there, and saw only the apostles Peter and James. That he calls upon God as witness of the truth of these statements (Gal. 1:20) is a sure sign that contrary allegations had been made.

Acts draws its account not from Paul but from a tradition embodying these contrary allegations. Acts knows nothing of his three years in Arabia but has him go, soon after his conversion, to Jerusalem, where he subordinates himself to the church and is in turn recognized as a missionary. Linton has plausibly argued (132) that what happened was that the hostile account of Paul (as subordinate to Jerusalem) had become current in some Christian communities but had lost its anti-Pauline polemical implications and formed neutral biographical material on which the author of Acts could draw. His purpose was not to oppose Paul's claim to independence (of which he surely knew nothing) but to allot him a place in the church's united front. It is not hard to see that the traditions which Acts' author collected would have suggested to him this version of the facts.

The visit to Arabia of which Paul himself wrote was not attended with any missionary success and did not lead to the founding of any Christian communities. This meant that this episode in his life was soon forgotten, and so was not represented in the traditions on which Luke drew. But once it had been dropped from Paul's biography, then his first journey to Jerusalem would naturally seem to follow his conversion quickly. If, then, he went to Jerusalem so soon after becoming a Christian, he would surely—so Luke must have reasoned—have made the journey to seek the approval of the mother church for his missionary work. This motive would have seemed the obvious one to Luke, for whom the early church was one harmonious whole, centered on Jerusalem, with no acrimonious disputes about leadership.

Another consequence of dropping the Arabian episode was that Paul's difficulties with Aretas' commissioner at Damascus also disappeared from tradition. Luke's sources seem to have told him that Paul had to leave Damascus because of some attempt on his life, but not who was responsible for this attempt. Thus Luke must have naturally supposed that the Jews, whom he regarded as Paul's ubiquitous enemies, were behind it. Accordingly, Luke's version of the facts is that Paul, immediately after his conversion, preached in the synagogues of Damascus (instead of going to Arabia), but so infuriated the Jews there that he had to flee to Jerusalem.

We see from such details not only that Luke drew his information from stories that bear little relation to Paul's own account of events in which he was, after all, personally involved, but also that Luke supplemented this defective material with conjectures, so as to make a coherent picture. Every historian does this, supplying (more or less critically) motives and events from his imagination in order to link together those reported by his sources. In Acts the need for conjecture was particularly great, as the source material was so sparse.

Of course, a modern historian is careful not to represent his conjectures as facts. But we cannot expect Luke to be circumspect in this way. He did not want to bore his readers with footnotes and hypotheses, but wished his story to read well and have a strong human interest. Nor did he have the modern historian's concern for strict consistency; he is quite capable of contradicting what he has said earlier for effectiveness later.[11] He does betray at times that he knows that the early church was not quite so harmonious as he represents it (see DJE, pp 129-30). But this amount of shading the truth is normal in any campaigner, then as now.

Acts' account of Paul as persecutor (before his conversion) again well illustrates how Luke supplements his sources. He knew from them that Paul had persecuted the church. But he had not read Paul's own statement that, even years after his conversion, he was "still not known by sight to the churches of Christ in Judea" (Gal. 1:22) and therefore must have persecuted Christians of other localities. On the contrary, for the author of Acts there was only one Christian community in existence at the time in question, namely the Jerusalem church. His sources told him of one Christian martyr (Stephen) there, with whose death Paul had no connection. But Luke adapted these sources so as to make Stephen one of many Jerusalem cases in which Paul is involved,[12] and by making him carry his anti-Christian activities to "cities outside" Jerusalem, even as far as Damascus (26:11–2).

Therefore Paul is represented as applying to the Jerusalem high priest for letters to the synagogues at Damascus authorizing him to arrest and bring to Jerusalem any members with Christian leanings (9:1–2). Commentators are baffled by this suggestion that the high priest had authority to order arrests in a Roman city 200 miles away, when the jurisdiction even of the Sanhedrin did not extend beyond Judea. But although unintelligible as history, this story of Paul persecuting at Damascus enabled Luke to link his account of Paul as persecutor with the tradition of his call to Christianity in the neighborhood of that city.

We have seen, in the case of relationships with Jerusalem, that Luke drew on stories that imputed to Paul behavior he himself had strongly denied. Another instance where Acts follows what was originally an anti-Pauline tradition is worth attention. In Gal. 5:11 Paul bitterly repudiates Judaistic allegations that he still occasionally preaches circumcision. Acts 16:3 seems to draw on precisely such a tradition when it represents him as circumcising Timothy (a convert of mixed Jewish and Greek parentage) so as not to offend the Jews. According to Acts (16:1) Timothy was already a Christian at the time, and it is clear from Paul's own statement in 1 Cor. 4:17 that he did know Timothy and probably converted him to Christianity himself. But he would not have circumcised a man who was already a Christian and therefore in Paul's view no longer Jew or Greek, for whom circumcision would constitute a lapse into the obsolete pre-Christian life under Jewish religious law.[13] Luke, then, drew this from an unreliable source.

This question of circumcision is prominent in Paul's letters. The Old Testament promises salvation only to those received into the chosen people by circumcision, which some Christians therefore regarded as essential, whereas Paul held that belief in Jesus sufficed (Gal. 2:16). He tells the Galatians of a second visit he made to Jerusalem — fourteen years after the first — to discuss this matter with the Christian leaders there. He stresses that he was not summoned, but went of his own free will, prompted "by revelation" (2:2) to "lay the gospel which I preach among the Gentiles" before Cephas (Peter), James, and John. They, he says, "added nothing" to it, and this means, as the sequel also shows, that they allowed his right to convert Gentiles without requiring them to conform to Jewish religious law.

Nevertheless, Paul did agree (so he says) at their request to collect money for the poor of Jerusalem. What he says in other epistles (1 Cor. 16:2; 2 Cor. 8 and 9) shows that he took great trouble to do this in his churches in Galatia, Macedonia, and Greece; and the last incident in his life that can be gleaned from his letters is his statement that he was again on his way to Jerusalem to deliver personally the money collected (Rom. 15:25-8).[14] This offering does imply a certain subordination, and the distribution of power is also indicated by the fact that, years before, when he went to Jerusalem to discuss circumcision, Cephas, James, and John did not come to him.

The occasion for this circumcision discussion was, Paul says (Gal. 2:1-10), that extreme Jewish Christians from Jerusalem — not in fact under the auspices of Peter and James, but "false brethren" who *pretended* to have the backing of these Jerusalem leaders — were unsettling his missionary work. Paul does not say in what locality, but the trouble obviously occurred at Antioch. The reason he makes no mention of Antioch in this section of his letter is that, at this time of writing to the Galatians, he had become a missionary independent of any Christian community and was anxious to give them the impression that, when he went to Jerusalem to discuss circumcision, he was equally independent.

In fact, however, he clearly went as a delegate of the church at Antioch, with Barnabas as another delegate with authority equal to his own. This is betrayed when he says, not that he "took" Barnabas with him (as he says he did Titus), but that Barnabas accompanied him (2:1) and when he concedes that the agreement reached with the Jerusalem apostles was not between them and him alone, but between them on the one hand and himself and Barnabas on the other (2:9).

Paul goes on to tell, in his letter, that after the Jerusalem agreement, Peter visited Antioch and at first ate with Gentile Christians there. But he and the other Jewish Christians of the city (including Barnabas) "drew back and separated" themselves, fearing the circumcision party, when representations were made by "certain men from James." The issue was not trivial. If Jewish Christians at a Gentile table ate pork (or a soup in which forbidden meat had been cooked), they would be repudiated by orthodox Jews and would moreover have to make the momentous admission that Jews could become Christians only by breaking with the Jewish community.

Paul, for his part, does not object to Jewish Christians keeping the Jewish religious law. But obviously, for them to stress its importance to the point of withdrawing from fellowship with Gentile believers could well undermine the doctrine that faith in Jesus suffices for salvation. He does not, however, allege that Cephas, Barnabas, and the other Jewish Christians deferred to his views, although he would surely have been very glad to have done so had it been the case, writing as he was in order to prevent Galatian Christians from rejecting his preaching in favor of that of advocates of the Jewish religious law.

What Paul says is thus quite obviously authentic. He would not have invented a serious disagreement with the circumcision party — a disagreement in which he is not able to allege that he came off best – in a letter written to dissuade Galatian Christians from accepting the gospel of circumcision. Paul thus broke with Barnabas on a serious question of principle. He makes no suggestion of any reconciliation, and he could hardly have remained in Antioch after thus having his own views repudiated.[15]

Luke knew that Paul and Barnabas had quarrelled and that subsequently Paul left Antioch without him to missionize elsewhere (whereas earlier the two had, according to Luke, gone out together). But Luke makes them part over a triviality. On the journey they made in common, they were (Luke says) deserted by one John Mark. When, back in Antioch, they were planning their next journey, Barnabas (according to Acts:14) proposed taking John Mark with them, but Paul refused to have this man who had let them down before. Whereupon Barnabas went with John Mark to work in Cyprus, while Paul (with Silas as companion) preached in Asia Minor.

I have already said why the account in Galatians of the quarrel must be authentic. How, then, can we suppose that Acts, which gives it an entirely different basis, was written by a companion of Paul? If, however, Acts was written a generation or more later, by someone who knew nothing of the real trouble, then we can understand how the author came to his version of it. He would have known from his sources that Paul worked first with Barnabas and then without him. If we can suppose that his sources also informed him that Barnabas and John Mark later worked together in Cyprus, then it would have been easy for him to suppose that what separated Paul from Barnabas was a quarrel about the suitability of John Mark.

Acts not only has its own version of the quarrel with Barnabas but also of the negotiations with Jerusalem. In Acts these are preceded by a vision in which Peter sees clean and unclean animals and is invited by a voice from heaven to "kill and eat" (10:13). A pious Jew such as he could well have reacted by selecting the clean animals for his meal. But the purpose of the narrator is to show that the Jewish food laws are obsolete, and so Peter is – implausibly enough – represented as refusing all the animals, on the ground that he has "never eaten anything that is common or unclean"; whereupon the voice explains: "What God has cleansed, you must not call common." On the basis of this vision, he becomes convinced that no man of any nation is "common or unclean" and that "God shows no partiality" (10:28, 34). Here speaks not the historical Peter but Gentile Christian theology of the late first century, which found no sense or truth in the idea of Israel as God's chosen people.

Paul (in Rom. 11:18-9) had begged Gentile Christians not to dispute the privileged position of the Jews (see p 121). What he feared would happen had, by the time of Acts, come to pass. The doctrine that "God shows no partiality" – put into Peter's mouth in Acts – solves the problem of table-fellowship with Gentiles, even before the first of them has been converted. On this basis Peter proceeds to convert a Roman centurion named Cornelius. Five chapters later we reach Acts' version of the Jerusalem discussion between Paul, Peter, and

James. Peter here says to the assembled Christians: "Brethren, you know that in the early days God made choice among you, that by my mouth the Gentiles should hear the word of the gospel and believe" (Acts 15:7). He can be alluding only to his behavior toward Cornelius, which seems to have been forgotten in the interval, for otherwise the whole discussion would have been unnecessary. Furthermore, he alludes to it in such a vague way that his audience could not possibly have appreciated its significance, which is, however, obvious enough to the reader who has gone through the earlier chapters of the book. The assembly then decides that Gentile Christians need not keep the whole law, but only four of its stipulations, including abstinence from certain foods.

Obviously, the subsequent quarrel which Paul (in his own letter) records as occurring in Antioch would not have broken out if a general ruling like this on the question of food had already been agreed upon.[16] Commentators have pointed out that the four stipulations are those which pagans living on Jewish territory had long been obliged to keep. They were presumably kept by Gentile Christians outside Judea in Luke's own day and attributed by tradition to the apostles. They could not have been unheeded in Luke's time, for he represents them as inspired by the Holy Spirit speaking through the apostles (15:28), and he would not have characterized the Gentile Christian communities of his age as disobedient to the Spirit.

In the first fifteen chapters of Acts, all roads lead to Jerusalem, and every area missionized is subordinated to it in one manner or another (cf. Haenchen, 94, pp 402–3). One reason why the author thus exaggerates the city's authority is his desire to show that Christianity had not lightly or readily broken away from its Jewish foundation. The rupture had occurred when Luke wrote; but he had to make clear that the rupture nevertheless did not jeopardize the continuity of God's dealings with the human race, since the Jews were entirely to blame for it and the Christians had done their best to retain their proper place within Judaism. It is in order to stress the church's fidelity to Judaism that he suppressed traditions (known to him from *Mark*) that the risen Jesus appeared in Galilee (see JEC, p 41). He made the risen one inaugurate the church in Jerusalem, where the apostles remain true to temple (Acts 3:1) and Torah, avoiding unclean food (10:14) and contact with the uncircumcised (11:3). They missionize Gentiles only when God forces them to it against their will and shows them — by a series of prodigious miracles during the Cornelius episode — that it is unmistakably in accordance with his will. These miracles culminate in the Holy Spirit resting upon Gentiles listening to Peter's preaching, enabling them to speak in tongues of ecstasy even before baptism (10:44–8). There could be no clearer indication of God's approval of the Gentile mission.

These experiences bring the apostles to think that Jewish religious law consists of such complex stipulations that no one, not even orthodox Jews, can really cope with them (15:10–2), a view of the Law which is quite un-Jewish and which reflects the Gentile standpoint from which Luke was writing.[17] However, Jews are not excluded from salvation, and Christianity has become an exclusively Gentile mission only because of Jewish obduracy in rejecting its gospel (13:46 etc.).

Luke, writing when Christianity had become predominantly a Gentile religion, naturally represented this development as planned from the first. For him, the Gentile mission was not promoted by Paul against considerable opposition but was an inevitable development in which all the leaders had played their part from the beginning. From this premise, he posits a harmonious relationship between Peter, James, and Paul. Paul, who had actually been involved in the beginnings of the Gentile mission and who was not writing about the problems involved from a respectable distance, saw the whole matter quite differently. The reasons he gave for not keeping the Jewish Law are unknown to Acts.

Paul never suggested the Gentile standpoint that the Law consists of stipulations so complicated as to be unfulfillable, but argues instead that those who keep it are led to boast of their own righteousness, instead of humbly accepting their utter unrighteousness before God (Rom. 10:3). His rejection of the Law is thus part of his basic theological position that man is essentially guilty before God and is saved by faith in Christ, not by achievements of his own. It was a later generation, for whom the Gentile mission was an established fact, that was reduced to accounting for its origin by positing a profusion of signs and miracles as divine sanctions of it; this later generation was entirely ignorant of the conflict and tensions the issue caused Christian leaders while it was still controversial.

Altogether, the account in Acts of relations between Jews and Christians is informed by two incompatible apologetic purposes. On the one hand, the author wishes to show that Christianity is really within Judaism, is indeed the true Judaism. Accordingly, the ordinary Jewish people (as against the Jewish authorities) are represented in the opening chapters as well disposed toward Christians. Peter's Pentecostal sermon is said to have converted 3000 Jews (2:41) and his next sermon another 2000 (4:4). Two speeches have thus sufficed to Christianize what has been calculated as one-fifth of the population of Jerusalem at that time (Haenchen, 94, p 174 n 3). When, in the next chapter, Christians clash with Jewish authorities, the people take the Christians' side (5:26). On the other hand, the author of Acts was concerned to denounce the Jews of his own day—in my view, the early second century—for having unequivocally rejected Christianity. Unlike Paul (Rom. 11:13-4, etc.) he retained no hope that they would eventually become Christians.

Thus Stephen, speaking in the spirit (Acts 6:5 and 7:55), turns on the Jews, ferociously calling them a "stiff-necked people" (7:51) who have always resisted the Holy Spirit, in that they first rejected Moses and practiced idolatry in the wilderness and then murdered their prophets. Stephen has prefaced these aggressive remarks with a summary (fifty verses long) of Israel's history from Abraham. This is the kind of material current in Luke's day as a synagogue sermon, but he has larded it with fierce anti-Jewish accusations. Later (Acts 12:3), the

Jerusalem Jews generally, and not just their leaders, are for the first time represented as anti-Christian.

When Paul leaves Jerusalem as a missionary, he is continually thwarted by Jewish opposition. Three times—once in Asia Minor (13:46), once in Greece (18:6) and finally in Rome (28:28)—he declares that the Jews have missed their chance, and that salvation will henceforth be offered to the Gentiles. Luke, like other Christian writers of the second century (Barnabas, Aristides, and Justin), wrote off the Jews and retained only their sacred scriptures—though not as testifying to God's covenant with them but solely because the Old Testament can be interpreted as foretelling the suffering and resurrection of Christ. As O'Neill has noted, the Old Testament has thus become a mere book of riddles, to which in every case the right answer is Jesus the Messiah (150, p 92).

Since Luke, then, no longer hopes for the conversion of the Jews, Jewish (as against Gentile) Christianity becomes less and less important in the later chapters of Acts. Jerusalem Christianity remains important only until Acts 15, when the terms of the mission to the Gentiles are agreed. After this the twelve Jerusalem apostles disappear from the narrative, and the emphasis is on Paul's missionary work outside Palestine. How any of the apostles met their end is not narrated, with the sole exception of the one who was martyred before Acts 15. The fantasy of later Christian writers sent the aging apostles away from Jerusalem on missions all over the world. Of that Luke knows nothing; for him it is Paul who carries Christianity around the Empire. After Acts 15 Jerusalem is only once again briefly prominent: when Paul returns there and is arrested by the Romans to protect him from a Jewish mob. We hear of Jewish plots against his life, but nothing of any attempt from Jerusalem Christians (who are supposed to number in the thousands [21:20]) to help him. After this the Jerusalem church is mentioned no further.[18]

The real Paul's attitude to Gentiles—and not just on the subject of the Jewish Law—is incompatible with the attitude he is made to strike in Acts. In Romans he says that all men at all times, by dint of their reason, have been able to discern God's true attributes, but have refused to honor him properly and have turned instead to idolatry (1:19 ff). In consequence, God has punished them by filling them with homosexual and other immoral desires. Three times he reiterates that God has "given them over" to their own worst tendencies for willfully and wickedly refusing to serve him whom their reason has from the first been able to discern truly. For the real Paul of this epistle, all men are guilty before God, and it is truly a miracle of grace that He nevertheless accepts Christians by virtue of Christ's sacrifice.

In Acts, however, Paul is made to tell the Athenians that they worship (albeit in a somewhat confused manner) the true God, in spite of their idolatry, for which God has not condemned them since they practiced it from ignorance: "The times of ignorance God overlooked" (17:30). All that is common to both standpoints is the view that man is, by nature, akin to God, although Paul stresses this much less than does Acts, for he retains the Jewish idea that

Jews occupy a privileged position as God's people. Thus in Romans he says—
on the subject of man's kinship with God—merely that God's power and deity
are manifest in all things of creation (1:20), whereas the Paul of Acts says,
more explicitly: "He is not far from each one of us, for in him we live and
move and have our being" (17:28). In Romans this kinship with God serves
merely to point to man's irresponsibility at having failed to acknowledge him,
whereas in Acts man is praised for having behaved essentially in accordance
with this kinship. Robinson denies that there is any incompatibility here, but
gives no evidence to support his view.

That Paul preached effectively in Athens and won followers (as Acts
alleges) before leaving for Corinth (17:34–18:1)—there is no suggestion that he
was driven out—is incompatible with Paul's own statement (1 Cor. 2:3) that he
reached Corinth in "fear and trembling," obviously after a very rough time in
Athens. If he ever did speak as Acts represents him, then he indeed went a long
way to accommodate his Christian views to pagans—so far as to eliminate the
redemptive significance of the cross, which he stresses at every turn in his letters.

Luke knows nothing of Paul's idea of the efficacy of the crucifixion. For
him, this event was a miscarriage of justice, a sin of the Jews, in that they per-
petrated it when they should have known from their scriptures that Jesus was
their Messiah.

Apologists have tried to argue that at Athens Paul modified his real views,
in accordance with his declared principle (1 Cor. 9:20) of becoming like a Jew
to win Jews and like a Gentile to win Gentiles. But the context shows that what
he had in mind when he wrote this was observation of the Jewish religious law
(which in his view is in any case unnecessary to salvation). In Jewish company
he is prepared to be bound, for instance, by Jewish food laws, but in pagan
company he feels free to abandon them. What he does not mean is that he is a
hypocrite who will change his theology so as to win converts. In Galatians he
insists that, as far as the theological substance of his preaching is concerned,
he will make no compromise: "Even if we, or an angel from heaven, should
preach to you a gospel contrary to that which we preached to you, let him be
accursed" (Gal. 1:8; cf. the whole of Gal. 2).

Apologists who reconcile Romans with Acts by making Paul modulate his
theology thus pay a heavy price for the consistency thus achieved. But if, in
fact, the author of Acts knew nothing of Paul's epistles and little of their theology, then the address to the Athenians becomes quite intelligible. Luke lived in
a world where the Christian mission had turned from Jews to Gentiles, and so he
naturally wished to show that Christianity is acceptable from Gentile premises.
To this end he makes Paul say that pagan religious ideas need but slight recasting
to become Christian, that Greek lore allows of Christian interpretation.

Acts also has its own account of the history of the conflict between Christians and Jews. What the Jews object to in Christianity is said to be its doctrine
of resurrection, and the Paul of Acts complains that the Jews arraign him
because of what he teaches about "the resurrection of the dead" (24:21). The

Jewish authorities likewise arrest Peter and John because "they were proclaiming in Jesus resurrection from the dead" (4:2). Paul, then, in Acts has to endure persecution not because of his obnoxious attacks (peculiar to his own theology) on the Jewish law, but because he proclaims the resurrection doctrine preached by all Christian missionaries. In his own letters, however, he tells a different story, and at times even Acts betrays some knowledge of it—as when Christian Pharisees demand that Gentile Christians be circumcised (15:5) and Jews complain that Paul encourages their Diaspora brethren to forsake the Law (21:21, 28). It was clearly his views on the Law that gave offense.

According to Acts, the Jews are grossly inconsistent in opposing Christian resurrection doctrine, for they themselves (so the argument goes) share the same hopes. Thus the Paul of Acts says that his resurrection preaching is in accordance with "all things which are according to the Law and which are written in the Prophets," and that it consists only of hopes which the Jews "themselves look for" (24:14-5). Acts tries to show how genuinely Jewish the Christian doctrine is by stressing that the Pharisees—the strictest faction within Judaism—believe in resurrection. Accordingly, in defiance of the anti-Pharisaic traditions represented in the gospels, Acts make them pro-Christian:[19] Gamaliel takes the apostles' side (5:35-9) and the Pharisees as a party speak up for Paul against the Sadducees, who deny resurrection (23:9).

This account of Christian-Jewish relations is so absurd that it can hardly have been designed to impress Jews. The author seems to have abandoned all hope of influencing them and is merely seeking reasons for blaming the rupture between the two religions, which by the time he wrote had already occurred, on the Jews' inconsistency and obduracy (cf. Haenchen, 94, p 674). A Jew would at once have countered that the Pharisees expect a *future* resurrection of the dead *at the end of time* and do not look back to a past resurrection of someone who allegedly died as the Messiah. Therefore they would not have leaped to the defense of Paul and of his doctrine of the risen Jesus because they felt they shared his views on resurrection. The Paul of Acts even calls himself a Pharisee and says he is on trial only for proclaiming the Pharisees' doctrine of "the hope and resurrection of the dead" (23:6).

Commentators have noted that one purpose Luke is pursuing here is to persuade the Roman authorities, who tolerate Judaism, likewise to tolerate Christianity as belonging essentially to it. Luke, then, insists that neither Pauline nor any other type of Christians clash with Jews over the Law, that Christians and Pharisees agree on fundamentals, such as resurrection, and that such disputes as they have are internal Jewish affairs and of no concern to Romans, who should therefore extend to the new religion the toleration they already accord to the old. Acts repeatedly represents Roman officials as doing precisely this and therefore as behaving as, in the view of the writer, they should.

At times, however, the real Christian hostility to Pharisees shows through, even in Acts, for example, in the polemic against them recorded in chapter 7. There is also, of course, the fact that Paul the Pharisee began as a persecutor of Christians. This real hostility was due to incompatible ideas about the value of Jewish Law. But since Luke greatly tones down the whole controversy over the Law, he is able to represent Pharisees as on the whole pro-Christian.

The Paul of the epistles, on the other hand, knows perfectly well that his Christian theology is incompatible with Jewish doctrine, and — far from claiming to be still a Pharisee — calls his pre-Christian Pharisaism "muck" (Phil. 3:8) that he gladly rejected when he embraced Christianity. Such a major discrepancy surely reveals the nullity of the traditional view that Acts was written by a Luke who had travelled with Paul. Acts is the product of a later age, which knew little of the real reasons for past conflicts.

The account Acts gives of Paul as a missionary is also much more positive than what Paul himself suggests in his own letters about his abilities. In Acts he is represented as working miracles as prodigious as those ascribed there to Peter. His handkerchiefs, applied to the sick, cured them (Acts 19:11-2), just as they expected to be cured when Peter's shadow fell on them (Acts 5:15). Paul is also, in Acts, as gifted an orator as Peter. For Luke, such traits belonged to the portrait of an apostle.

Paul himself, however, informs us otherwise. He implies in 2 Corinthians that rival Christian teachers had questioned his ability to perform miracles.[20] He also reports their criticism that, although he was influential in writing, he could make but a poor impression as a speaker (2 Cor. 10:10), a criticism he seems to accept as just when he comments: "Even if I am unskilled in speaking, I am not in knowledge" (2 Cor. 11:6). It is clear, then, that Luke knew only the ideal picture of an apostle current in later days. The Paul of Acts is always on top of it all. He may be stoned, but he is on his feet again at once (Acts 14:19-20). On his voyage to Rome he never despairs, but adopts a commanding position (although he is supposed to be in chains as a mere prisoner), encourages, advises, and saves the lives of all. The real Paul was no such superman, but confessed to being "so unbearably crushed" by his afflictions that he "despaired of life" (2 Cor. 1:8). He confessed repeatedly to his own "weakness" (2 Cor. 11:29 and 12:9) and was all too familiar with "fear and trembling" (1 Cor. 2:3).

I have said repeatedly that the author of Acts had not read Paul's letters. He would surely have hesitated to set aside so much of what he must have known (had he known it at all) to be authentic tradition merely to write something edifying. Yet Paul's letters undoubtedly existed when he wrote, although they may not have been circulating as a collection at that time (see p 20). Luke's ignorance of Paul's letters probably means that documents which were prized in some Christian communities were unknown or ignored in others. Although Paul is mentioned more often in the Christian writings of the second century than any Christian personage other than Jesus, Justin Martyr, who wrote as late as about 150, never quotes Paul, nor even mentions him.[21]

Luke knew of Paul as the great missionary of the early church, the man who carried Christianity into Asia Minor and Greece. He did not know the details of his theology. Of course he and other Christians of his time knew enough to be aware that Paul had preached justification by faith. And Luke is clearly attempting to reproduce this theology when he makes Paul tell Jews (Acts 13:39) that by Jesus "everyone that believes is freed from everything from which you could not be freed by the law of Moses." Luke and the Christians for whom he wrote firmly believed that only Christians, and not the non-Christian Jews, were justified. And so this Pauline view was quite acceptable to him. Since, for him, Peter and Paul worked in complete harmony, he does not hesitate to represent Peter, in the course of his argument that Christians need not keep the Jewish religious law, as making the Pauline-sounding comment that "we believe that we shall be saved through the grace of the Lord Jesus" (15:11).

This is not a historical documentation of Peter's beliefs but represents the faith of Luke and of the Christians for whom he wrote. Paul himself had said (Gal. 2:15–6): "A man is not justified by works of the law, but through faith in Jesus Christ." This genuinely Pauline contrast between reliance on one's own achievements (one's own moral excellence at keeping the Law) and reliance on God's merciful saving grace (which Paul espoused), is nowhere made clear in Acts. The two passages in Acts which I have just quoted (Paul's statement at 13:39 and Peter's at 15:11) are the only ones that mention the Law's limitations. The Paul of Acts does not attack the Law, as does the Paul of Galatians. In Acts Paul's hostility to the Law is a Jewish libel and a charge (21:21, 28) he is made to repudiate. In sum, Pauline ideas are at times taken over by Luke, but not the Pauline theology underlying them.

V   CONCLUSION

At the end of his survey of the scholarship concerning the value of Acts as a source for the study of Paul, Mattill notes that the "dominant" view today, and the one which "has succeeded in putting the burden of proof on others," is the view that "in Acts and the epistles there are two Pauls, the historical Paul of the authentic epistles and the legendary Paul of Acts" (196, pp 88, 98). As exponents of this view he mentions not only Haenchen (on whose work I have drawn very substantially) but a whole series of scholars from Zeller to the present day. On the other hand, the view that Acts and the epistles complement each other, without contradiction, is, he says, still "strong among conservative scholars," while yet others adopt a mediating position. My readers must decide for themselves which position is best served by the evidence.

8

New Testament References
to Jesus' Family

I JESUS' BROTHERS

I have argued that Paul (writing not later than AD 60) does not speak of Jesus as of a contemporary and seems to have no clear idea as to when or where he lived his incarnate life; and that it is only later Christian tradition, as represented for instance in the canonical gospels (all written after AD 70 and, in my view, as late as AD 90), that places this life in first-century Palestine. However, in Gal. 1:19 Paul does claim personal acquaintance with "James the Lord's brother," whom he describes as one of the leaders of the Jerusalem church.

If Paul means blood brother of a historical Jesus, then it would suffice to establish—against my view—that Jesus had really lived in the first half of the first century. Furthermore, I must admit that this interpretation of Paul's words does seem the immediate and obvious one. Here, then, is a case where what seems to be the plain sense of a text does not support me. It has to be weighed against other texts where my theory makes better sense of the evidence. If the only reasonable interpretation of what Paul says implies that James and Jesus were physical brothers, then this passage would weigh very heavily indeed against my view of Christian origins. But is this the only reasonable sense in which Paul's words can be taken?

Paul writes not of Jesus' brother, but of "the brother of the Lord"; not of Jesus' brethren but of "the brethren of the Lord" (1 Cor. 9:5). The phrase could designate a group of Christians who were, like the Lord himself as Paul conceived him, members of the house of David. But it is unlikely that this is what Paul means. It is more likely that the phrase "brethren of the Lord" designates a

167

small group or fraternity of Messianists not related to Jesus but zealous in the service of the risen one. (This suggestion was made fifty years ago, with his usual discernment, by J. M. Robertson, 161, pp 140 ff.) Brandon, who emphasizes the preeminence of James at Jerusalem, refers to evidence that the term *brother* could in those days mean "principal servant" (23, p 20 n and refs.). Strabo states (Bk. 16:4, 21) that the vizier of the Nabataean kings regularly bore the title "brother of the king"; and Cerfaux mentions inscriptions which confirm that *brother* was used as a title (38, p 141). In the pagan world, *brethren* was certainly used to denote members of a particular religious society. Examples from papyri are given by Moulton and Milligan (146, p 9).

At 1 Cor. 1:11–3 Paul complains of Christian factions at Corinth which bear the titles "of Cephas," "of Apollos" and—most significant of all—"of Christ." What do these expressions imply? That certain Christians in the city made themselves into a Cephas (Peter) party does not mean that Peter had been in Corinth to preach to them. They may merely have adopted some variety of doctrine that had been represented to them as Peter's teaching (which, we know from what Paul says in Galatians, was not identical with Paul's). Apollos, however, had actually preached at Corinth, and had inculcated doctrines which went beyond what Paul regarded as true Christianity.

Paul regarded himself as the "father" of the Christian community there (1 Cor. 4:15), who had "planted the faith" (3:6)—not as the very first missionary, but by laying a "foundation" in that he preached the true gospel: "For no other foundation can anyone lay than that which is laid, which is Jesus Christ" (3:10–11). During his absence from Corinth, Apollos "built" on this foundation, and whether he has built correctly will, says Paul, be manifest on the Day of Judgment (vss. 12–5). Haenchen notes (94, pp 490–1) that Paul's view is clearly that, while his own foundation has been approved by God, Apollos' superstructure still awaits vindication. He adds that Paul repeatedly mentions qualities in which he himself has been found lacking—such as ability to speak effectively (2 Cor. 10:10) and the gift of "wisdom." Acts 18:24–5 preserves a tradition that Apollos was "an eloquent man, well versed in the scriptures, fervent in spirit," and on this basis one can well understand friction between him and Paul.

So much, then, for the Cephas and Apollos parties. That there was also a "Christ" party at Corinth is more perplexing, and some have dismissed Paul's reference to it as a manuscript error. (It is admittedly striking that when, at 3:22, Paul again alludes to the factions, he mentions Cephas and Apollos, but not Christ.) But many commentators (for example, Thrall, 201, p 18) concede that he did mean to refer to a Christ party. Now if there was a Corinthian group called "those of the Christ," there could also have been a Jerusalem one called "the brethren of the Lord," who would not necessarily have had any more personal experience of Jesus than Paul himself. And James, as "*the* brother of the Lord," could have been the leader of this group.

In this connection it is of interest that in two gospels the risen Jesus is made to call a group of followers who are not his blood relatives his "brothers."

In Matthew's resurrection narrative, when Jesus appears to the women near the empty tomb: "they took hold of his feet and worshipped him. Then Jesus said to them, 'Do not be afraid; go and tell my brethren to go to Galilee, and there they will see me'" (Mt. 28:9–10).

Matthew has here supplemented Mark's empty-tomb narrative with this evidence of the corporeal reality of Jesus' feet as further proof of the reality of the resurrection. Jesus' designation here of his disciples as his "brethren" is not in accordance with Matthew's previous usage, and comes as a surprise. That the disciples (and not Jesus' family) is meant is clear from the sequel. "The eleven disciples went to Galilee," where they saw and worshipped the risen one (vss. 16–7).

In the fourth gospel, Jesus says, in the same circumstances: "Do not hold me, for I have not yet ascended to the Father; but go to my brethren and say to them, I am ascending . . ." (Jn. 20:17).

If we accept the good grounds which many theologians give for thinking that John did not know the other gospels directly, but at times drew on sources very similar to theirs and reworked them so as to express his own theology (cf. p 130), then the present parallel may well be due to a common source, a resurrection narrative in which Jesus made some statement about his "brethren." Each evangelist has made something different of this underlying unit of tradition. Matthew makes the women touch Jesus to show that he is risen in body; John makes him say, in effect: stop clinging to me and so hindering my ascension. But both include the word *brethren* in the sense of disciples, and this word was presumably in the source from which both drew.

What did it mean in that source? If it there meant Jesus' blood brothers, then we must suppose that both evangelists independently of each other changed its sense so as to make it mean a group of disciples. This seems very unlikely, as neither Matthew nor John use the word in this sense in other contexts. Thus we are driven to suppose that, already in the source, it meant a group of disciples. If so, then Jesus' words about "my brethren" constitute evidence for an early (pre-gospel) use of the title *brethren* as meaning a Christian group serving the Lord.

One reason, however, for taking Paul's statement about "the brethren of the Lord" to refer to Jesus' own blood brothers is that this interpretation is supported by what the gospels say about Jesus' incarnate life. Mark (writing, it is often held, only ten or twenty years later than Paul) and also Matthew and Luke (who adapted *Mark*) state that Jesus had blood brothers; Mark and Matthew (but not Luke) agree that one of them was named James. If this is a true chronicle of historical fact, then it constitutes strong support for interpreting Paul to mean that James was one of Jesus' physical brothers. But did the evangelists supply Jesus with a family in order to argue a theological point rather than to chronicle actual facts?

We have seen that one heresy which had to be combatted in early Christian times was Docetism, the view that the historical Jesus only *seemed* to have a real body. One way for opponents of Docetism to underline the reality and the completeness of his incarnation would be to allege that he had real brothers and sisters like any normal child. And once such stories had entered the tradition, they would be repeated and assimilated to others, even when anti-Docetic motives had been lost from sight. But let us leave conjecture, and study what the gospels say about these brothers and sisters.

Mk. 3:31–5 introduces Jesus' "mother and brothers." They seek him, but he shows no interest and declares instead that the "crowd sitting about him" are his true kin: for "whoever does the will of God is my brother, and sister, and mother." Matthew and Luke also give this story, and, as already noted, they are not independent witnesses to its truth, but have taken it from *Mark*.

Now one of the most oft-repeated doctrines in the New Testament is the supreme importance of faith in and service to Jesus. Jesus, for instance, turns to a vast multitude, and tells them that they cannot be his disciples unless they are prepared to hate their parents and brothers as well as their own lives (Lk. 14:26; cf. Mk. 10:29–30). What, then, could be more appropriate, from the evangelists' point of view, than to represent him as implementing his own precept by neglecting his family for the sake of his followers? In this connection Best has argued that Mark's purpose here was to set down, for the Christian community for which he wrote his gospel, the nature of true discipleship, and that, to this end, he "used the family of Jesus homiletically" (15, p 317).

In Mk. 3 and parallels there is, then, mention of Jesus' brethren, but in this gospel these personages are specifically named only in the episode (Mk. 6:1–3) where Jesus amazes the Jews of his "own country" by his teaching. The ground of their amazement is that they know him as a perfectly ordinary local personage, with entirely undistinguished connections: as "the carpenter, the son of Mary,[1] the brother of James and Joses and Judas and Simon" and as a man whose sisters are also known. Matthew repeats this story (with "Joseph" instead of "Joses" as the second of the four brothers). Luke, as we shall see, places it earlier in Jesus' public career, and makes no mention of his brethren; in Luke's version, the Jews simply ask: "Is not this Joseph's son?"

As for Jesus' rejection in his own country, I have given reasons elsewhere (DJE, pp 149–51) for believing that all that was available to Mark was a tradition that he had preached there without success, and that the concrete details of the rejection are Mark's own construction. I have already argued in this volume that the earliest extant traditions about the historical Jesus represent him as living an obscure life which ended in humiliation and rejection by men, and that Jewish wisdom literature had already told—without giving details of time or place—of agents of God's saving purpose who came to earth and were rejected by man. In a climate of opinion where Jesus was similarly regarded, it would be easy for stories to arise to the effect that he had preached in his homeland without success. Indeed, the Jewish wisdom literature may have influenced Mark's narrative more directly. In Mk. 6:2 Jesus figures as an exponent of wisdom, and a recent student of this Jewish literature, Hamerton-Kelly, has discreetly suggested that "the myth of Wisdom's messengers exercised some influence on Mark's Christology" (96, p 50).

That Jesus' rejection in his own country was originally vaguely conceived, without reference to time or place, is suggested by the fact that different evangelists supply different settings to the scene. Mark names no locality (merely his "own country"). Luke, in adapting *Mark* specifies Nazareth; while John (writing independently of the other three gospels) certainly understood Jesus to hail from Nazareth (1:45–6), but represents his rejection as effected by the Jews at their religious center (of which he is the rightful king), and therefore hints that it occurred at Jerusalem (4:43–5; cf. Lindars, 130, pp 200–1). All three evangelists make Jesus speak words to the effect that "a prophet has no honor in his own country." Mark and John, then, were drawing independently on a unit of tradition which did not specify any particular locality.

The two incidents—Mk. 3 and parallels and Mk. 6 and parallels—are the only ones in the Synoptics in which Jesus' brethren figure. Mk. 3 makes clear not only that he showed some indifference to his family, but also that his family was hostile to him. Thus Mk. 3:21 has it that "the ones from beside him" (or "those alongside him") went out to seize him, thinking he had lost his senses. Some older English versions translate the Greek here as though the reference were to "his friends." However, the meaning in this context is "his family," for when they reach him in verse 31 (and thus occasion his comment that his true family are those who do the will of God) they are identified as his mother and brothers. The fourth gospel also knows of a tradition according to which "his brethren did not believe in him" (Jn. 7:5). In this gospel (as in *Luke*) these brethren are never named; but, as Telfer has noted (200, p 21), their indifference to Jesus is later stressed when the evangelist underlines their absence at the time of the crucifixion by making him consign his mother to the care of the beloved disciple (Jn. 19:26–7).

That Jesus was rejected not only by his own countrymen but even by those closest to him is an idea that could easily arise from the premise that he led a life of humiliation. Mark himself believed (9:12) that the Jewish scriptures foretold suffering for him, and there are obvious Old Testament passages which were adduced in early Christian times in support (for example, Isaiah 53:3, "he was despised and rejected"). And in any case, rejection by neighbors is a fate usually ascribed to divine men. Apollonius of Tyana is represented as complaining that his "native place" ignored him. Burkill has suggested that Mark saw, in the hostility of Jesus' kinfolk, a symbol of the Jewish nation as a whole. On this view, "the passage dramatically exemplifies two motifs that figured prominently in the thought of primitive Christianity, namely the theme of the Messiah's rejection by the Jewish people, and the concept of the Church as the New Israel, transcending all racial and sexual distinctions," in that the multitude seated in the house with the Lord—and not his mother and brothers who stand aside—represent his genuine relatives (33, pp 234–5). Nevertheless, and understandably enough, some Christian communities could not believe that Jesus' family had ever rejected him. This seems to have been the case with the communities for which Matthew and Luke wrote; for they did not incorporate Mk. 3:20–1 into their gospels, and they deleted the words "among his own kin" in their adaptations of Mk. 6:4.

The evidence, then, shows that when Mark wrote, he was able at two points to draw on traditions which may already have referred to Jesus' family, including brothers. I have said enough to show that such traditions, and Mark's use of them, may well have arisen as support for the Christology of a Christian community. The theologians whose views I have mentioned do not, of course, suppose that the traditions arose in that way. Their view is that the traditions are based on historical facts, and were merely exploited for Christological purposes.

Let us now see what Luke makes of these traditions, both in his gospel and in Acts. As already noted, he does not include Mk. 3:21, which makes Jesus' family hostile to him. He does (at 8:19) include Mk. 3:31, where Jesus' brothers are mentioned but not named. As for the rejection of Jesus narrated in Mk. 6:1–6, Luke tells this story, in a highly modified form, at an earlier point in his narrative (Lk. 4:16–30). It is not universally agreed that he is here telling the same story as the one in Mk. 6, but there is strong evidence that in fact he is. Mark places the story of the rejection between Jesus' raising a girl from the dead and sending out the disciples preaching, while Luke makes the dispatch of the disciples follow directly after the raising (8:54–9:1). This shows that he considered that he had already dealt with Mark's story of the rejection of Jesus in his earlier narrative of 4:16–30, where, as Creed has noted, he has in fact reproduced "the essential features" of Mk. 6:1 ff: "Jesus preaches in the synagogue and impresses his hearers, who, however, take offence at the 'wisdom' of their fellow-townsman. Jesus retorts with the saying that a prophet is not without honour except among his own people" (47, p 65).

The changes Luke has made have been studied in detail by Haenchen (92, pp 156–81), who argues that one reason why Luke placed the incident earlier than Mark is that he wanted Jesus' synagogue sermon to be followed by a physical attack on him, which could hardly have developed had he arrived accompanied by his disciples (as in *Mark*); therefore Luke transferred the incident to the beginning of Jesus' ministry, prior to their call. The reason for the attack is that he infuriates his audience by hinting that the Jews have missed their chance of salvation. Luke could not enunciate this—his own—view as clearly here (when Jesus has hardly begun to preach to the Jews) as he does in the later chapters of Acts, where he uses Paul as his spokesman to declare that, after repeated rebuffs from the Jews, "this salvation of God has been sent to the Gentiles" (Acts 28:28). But Luke gives hints enough and has thus made of Mark's simple narrative a story which intimates the development of Christianity up to the time of its decisive break with Judaism. This, argues Haenchen, is another reason why Luke placed it so early; the development actually achieved in Luke's own time, and stated as a fact at the end of Acts, is heralded at the very beginning of Jesus' ministry.

In the course of this incident Jesus' audience asks: "Is not this the son of Joseph?" (Lk. 4:22). The corresponding question in Mk. 6:3 was, we recall: "Is not this the carpenter, the son of Mary, and brother of James and Joses and Judas and Simon, and are not his sisters with us?" Luke, then, has deleted all reference to these persons and replaced it with a reference to Jesus' father. This was surely deliberate; for Luke, as one of the two evangelists who begins his gospel with a virgin-birth story, did not himself believe that Jesus was Joseph's son. That he makes the Jews regard him as such is a neat way of indicating how completely they fail to comprehend his true nature.

After 8:19 where, as I have noted, Luke follows Mk. 3:31 in mentioning but not naming Jesus' brothers, he never again mentions them in his gospel. And because he would not credit them with any hostility to Jesus he seems to have inferred from Psalms 38:11 and 88:8 ("my kinsmen stand afar off" and "thou hast put mine acquaintance far from me"), not that Jesus' family failed to accompany him to Jerusalem, but that they witnessed his death only at some distance from the cross. Hence Lk. 23:49 has it that, at the crucifixion, "all his acquaintances and the women who had followed him from Galilee stood at a distance." Luke obviously supposed that, subsequently, the family and the women remained in Jerusalem with the eleven. And so in Acts he states (1:14) that after the ascension the eleven "continued steadfastly in prayer with the women and Mary the mother of Jesus, and with his brethren." Here again the brothers are not named, and they are never subsequently mentioned. The author's aim is clearly, as Haenchen notes (94, p 122), to give the edifying impression that Jesus' family belonged to the earliest church from the first. As, however, he had no real information about this family, he was not able to work them into any further narrative.

Luke and Acts thus, on two occasions, mention brothers of Jesus, but has adapted *Mark* so as to avoid suggesting that they were hostile to him. *Luke-Acts* also never names them, even though the author would have known from *Mark* that one of them was allegedly named James. Furthermore, although the author does, in Acts, represent a certain James as leader of the Jerusalem church, he never suggests that this person was Jesus' brother. After having narrated the martyrdom of James the son of Zebedee (one of the twelve and, of course, no relation of Jesus) in Acts 12:2, he makes Peter, as he goes into hiding, bid that news of his affairs be conveyed to "James and the brethren" (verse 17). Here, for the first time, is mentioned someone simply called James, and who, by chapter 15, functions as the leader of the Jerusalem church.

Telfer argues that (1) the reference is to Jesus' brother, and (2) the position he occupied, as leader of the church, was so obviously known to any Christian reader that no explanation of his identity was called for, even though another James, the son of Zebedee, had been the subject of reference only a few verses earlier (200, p 6). But I think that if Luke had wanted his readers to regard the James of Acts 12:17 (and of later chapters) as Jesus' brother, then he would either have called him such, or at least have been careful to include in his gospel the statement (known from *Mark*) that Jesus had a brother named James. I argued that in his version of Mk. 6 Luke had good reason to drop the names of Jesus' brothers and make the Jews ask instead a question about his father Joseph. But so careful a writer would surely have not left us entirely without clues had he regarded (and wished us to regard) the Jerusalem leader of Acts as Jesus' brother. I thus infer that he did not regard this person as such, even though what he tells (in Acts 15) of this James' dealings with Paul shows that this person is the one whom Paul, in his letter to the Galatians, calls "the brother of the Lord."

In sum, Paul writes of "James the brother of the Lord," who was one of the Christian leaders at Jerusalem; and Luke (in Acts) writes of a James who is not more specifically defined, but who led the church at Jerusalem and who had (according to Acts 15) negotiations with Paul which obviously represent Luke's version of the negotiations between James and Paul mentioned in Galatians. In none of these texts is it necessary, in my view, to regard James as Jesus' brother. But this would be an easy and natural inference for anyone who tried to harmonize them with *Mark* or *Matthew*.

Statements of the Christian writer Hegesippus, made about AD 180 but based on earlier material, give some indication of how the interpretation that a blood brother was meant was encouraged. Hegesippus (whose work survives only as quotations in other writers, notably Eusebius) was writing about James and about the subapostolic Jerusalem church of the AD 60s, more than a hundred years after the destruction of the city in AD 70 and some fifty years after Hadrian had rebuilt it as a pagan city which no Jew was allowed to enter. It is obvious, then, that his information could not have been firsthand and that he drew it from a written source. Telfer has given evidence (199) that neither Hegesippus nor his source knew much of anything about Jewish language or customs, and that it was this source which attributed the relative orthodoxy of the Jerusalem church to the fact that it had long been governed by a succession of kinsmen of Christ: first James, the brother of Jesus, and then Simon or Simeon, "a cousin of the savior." This seems to indicate a sufficient motive for the fostering of the idea that the brother of Jesus was Jerusalem's first bishop.

Morton Smith, who like most commentators regards the James who led the Jerusalem Christians in Paul's day as Jesus' brother, explains his accession by arguing that Jesus' title of Messiah was hereditary, "so his brothers found themselves saddled with his claims" after his execution (184, p 25). So we are to believe that James led the Jerusalem Christians as their Messianic king without Roman interference! In my view, the fact that the Jewish and Roman authorities permitted Christians to practice their religion at Jerusalem in the 50s is itself evidence against the view that the founder of the faith had a few years earlier been executed as a result of Jewish or Roman hostility.

II   JESUS AS SON OF DAVID

The historicity of Jesus has been defended on the ground that he was from the first regarded not as of unknown origin, but specifically as of Davidic descent.

Such a concrete detail, it is suggested, tells against arbitrary invention, even though it is conceded that many Jews expected the Messiah to be in David's line and that any supposed Messiah might therefore have had descent from David imputed to him.

The New Testament evidence for Jesus' Davidic origin has been studied closely by Burger, and throughout this section I shall be following his valuable monograph (31).

The earliest mention of Jesus' Davidic descent is Paul's statement (Rom. 1: 3–4) that he is God's son, "descended from David according to [i.e., in the sphere of] the flesh, and designated son of God in power according to the spirit of holiness [that is, in the sphere of the holy spirit] by his resurrection from the dead." Paul, we recall, believed that Jesus had always existed as son of God before coming to earth. Hence he is not here saying that Jesus was "designated" or "appointed" son of God only after his resurrection, but rather that he was designated son of God *in power* after that event (cf. p 35). On earth he lived, according to Paul, obscurely and humbly, but after resurrection was properly enthroned as God's son. Thus his Davidic existence on earth was part of his act of humbling himself by assuming human form. Paul says that Jesus, "though he was in the form of God," nevertheless "emptied himself, taking the form of a servant, being born in the likeness of men" (Phil. 2:6–7). Thus "descended from David according to the flesh" of Rom. 1:3 is parallel to "born of a woman, born under the law" of Gal. 4:4, in that in both cases submission to something humiliating is implied.

Conservative scholars conjecture that Paul derived his information that Jesus was descended from David from the original community of Christians at Jerusalem, who, they believe, had known Jesus personally. But nothing that Paul says supports this. When he affirms Jesus' Davidic descent, his intention is surely to state an article of faith on which both he and the Christian community at Rome which he is addressing (and which he had never visited) are agreed. He must therefore have reckoned that this tenet was current there, and it is clear from his letter that—as one would in any case have expected—Christians at Rome about AD 60 were Gentiles or Diaspora Jews (in both cases Greek-speaking). And so nothing in the evidence necessarily points to any connection with a Palestinian Jesus and Aramaic-speaking disciples.

Mark, like Paul, is anxious to represent Jesus as son of David, but little of the material at his disposal could be made to serve this end. Mark, of course, gives no account of Jesus' birth or early life, but introduces him as an adult at his baptism by John. The evangelist does not in any way suggest that he is of the line of David until just before he reaches Jerusalem in his final days. I quote Mark's version of this incident, side by side with the Lucan parallel, from the RV:

Mark: 10	*Luke: 18*
46a And they come to Jericho	35 And it came to pass, as he drew
	nigh unto Jericho

46b   And as he went out from Jericho, with his disciples |and a great multitude, the son of Timaeus, Bartimaeus, a blind beggar, was sitting by the way side.

a certain blind man
sat by the way side begging.

36   And hearing a multitude going by, he enquired what this meant.

47   And when he heard that it was Jesus of Nazareth, he began to cry out, and say, Jesus, thou son of David, have mercy on me.

37   And they told him that Jesus of Nazareth passeth by.

38   And he cried, saying, Jesus, thou son of David, have mercy on me.

48   And many rebuked him, that he should hold his peace: but he cried out the more a great deal, Thou son of David, have mercy on me.

39   And they that went before rebuked him that he should hold his peace: but he cried out the more a great deal, Thou son of David, have mercy on me.

49   And Jesus stood still, and said, call ye him.
And they called the blind man, saying unto him, Be of good cheer;
50   rise, he calleth thee. And he, casting away his garment, sprang up and came to Jesus.

40   And Jesus stood, and commanded him to be brought unto him.

And when he was come near

51   And Jesus answered him and said What wilt thou that I should do unto thee?
And the blind man said unto him, Rabboni, that I may receive my sight.

he asked him
41   What wilt thou that I should do unto thee?
And he said,
Lord, that I may receive my sight.

52   And Jesus said unto him,
Go thy way; thy faith hath made thee whole.
And straight away he received his sight, and followed him in the way.

42   And Jesus said unto him,
Receive thy sight: thy faith hath made thee whole.
43   And immediately he received his sight and followed him, glorifying God; and all the people, when they saw it, gave praise unto God.

Striking is Mark's double introduction: "They come to Jericho," followed by "he went out from Jericho," with no intervening report of any incident which happened there. This was unacceptable to the other synoptics. (Luke, for instance, deletes the substance of Mark's verse 46b.) Burger infers from the clumsiness of Mark's introduction that his sources included a story of Jesus (with his disciples) curing a blind man on leaving Jericho—a story which probably began with the words Mark has utilized as verse 46b. But in order to make him leave Jericho, the evangelist has first to make him enter it, and therefore wrote 46a.

The story in Mark's source probably included all the material in his narrative except that in the quotation above which I have placed in a box outline.

If we subtract these verses, there remains a miracle story which is complete but for its failure to indicate how the patient first drew Jesus' attention. This too may well have been included in the source-story, but if so Mark has deleted the relevant material in order to supply his own version of how this happened, as an insertion (in the box outline). Burger's evidence that this is in fact a Marcan insertion is as follows:

(1) In the insertion, the patient twice addresses Jesus as "son of David," whereas in the miracle story (from the source) he uses a different title: "Rabboni" (master).

(2) The crowd is prominent in the insertion (there is a "great multitude" and "many" rebuked the patient), but in the miracle story there is no mention of a crowd, only of Jesus, his disciples, and the patient.

(3) In the miracle story the patient is told to "rise" and "be of good cheer" (verse 49), as if hitherto he had been sitting in silent gloomy dejection. This clashes with the insertion, which makes him shout and in need of restraint.

All three of these unevennesses are sufficiently prominent to have caught the attention of Luke, who smoothes them out. In his version

(1) The patient no longer addresses Jesus as "Rabboni," but as "Lord" (18:41), which does not clash with the previous allocution "son of David," as both are Christological titles.

(2) The crowd is not lost from sight but functions as a witness in 18:43b (which has no equivalent in *Mark*).

(3) The Marcan injunction to the patient to "rise" and "be of good cheer" is deleted, and so there is no contradiction with the earlier injunction to "hold his peace."

Returning now to *Mark,* the allocution "son of David" occurs only in the insertion (where it is repeated). It is the first time in his gospel that Mark has used the phrase. Burger claims that the words which follow it ("have mercy upon me") are nowhere else in the Bible used to address a human being (except of course in passages in *Matthew* and *Luke* obviously dependent on *Mark*. Lk. 16:24 is only apparently an exception, for the person here addressed is not the man Abraham, but Abraham exalted into heaven). They are, however, frequently used in the Psalms by suppliants addressing God, and so Mark would regard this as an appropriate way of addressing Jesus.

Mark, then, added "have mercy upon me" and "son of David" to a story about the miraculous cure of a beggar which reached him from tradition. His purpose seems to have been to show, by these additions, that Jesus was first recognized as son of David immediately before his entry into Jerusalem, and thus to prepare the words of acclamation with which he is greeted as he rides into the city (Mk. 11:9–10, RV):

> Hosanna:
> Blessed is he that cometh in the name of the Lord:
> Blessed is the kingdom that cometh of our Father David:
> Hosanna in the highest.

The blind Bartimaeus prepares this acclamation, since Mark represents him as following Jesus "in the way" (10:52) to Jerusalem (to which they all "draw near" in the very next verse, 11:1) as soon as he has been cured.

"Hosanna" is another cry of supplication from the Psalter, meaning "please help." Mark took it as an expression of joy—a misunderstanding, notes Burger, that persists in the Christian liturgy. The cry is thus, in this gospel context, not a record of a historical occurrence, but a construction of the evangelist. And Mark's "blessed is he that cometh in the name of the Lord" is quoted from Psalm 118:26, which was used at the annual festivals in Jerusalem and understood as a blessing on pilgrims coming up to the city.

The next sentence in *Mark* is designed as a comment on this blessing. In literal translation from the Greek, "blessed is the coming one," from the Psalm, is echoed by "blessed is the coming kingdom." Burger regards this wording as Christian, for Jewish tradition speaks of the "restoration," not the "coming" of the Davidic kingdom, and believes that God's kingdom—not David's—is coming. This passage too, then, is a literary construction, not a report of the actual behavior of a Jewish crowd.

Burger's inference from all this is that a pre-Marcan Christian narrator has made a traditional cry of welcome to Jewish pilgrims into a Messianic acclamation by adding a reference to David's kingdom that in fact ill accords with Jewish ideas. That the narrative existed before Mark utilized it is clear from the fact that it is but poorly adapted to his purpose. That Jesus' entry is to be linked with the coming of David's kingdom is but a very oblique way of calling him son of David. The crowd does not call him this at all, but only claims David as *their* father. (That this is unsatisfactory was felt by Matthew, who rewords what the crowd says as "Hosanna to the son of David," 21:9). All that Mark has done with this unit of earlier Christian tradition is to make clear—by prefacing it with the Bartimaeus incident—how he wants it understood: namely as establishing that Jesus is the son of David.

Inside Jerusalem Jesus is himself made by Mark to use the phrase "son of David" in a discussion of Psalm 110:1 and its implications concerning "the Christ." He says in the temple (Mk. 12:35-7): "How can the scribes say that the Christ is the son of David? David himself, inspired by the holy spirit, declared, 'The Lord said to my Lord, sit at my right hand, till I put thy enemies under thy feet.' David himself calls him Lord; so how is he his son?"

The passage quoted here from the Psalter seems to have been originally an assurance of divine protection to the king on his enthronement (62, p 13). In this sense "the Lord" (Yahweh) bade "my Lord" (the king) sit at his right hand. As, according to many modern commentators, this Psalm 110 is of Maccabean date, "my Lord" may well mean Simon Maccabeus, who reigned 142–134 BC (148, p 332). But the Psalm came in time to be ascribed to David, and "my Lord" to mean "David's Lord," the Messiah, so that the passage looked like a flat denial of the Messiah's Davidic descent. For if David in an inspired Psalm calls him "Lord," he can hardly be David's son.

The whole context in *Mark* in which this verse from Psalm 110 is quoted probably reached the evangelist as a tradition from a Christian community which denied Jesus' descent from David. That such communities existed is indicated, perhaps by the fourth gospel[2] but certainly by the non-canonical *Epistle of Barnabas* (written after AD 70, as it comments on the destruction of the Jerusalem temple). This eminently anti-Jewish work alleges (chapter 12) that David was inspired to speak Psalm 110 in order to provide means of refuting those who "in after times will assert that Christ is a son of David."

These words also show that Christian use of the Psalm apropos of the ancestry of the Messiah derives from the doctrinal needs of a Christian community, not from anything said by Jesus, for the epistle does not allege that Jesus himself used the Psalm in this or any other connection. Mark, however, has not only put the doctrine into Jesus' mouth, but also, in placing it after the Bartimaeus episode and the triumphal entry, can hardly have meant it to be understood in its original sense as a denial of his Davidic descent. Mark's intention seems rather to be to indicate that "son of David" is not a sufficiently exalted title for the Messiah, who is a supernatural being in heaven, sitting at God's right hand. (The same words from Psalm 110 are quoted in Hebrews 1:13 and in Acts 2:34–5 in order to emphasize this.) He is therefore far superior to David, who himself acknowledges this by calling him Lord, and so cannot be subordinate to him (as his son). If, then, he is given the title "son of David," he must nevertheless be regarded not as a mere earthly prince but as transcendental Lord.

In sum, by means of the incident with Bartimaeus and the triumphal entry, Mark represents Jesus as son of David, and yet shows from Jesus' own words in Jerusalem that this title does not do him full justice. In this connection Burger reminds us of Paul's formula "son of David according to the flesh" but "son of God in power according to the spirit of holiness by his resurrection from the dead." From *Mark,* then, the only evidence of Jesus' Davidic descent is:

(1) In chapter 10 a miracle story in which Mark has contrived to have Jesus addressed as "son of David."

(2) In chapter 11 a greeting from the crowd which does not state directly and unambiguously that he was the son of David.

(3) In chapter 12 a discussion of the title "son of David," which culminates in its rejection.

Furthermore, we saw that Mark records in chapter 6 an incident where Jesus is rejected as a nonentity because his family connections are known to be quite ordinary. The people who thus reject him show no consciousness that his lineage marks him out for a special role. All this shows that the individual traditions collected in the gospel do not all presuppose the idea of his Davidic descent.

Matthew and Luke supplement this Marcan material with genealogies tracing Jesus' ancestry back to David through Joseph (who, however, is nevertheless not represented as Jesus' physical father, as he is said to have been virgin-born). However, each of these two evangelists supplies Joseph with entirely different forefathers, and this (among other considerations) makes it obvious that the genealogies are fictions, not real family registers. Many theologians have given up trying to defend them.[3] Johnson, for instance, in a monograph devoted to the genealogies, reviews the various attempts to claim full historical authenticity for both and rejects them all as "unconvincing and strained" (112, p 144).

Johnson also discusses why Matthew's genealogy should include four women who—since the ancestry goes through the male line—could be deleted without impairing its continuity. They are Tamar and Rahab (both harlots), Ruth, and "the wife of Uriah," that is, Bathsheba, an adulteress, hardly the kind of ladies one would expect to find named in a genealogy of Jesus. Johnson shows that all four were much discussed in Jewish tradition, and that the judgment of the rabbis concerning them was by no means uniform. He suggests that Jews who favored a Levitical Messiah, as many did prior to AD 70, mentioned the four women as "blots in the Davidic ancestry," while those who thought the Messiah would be in David's line (particularly the Pharisees, who dominated the scene after the elimination of Sadducee and Essene influence in AD 70) had to admit that Tamar, Ruth, and Bathsheba were ancestors of David, and that Rahab had also been connected with the Davidic line.[4] They simply tried to "put the most charitable construction on them as was possible." He adds:

> Matthew wrote after AD 70 to Jewish or Jewish-Christian readers who were aware of [this] polemic on the ancestry of the Messiah which had been carried on within Judaism . . . . It was apparent to our author that the Pharisaic element within Judaism had become predominant—perhaps he himself had belonged to their number. Thus Matthew wrote to show that in every respect the Pharisaic expectation of the Messiah had been fulfilled in Jesus (112, pp 176–7).[5]

Matthew and Luke also represent Jesus as born in Bethlehem, which Luke (but not Matthew) describes as "David's city" (Lk. 2:4 and 11). The Old Testament makes David spend his youth in Bethlehem, but does not suggest that he was there as king; for Jewish tradition up to Matthew's time, Jerusalem, not Bethlehem, was the city of David. The prophecy of Micah 5:1 ff, which states (without mentioning David) that a ruler of Israel will come forth from Bethlehem, does not seem to have been understood by pre-Christian Jews as referring to the Messiah, for it is interpreted Messianically only in the Targum and not, for instance, at Qumran, even though Micah was used there. Hence, as Burger notes (31, p 24), the location of the Messiah's birth at Bethlehem was not common Jewish tradition ready and waiting for Christians to assimilate. He thinks (p 105) that the name "Bethlehem" was important in pre-gospel traditions about Herod's dealings with wise men from the East and about his ferocious behavior towards royal pretenders. Christian readers of the Old Testament would then have discovered Micah's prophecy about Bethlehem, and would also have known from 1 Samuel 16 that David had been there. In this way, the location of Jesus' birth there (in the traditions about Herod which had already been linked with him) would seem especially significant.[6]

Apart from these questionable stories about Jesus' origin and birth, Matthew and Luke are entirely dependent on *Mark* for what they say concerning his descent from David. Matthew, for instance, has frequently had him addressed as "son of David" in passages taken from *Mark*.[7] Mark's story of Bartimaeus' cure seems to have given Matthew the idea that as son of David Jesus works miracles. And so a crowd is made to react to the cure of a blind and dumb man (the incident does not occur in *Mark*) by asking: "Can this be the son of David?" (Mt. 12:23). Again, he adapts *Mark*'s account of the cleansing of the temple by making this incident simply a prelude to miraculous cures. Hardly has Jesus cleared the traders away when, in an incident lacking in *Mark,* the blind and lame come to him, and he is addressed as "son of David" as he cures them (Mt. 21:14–6).

Luke makes the cure of Bartimaeus occur while Jesus is still on his way to Jericho (see Lk. 18:35, the first verse I have quoted from *Luke* in the column on p 175). Luke follows it with an incident in Jericho (a story of a visit to a publican) not recorded in any other gospel; and this is in turn followed by the parable of the talents, which is also represented as told in Jericho. (Matthew, the only other evangelist to record it, places it later, when Jesus is already in Jerusalem.) Only then does Luke record Jesus' entry into Jerusalem.

Luke, by interposing two incidents between the cure of the blind man and the triumphal entry, destroys the linkage established between them in *Mark*; and he carefully deletes Mark's statement that the cured man took the "way" to Jerusalem with Jesus. He does not need this man's services at the triumphal entry, in Luke's version of which there is no mention of David, let alone of David's "kingdom." Commentators are agreed that one motive which guided Luke here was his desire to represent Jesus as politically inoffensive, to convince the Roman authorities that Christianity did not in any way imply disloyalty to Rome. Hence, anything in his sources which could be construed as militant Jewish Messianism he revised or deleted.[8]

Nevertheless, Luke does stress, in his story of Jesus' birth, that he is David's son. What this term signified to Luke is clear from his treatment of the third Marcan passage about the son of David, where Psalm 110 is quoted. In his gospel, he records this incident unaltered, but in Acts 2:32–6 he gives his answer to the question Jesus there asks, and says: the Messiah is David's son because born a descendant of David; but he is also David's Lord because God raised him from the dead and set him at his right hand. Obviously, if this is the answer to the question Jesus asks in the gospel, it could not be given at the time of asking, but only after his resurrection, in the situation presupposed by the narrative in Acts. In Luke's view, then, Jesus, while alive on earth, was of David's line, but his enthronement as Davidic Messiah came only with his exaltation after his resurrection.

We are now in a position to see how baseless is the argument that Jesus' Davidic descent must be historical fact because it is recorded as early as the Pauline letters. Mark, we saw, at two points imposed the idea onto his material, and at a third adapted to his own purposes a tradition which expressly denied it. The rest of his gospel does nothing to link Jesus with David, and even includes material which militates against any such link. Matthew and Luke knew of no additional relevant traditions except their obviously legendary genealogies and birth stories. And John seems not to accept Jesus' Davidic origin at all. As for Paul, his statement on the matter is not put out as historical information, but as an article of faith.

9

The Shroud of Turin in the Light of the New Testament

I THE HISTORY AND NATURE OF THE SHROUD

The holy shroud of Turin has been called the one relic claiming to be associated with the life of Jesus that has "a serious claim to be considered genuine."[1] It is a strip of cloth, about 14 feet long and 3½ feet wide, bearing on half its length the impression of the back, and, on the other half, of the front of a naked man. It is argued that Jesus' body was laid on the unrolled cloth (so as to cover half its length) and that the remaining length was then drawn over the face and chest down to the feet, so that the whole came to receive impressions of both front and back of the corpse. The champions of the shroud offer it not as evidence of Jesus' death and burial — for we are repeatedly told that "no serious scholar" now doubts that he existed and was crucified by the Romans (Nineham, 149, p 76) — but as testimony to his resurrection. For, if the impressions on the cloth were truly made by a corpse, then this corpse must have remained in the shroud for a day or so (the time needed to form the impressions) but not long enough for putrifaction to set in, which would have destroyed the impressions and eventually the cloth.

Head, trunk and limbs are clearly recognizable on the Turin cloth, and the face, hands, side, and feet are marked with stains which correspond well with wrist and foot wounds which one might expect in a crucified man,[2] with the side wound of the fourth gospel, and with blood trickles from a crown of thorns. That the relic thus harmonizes a detail known only from the fourth gospel with details from the synoptics is, to my mind, a ground for suspicion. A pathologist, Dr. M. M. Baden has recently pointed to the blood trickles from the scalp as evidence of forgery—on the ground that blood from a scalp wound does not flow in rivulets but mats the hair (*Medical World News*, Dec. 22, 1980).

Much has been made of the fact that the figure on the cloth stands out more sharply when one looks at a photographic plate or negative of it, as was discovered when it was first photographed in 1898. What gives the markings the character of a good negative is that the upstanding or protruding areas (for example, the brow and nose) have imparted darker stains to the cloth than the cavities and depressions. Normally on any object or person the "highs" are well lighted, while the "lows" are shaded. In the case of the shroud's images, the "highs" are dark, while the "lows" are light—hence, the typically negative character of these images. Obviously, a medieval forger could not have *aimed* at painting the face in a way which would look crude on the actual shroud but majestic (as it does) on a photographic plate. To this I shall return.

Historical evidence does not inspire confidence in the relic's authenticity. Its known certain history begins as late as the fourteenth century, although there is evidence that it may have been in Constantinople 150 years earlier. Robert de Clari, a chronicler of the Fourth Crusade, said that a monastery of the city exhibited the cloth in which our Lord was wrapped, on which his figure could plainly be seen. Clari added that no one knew what happened to this relic after the sack of the city by European crusaders in 1204.[3]

There is no earlier record of the shroud, as is admitted by the more sober of its advocates.[4] About 1200 Constantinople was so crammed with relics that one may speak of a veritable industry with its own factories. Blinzler (a Catholic New Testament scholar) lists, as examples: letters in Jesus' own hand, the gold brought to the baby Jesus by the wise men, the twelve baskets of bread collected after the miraculous feeding of the 5000, the throne of David, the trumpets of Jericho, the axe with which Noah made the Ark, and so on (19, p 40).

The certain history of the shroud begins in the 1350s. In 1353 the French knight Geoffrey I of Charny founded the abbey of Lirey, near Troyes, and a few years later he or his widow presented it with the shroud, doubtless to encourage pilgrims as a source of revenue. He never indicated how it had come into his possession, and his heirs did not seem to know either; for while his son said it was given him as a present, his granddaughter held that he had acquired it as war booty. (He had participated in the crusade of 1346.)

During war disturbances of 1418, the abbey clergy of Lirey gave the shroud for safekeeping to the then Lord of Lirey, and in 1452 his widow sold it to the House of Savoy. It came to be kept in the Court Chapel at Chambéry, where it was damaged and very nearly destroyed by fire. It was transferred to Turin in 1578 and is today kept in the Chapel of the House of Savoy, adjoining the Cathedral there, with the archbishop of Turin as its official custodian.

If we accept that the shroud was in Constantinople and disappeared in the sack of that city in 1204, where was it between then and its appearance in

France about 1355? It may have been taken from Constantinople to Syria or even Palestine, for Christian Templars were in Jerusalem until 1244, and the Latin Kingdom of Jerusalem survived until the fall of Acre in 1291. The relic could have been taken to France on the Christian withdrawal from these territories, or it may have remained in the Near East until falling into the hands of its first known possessor, Geoffrey of Charny, who, as we saw, had been in the East in the Crusade of 1346.

In the early part of the present century, textile experts identified the fabric of the Turin shroud as herringbone twill of a type unknown in France until after the fourteenth century, but evidenced for Roman times in Syria, Pompeii, and Mainz, and still made in Syria today (see Blinzler, 19, p 32). Clearly then, the shroud could not have acquired its markings in medieval France unless the cloth had been imported; but it could, from this evidence, have been painted or otherwise treated in Constantinople at any time.

In 1969 the church authorities in Turin permitted scientists to examine the shroud. Their names were not divulged until 1976, and this makes one wonder whether the authorities are anxious not to publicize any findings except those which favor the relic's authenticity, or which turn out to be irrelevant to the case against it. The best way of establishing whether the cloth derives from the right century to be the shroud of Jesus would be a carbon-14 test. But this has not been permitted, neither in 1969 nor in the next round of tests which took place in October 1978. In 1973 samples (mainly threads) were taken from the cloth, and by 1976 a number of reports had been made. Professor Raes (of the Ghent Institute of Textile Technology) reported minute traces of cotton in the linen, showing that it had been made on equipment used also for weaving cotton. This makes it likely that the fabric came from the Middle East, as cotton is not grown in Europe (although we should not overlook that the cotton-manufacturing industry was imported into Europe and flourished in Spain as early as the thirteenth century). It does not, of course, prove that the imprints on the shroud were made in the Middle East. A European or Byzantine forger could have used imported cloth. It is not necessary to suppose that he would deliberately have chosen such material for the purpose of associating it with Palestine,[5] for international trade was well developed in the Middle Ages and earlier, and linen which might come his way was as likely as not to have been imported.

Dr. Max Frei, a Zürich forensic scientist and botanist, examined the pollen on the shroud, and was widely reported in the international press as having found evidence of plants which grew only in Palestine in the first century of the Christian era. Frei in fact made no such claim. He stressed that the pollen on the shroud does not enable us to date it, but may identify the localities at which it has been exposed to the air. He did find pollen from desert halophytes — "salt plants" which grow only in very saline desert soils such as those in the Jordan valley. I have noted that the shroud could have been in Palestine between 1204 and 1355. Another possibility is that it was manufactured in Palestine or

Syria, and exposed to the open air then, before acquiring its peculiar markings (in Constantinople or anywhere it had been sent by way of trade.) Frei also found pollen characteristic of the Anatolian region of Turkey. As the shroud may well have been in Constantinople, this is not particularly significant. Furthermore, Crusaders captured Smyrna, even nearer the region suggested by Frei's pollen, in 1345, and if the shroud had remained in the Middle East after its disappearance from Constantinople, it might then have fallen into hands which brought it to France.

Concerning the dark stains which look like blood from a crucified body, standard forensic tests made on specimens from the cloth have failed to reveal any traces of blood. Some of the shroud's advocates have argued that the original blood has been destroyed by some kind of force released at the resurrection. Wilson in his recent book speaks in this connection of "some form of thermonuclear flash" (218, p 210) which occurred at the resurrection and dissolved the blood on the cloth. In other words, markings we ought to find and do not are explained in terms of a process we understand still less.

The latest scientific discoveries have frequently been invoked by religious enthusiasts over the ages. "In the 1920s, people with a degree of religious dottiness thought they were receiving divine or demonic messages through wireless waves, just as in the nineteenth century they had similar obsessions about domestic gas" (227a, p 151). Wilson is appealing to miracle. The resurrection was a miracle during the course of which power emanated from Jesus' body, comparable with that released in an atomic explosion. Of course, once miracles are accepted as accounting for the markings, then there need be no embarrassment, even if it had to be argued that what once had conceivably been bloodstains had changed into rhubarb.

Since Wilson's book appeared, the microscopist Dr. Walter McCrone has published the results of a study of thirty-two samples taken from the shroud. He found significant amounts of a very fine red iron oxide used since prehistoric time as a paint pigment, but only in those portions of the cloth which are marked with an image, not in the material as a whole. He also found an "animal tempera, a common paint medium during all of the past several thousand years." He inferred that "the entire image appears . . . to be the work of a skilful, well-informed artist." The only alternative inference, he says, is that this artist merely enhanced an earlier image that is authentic, but he thinks this unlikely. (See his two papers in *The Microscope,* 28 [1980], pp 105–28.) Joe Nickell, a professional stage magician, has achieved some interesting results in experimenting with cloth in order to find what conditions would produce an image comparable to that on the shroud. He realized that a bas-relief would, more readily than a statue or a real human body, give an undistorted image with the perspective of a human face and figure seen from the front. He says:

> Soaking cloth in hot water, I carefully moulded it to a bas-relief, allowed it to dry, and then applied pigment—rather as one would do a rubbing of a gravestone . . .

I selected a mixture of myrrh and aloes as my pigment, stroking it on with a dauber. Careful application produces the negative images illustrated [in Nickell's article]; and photographic negatives returned positive images of remarkable fidelity.

He adds that all this is consistent with medieval technology, since rubbings originated in China in the second century BC and had been used in Europe as early as the twelfth century (147, p 31).

II THE SHROUD AND THE GOSPELS

Attempts have naturally been made to correlate the evidence of the markings on the cloth with the gospel Passion and burial narratives. But few who have attempted this are acquainted with critical theology, and in consequence all four gospel narratives have naively been treated as basically reliable and as differing only as one might expect eyewitness reports of the same events to differ. In fact, however, as readers of my earlier chapters will be aware, critical theologians have long since acknowledged that the gospels are tendentious, in that each gives, for example, a different twist to a parable or teaching (put into Jesus' mouth in some earlier document or tradition) in order to inculcate the view of Jesus current in the Christian community to which the writer happened to belong. Mark, we saw, is well removed in time from the events he narrates, and Matthew and Luke are secondary to him and adapt his narrative in order to argue views of their own—not because they are better informed concerning the alleged historical facts underlying *Mark*. The fourth evangelist gives yet another version because his theological premises are again different.

All three synoptics, for instance, agree in representing Simon of Cyrene as carrying Jesus' cross, whereas the fourth gospel makes him carry it himself. Commentators have repeatedly observed that, unlike the synoptics, the fourth evangelist is anxious to represent Jesus as strong and triumphant at his crucifixion, and for that reason could not accept any tradition that the Lamb of God who takes away our sins needed to have his cross carried for him. The shroud's advocates resort here, characteristically, to harmonization. Thus Wilson interprets features in the shoulder region of the cloth as due to the chafing of the cross Jesus carried, while markings on the knees of the figure are taken to mean that he fell repeatedly under the burden, so that Simon was called in to relieve him of it (218, pp 25, 37).

Mark follows this story of the walk to Golgotha with a brief account of the crucifixion. As Jesus breathed his last, "the curtain of the temple was torn in two, from top to bottom" (Mk. 15:38). Commentators concede that this is "not a historical reminiscence but a symbolic declaration of the meaning of Jesus' death" (Anderson, 2, p 347). The centurion at the cross, seeing him die, acknowledged him as "truly the son of God" (15:39). Before the evangelist passes on to the next incident—how he came to be taken from the cross and buried—he notes that his death was witnessed "from afar" by a number of women who had ministered to him in Galilee and accompanied him to Jerusalem (15:40–1). Now Mark's account of both crucifixion and burial may well be based on earlier documents; but these two verses about the women witnesses, placed between the narratives of the two main events, are likely to be entirely from Mark's own hand, for they are clearly, as Taylor says (198, p 598), an addendum to the crucifixion narrative (after this has terminated in the climax of the centurion's cry) and preparatory to the accounts of the burial and resurrection, where the women are also introduced as witnesses.

In these same two verses, three of the Galilean women are named: Mary Magdalene, "Mary the mother of James the younger and of Joses," and Salome. To us who know post-Marcan Christian tradition, the first of these three names (if not the others) has a familiar ring; and it comes as something of a shock to learn that none of the women (nor, for that matter, James and Joses) has earlier been mentioned by Mark.

It is an essential part of Mark's Christology that Jesus should die alone, deserted by man and even by God. It is in order to show both the magnitude of the burden he assumed, and his strength in bearing it, that the evangelist makes him speak (as his sole utterance from the cross) the opening words of Psalm 22, "My God, why hast thou forsaken me?" Since Mark wants him to die alone, his disciples are represented as deserting him at his arrest: "they all left him and fled" (14:50). Hence only the Galilean women who had come up with him to Jerusalem are available as Christian witnesses of his death. Mark's statement that they stood "afar off" from the cross is not, as some commentators suppose, to be accepted as historically correct because of its modesty (in contrast with the claim of the fourth gospel that both women and disciples stood right under the cross). Mark's "modesty" is here due to the conflicting motives that inspire his narrative. He wants the women present so that his readers do not doubt that Jesus really died on the cross; yet they must stand "afar off" because he also wants him to die forsaken and deserted.

Galilean women, then, see Jesus die (Mk. 15:40). They also see him buried (15:47), and, according to Mark's next verse (16:1), they go to the tomb on Easter morning and find it empty. Mark is anxious to convince his readers that the tomb found empty was really Jesus' tomb, and that the women did not find an empty tomb because they went to the wrong one. Hence the evangelist is careful to stress that they had witnessed the burial: "they beheld where he was laid" (15:47). The witnesses are named in this same verse as Mary Magdalene and Mary of Joses. In the next verse the women who find the tomb empty are said to be Mary Magdalene, Mary of James, and Salome. It seems then, that the traditions on which Mark drew supplied him with one list of names for the burial and another list for the discovery of the empty tomb (only Mary Magdalene being common to both lists). In 15:40, which we have already suspected to be Mark's own original writing—placed as it is after his narrative of the crucifixion but before his account of the burial—he clearly tries to combine the two lists into one, by specifying (as witnesses of Jesus' death) both Mary Magdalene and Salome, and by making the Mary of Joses of 15:47 and the Mary of James of 16:1 into one person: Mary the mother of James and Joses (cf. Taylor, 198, p 652).

The point of this analysis goes beyond the mere details; for if my suggestion is correct, Mark's narrative of the death, burial, and empty tomb is thereby shown to be, not straightforward historical reporting, but an attempt to synthesize earlier traditions—and we can know nothing of their provenance or reliability. Nobody knows who was Joses, whose Mary (his mother?) witnessed the burial, or who was James, whose Mary found the tomb empty. But they were presumably known (at any rate by hearsay) to the Christian community in which the underlying traditions (on which Mark drew) arose. If "Mary of Joses" means that Mary was his mother, then the upshot is that in some Christian community the mother of a man himself known perhaps only from tradition was believed to have witnessed Jesus' burial.

I have noted that the shroud shows markings which can be correlated with the wound in Jesus' side recorded only in the fourth gospel. The story there is that the soldiers broke the legs of the two victims crucified with him; then, seeing that he was already dead, they did not treat him in the same way, but one of them pierced his side with a spear, "and at once there came out blood and water" (Jn. 19:34). The shroud's advocates take all this as historical. But there are difficulties.

First, the incident is alleged to have occurred in fulfillment of Old Testament "prophecy," and may therefore be one of the many gospel details that were fabricated to give such an appearance. Two Old Testament texts are alleged by the evangelist to have been fulfilled by the soldiers' behavior towards Jesus: the direction in Exodus 12:46 for the preparation of the paschal lamb ("Not a bone of him shall be broken") and Zechariah 12:10 ("They shall look on him whom they have pierced").

Second, the whole story in Jn. 19:31-7 of the leg breaking and the spear thrust is a tradition which the evangelist was not able to work with complete consistency into the next section of his own narrative. For the story begins (verse 31) by stating that the Jews, anxious that the bodies should not remain exposed during the Sabbath, requested Pilate to have the sufferers killed and their bodies taken down. But after the leg breaking and the spear thrust, and the explanation of their scriptural significance, we read (verse 38), that Pilate was approached by Joseph of Arimathea, who asked permission to take Jesus' body down; "and Pilate gave him leave." But if we are to believe verse 31, Joseph came too late, for the Jews had already persuaded the governor to have the bodies removed. Commentators note that the repetition of the verb "to take" (from the cross) in these two verses shows that the intervening passage (about the leg breaking and spear thrust) represents an insertion, after which the evangelist has to work back to the topic of verse 31 (taking the body down).

In Mark's version of Joseph's approach, Pilate is surprised to learn from him that Jesus is already dead (Mk. 15:44). This is certainly irreconcilable with the inserted story of Jn. 19:31-7, according to which the governor had himself earlier agreed to have the deaths of the sufferers expedited. In sum, John's story of the leg breaking and spear thrust is not only absent from the synoptics, but also includes a detail which is excluded by Mark and which does not harmonize even with the next section in *John*.

Furthermore, contrary to what has often been affirmed, modern medicine is unable to explain the issue of water (together with blood) from Jesus' side, as a comprehensive article on the subject in a Berlin medical journal conceded in 1963 (176). On this point advocates of the shroud have resorted to desperate expedients. Barbet, a Paris surgeon who wrote on the shroud in 1940, explained the water as pericardial fluid, although not more than about half a thimble full of fluid could come from the pericardium. It has also been suggested that Jesus was suffering from a pleural effusion. In fact, the lungs are at sub-atmospheric pressure, so that if a man's side is perforated when there is fluid in the pleural cavity, air will go in, not fluid come out. To remove the fluid, it has to be sucked out through the perforation under pressure. It is sad to think how much ingenuity has been expended to authenticate what is obviously a legend.

The shroud's advocates agree that, only if Jesus was buried unwashed can the authenticity of the relic be upheld; for washing would have removed all blood from the corpse, and there would then have been no markings on the cloth from wounds. Accordingly, Wilson argues that Joseph of Arimathea was unable to wash the body as he had to bury it quickly. He also argues that the very good quality of the Turin linen—three-to-one twill known in silks but not in linens from the first century, and differing from the plain weave most common then—is perhaps to be expected, as Joseph was a wealthy man (218, p 53). But analysis of the gospels' burial narratives strongly suggests that the whole idea of Joseph working in a hurry was imposed by Mark on earlier tradition which in no way suggested it; and Joseph's wealth was introduced by Matthew, expanding Mark's narrative for purposes of his own. Let us study the details.

Joseph is not known apart from the incident where he asks Pilate if he may take the body from the cross and bury it. Mark represents him as a pious Jew, "a respected member of the council who was also himself looking for the kingdom of God" (Mk. 15:43). "The council" could mean the Jerusalem Sanhedrin or some local council elsewhere. And in "looking for the kingdom" he was simply sharing the Messianic expectations of other Jews. As a pious Jew, he would naturally wish Jesus to be buried before nightfall, for the Law stipulates that a criminal's body shall not remain at nightfall on the gibbet (Deuteronomy 21:23). Some have argued that this story must be authentic, since no Christian would have fabricated a tradition which made Jesus receive burial from a Jew instead of from his own supporters. But the oldest extant Christology (that of the Pauline letters) represents him as dying in shame and humiliation, and it is in the spirit of this early tradition that his supporters should desert him at the end, as (we saw) they do in Mark's account.

In *Mark* Joseph has an additional motive for completing the burial by nightfall: the Sabbath will commence at 6 P.M. (In the Jews' reckoning, a day runs from evening to evening, not from one midnight to the next.) However, according to Mark's preceding Passion narrative, the day of Jesus' death and of Joseph's approach to Pilate was the Passover, and, as Nineham says, "the prohibitions with regard to Passover were nearly as strict as those relating to the Sabbath" (148, p 433). Nineham thinks that the burial story reached Mark "from a cycle of tradition which knew of *no chronological* tie-up between the crucifixion and the Passover," and that Mark has simply incorporated it, without adapting it to his Passion chronology.

Mark makes Joseph's task of completing the burial in time impossible by delaying his approach to Pilate until "evening had come" (that is, 6 P.M.). Mark chooses this hour for the first incident in his burial narrative because throughout Chapter 15 he is imposing an artificial scheme on the principal events, making them occur at three-hour intervals. Thus Jesus is delivered to Pilate "as soon as it was morning," and is crucified "at the third hour" (9 A.M.); from the sixth to the ninth hour darkness covers the land, and at the ninth hour (3 P.M.) Jesus utters his last cry and dies. Then, "when evening had come," Joseph seeks permission to take the body from the cross.

Clearly, then, this artificial time scheme leaves Joseph with no opportunity of completing his task before the Jewish Sabbath begins. Mark nevertheless represents him, after his approach to Pilate, as embarking on the further errand of "buying a linen cloth" before he proceeds to take the body down, wrap it in this shroud, and place it in "a tomb which had been hewn out of a rock." Mark is here presumably reproducing the story as he found it in some earlier tradition, where there would have been no three-hour intervals, where Joseph could therefore have approached Pilate before evening, with sufficient time for all the operations alleged.

How quickly tradition about Jesus grew and changed can be seen from the ways in which Matthew and Luke have adapted Mark's account of Joseph. Luke took Mark's phrase "a respected member of the council" to mean that Joseph was a member of the Jerusalem Sanhedrin, which had handed Jesus over to Pilate. (Perhaps Luke did not know that there were councils in other Jewish towns.) And so Luke is at pains to explain that Joseph was "a good and righteous man," who had not consented to "the purpose and deed" of his Sanhedrin colleagues (Lk. 23:50-1). Matthew (who knew *Mark* but not *Luke*) read in *Mark* that Joseph was "looking for the kingdom" and supposed that this meant that he was expecting the kingdom to be brought by Jesus, and was therefore "a disciple of Jesus" (Mt. 27:57).

Wilson describes Joseph of Arimethea as a "wealthy and influential secret disciple of Jesus" (218, p 40) and is apparently unaware that both his Christianity and his wealth are Matthew's own additions to tradition; for it is Matthew who makes Joseph not—as did Mark—"a respected member of the council," but "a rich man." Commentators explain this change as due to the evangelist's desire to link Jesus' burial with that of the suffering servant of Yahweh, who had his grave made "with a rich man in his death" (Isaiah 53:9). So Joseph's wealth, invoked by Wilson to explain the exceptionally fine quality of the shroud's fabric, is not known historical fact but probably a twist given to an earlier tradition about him to make a theological point.[6]

Mark does not say that Joseph anointed the body for burial. On the contrary, it is because no anointing had taken place that the women came to the tomb a day and two nights later with "spices, so that they might . . . anoint him" (16:1). Most commentators agree that it is hard to credit the women with the intention of anointing a body that had been dead in a Middle Eastern climate for this long; but Wilson accepts what Mark here says as true. As they approach the tomb, they wonder "who will roll away the stone for us from the door?" (Mk. 16:3). Since, according to this same gospel, they had witnessed the burial on Good Friday, it is strange that this difficulty crosses their mind only on Easter morning. But, as we saw, Mark had his own motive for making them witnesses of the burial, however much their doing so may create difficulties in what he later narrates. Taylor says that the women's question, "who will roll away the stone?" arises from their purpose (to anoint the body), and if this is held to be improbable, then their question "must be dramatic and imaginative rather than historical" (198, p 605).

The women find the stone already rolled away, and when they enter the tomb a young man dressed in a white robe tells them that Jesus is risen. In the scriptures supernatural beings habitually wear white; and Nineham gives evidence that "young man" was a not uncommon designation of an angel at the time when Mark wrote. It is clear that the assurance of this angel is a necessary part of Mark's proof of the resurrection—the mere emptiness of the tomb would not have sufficed to evidence the fact. That the angel's testimony is thus an integral part of the empty-tomb story does not inspire confidence in the historicity of the whole. This is recognized by Christian commentators. Beare, for instance, says:

> If we do not share the early Christian belief in angels who take part with human form and human speech in incidents of human life, there is no reason for us to attach any historical value whatsoever to the story, even to the minimal element that women came to the tomb and found it empty (12, p 241).

Jesus, then, can be regarded as having been buried unwashed if we accept the improbable narrative of Mark. But it is flatly contradicted by the fourth gospel, which states that the burial was a normal one—"according to the custom of the Jews" (Jn. 19:40)—and that Joseph, assisted by Nicodemus (one of the group of characters known only from this gospel) anointed the body in the process with "about a hundred pounds' weight" of substances. John habitually exaggerates quantities in this way. (At 2:6–10 he makes Jesus turn into wine water in six jars "each holding twenty or thirty gallons.") But Wilson accepts

Nicodemus' one hundred pounds as historical, and harmonizes this with the synoptics by supposing that the spices were not used for washing or anointing the body, but were packed round it as anti-putrifacients, leaving the washing to be attempted, as in the synoptic narrative—not, of course, in John's resurrection narrative—by the women on Easter morning (218, p 41). So he wants spices to be used at the burial (as John alleges), but the washing to be delayed (as the synoptics allege).

This harmonization supplies the answer to a further problem. If cloth is wound round a body, any image produced will be grossly distorted. But the impressions on the shroud show no distortion, and could have been produced only if the cloth lay flat, like a photographic plate, under and over the whole body. Wilson argues that the great quantity of spices packed around the body did enable the shroud to rest flat on top of it. Unfortunately for this view, the fourth evangelist, who alone supplies these spices, makes clear that no shroud was used for the burial. I will summarize the details briefly.

Mark does at least assert that a shroud was used, but says that the body was "wrapped" in it (15:46). The Greek verb used means "press in," "pack," "force in." Matthew and Luke obviously found the word somewhat unseemly and replaced it with one that means "envelop." But the clear implication of all three synoptics is that the material was bound tightly round the body. In John's account, however, there is no shroud, but "linen cloths" (bandages). Wilson recognizes the difficulty, but decides that the word used by John means "cloths in general, which could incorporate shroud and bands" (218, p 42).[7] Earlier this century Vignon had indulged in similar fanciful harmonization. He understood the impressions on the shroud as produced by emanations from the body. But impressions can be made on cloth only if it has been sensitized in some way, for example, by impregnation with oil or aloes. He therefore interpreted John's account of the anointing of the body as an anointing of the shroud, even though there is no shroud in John's narrative (204, p 164).

The fourth gospel only mentions grave clothes for a theological, not a historical purpose, namely to dispose of any suggestion that the body had been stolen from the tomb by his disciples. (That the earliest Christian apologists were anxious to refute this charge is clear from Matthew's clumsy story that the tomb was guarded by soldiers. To accommodate this story Matthew has to change the motive of the women's Easter visit to the tomb. They could not be represented as expecting to get past an armed guard, so in this gospel their purpose is said to be to "see the sepulchre," not to anoint the body.) In John's narrative Peter enters the tomb and sees "the linen cloths lying, and the napkin, that was upon his head, not lying with the linen cloths, but rolled up in a place by itself." Clearly, robbers would not have troubled to remove cloths from the body, still less to fold the napkin. Haenchen notes that the narrator is at any rate prevented by his good genius from asserting that the cloths too were rolled up tidily (93, p 556).

There is an obvious motive for the concoction of all the gospel empty-tomb stories. Paul (at an earlier stage in the growing traditions about Jesus) had based the resurrection faith solely on the recorded appearances of the risen Jesus to named individuals (including Paul himself). But mere appearances could be dismissed by skeptics as hallucinations. An empty tomb was obviously a more objective warrant. That Mark's story was dictated by this motive is clear not only from its internal implausibilities, but also from the fact that the three later evangelists are not content with an empty tomb. They elaborate Mark's tendency to posit objective and tangible evidence of the resurrection by insisting on the physical reality of the risen body. Matthew, for instance, says that, immediately after the angel's message to the women, Jesus himself appeared to them, and "they took hold of his feet." (This incident is in part but an expansion of Mark's empty tomb story; for the risen one simply gives the women exactly the same message they had already received from the angel at the tomb, namely that they are to tell the disciples to go to Galilee, where they will see Jesus: Mk. 16:7; Mt. 28:7 and 10; cf. p 169.) Luke establishes the physical reality of Jesus' resurrection by making him eat "broiled fish" in front of his disciples (cf. p 45). John has it that he showed them the nail marks in his hands (Jn. 20:25–6).

Again, these discrepancies are of interest not in themselves, but because they show how different apologists made up different stories for a given theological purpose. The stories they offer are so divergent that they were obviously either freely composed to illustrate the required thesis, or, as Haenchen suggests, drawn from "a flood of local traditions which had established themselves in one place or another" (93, p 558). Robinson has argued that the differences in the empty-tomb traditions are but relatively minor legendary accretions, and no more than what one would expect in genuine accounts of so confusing a scene. Evans has replied that the differences can be accounted for in terms of "conscious editorial modification," which governs each evangelist's whole version (see p 15).

Wilson suggests that the evangelists wrote about an authentic tomb, which has been identified by archaeologists. This is grossly misleading. There is not a single existing site in Jerusalem which is mentioned in connection with Christian history before 326, when Helena (mother of Constantine) saw a cave that had just been excavated, and which was identified with Jesus' tomb. The fourth-century Christians explained away earlier ignorance of it by alleging that Hadrian had covered over the original sites of the crucifixion and resurrection. Kathleen Kenyon, the authority to whom Wilson refers, claims no more than that the available evidence does not prove that the traditional sites cannot be authentic (120, p 154).

Is the shroud a forgery? Bulst rejects such "realistic" and "cunning" forgery as unparalleled in the Middle Ages (29, p 37). Rinaldi declares that "it implies a knowledge of chemistry, anatomy and physiology . . . quite inadmissible" (160, p 48). This seems to me quite untrue. In former times as now, results are obvious to many who have no idea of how the processes resorted to can be explained scientifically. Furthermore, although it is known that the arts of deceit have been practiced, often with great success, throughout human history, it is very difficult to write a technical history of forgery in the way one can write a history of the techniques of shipbuilding. Forgers and magicians are not given to publishing the secrets of their craft, and a modern scientist is not in a good position to say what knowledge and technical resources were available to a forger in the Dark and Middle Ages. One thing, however, can be taken for granted—that men were then as inventive, ingenious, dishonest, and acquisitive as they are now.

Postscript: Since this chapter was written, the *Skeptical Inquirer* (v. 6, 1982, pp. 15–36) has published three important articles, grouped together as a "Special Critique on the Shroud of Turin." In the first, Marvin M. Mueller summarizes the work and findings of Joe Nickell and Walter McCrone, to which I have referred above, and stresses the need to date the shroud cloth by radiocarbon methods. He notes, however, that even a date of AD 30 plus or minus 100 years could not rule out forgery, since an artist might well have obtained ancient linen. In the second article, McCrone states, on the basis of his previous work, that "the entire image was produced by an artist using iron earth and vermillon pigments in a tempera medium during the middle of the fourteenth century." The third article, by Steven D. Schafersman, critically reviews recent publications (including the book by Wilson) which defend the authenticity of the shroud.

10

Myth and Authenticity in
the New Testament

I REINTERPRETATION OF NEW TESTAMENT MYTH

In the twenty-seven books of the New Testament there is not one Jesus but many, and from the beginning Christians were deeply divided about his fundamental nature. I said in *Did Jesus Exist?* (p 120) that, if he had really lived, early Christian literature would not disagree so radically as to what kind of person he was.

Reviewers replied that such disagreement is not unknown in sectarian literature, religious or otherwise, and that no one infers from the quarrels between Marxist groups that Marx did not exist. But were there many such groups within a generation of Marx's death? Did they all have different versions of his biography? Did each have a different text of *Das Kapital*? If none of these suggestions is the case, I cannot see the relevance of citing Marx. If the controversy was simply about the interpretation of documents agreed to have been written by Marx, then it is not relevant to his historicity, any more than the existence of various schools of thought about what Aristotle meant impugn his historicity.

Today many theologians do not believe that Jesus was a superhuman figure whose life was a pageant of supernatural events of revelation. As Goulder puts it: his "miracles" and his "resurrection" now find "this-worldly explanations," with the concomitant that "the belief that the Bible is infallible truth is discredited" (83, p 55). For instance, Goulder explains the belief in the resurrection by supposing that, within two days of Jesus' death, Peter became convinced that he must have been raised to God's right hand, and would return

197

soon in power. When this idea was passed on to others, "the power of hysteria in a small community" made them think that he had actually appeared to them briefly by passing through locked doors (101, p 59).

Bultmann and his pupils have shown how much in the gospels consists of material created by and shaped to fit the needs of the early church, and that, even if the records do preserve a few of Jesus' actual words, these have been put into new contexts and reinterpreted. But the same theologians who concede that much of the behavior ascribed to him in the gospels is mythical, claim nevertheless to have—in Cupitt's phrase—"found salvation" through his "voice and person" (83, p 169). Cupitt meets "the historical objection that we do not have one single certainly authentic saying" of his by replying: "Though particular words are uncertain," Jesus' "voice" is clear. "The voice precipitates the hearer into a final confrontation with God" (p 39).

The method which leads to such conclusions consists in regarding a myth not as "a fairy-tale, not true," but as "a story of profound meaning by which men guide their lives" (Goulder, 83, p vii). Myth, then, is not simply to be set aside as error. The traditional doctrine of the atonement is a myth, but it nevertheless remains true that "God has somehow dealt with evil" (Frances Young, 101, p 35). Rodwell urges that "the line between science and non-science should not be drawn too sharply," and that "most scientific theories, after all, originated in myths" (83, p 71). But in science obviously false hypotheses are dropped when better ones become available, not reinterpreted so as to be understood as expressions of profound truths.

Frances Young tries to build on the fact that physicists have discovered that light seems to possess some of the properties of particles and some of the properties of waves; that its behavior cannot be explained in terms of a conceptual model based exclusively on the one or the other. Likewise, she says, Christians explain the world with two kinds of models: "the scientific model," which posits natural causes, and "mythological or symbolical models" which (albeit inadequately) represent "the religious and spiritual dimension of our experience." These latter models are "indefinable in terms of human language, and in their totality inconceivable within the limited powers and experience of the finite human mind" (101, p 34). It is already clear that she does not realize that the purpose of a conceptual model is to explain the unfamiliar in terms of phenomena which *are* familiar (waves, particles, etc.). Explanation in terms of an "inconceivable" model will inevitably be a fruitless undertaking. And if the model is "indefinable in terms of human language" we shall not even be able to talk accurately about it.

A good example of reinterpretation of gospel myths as pointers to something more subtle than what they literally affirm is Perrin's "new approach" to the resurrection narratives. He begins by noting the following facts. In *Mark* (which originally ended at 16:8) the risen Jesus does not appear to anyone at all; in *Matthew* he appears to his disciples only in Galilee; and in *Luke* he appears only in Jerusalem and its environs. These contradictions make it impossible to accept all three versions as literally true. Perrin therefore decides that, rather than ask whether there was any resurrection at all, and if so what Jesus did subsequently, it will be more profitable to inquire what the evangelists believed happened, and how their beliefs differ.

Following this lead he argues that Mark understood God to have taken the risen Jesus straight to heaven, where he was to stay until his return to earth to effect the final judgment; that Matthew agreed with this except that he believed Jesus to have appeared to his disciples in Galilee "as it were proleptically, in anticipation of his final glory, having been given 'all authority in heaven and earth' (Mt. 28:18) and as founding a church by virtue of his authority"; whereas Luke thought that the risen Jesus did not go straight to heaven, but first returned to normal life in order to instruct his disciples in their new responsibilities of preaching the gospel from Jerusalem to the end of the earth.

I am not here concerned with the merits of this exegesis, although I may note that that of *Mark* is not without its difficulties.[1] I wish rather to point out that Perrin does not expect Christians to accept any of these three views that a resurrection actually happened, but thinks they can nevertheless be interpreted as conveying three messages that are meaningful today. His reinterpretations are in fact no more than a form of words so vague and uncertain in meaning that anyone can subscribe to such propositions without feeling that he is saying what he does not believe. Here, for instance, is what he considers to be the truth underlying Mark's myth:

> For me to say "Jesus is risen" in Marcan terms means to say that I experience Jesus as ultimacy in the historicity of my every-day, and that that experience transforms my every-dayness as Mark expected the [second] coming of Jesus to transform the world (157, p 40).

What does such an interpretation leave except the name of Jesus and the organization which depends on it?

In an earlier book, Perrin distinguishes "historical" knowledge of Jesus from what he calls "faith-knowledge" of him. The latter "introduces a reference to a . . . non-historical reality," that is, "the idea of God and his activity." Religious or faith-knowledge "mediates the understanding of ultimate reality" (155, pp 237–41). The technique employed here is worthy of note. Certain words (such as *God*) have by long association with religious ideas acquired a certain sanctity which is not at all diminished by any uncertainty as to meaning. Other words (for example, *ultimate reality*) have, by use in philosophical contexts, acquired a certain air of rational and logical precision. By equating the religious word with the metaphysical word, inferences which appear justified from the latter are transferred to the former.

One can understand Christians' dilemma. They cannot retain indefensible traditional views, but, on the other hand, if they drop the tradition altogether, they are left with no justification for calling themselves Christians. Chemistry has developed from earlier traditions that it has cheerfully abandoned. But if it had to call itself *alchemy* or *phlogistology*, it would be hard put to find a justification for the title.

II CLAIMS CONCERNING THE "AUTHENTIC" JESUS

Jesus the Deluded Apocalyptist: Schweitzer

However many concessions today's theological critics of the New Testament make, most of them will not surrender Jesus' religious importance. In this they are no different from Albert Schweitzer (1875-1965), who is a particularly striking example, since he regarded the Jesus of history as no more than a man who acted under the influence of gross delusions.

According to Schweitzer Jesus himself believed that he would be transformed into a supernatural personage who would then come down from the clouds, bring the world to a catastrophic end, and inaugurate the kingdom of God with a universal judgment of the living and the dead. Further, that when these expectations that the last days were at hand were disappointed, he arbitrarily decided that God had singled him out to suffer tribulation alone, and that it therefore behooved him to undergo crucifixion, after which the kingdom would come. Again his hopes remained unfulfilled, for his death was not followed by the end of the world.

It is hardly surprising that (I quote *The Oxford Dictionary of the Christian Church*) such a "view of our Lord's Person aroused much opposition, not only among conservative theologians." Käsemann has justly said that Schweitzer's Jesus is no more than "a wild apocalyptic figure" (116, p 42). Schweitzer did however try to make his views more acceptable by cloaking them in vague and mystical language that obscures their unorthodoxy. He does not say that Jesus was deluded, but rather that his behavior rested on "considerations lying outside history," on "dogmatic eschatological considerations" (180, pp 351, 357).

Eschatology means theories about the end of the world, how it will come about, and what circumstances will attend it. That Jesus was determined by eschatological considerations must mean that he was actuated by a belief in the coming of the kingdom or by the conviction that he was the Messiah who would inaugurate the kingdom. But instead of putting the matter thus plainly, Schweitzer says: "Eschatology is simply 'dogmatic history'—history as molded by theological beliefs—which breaks in upon the natural course of history and abrogates it" (180, p 349). He means simply that Jesus' behavior was determined by his religious ideas.

But the behavior of every man is determined by his own beliefs as much as, or more than, by the "natural course" of events. Of the real events of his time no man can have anything but a very imperfect notion collected by reports or by inference from his own restricted experience. And it must be on the basis of his own inadequate notions that he acts. If, in addition to the inevitable limitations thus imposed, he suffers from positive delusions, then his behavior will be even less adapted to the real conditions in which he is living, and in such cases we cannot hope to explain or predict his behavior unless we know what his delusions are.

Schweitzer writes so as to suggest that Jesus' theological beliefs are an objective force, outside history, whereas other people's ideas belong to the natural course of history. He says, apropos of Jesus' identification of John the Baptist with Elijah (Mt. 11:14): "We see here, too, how, in the thought of Jesus, Messianic doctrine forces its way into history and simply abolishes the historic aspect of events" (180, p 373). The casual reader is not likely to interpret this as meaning that Jesus was under a delusion; rather he will suppose that there is some supernatural, metaphysical, "eschatological" aspect of the events which is just as real, or perhaps more real, than the historical aspect.

Instead, then, of saying plainly that he regards Jesus as a deluded fanatic, Schweitzer writes of "the largeness, the startling originality, the self-contradictoriness and the terrible irony" in his thought (p 208). He even makes a virtue of the inconsistencies and incredibilities of the gospel portrait of Jesus by claiming that he is a supreme personality whom we really cannot expect to understand. Thus he holds that the "chaotic confusion" of the gospel narratives "ought to have suggested the thought that the events had been thrown into this confusion by the volcanic force of an incalculable personality, not by some kind of carelessness or freak of the tradition" (p 349).

The discrepancies in the gospel are no doubt due to a number of causes: the purpose and intelligence of the authors or editors, the disparate sources from which they drew their material, the interests of those who preserved and copied the manuscripts, and so on. But it seems unhelpful to say that everything can be accounted for by supposing that the subject of the story was an incalculable personality. By this method any myth could be taken as plausible history. The whole manner of argument savors more of evangelical pulpit oratory than of scientific discussion.

The second German edition (179) of Schweitzer's *Quest of the Historical Jesus* includes a discussion (omitted in the English translation cited above) of contemporaries who denied that Jesus ever existed. Schweitzer's overconfidence is typified by his inclusion of English works (for example, J. M. Robertson's *Christianity and Mythology*) in this review, even though he knew no English. Robertson was able to reply (in the second edition of his own book) that the summary of his book given by Schweitzer was "impossible to anyone who has read it." In this section of his work Schweitzer does, however, make some unexpected concessions. He notes that all our information about Jesus comes from Christian sources, for the sparse pagan and Jewish notices of him are clearly dependent on Christian tradition. For instance, Tacitus' reference (about AD 120) to the crucifixion under Pilate at best establishes that the church of the early second century believed in that event (179, pp 453, 512).

Schweitzer even declares that Christianity must reckon with the possibility that it will have to surrender the historicity of Jesus altogether, and must have—in readiness for such a contingency—"a metaphysic, that is, a fundamental philosophy of the nature and significance of being that is completely independent of historical fact and of knowledge imparted by tradition, and which must be created anew every moment in every religious person" (p 512). He adds that if the gospel Jesus did exist, then it must be admitted that he displays some traits which may be found morally and religiously offensive—for example, his ethical teaching is impaired by its constant appeal to the prospect of heavenly rewards as incentives for good behavior, by Jewish particularism, and by assumptions concerning predestination (p 516; cf. pp 595–6). However, he notes earlier in his book that "the apologists, as we learn from the history of the Lives of Jesus, can get the better of any historical result whatever" (180, p 233). This is as true of his own performance as of those he criticizes; and it is equally true of more recent apologists.

Jesus the Moral Teacher

The quest for authentic words of Jesus has not proceeded without occasional blurring of the issues. Just as myth has been redefined as truth for certain theological purposes, so discussion about Jesus' authentic words has seen some attempt to put a new sense on the term. J. M. Robinson, for instance (not to be confused with J. A. T. Robinson, to whose views I have so frequently referred), suggests that a saying which Jesus never spoke "may well reflect accurately his historical significance, and in this sense be more 'historical' than many irrelevant things Jesus actually said" (162, p 99). He goes on likewise to use the word *authentic* in the sense of "of historical importance" or "relevant in the light of subsequent developments." Then he complains of what he calls "the helpless ambiguity of the old term 'unauthentic.'" As Calvert has appropriately commented: "Ambiguity . . . is avoided if the word 'authentic' is reserved for those words which Jesus actually spoke," as against those which have been put into his mouth (35, p 209).

Even if we were to accept what the gospels allege of Jesus as authentic (although contradictions in the material would still force us to be selective) we could not say that his life or teaching were ethically novel in any way. Let me try to justify this view.

The so-called "Golden Rule" ("Whatever you wish that men would do to you, do so to them," Mt. 7:12) is admitted to have been proverbial before Jesus.[2] Among others, Confucius, the Rabbi Hillel, and the *Book of Tobit* (4:15) had already given this doctrine in a negative formulation: "Do not do to others what you would not wish them to do to you." It has sometimes been claimed that this formulation is inferior. But what would be the difference between: "Treat people kindly if you would like them to treat you kindly" and "Do not treat unkindly if you would not wish to be treated unkindly"? It depends on the peculiarities of language whether a particular action is expressed by a positive or a negative.

Luke also records Jesus' teaching of the Golden Rule, in a context where it is followed by a passage in which the generous action is advocated as a means of ensuring similar treatment for oneself: 'As you wish that men would do to you, do so to them . . . And your reward will be great, and you will be sons of the most high" (Lk. 6:31-5). In the intervening verses, however (6:32-4), no reward is implied; indeed, it is recognized that to do good merely in the hope of reciprocal treatment is not exceptionally virtuous. The writer is obviously putting together a number of common maxims with different implications. Some suggest that the reward is now and at the hands of one's fellowmen; others that it is hereafter and from God. We saw (p 202) that, in Schweitzer's view, Jesus' ethical teaching is compromised by its stress on heavenly rewards for good behavior. Jesus teaches poverty, renunciation, abandonment of friends and relatives (Lk. 14:26), universal abnegation. These are the ideals, and for these the reward will be power, majesty, authority—in short everything that on earth has been renounced, but multiplied a hundredfold (Mt. 19:29).

Some of the rules Jesus proposes as a revision of the Mosaic Law are scarcely reasonable. They include: turn the other cheek, give your coat to him who takes your cloak, give to everyone that asks (Mt. 5:39-42), sell all your property and give the proceeds to the poor (Mk. 10:17-22). Some commentators say that such maxims would make sense for those who were expecting an almost immediate end to the world and the return of Jesus as its judge and that either he himself, believing in such developments (long since falsified by history), delivered such teachings, or else they were put into his mouth by an apocalyptically minded Christian community.

Other commentators prefer to argue that he did not mean to be taken literally here—a view which involves the surrender of any claim that his teachings constitute a guide to behavior. For it is difficult to see how we are to know when to take him literally unless we have some independent criterion of what is right and wrong. And if we do know, independently of him, what is right, then we do not need him as an ethical guide. Furthermore, it would not be reasonable to take his words literally when we approve of them, and non-literally when we do not, and then pretend that his teaching constitutes the ethical ideal.

Side by side with Jesus' sharpening of the requirements of the Mosaic Law, with his demand for "a righteousness exceeding that of the scribes and Pharisees" (Mt. 5:20), he preaches an equally radical grace, and represents God as rejoicing particularly in the dissolute man's change of heart. This is the lesson of the parable of the prodigal son (Lk. 15:11-32). So on the other hand we can be saved only by being ever so holy; yet on the other it is the dissolute whose repentance gives God most pleasure. Braun (among other Christian commentators) calls this a "paradox" (24, p 248) and says it has not been "theologically thought through to its consequences." Thus he admits to difficulties in this connection.

My main concern, however, is not whether Jesus' teaching is acceptable, but whether any of it must be taken as authentic. If teachings were from the first imparted to Christians by the spirit, by the voice of the risen Jesus speaking through a Christian prophet, then it is understandable enough that in time, Jesus should come to be regarded as having taught during his incarnate life. We found some suggestion in Ephesians and in Hebrews that the authors of these letters may have believed the historical Jesus to have preached (pp 55, 62). But *what* he preached is not evidenced before *1 Clement. Earlier writers do not ascribe to him the ethical teachings he gives in the gospels.* Paul, we saw, says "bless those who persecute you," with no suggestion that Jesus had taught this doctrine.

I was able to show repeatedly in chapters 2 and 3 that Paul is in this respect typical of many early Christian writers and that some of these even urge ethical views that contradict those which later came to be ascribed to Jesus in the gospels. Could the author of 2 John or Ignatius, who stipulate that those who do not bring the true doctrine should not be received, nor even greeted, have known anything of Matthew's Jesus, who tells his audience that they must greet and even love their enemies? And is it not likely that Matthew has simply put this doctrine into Jesus' mouth, since—in arguing against the Pharisees of his own day, and against their interpretation of the Jewish religious law—he stamps the Levitical command to love one's neighbor as the Law's most imperative stipulation (Mt. 5:43–8 and 22:40), in the light of which some of its other stipulations must be reinterpreted?

It is in this connection sad to note that, although Matthew thus posits love of neighbor as the essence of the Law, he goes on, in chapter 23 (in the interests of his polemic against the Pharisees' interpretation of it), to ascribe to Jesus unqualified hatred of his neighbors, the scribes and Pharisees.

I have been told that the fact that Jesus' teaching in the gospels includes parables argues for his historicity. But parables could easily have emanated from Christian theological schools comparable to the rabbinic ones. Trocmé finds "something academic," smacking of such schools, about some of the parables in *Mark* and *Matthew* (for example, in their allusions to scripture). He also thinks that Luke found many of the parables he records in the preaching of the churches where he gathered his material. They served as "illustrations and examples for a message which emphasized piety, religious emotion and a morality based upon repentance and forgiveness" (202, p 86). *Mark,* the earliest gospel, has few parables and lacks most of those included in the other two synoptics. Half the parables in *Luke* are peculiar to it, and half of those in *Matthew* are not paralleled in any other canonical gospel. *John* has no parables at all. All this prompts us to ask, with Trocmé (pp 88–9), "why the parables came so slowly to form part of the tradition which the evangelists gathered together?"

The discussion between Jesus and a lawyer (Lk. 10:25–37), which terminates with the parable of the Good Samaritan (recorded only by Luke) cannot have been spoken by Jesus. The purpose of the parable (that is, of vss. 30–7) is to inculcate love of neighbor. But the evangelist, by making this part of a discussion which begins already at verse 25, has combined it with another (originally independent) unit of tradition and thereby blurred its lesson. Let us study the details.

At Lk. 10:25 a lawyer asks Jesus what he must do to have eternal life, and is told to love God and his neighbor. When he asks "who is my neighbor?" (v. 29), Jesus in reply tells him the story of a man who is set upon by robbers who leave him half dead. A priest and a Levite pass by without going to his assistance—part of the purpose of the parable seems to be to cast a slur on priests and Levites—but a Samaritan binds his wounds, takes him to an inn and pays the innkeeper to look after him. At the end of the story, Jesus asks: "Which of these three do you think proved neighbor to the man who fell among the robbers?" The lawyer replies: "The one who showed mercy on him."

Is this the answer to the lawyer's question "who is the neighbor I must love to have eternal life?" Is it the man who aids and looks after him that he must love, and not the priests and Levites who pass by on the other side? Earlier (Lk. 8:32-5) Jesus is reported to have repudiated such a view. ("If you love those who love you, what credit is that to you? For even sinners love those who love them. And if you do good to those who do good to you, what credit is that to you? For even sinners do the same . . . But love your enemies and do [them] good.") However, his last words, when he has told the parable of the Good Samaritan, are: "Go and do likewise" (10:37).

So the action of the Samaritan is an example to be imitated, and the question which gave rise to the parable has been forgotten. Commentators such as Barclay say: "The question . . . was 'Who is my neighbor?' and the answer of the parable is 'Anyone who needs your help'" (4, p 82). But it was the Samaritan who was the neighbor according to what the lawyer says at the end of the parable, not (as Barclay says) the victim of the robbers. Crossan notes that, in the dialogue before the parable, *neighbor* means he to whom love must be offered (10:27 and 29), whereas after the parable, *neighbor* is he who offers mercy to another's need (verses 36-7). The parable itself is placed in between, with the result that it blurs this distinction. What precedes the parable would indicate that the neighbor in it is the wounded man by the roadside; whereas what follows it would mean that the neighbor is the Good Samaritan.

Crossan concludes: "The parable of 10:30-5 would fit quite well with 10:27-9 showing that the neighbor is anyone in need; and it would also fit well with 10:36 indicating that the neighbor is one who assists another's need; but it cannot go with both 10:27-9 and 10:36 simultaneously" (48, pp 288-9).[3] Probably what we have here is some sort of literary combination, on the part of the evangelist, of divergent source material, certainly not an authentic dialogue between Jesus and a questioner.

What the gospel Jesus emphasizes more than neighborliness is the importance of belief in him (Mt. 25:40 and 45). It is for men's behavior to him, or to his Father, that, in this context of *Matthew,* they will be sent to heaven or hell. The cardinal crime is unbelief (Jn. 3:18 and 36) and whole communities will be most frightfully punished for it (Mt. 10:14-5). If belief is all-important, then leading others to unbelief is unforgivable (Mt. 18:6). The conviction that the faithful must be protected at all cost from unbelief has repeatedly led to ferocious persecution of the unorthodox. In 1 Corinthians 13 we have happily (and without ascription to Jesus) another doctrine: "I may have faith strong enough to move mountains, but if I have no love I am nothing."

Theologians who have come to regard Jesus as no more than a man continue to make excessive claims for his teaching. Goulder, for instance, thinks that "unprejudiced humanists" may well be willing to admire him "as the prime historical source for the first full teaching of love, and its realization in an ongoing human community" (101, p 60). It is, however, refreshing to find Nineham pointing out, in the very same volume, that such claims are not merely not justified by what is said of Jesus in the gospels; they also could not be "justified to the hilt by *any* historical records" (101, p 188). The gospels are about as imperfect as historical records can be. Nineham says:

> B. H. Streeter once calculated that, apart from the forty days and nights in the wilderness (of which we are told virtually nothing) everything reported to have been said and done by Jesus in all four gospels would have occupied only some three weeks . . . . Those who transmitted the gospel material were primarily concerned to vindicate certain supernatural claims for Jesus . . . . No doubt they took his moral perfection for granted . . . but that very fact means that they retailed very little information relevant to the establishing of it now (p 189).

Nineham is unwilling to "join those who deny . . . the historicity of Jesus" (p 191). But he at any rate insists that "modern historical methods have rendered obsolete any talk of 'assured results' in relation to the figure of Jesus" (p 192).

Jesus as Miracle-Worker or Magician

The difficulties in accepting the evidence of the gospels and of Acts that Jesus and his disciples worked miracles are considerable. Earlier Christian documents in no way suggest that he did so, and the Pauline letters and the letter to the Hebrews rather imply the contrary (cf. pp 35, 61). The gospels are widely agreed to have been written between forty and eighty years after his supposed lifetime by unknown authors who were not personally acquainted with him. And their miracle stories are nearly all couched in general terms, with no indication of time or place or details concerning the person or persons who benefited. Petzke has justly said that "these traditions are a picture in narrative form of the christological title 'miracle worker'" (158, p 201). Their point is to glorify the earthly life of Jesus, not to report on it. They were clearly good propaganda for Christianity, as is conceded at Jn. 20:30-1: "Jesus did many other signs in the presence of the disciples which are not written in this book; but these are written that you may believe that Jesus is the Christ, the Son of God, and that believing you may have life in his name."

They are motivated too by the desire to stamp his lifetime as the beginning of the age of salvation; for according to Jewish tradition, power to work miracles was to return in Messianic times. "As in the days of your coming forth out of the land of Egypt, I will show him marvellous things" (Micah 7:15). As Grant has said, the primary reason why miracles stories are so prominent in early Christianity is that it was an eschatological movement within Judaism: as in apocalyptic movements generally, miracles came to be expected just before the imminent reign of God, when he would renew his favor toward Israel as in the days of the Exodus (85, pp 163, 172). The association of miracles with Messianic times is actually alluded to at Mt. 11:2–5. Disciples of John the Baptist there ask Jesus "Are you he who is to come?" and are told in reply: "Go and tell John what you hear and see: the blind receive their sight and the lame walk, lepers are cleansed and the deaf hear, and the dead are raised up."

When we find Isaiah (35:5) depicting the era of salvation with "then the eyes of the blind shall be opened and the ears of the deaf shall be unstopped," it is pretty obvious on what basis Christians came early to believe that Jesus had cured blindness and deafness. We saw too that some gospel miracles are conscious parallels to Old Testament ones: the miraculous feeding parallels a story of Elisha and the walking on the water, a statement in the book of Job (see pp 132, 134).

As for the apostles' miracles recorded in Acts, these are narrated in a late first- or early second-century work by an author who had little real knowledge of the church of the 30s which he describes, who did not know the original apostles but only the ideal conception of an apostle current in his own day; and to such an ideal picture the power to work miracles certainly belonged. These stories, in both gospels and Acts, were written in an age of credulity concerning miracles of all kinds.

Grant notes that the content of the gospel miracle stories is not uniquely Jewish or eschatological, and that they can be paralleled in Greek and Roman literature. There were so-called "divine men" in the Greco-Roman world who revealed their divinity through the miracles which accompanied their births, characterized their lives, and made them triumph over death. These miracles were very similar to those ascribed to some of the heroes of the Old Testament; when Greek-speaking Jews such as Philo and Josephus came to rewrite the Old Testament stories for a Greek audience, they described the Old Testament "divine men" in terms of their Greco-Roman equivalents. Thus the way was prepared for the Christian interpretation of Jesus in similar terms (Windisch, 219, pp 101–14).

All these objections seem to me to amount to more than mere "rationalist bias," of which those who reject all the New Testament miracle stories are commonly accused. Even apologists are inclined to some skepticism in regard to Jesus' nature miracles: his stilling of the storm, walking on the sea, multiplication of bread and cursing of the fig tree; and also toward the story of the coin in the fish's mouth and John's narrative of the changing of water into wine.

But many hold with Grant that, whatever may be said about these, the tradition of his healing miracles is "unquestionably reliable" (85, p 168). Some apologists would agree that it is not necessary to assume that any miracle was involved, merely that he did acquire a reputation for curing disease, particularly by "casting out" the demons or "unclean spirits" believed responsible for it. But the real reason why he is made to cure demoniacs may be merely that "according to Jewish tradition, demonic power was to be crushed in the Messianic age" (Ellis on Lk. 4:31–44; 58, p 99). Mark's miracle stories were told "in a community in which Jesus is regarded as an agent who has come in the end of time to defeat the powers of Satan" (Kee, 117, p 36).

We saw that in the earliest documents, the manner in which this belief was applied to him did not make him a miracle-worker during his incarnate life. Paul and the author of Hebrews represent him as crushing the power of demons by submitting to a shameful death at their instigation. Since, however, Paul and early Christians generally took the working of miracles in their own day as one of the gifts of the spirit vouchsafed in the last times, it is intelligible enough that, in the course of developing tradition, it should come to be supposed that Jesus, in his lifetime, had mastered demons in the same manner that the leaders of the post-resurrection churches claimed to do so. It is, then, very relevant to ask (with Roloff, 167, p 141) how far the idea that he worked miracles was dependent on the pneumatic experiences of the post-Easter community.

Let us next study a typical synoptic healing miracle—the curing of the epileptic boy reported at Mk. 9:14 (and its parallels in *Matthew* and *Luke*). A short while before, Jesus had gone (ch. 8) from Bethsaida (on the northern shore of the Sea of Galilee) to Caesarea Philippi (about 25 miles further north), and thence to a "high mountain" (9:2) where, in the presence of Peter, James, and John, he was transfigured. There are indeed mountains (for example, Mt. Hermon) in this lonely northern area. However, when he descends from it with the three, he finds the other nine arguing with a "great crowd" (9:14). The argument had developed because the disciples had been unable to cure a boy brought to them. Already it is clear that the location Mark gives this story is not authentic. In the sparsely populated north there would be no great crowds, nor would any of the population have known of the powers of Jesus and his disciples in this area well away from what Mark himself had represented as the scenes of his activity hitherto.

In Mk. 6:7 the disciples had been given power to drive out unclean spirits. Only here, three chapters later, is there any mention of failure on their part to effect miracles; even here, it is made clear that their failure is unusual, so that the idea that they can effect cures is presupposed. Their failure on this occasion is not to be taken as indicating the story's authenticity. It is simply a foil to the greater power of Jesus, here able to cast out a particularly powerful demon.

When Jesus is told by the boy's father, who is "one of the crowd," of the disciples' failure, he says: "O faithless generation" (9:19). This seems to be directed against the father (or the crowd generally), not against the disciples;

for he later (vss. 23–4) expressly chides the father with insufficient faith. Verse 19 continues with: "How long am I to be with you? How long am I to bear with you?" This interrupts the simple sequence of the miracle story by drawing attention to his supernatural status as a pre-existent being who is finding it a strain to keep company with his inferiors on earth who do not believe in him. Mark himself may well have inserted this comment into the story as it reached him from a source. The weariness Jesus is made, in the comment, to express could explain why Mark has placed the whole story *after* he has had some experience with crowds in Galilee, even though this meant placing it inappropriately in the lonely north. An even stronger reason for this siting is that the allusion to Jesus' true supernatural status in verse 19 makes good sense to the reader at this point, for he has just been informed of the transfiguration and of the injunction to its three privileged witnesses not to tell of it "until the Son of Man should have risen from the dead" (9:9).

In its pre-Marcan form the story would have passed straight from the statement of the disciples' failure and Jesus' complaint about the people's faithlessness to his instruction "bring him [the boy] to me," and the description of the fit the boy then had (vss. 20–1). The severity of this fit, and the previous failure of the disciples to drive out the demon, make it understandable that the father is far from confident that Jesus will be able to help. And so he asks him to help the boy "if you can." This enables Jesus again to stress the need to have faith in him. "All things are possible to him who believes." He then rebukes the "unclean spirit" and instructs it to "come out" of the boy and "never enter him again" (v. 25).

By verse 27 the boy is cured and the story has ended. But two verses have been added in which the disciples ask Jesus privately why they had not been able to cast the demon out, and are told: "This kind cannot be driven out by anything but prayer." Most manuscripts add "and fasting." Prayer and fasting are what the Jews believed conferred power over demons. The hand that added the reference to fasting has done a particularly clumsy job, as Jesus was earlier represented (2:18–20) as explaining why his disciples do not need to fast. The two added verses conflict with what we are told in the miracle story. Verses 22–4 have argued that lack of faith (on the part of the father who requested the miracle) was responsible for the disciples' failure; for not until that point is this lack of faith remedied, and the father able to say "I believe." The added verses seem to have been written by someone who felt that the story as it stood did not explain why the disciples had been unsuccessful. In this connection the parallels in *Luke* and *Matthew* are of interest. Luke simply omits the added verses and terminates the story by making Jesus give the cured boy back to his father, to the astonishment of the crowd (Lk. 9:42–3). Matthew has the disciples ask Jesus privately to explain their failure; but Jesus then replies not with references to prayer and fasting, but by complaining that they—the disciples, not the father—had insufficient faith (Mt. 17:20). The verses in which Mark's Jesus chides the father with lack of faith are omitted by Matthew, who retains

Jesus' complaint that he has to live on earth with a "faithless generation" but interprets it as a criticism of the disciples, not of the crowd.

Roloff sums up all this when he says that a story of the disciples' failure, in which their impotence was contrasted with Jesus' power, has been expanded, as the tradition developed further, in two quite different directions, so as on the one hand to instruct the disciples on how to work miracles and on the other to inculcate the need for faith in Jesus (167, p 147). In fact, a not inconsiderable number of Mark's miracle stories aim at underlining the need for faith, as the following passages show:

> And when Jesus saw their faith, he said to the paralytic . . . (2:5).
> He said to them "Why are you afraid [of the storm]. Have you no faith?" (4: 40).
> Jesus said to [him], "Do not fear, only believe" (5:36).
> He could do no mighty work there . . . and he marvelled because of their unbelief (6:5–6).
> And Jesus said . . . "Your faith has made you well" (10:52).

The Christian community for which such stories were written was perhaps not free from doubts and misgivings, and needed to be told again and again of the paramount importance of faith.

Scholarly defense of belief in miracles comes today only from those who make religious beliefs their fundamental premise for interpreting their whole experience. Thus the theologian G. F. Woods says: "It cannot be denied that the evidential value of the miraculous is closely interwoven with the metaphysical views of those to whom the evidence is offered. Those who reject theism and do not believe in the divinity of Christ have many alternative interpretations of the reported miracles" (221, p 30). R. Swinburne notes, in a similar vein, that whether one is convinced by evidence for a miracle depends to some extent on one's overall worldview (195). Each of us tries to fit his views and experiences together into a coherent system, so that they do not contradict each other, and we must all judge the credibility of any given report according to the system of beliefs by which we live.[4]

Morton Smith has recently tried to show that the Jesus of history was a magician, a man who claimed supernatural powers and did in fact effect cures of psychological illnesses, though not by supernatural means. Smith confidently declares that all theories that Jesus never existed "have been thoroughly discredited" (184, note on p 166) — he does not say by what considerations — so that "Jesus unquestionably started the process that became Christianity" (p 5). Perhaps he thinks Jesus' existence is assured because he assumes throughout his book that stories which could be taken as discreditable to him — and there are a not inconsiderable number of them in the gospels — cannot be Christian inventions. We have, however, seen that Jesus' rejection by his family, his crucifixion, and his burial by a non-disciple are all intelligible as elements of a

Christology inspired by Jewish wisdom literature, by Isaiah's suffering servant who was "despised and rejected," and by historical events of 100 and 200 years before Christian times and known through tradition to the earliest Christians. In DJE I discussed further, other apparently discreditable incidents: Jesus' betrayal by a close disciple (pp 132 ff), his refusal to be called good and his confession of ignorance concerning when the world would end (p 148).

Jesus' baptism is commonly regarded as another such incident. Smith says that it "shows the master going to another prophet for sanctification" (p 166) and therefore cannot be a Christian invention. He makes no mention of obvious factors which have led a number of theologians to deny its historicity. There was, for instance, a Jewish belief that the Messiah would be unknown as such to himself and others until anointed by Elijah his forerunner, and Jesus himself is made to designate John the Baptist as Elijah (cf. DJE, pp 156–7). We have seen (p 103) that Ignatius also betrays how belief that Jesus had been baptized could have arisen. Mark, whose account of the incident is the earliest extant, shows no sign of embarrassment at Jesus going to another prophet. I have already mentioned Enslin's argument that "the whole story of the contact of Jesus and John" is "the creation of later Christian thinking" (cf. p 15). Gager, in his critical survey of attempts to reach back to the historical Jesus, finds Enslin's case impressive (226a, p 263).

Smith further argues: unless Jesus had had a large following, he would not have been crucified (p 24), and it must have been his success in curing hysterical patients that drew the crowds. If he had started as a teacher, he would not later have been credited with miracles; whereas if he initially gained a reputation as a miracle-worker, later he could easily have been credited with teachings (p 16).

In criticism of all this, I would note:

(1) If he in fact drew large crowds, why does Josephus not mention him? Smith says that "Christian propaganda shows that Christians themselves expected Jesus to be seen as a figure of the same social type as Judas [the Galilean] and Theudas" (p 20). These two *are* mentioned by Josephus, whereas his two references to Jesus can fairly be set aside as interpolations (see DJE, pp 10–1). Smith quotes (p 45) the reference in Josephus to "Jesus the so-called Christ" and comments: "No Christian would have forged a reference to Jesus in this style." But the Greek does not have "so-called" but "him called Christ," and this, so far from being non-Christian, is the exact wording of Mt. 1:16.

(2) If Jesus worked miracles or pretended miracles, why does Paul (among other early Christian writers) give no hint of this, and even—like the author of Hebrews—come close to denying it? Smith admits that he has to discount the relevant Pauline evidence. According to Paul, the Jews refuse to accept Jesus as Messiah because he was crucified, not because of his practices. "On this point," says Smith, "Paul cannot be believed" (p 15).

(3) Mohammed was a teacher who worked no miracles but was later credited with them. It is not a priori inconceivable that the same could have been

the case with Jesus. I do not believe that he was either a teacher or a miracle-worker, but Christian tradition represents him as the former before it imputes miracles to him (see pp 203–4). None of the documents discussed in chapters 1–3 alleges that he worked miracles, although 1 Timothy gives some indication of how, in time, miracles came to be attributed to him (see p 96). Smith makes much of the fact that non-Christian documents of the second century and later say that Jesus was a magician and therefore admit that he did effect cures. But as Petzke has pointed out (158, p 202), belief in miracles was, in antiquity, part of the way in which everyday reality was comprehended. Allegations that a particular person worked miracles would therefore be met by hostile commentators with a denigration of his miracles as mere magic, not with a denial that he worked any (cf. p 16).

Smith asserts that, if Jesus' miracles be denied, then we have to suppose that "within 40 to 60 years of his death, all [sic] the preserved strands of Christian tradition had forgotten or deliberately misrepresented the most conspicuous characteristic of the public career of the founder of the movement" (p 14). This statement that all chronological layers of Christian tradition represent him as a miracle-worker is simply untrue, and can be made only by those who ignore the epistles and concentrate exclusively on the gospels and their presumed sources. It is because this is so often done by those who try to find out what we can know of Jesus that I have devoted the opening three chapters of this present book to a detailed study of the epistles. Smith is sternly critical of present-day theologians for restricting themselves to the New Testament and for not checking what they find in it against a wider background of known fact (p 17). But he himself does not check the gospels against earlier tradition.

III CHRISTIANITY WITHOUT THE HISTORICAL JESUS: SCHMITHALS

Finally, I turn to a Marburg theologian, Walter Schmithals. I do so because in a book published in 1972 he has squarely faced the evidence I have stressed here by asking: If Christianity was inaugurated by Jesus' own preaching, why is it that not only Paul but early Christians generally—although they believed that he did live and die on earth—did not seem to care what he had taught, believed, or done, or what sort of man he had been? How can we explain, given such antecedents, the interest in his doctrines and biography which the gospels suddenly seemed to bring into Christian tradition late in the first century, and which established itself as an essential part of Christian thinking and teaching only with Justin and Irenaeus from the mid-second century? Schmithals describes this as "the real riddle of the New Testament" (174, p 82).

To answer these questions Schmithals first sets aside material other than straight biography that is contained in the gospels. The Passion and resurrection story, for instance, he regards as a mere expansion of the statement, iterated in the earliest creeds or affirmations of the faith, that Jesus died for our sins and was raised. The expansion manipulates earlier tradition so as to make it serve apologetic ends of the evangelists' own period. (Thus, if Pilate is represented as finding Jesus guiltless and as having been bullied by Jewish leaders into ordering his crucifixion, this is because the evangelists wished to represent Christianity to the Roman authorities of the late first century as politically harmless.)

Another prominent component in the gospels is the miracle stories and the so-called "apophthegmata" (incidents where Jesus' situation enables him to give a definitive ruling on some issue). This too, says Schmithals, is not real biography; the historical Jesus did and said no such things. It was the post-Easter church that ascribed such behavior to him in order to show the Lord of their faith acting with the heavenly power appropriate to him. Thus the miracle stories are concerned not to record the cure of few individual sick persons, but to point to the salvation which has come in the person of Jesus and which is available to all who believe in him. And the apophthegmata show that he is no mere rabbi, relying on the authority of earlier teachers or scriptures, but that he speaks with supernatural authority.

The only genuinely biographical material in the gospels, says Schmithals are the "logia"—that is, Jesus' sayings as represented above all in those sections common to *Matthew* and *Luke* that are absent from *Mark* and which Schmithals (and many others) think were drawn from a lost source (known as Q) of which Mark was ignorant.[5] A very remarkable thing about Q (in so far as one can reconstruct it from *Matthew* and *Luke*) is that, although it sets Jesus' life in first-century Palestine by associating him with John the Baptist, it makes no mention of Pilate and gives not the slightest hint of the Passion, crucifixion, and resurrection. Nor does it represent Jesus as a great miracle-worker but rather as an obscure and rejected preacher. The Jesus of Q suffers in so far as he is rejected by men, but his suffering has no atoning power. The suffering stressed in Q is the tribulation which is to befall men in the last days, but it has no redemptory effect. Q consists mainly of sayings in which Jesus predicts the coming of the kingdom and insists that only those who accept him and what he says will be saved when the Son of Man (a supernatural personage familiar in Jewish apocalyptic literature) comes to inaugurate it. He also provides a moral code ("love your enemies," "judge not") by which men are to live in preparation for the coming judgment. From Q, then, we can infer—according to Schmithals—that the historical Jesus called upon men to repent quickly before God brought the world to an end. He did not—any more than did the Baptist, whose preaching he reiterated—expect to bring about the end himself nor to figure as judge when it came. He did not identify himself with the Son of Man, nor suppose that he was in any sense the Messiah. Schmithals thinks that, after preaching in Galilee, he went with his followers to Jerusalem—perhaps expecting there the first manifestations of the end—and was crucified there. (This of course, is an inference from other Christian traditions, not from Q.)

The first part of Q includes the story of Jesus' temptation, a miracle story, and some sayings where he is made to speak with more than human authority. Schmithals thinks that all this material betrays that the author's intention was to integrate the genuinely biographical sayings of Jesus into the stream of tradition which accepted him as the risen Lord. Thus, by prefacing the genuine, unpretentious sayings with incidents which give him supernatural status, the author could represent all the sayings as having supernatural authority.

But what Christian community had preserved the genuine sayings so that they could in due course be drawn upon by the author of Q and then by Matthew and Luke? Schmithals answers: There must have been a Christian group that "took no notice of the Easter events and of the resulting developments in the Christian creed" (p 71). All Jesus' companions regarded him, in his lifetime as a prophet (not as Messiah, still less as Son of Man), and a certain group retained this modest view of him after his death, which they regarded as characteristic of the prophet's fate and which, in their eyes, did no more than set the seal on what he had taught while alive. They therefore continued to promulgate his view that the world would soon end and the Son of Man come to sit in judgment—without believing that Jesus himself had been raised and would function as judge. Such a sect could have existed well apart from the main Christian centers known to Paul (including Jerusalem), and perhaps, Schmithals suggests, be assigned to Galilee. (Paul significantly says nothing of Galilean Christianity.)

Schmithals finds (p 72) that patristic references to Jewish-Christians called Ebionites support his view that there was a Palestinian sect that regarded Jesus as a mere man who had died on the cross, but whose resurrection would occur only when all the dead were raised. All the other Christian groups, however, accepted what Schmithals called "the Easter events" and therefore held that God, in raising Jesus, had made his preaching obsolete, so that it was no longer appropriate to repeat his teaching that a new aeon would be coming. Jesus himself—contrary to his own expectations—had been made at his resurrection to inaugurate this new aeon, so that the kingdom of God was not (as he had taught) purely of the future. By raising him, God had given assurance that his final intervention in the affairs of this world had already begun. The mainstream early Christians, then, did not deny (as the Gnostics were later to do) that Jesus had been a man with a real human biography. What mattered in their view was not what he had done on earth, but *what God had done by means of him after his death.*

It remains for Schmithals to explain why the post-Easter traditions, in which Jesus figures as the Lord, were in time fused with the pre-crucifixion traditions of his preaching. He has argued that some integration of the two is already discernible in Q, but he finds that Mark (although ignorant of Q) includes some biographical teaching material and also reveals how it came to be combined with the traditions inspired by the Easter events. It has long been recognized as one of the peculiarities of *Mark* that—although in this gospel

Jesus appears as the Messiah and works many miracles — he repeatedly enjoins people to keep silence about his Messianic status and his miracles, even in circumstances where the injunction could scarcely be obeyed because the miracle was so public. Mark's purpose is to show that, although Jesus was Messiah, he was not recognized as such by his Galilean audiences.

Schmithals argues that, perhaps as a result of the disruption occasioned by the Jewish War (AD 66–73), the Galilean community (which had retained the view that Jesus was a mere prophet whose activities ended at his death) was brought into contact with the Christian community in which Mark lived and which accepted the Easter events. Mark wrote in order to win this Galilean community for the faith as he understood it. His gospel therefore admits that Jesus was indeed active in Galilee and not accepted as Messiah there, and contrives to show that this was because he himself kept his Messiahship secret — except to his three most intimate disciples (Peter, James, and John), who according to Mark witnessed his transfiguration and were thus in a position later to appreciate the significance of the Easter events. After Mark — and on the basis of knowledge of his gospel — a more exhaustive collection of traditions of Jesus' preaching was undertaken and integrated in Q with the mainstream view of him.

Schmithals does not wish to base the Christianity of today on the historical Jesus. He points out that it is impossible to be quite sure about the opinions of this person, since they are recorded only in gospels which adapt them to the Easter faith. He even says that, since the church, in effect, launched itself by falsifying the record of the historical Jesus, one should not try to base the church of today on what this record really was (p 75). What matters for Schmithals, as for the early church, is not the historical Jesus but the "Easter events"; and he is quite clear (pp 22, 75) that these can be authenticated only by faith, not by historical evidence.

I have tried to show that, in the course of his argument, he highlights a very serious problem about Christian origins, and one must welcome the lucidity and the uncompromising honesty of his exposition. The principal criticism I would make of it — and I am concerned with his historical analysis, not with his faith in the Easter events — is that he is not justified in insisting that the Galilean preacher of Q and of the gospels is the same person as the Pauline Christ who, according to the earliest Christian writings, was crucified and resurrected. Schmithals is not entitled to say (as he does, pp 73–4) that these documents affirm belief in Jesus "of Nazareth," for they make no mention of the place nor even of the time of Jesus' earthly existence. (He may have in mind Peter's words in Acts 2:22 ff, but he must know that there are good reasons for not accepting Peter's speeches in Acts as early material.)

Schmithals' theory — that the Easter events made Jesus' preaching obsolete — could explain why the earliest documents do not record this preaching but *not* why they fail to mention the when and where of his earthly existence, and even the historical setting of the crucifixion of this person who (they nevertheless insist) did live on earth and die on the cross.

I find it more satisfactory to regard the Jesus of the earliest documents as someone about whose life nothing was known, who had certainly not been a contemporary or near-contemporary of Paul, but who was *later* regarded as having lived about AD 30 and as having preached in Galilee before his death in Jerusalem, perhaps because he was identified with an obscure Galilean preacher of the same name (which after all was a common one).

11

Conclusion

That it is not possible to write a biography of Jesus is today widely conceded. Gager has recently noted, in an article on the methodology of Jesus research, that we lack all the essential data for such an undertaking:

> We know virtually nothing of parents, siblings, early years (childhood, adolescence, early adulthood), friends, education, religious training, profession, or contacts with the broader Graeco-Roman world. We know neither the date of his birth, nor the length of his public ministry (the modern consensus of two or three years is an educated guess based largely on the Gospel of John), nor his age at death (Luke 3:23 states that he was "about thirty when he began"). Thus even an optimistic view of the quest [of the historical Jesus] can envisage no more than a collection of "authentic" sayings and motifs devoid of context (226a, p 261).

Gager goes on to say that there is little ground even for this amount of optimism. Having pointed out numerous defects in methods which have been employed to reach back to the historical Jesus, he says that "when these failures have been remedied, the result will be greater rather than less scepticism about the possibility of the quest" (p 272).

I have argued here that, if we arrange extant early Christian documents into a chronological series, we find that only from about 90 did Christians regard Jesus as a teacher, miracle-worker and a near contemporary, crucified under Pilate. In the earliest documents (which do not include the gospels, which I give reasons for dating from 90 to 110) Jesus figures simply as a supernatural personage whom God had sent in human form into the world to redeem it and

217

who was crucified there in unspecified circumstances. These early writers are so vague in what they say about his life that they may well have believed only that he had been crucified in obscure circumstances long ago. I show that such a view is likely to have been suggested to them by the Jewish wisdom literature they knew well and by traditions they must have known concerning actual crucifixions of living men in Palestine one and two centuries before their time. And I argue that they were in fact probably wrong in believing even this much of him.

The silence of the early material about so much of what Jesus (according to the later material) said and did, is widely admitted to be something of a problem. Of course, silence does not always imply ignorance. But a book on transport in Cologne which, though written after 1965, made no reference to an underground railway, might reasonably be presumed to have been written in ignorance of the underground then constructed there. In other words, silence on a topic is significant if this silence extends to matters obviously relevant to what the writer has chosen to discuss.

I have been able to show that there is much that Jesus—according to the gospels and to other Christian writings of roughly the same date—said and did that would have been relevant to the concerns of the earlier writers, and that they would not have ignored it had they known of it. I have also been able to show that it is not merely a question of silence, and that the earlier writers sometimes make statements which positively exclude the idea that Jesus worked miracles, delivered certain teachings, or suffered under Pilate.

Nevertheless, the view that there was no historical Jesus, that his earthly existence is a fiction of earliest Christianity—a fiction only later made concrete by setting his life in the first century—is today almost universally rejected. One reason for this is the obvious extravagance of many attempts (from Dupuis in the late eighteenth century to John Allegro of today) to explain Christian origins without a Jesus of history. I have not tried in this book to survey these attempts. My purpose has been rather to show that recent work from critical theologians themselves provides a basis for taking more seriously the hypothesis that Christianity did not begin with a Jesus who lived on earth. Nevertheless, I owe it to my readers to give, in these final pages, some indication of the arguments of other writers who have denied Jesus' historicity. I will restrict detailed comment to works on which I have not already commented in DJE.

Whether Jesus existed was fiercely debated at the beginning of this century, and Archibald Robertson's *Jesus: Myth or History* (London, 1949) gives a good account of this controversy. The account of it in H. Cutner's *Jesus, God, Man or Myth?* (New York, 1950) is also of interest, in spite of the polemical tone it adopts in supporting scholars who had argued that Jesus is a myth. Those who took this negative view in the early years of this century (with J. M. Robertson as the ablest) made two mistakes: they set aside as interpolations all New Testament passages they found inconvenient and they tried to explain Jesus away in terms of pagan parallels (as simply another Osiris or Hercules), when the Jewish background is clearly of greater importance. The negative view gained some support from radical Dutch theologians of the day (for example, W. C. van Manen and G. A. van den Bergh van Eysinga) who regarded all the Pauline letters, the earliest witnesses to a human Jesus, as second-century forgeries.

One reason why New Testament scholars of today treat present-day rationalist writers on the New Testament with some disdain is that so many of the latter continue in the mistakes made early in this century. This is particularly true of French rationalism. For instance, G. Fau, whose *La fable de Jésus Christ* went into a third edition in 1967, makes the man Jesus into a construct of the mid-second century by arbitrary dating of the documents, by interpreting as "purely symbolic" some of the references to Jesus' life on earth in the few documents which he admits to be as early as the first century, and by setting aside the remaining such references in this early material as interpolations. He allows only the four principal Paulines, the letter to the Hebrews, and the Revelations to belong to the first century. Paul's statement that Jesus was crucified at the instigation of evil supernatural powers (cf. p 34) is taken as implying that his death was not a historical event but "pure symbol" (pp 117, 124).

Fau has avowedly followed G. Ory, who likewise holds that the crucifixion was "divine and cosmic" and "did not take place on earth"; that "the enemies of the cross of Christ" of whom Paul complains (Phil. 3:18) are those who insist on taking it as history instead of as a "mystery"; and that "the blood of his cross" and "his body of flesh" (Coloss. 1:20, 22) must be understood in a spiritual sense (*Le Christ et Jésus*, Paris, 1968, pp 72, 160, 164).

Fau takes the references to the cross in the letter to the Hebrews and other indications of Jesus' humanity both in this letter and in the Paulines as interpolations. Here again he follows Ory, who regards, for instance, the statement that Jesus was "born of a woman, born under the law" as interpolated at Gal. 4:4, and who thinks that Gal. 3:13 (where it is implied that Christ "hung on a tree" and was therefore really crucified) was inserted perhaps by a Jew who wanted to show that Jesus, though a man, could not be the Messiah because his crucifixion had made him accursed (pp 69, 160 and note).

Fau regards documents replete with references to the man Jesus as either forged or as late, even if genuine. He dates *1 Clement* at 140 (instead of 95) and rejects the letters of Ignatius and the epistle of Polycarp as forgeries in their entirety. He puts the gospels 100 years later than Paul's letters (pp 76, 86 f) and dates Acts at the very end of the second century (p 68). Tacitus' mention, quite early in the second century, of Christ's crucifixion under Pilate he regards as "very probably a forgery of the fifteenth century" (p 41).

His grounds for dating the gospels so late are quite unconvincing. For instance, he places *Mark* later than 140 because he interprets "the abomination of desolation" in Mk. 13 as an allusion to Hadrian's building of a pagan shrine on the site of the Jerusalem temple (p 89). One could just as well date *Mark* almost a century earlier by taking "the abomination" to refer to Caligula's threat to have a statue of himself erected in the Jewish temple. Fau also claims that there are no extant copies of the gospels earlier than the fourth century (p 82). This was true in 1910, but recent papyrus discoveries have brought earlier copies to light. (For details, see p 2 ff.) Christian scholars commonly complain that rationalists of today do not seem to have read any theological (as opposed to rationalist) literature published since the early part of this century. Fau is certainly open to this charge. The authorities on whom he relies are French rationalists (from Couchoud to Ory) and French theologians of a generation or more ago (Renan, Loisy, Guignebert).

Only apropos of the Dead Sea Scrolls does Fau refer to more recent literature which is not exclusively rationalistic. He offers the hypothesis that Paul's crucified savior is the Essene Teacher of Righteousness of the Scrolls (p 75). This, after his premise that the Jesus whom Paul worshipped had never been human, is surprising, since, according to Fau himself, the Teacher of Righteousness was a Jewish priest. But, says Fau, he soon came to be regarded as a supernatural personage (p 213), and Paul was converted at Damascus not to straightforward Essenism but to an advanced form which was permeated with the ideas of the Hellenistic mystery religions (pp 218–9). He finds evidence of Paul's connection with what he takes for Damascus Essenism, not in Paul's own writings but in Acts, which, we recall, he regards as written more than a century after Paul's time. He has to suppose that, although in general unreliable, Acts drew what it says about Paul and Damascus from older and more accurate tradition. But I have shown (in chapter 7) how unreliable Acts' portrait of Paul is, and there is no need to date this work at the end, instead of at the beginning, of the second century.

The work of these French rationalists shows the opposite of what they intended. It shows that the earliest Christians really *did believe* that Jesus had at some time assumed human flesh; and that to deny this requires arbitrary interpretation of some of the early texts that affirm it, arbitrary excision of others as interpolations, and arbitrary dating of the majority of the documents. The questions that remain are: (1) whether this belief of the earliest Christians was founded on fact; and (2) in particular, whether they thought that Jesus had lived so recently as to be a contemporary or near-contemporary, as the gospels allege is the case. This book has aimed to establish that there are good reasons for answering these questions negatively.

In the English-speaking world the few who have recently challenged Jesus' historicity have allowed that Jesus was, from the first, *said* to have existed as a man. But they have argued, very unconvincingly, that the earliest Christians did not believe this statement to be literal truth but meant it as elaborate allegory. This view is argued by W. B. Smith and J. M. Allegro. Smith, who had contributed to the controversy at the beginning of this century, completed a further book in 1927. This was published posthumously as *The Birth of the Gospel* (ed. A. Gulick, New York, 1957). It is, then, if not a recent work, at any rate only recently before the public and not untypical of a recent trend.

Smith's argument is that Christianity emanated from the Jews of the Diaspora, who saw their function in the world—harassed as they were by Gentile oppression—expressed in Isaiah's story of the suffering servant of Yahweh, whose persecution and death made atonement for the whole world's sins. In other words, this story showed them that Israel was to be dispersed among pagans so that God.could illuminate all the world's dark places with Jewish monotheism. The suffering and afflicted Messiah was thus, for them, a spiritual interpretation of the history of Israel. Since they did not find it expedient to say bluntly to Gentiles that the nation of Israel had the role of enlightening all others, they dressed up Israel's history in the form of the life-history of an individual, Jesus, and invented incident after incident in his life to reflect the history and character of Israel, as known to them from the Old Testament.

For example, the demons which Jesus casts out from persons in whom they have lodged symbolize heathen gods vanquished by Jewish monotheism. His crucifixion and resurrection represent the suffering of Israel at heathen hands, the political burial of the Hebrew state, to be followed by the spiritual triumph of Israel and its ideal monotheism. The original apostles, says Smith, intended this personification of the role of Israel only as a transient expedient and hoped that at a later time the Gentiles would be able to accept the unvarnished truth. But soon the allegorical basis of the story was lost from sight, and Jesus was accepted as a historical personage by Christians themselves.

It is always difficult to produce decisive evidence against scholars who insist on finding hidden meanings in plain statements, although it must be said that the onus is on them to support interpretations that seem forced and arbitrary. Furthermore, in deriving Christianity from Jewish proselytism in the Diaspora, Smith does not do justice to the fact that, already in Paul's time, Jerusalem was an important Christian center.

J. M. Allegro also sees the gospels as allegory, but as allegory of a very different kind. In *The Sacred Mushroom and the Cross* (London, 1970) and *The End of a Road,* published in the same year, he argues that primitive man imagined the rain which fructified the crops as analogous to the semen which fructified his own kind. The rain was God's seed, and God himself a mighty penis in the sky. The function of religious rites was to bring this penis to ejaculation. Allegro also thinks that the Jewish and Christian religions originated as fertility cults. His basis for this claim is that he can trace such names as Zeus, Yahweh, and Jesus to a Sumerian root which, about 3,500 BC, meant "semen." He supposes that this root provides a guide to the meaning of the word over the whole of its history. But, as he well knows, words often persist while the ideas associated with them change radically.

Even if the root of the word *Jesus* means "semen" in what Allegro says is the earliest written language of the world, it does not follow that the word had that meaning at the time when Christianity originated—any more than the word "hysterical" today suggests a disordered womb, notwithstanding the meaning of the Greek *hustera.* Allegro tries to discount considerations of this kind by implying that rapid change in the meaning of religious words is characteristic only of modern times. "In antiquity people and ideas did not move quite so fast." But, surely, before literacy and even writing were established, and before there was much centralization, the meanings of words would change more, and not less, rapidly. If the meaning of the Sumerian root of a Biblical word is merely one phase in a sequence of meanings, and if it is the original meaning that is important for Christian origins, then we shall have to refer the matter to the paleontologists.

Allegro argues, doubtless correctly, that religious terminology and liturgies were handed down unchanged over long periods, with the result that hymns and religious epics "differ considerably from the common tongue of the same period." The common language of daily intercourse gradually changed, while the language of religious transactions has been preserved from a remote past. The philologists, he says, study such liturgies because it is in them that "we can expect to find words used in their most primitive sense." But it is precisely because the archaisms of these liturgies could no longer be understood by the worshippers that the old words came to be reinterpreted and associated with new ideas.

What is true of words is equally true of rituals. J. G. Frazer and others have shown that rites which were originally intended to promote the growth of crops persisted in urban environments which had lost all direct concern with agriculture, and where, therefore, their original purpose was no longer understood. By the beginning of the Christian era such rites had been widely reinterpreted as ensuring the performers some kind of immortality. Allegro, however, seems to suppose that a fertility ritual continued to be regarded as such, even in adaptation. He does not deny that, as civilization developed, "the aim of religious ritual became less to influence the weather and the crops than to attain wisdom and the knowledge of the future." But he nevertheless supposes that the later worshippers, as much as the earlier, were consciously concerned with a divine penis. His justification for this view is that "the heavenly penis . . . was not only the source of life-giving semen, it was the origin of knowledge."

This idea—namely, that for the ancient mind knowledge and fertility derived from the same source—is vital to Allegro's whole theory. He insists, then, that to assimilate the divine semen is to have divine knowledge and thus power. He holds that this power was often sought from drugs. There were some plants and trees, he says, which seemed to contain more of the god's sperm in their sap than others, for some had no power, while others could heal and yet others kill. Thus by eating the right plants the prophet could induce within himself a hallucinatory state which he explained as direct communion with God. One particular drug source which, Allegro says, was specially favored was the red-topped mushroom Amanita Muscaria.

Allegro's evidence for the importance of this plant is, of course, philological. Greek and Latin plant names can be traced to "a common source in Sumerian," and these roots can be interpreted as allusions to certain features of a mushroom. For instance, one of the Greek names for the mandrake is "traceable to a Sumerian original meaning 'heavenly shade,'" and this is clearly "a reference to the canopy of the opened fungus." If we object that a mandrake is not a mushroom, Allegro will reply that "the ancients did not always differentiate the mushroom from other plants, so that its names have to be disentangled from those of quite unrelated species." His method, then, is to take any plant name in Greek or Latin, trace it to a root which suggests, however remotely, one of the real or supposed characteristics of a mushroom, and then claim that the original meaning of the Greek or Latin word was "mushroom."

Allegro seems to think the theory that God was a penis in the sky was universal. We would need a lot of evidence to be convinced — something on the scale of Frazer's *Golden Bough*. He similarly supposes that resort to drugs, particularly to Amanita Muscaria, was almost universal in the ancient world. Yet he holds that the identity of this plant that provided the divine semen was a closely guarded secret, and that the manner of using the herb, the accompanying incantations, etc., were equally secret. Such secrets were normally passed on by word of mouth from believer to initiate. But since a crisis such as the Jewish War of AD 66–70 would disperse the faithful, the secrets would have to be recorded in writing if they were to survive. Naturally, these writings must betray nothing to outsiders and be intelligible only to those within the dispersed communities. Allegro believes that the New Testament was written as a disguised herbal of this kind, to meet the crisis created by the Jewish War. It is thus an elaborate cryptogram to be deciphered by philologists.

These books by Fau, Smith, and Allegro do much to explain why serious students of the New Testament today regard the existence of Jesus as an unassailable fact. It is felt that, if the only arguments impugning Jesus' historicity are of the caliber these writers offer, then it is firmly enough established. Thus it is customary today to dismiss with amused contempt the suggestion that Jesus never existed. I have tried to show in this book that, whatever the final upshot of the debate may be, there is no ground for such a confident attitude.

Notes

INTRODUCTION

1. It is severely criticized by Klijn (123, p 66).
2. Notably by Menoud (136) and Epp (61).
3. On the "Western non-interpolations," see Metzger, 139, pp xix, 191-2.
4. The best mss. of *Mark* end at 16:8. The remainder of ch. 16 is an appendix (distinguished as such in the RV, the RSV and NEB), which makes the risen Jesus promise (among other things) that believers will be able to handle snakes and drink deadly poison without coming to harm. For a full study of this Marcan appendix, see Farmer, 65. John's story of the woman taken in adultery (Jn. 8:1-11) is also absent from the best manuscripts, and breaks the sequence of the narrative in which it occurs. It was presumably inserted from some apocryphal source by a late editor who thought it too good to miss.
5. I mention Hoskyns and Davey only because their book has been "immensely influential" (Evans, 64, p vii) and was translated into 18 languages.
6. For an excellent account of recent discussion of these problems see Tyson (196); also note 5 to ch. 10.
7. That *Luke* is secondary to *Mark* in an account of Jesus' appearance before the Sanhedrin is argued by Creed (47, pp 276 ff), Haenchen (93, pp 504 ff), and, as Catchpole himself stresses, by Lietzmann, Lohse, Blintzler and others; cf. Franklin, 70, p 92.
8. One may think in this connection of Sherwin-White's attempt (181) to show that what the gospels allege about Jesus before Pilate reflects Roman juridical practice. This has been sharply criticized by Burkill (32).

CHAPTER 1

1. Before and after Gal. 2:7-8 Paul uses only the name Cephas, not Peter. O'Neill

thinks that the references to Peter in these two verses were originally glosses designed to incorporate into the epistle the view (expressed in *Matthew,* where, as in the other synoptics, there is no mention of Cephas) that Peter (not James) was the leader of the Jewish church (151, p 37). On the two names *Cephas* and *Peter* see DJE, pp 124–5.

2. By Klein (121) and by Linnemann (to whom Klein refers, 121, pp 94 ff).

3. Grayston, however, thinks (p 75) that the passage may mean not that the final fate of the Jews is now settled, but merely that God's appointment of the Jewish people to be his servant to enlighten the Gentiles (cf. Isaiah 49:6) was now cancelled – in which case there is no contradiction with the teaching of the letter to the Romans. Pearson, however, has pointed out that the passage does indicate the finality of the wrath that has come upon the Jews (154, p 81).

4. The Eucharist approved by Paul was, then, not the only type practiced in his day. There is even evidence that the Christians addressed in the letter to the Hebrews had no Eucharist (see Williamson, 217).

5. At Rev. 19:10 an angel tells the author (in the rendering of the NEB) that "those who bear testimony to Jesus are inspired like the prophets"; and at 22:8 the author is himself classed among the prophets.

6. The ruling on divorce which Paul gives at 1 Cor. 7:10 as a word of the Lord is surely another of the "words of the (risen) Lord given to some Christian prophet such as Paul" (Ruef, 169, p 56); cf. DJE, pp 27–8.

7. When I made this criticism in a review of his book, Mr. Schonfield retorted that my comments "reveal an unfamiliarity with the techniques of historical inquiry. . . . That one source is later than another does not necessarily mean that it is less reliable. It may have had access to more primitive factual material." To this I replied that I am well aware that a later writer may use more reliable sources than an earlier one, and that I had illustrated the phenomenon in JEC, ch. 8; but that this does not justify Schonfield's method of drawing freely from any documents – early or late – to construct what he regards as a plausible biography of Jesus. In his *The Passover Plot* (London, 1965), for instance, he concedes that the fourth gospel is unreliable. But as he needs it for evidence of much that he regards as genuinely Jesuine, he simply supposes that its author "had access to some genuine unpublished reminiscences of the unnamed Beloved Disciple." (On the Beloved Disciple, see pp 128 ff.)

8. This idea that Satan rules the world is also represented in Luke's story of Jesus' temptation (4:6–7) and elsewhere in the same gospel (10:18 and 13:16).

9. Cf. further DJE, p 97. When Paul speaks of "the life of Jesus" as delivering us from perils (2 Cor. 4:7–12), he is not representing his incarnate life as powerful, but (as Tannehill shows, 197, p 85) is referring to the divine power of his resurrection life. The "life of Jesus" (v. 11), which is "at work" among the Corinthians (v. 12) corresponds to "the power of God" in v. 7; cf. 13:4, where Paul says: Jesus "was crucified in weakness but lives by the power of God."

10. I am sometimes asked why I accept the historicity of John the Baptist if I reject that of Jesus, as though the evidence were equal for both. John the Baptist is mentioned as a historical character by Josephus in a passage which makes no mention of Jesus and which, I have elsewhere argued (DJE, pp 11, 152) can be accepted as genuine. If it had been interpolated by a Christian scribe familiar with the gospels, its account of the motives for John's imprisonment and execution would not be (as they in fact are) entirely different from those specified in the gospel version of these events. Josephus and the

gospels are, therefore, two independent witnesses about John the Baptist. Concerning Pilate, there is both substantial literary evidence and also an inscription.

11. Trocmé, criticizing writers who have denied the historical existence of Jesus, complains of the "picturesque fantasies" of their attempts to seek out pagan influences, and of their "contortions, allegedly based on a study of comparative religions" (202, p 7). It is true that denial of Jesus' historicity has often been founded on grotesque exaggeration of pagan influences. But these latter cannot simply be discounted (see DJE, ch. 8). Braun gives a brief but informative account of significant parallels between Jesus and pagan savior gods (24, pp 254-63) in the course of showing how Hellenistic religions influenced ideas about Jesus. The parallels are so marked that he does not find it easy to say how the Hellenistic pre-Pauline Christian differed from his pagan contemporary, for although they gave different names to their cult lords, their ideas concerning salvation would have been "largely similar" (p 267).

12. It has been shown repeatedly (and recently by Evans) how many incidents in the Passion the evangelists link with the Psalms. Evans thinks that the dying Jesus actually did (as Mk. 15:34 alleges) quote Psalm 22:1 ("My God, . . . why hast thou forsaken me?") and that, on this basis, early Christian writers searched in this and other Psalms for more information about the Passion and "found a great deal there" (64, p 8). But there is no need to take Jesus' cry from the cross as historical: see DJE, p 102, and in this volume, p 188.

13. The Catholic writer Feuillet (see 226) has given very considerable evidence to support the view that Paul's Christology is dependent on wisdom literature. Another Catholic, Larcher, reviewing discussion on the subject, agrees that Feuillet has made out a strong case (126, pp 19, 412 n.).

14. This in itself shows that, in the earliest Christian literature, *apostle* did not mean what it later came to mean, namely "companion of the historical Jesus." At Rev. 2:2 the church at Ephesus is congratulated for having "tested those who call themselves apostles but are not" (cf. the testing of charismatics, p 30). If *apostles* here meant (twelve) companions of Jesus," they could have been identified without being put to the test and "found false." Cf. further p 63 f.

CHAPTER 2

1. For details, see Whiteley, 213, p 9.

2. This is the view argued by Friedrich in his recent commentary (72).

3. Irenaeus said (as late as AD 180) that, before the end, the man of lawlessness will take his seat in the temple. But he was here (Bk. 5, chaps. 24-30) modeling his views of the end-events on 2 Thessalonians, and reckoned that the temple would be rebuilt for the Antichrist.

4. Polycarp wrote in ch. 11 of his letter to the Philippians that "the blessed Paul" had written them a letter at the beginning of which he had praised them by saying that he "boasts" of them "in all the Churches." These words in fact occur not in Paul's letter to the Philippians, but near the beginning of 2 Thessalonians: "We ourselves boast of you in the Churches of God for your steadfastness." We may infer that Polycarp knew 2 Thessalonians but confused it, by an understandable lapse of memory, with Paul's letter to another Macedonian church, that of Philippi.

5. "Do not be anxious about . . . what you shall eat . . . Look at the birds of the air: they neither sow nor reap nor gather into barns, and yet your heavenly Father feeds them" (Mt. 6:25–6, paralleled in Lk. 12:22–31). This doctrine has regrettably saved neither bird nor man from starvation.

6. The vocabulary of Hebrews is different from Paul's even where the ideas expressed are similar. Hebrews, for instance, speaks of Christ's "exaltation" to heaven, whereas Paul would have put "resurrection." Kümmel notes (125, pp 394–5) that Hebrews is among those letters written in the best Greek in the NT, in a style very different from Paul's, and shows "dependence on the modes of expression of Greek rhetoric."

7. See Theissen, 233a, pp 34–7.

8. Montefiore notes (143, p 98) that "desperate attempts" have been made to harmonize the statements in Hebrews with the gospel Gethsemane story. Among them we may perhaps include his own, which consists in rendering the Greek not as stating that Jesus' prayer to be saved from death "was heard for his godly fear" (RSV), but as implying that, although he did in fact die, he was set free from fear (p 99).

9. Grässer notes (86, p 268) that the Greek at 2:4 has a present participle ("bearing witness by signs," etc.), and that this does not restrict God's supporting witness of miracles to the time of "those who heard" Jesus, but leaves open the possibility that God may be bearing similar witness at the time of the writer.

10. See DJE, pp 126 ff. Luke does, however, in Acts 14:4 and 14 call Paul and Barnabas "apostles"; this is quite against his normal practice. Some commentators think that he drew on a tradition in which these two men figured as apostles in the nontechnical sense of missionaries (the Greek term means "those sent"). It is still perplexing that he assimilated the term from a source document when it so clearly conflicts with his own understanding of the term. Lindemann has suggested that as, for Luke, the "apostles" figure primarily as the leaders of the Jerusalem church, he did not feel it inappropriate to call by the same term those who later carry Christianity to pagans (232, p 62).

11. Best (14, p 35), Leaney (127, p 20), and Mitton (see p 53) all regard the dependence of 1 Peter on Ephesians as very probable.

12. "She who is in Babylon who is likewise chosen, sends you greetings" (1 Peter 5:13). "She" means the local church from which the letter was written. This is clear from similar phases in 2 John where "the elect Lady" is the church addressed, and fellow Christians of the author's own church are described as "children" of the recipients' "elect sister." The church in Babylon is said in 1 Peter to be "likewise chosen" because, like the Asian churches addressed (1:1 and 2:9), it has perceived and responded to God's saving call.

13. Jesus' pre-existence is implied by the statement (1 Peter 1:11) that the OT prophets were prompted to utterance "by the spirit of Christ within them"; and also by 1:20 (on which, see p 69).

14. The author writes for instance of the addressees' "good behavior in Christ" (1 Peter 3:16); and we saw that when he says that they are "in Christ," he means that baptism has regenerated the believer and moved him into a new sphere of existence, where he is united with Christ and shares his risen life. Cf. 3:21. "Baptism now serves you . . . through the resurrection of Jesus Christ."

CHAPTER 3

1. To give but a few examples: Paul complains of "false apostles" and of Christian

missionaries who preach "another Jesus than the one we preached" (2 Cor. 11:4 and 13). Hebrews 13:8–9 warns the faithful not to be led astray by "diverse and strange teachings" about Jesus; the pastoral epistles repeatedly complain of "false teachers," and Jude and 2 Peter also castigate heretics. 2 John 10–11 warns against Christians who do not bring the true doctrine.

2. I discuss this matter in JEC, ch. 8 (see especially p 220).

3. In ch. 9 of Ignatius' letter to the Magnesians, *we* are contrasted with Jewish Christians.

4. On Mark's ignorance of Palestinian geography, see note 2 on p 230.

5. The letter of Jude admittedly had some initial popularity. It was used by the author of 2 Peter and widely acknowledged as scripture about AD 200 (see Kelly, 119, p 223 for details), but then was long discarded or ignored. On James, see p 70.

6. Paul refers Roman Christians to "the standard of teaching" to which they were committed (Rom. 6:17), but does not use the word *faith* to denote a whole body of doctrine. On the few occasions, when, for him, "faith" does mean the content of what is believed (for example, Rom. 10:8, "the word of faith which we preach") the reference is probably to some simple formula such as "Jesus is Lord."

7. On Jewish and early Christian valedictories, see Fornberg, 67, p 10. Leaney argues (127, p 111) that the early church's doubts about the authenticity of 2 Peter may well have been due to familiarity with this genre, which was known to be pseudonymous.

8. Schmithals, however, thinks that, in the original version of the story, Peter's reference to the shelters or tents was meant to indicate that, in his view, with Christ's translation to heaven, the end-time had come; for some OT passages were held to imply that tents are to be the dwellings of the end-time (173, p 391 and note).

9. For details see Kümmel, 125, p 370. It has been claimed that Polycarp quoted the Pastorals (about AD 120) in two passages. But these do no more than state commonplaces (for example, "the love of money is the root of all evil") which could have belonged to the intellectual background of both Polycarp and the author of the Pastorals.

10. The Pastorals "lack many shorter words that are used with great frequency by Paul" (Kümmel, 125, p 373, who lists them there) and resemble standard Hellenistic Greek (the so-called higher Koine) more than do the generally acknowledged Paulines.

11. For instance, where Paul would use the word *gospel,* 1 Tim. 1:10 speaks of "sound teaching." The phrase is very characteristic of the Pastorals but is found nowhere else in the NT.

12. Kelly, however, thinks that Paul intended the letters to be read out publicly to the congregation and then preserved in the church's archives (118, pp 42–3) and that these were sufficient motives for writing.

13. 1 Tim. 3:4–5 gives the bishop and 1 Tim. 5:17 the elders a superintendent role. And Titus 1:5 and 7 mentions elders and bishops in such a way as to imply that the bishop is himself an elder.

14. Timothy is told to "guard what has been entrusted" to him (1 Tim. 6:20), and the Greek noun translated by the verb *entrust* (reiterated in 2 Tim. 1:12 and 14) is "a legal term denoting something which is placed in another man's keeping. The suggestion is that the Christian message ('the faith' or 'the truth' as it is so often called in these letters) is not something which the Church's minister works out for himself or is entitled to add to; it is a divine revelation which has been committed to his care" (Kelly, 118, p 150).

15. Kelly notes that a literal translation from the Greek would be "wholesome words, those of our Lord Jesus Christ," with no definite article before *wholesome.* He

thinks that the meaning is not "the sayings of Jesus" but "the sound Christian message" (118, pp 133–4).

16. It was surely because this doctrine is included in Scripture that the clergy in Scotland taught in the 17th century that food or shelter must not be given to a starving man unless his opinions were orthodox. See H. T. Buckle, *History of Civilization in England*, in 3 vol., III, 277.

CHAPTER 4

1. For an example of Matthew's adaptation of *Mark* see p 13 f. Such examples show that the word of God, which every evangelist claimed to speak, was not identified with a particular document. Old traditions were reinterpreted so as to be relevant to the particular circumstances of later evangelists (Haenchen, 92, p 131).

2. Mark makes serious mistakes in his geographical references to Palestine. He knows the Galilean place names and the general relative positions of the localities, but not specific details. Hence he "represents Jesus as traveling back and forth in Galilee and adjacent territories in a puzzling fashion" (Kee, 117, pp 102–3). To go (as Jesus is said to in Mk. 7:31) from the territory of Tyre by way of Sidon to the Sea of Galilee "is like traveling from Cornwall to London via Manchester" (Anderson, 2, p 192). Again, Mark's "references to movements across the Sea of Galilee are impossible to trace sequentially. Mention of specific locations near the sea are either unknown sites, such as Dalmanutha (8:10), or are patently inaccurate, as in the designation of the eastern shore of the lake as the country of the Gerasenes (5:1)" (Kee, loc. cit.). Gerasa is more than thirty miles southeast of the lake, too far away for the setting of the story which demands a city in its vicinity, with a precipitous slope down to the water. Probably all that concerned Mark, collecting and adapting pre-existing stories about Jesus, was that the lake and its surrounding territories, some Jewish and some mainly Gentile, was an ideal setting for journeys of Jesus and his disciples, showing how both Jews and Gentiles responded to him with faith. That place names in *Mark* caused perplexity among early readers is shown by the wide range of variants in the textual tradition where names occur in the gospel. Perplexity is also evidenced by Matthew, who changed Mark's *Gerasenes* to *Gadarenes* (Mt. 8:28), Gadara being a well-known spa only eight miles from the lake.

3. Robinson (164, p 16) takes Mark's instruction to Judaeans to "flee to the mountains" as evidence that he wrote when Christians in Judea were still free and able to flee — that is, before the Roman conquest, AD 70. Another reason why he thinks the passage must have been written before the Jewish War is that a tradition, preserved by the 4th-century church father, Eusebius, informs us that Christians in Jerusalem were instructed by an oracle *before* the war to head, not for the hills, but for Pella, a city below sea level. The argument, then, is that the Pella tradition is true (that is, Jerusalem Christians fled there before the encirclement of Jerusalem by Roman armies). Therefore since Mark's account conflicts with it, he wrote earlier, in ignorance of what actually happened in the war, which began in AD 66. But the Pella tradition is in fact most dubious. The fact that Eusebius may have taken it from the 2nd-century Christian writer Hegesippus does nothing to enhance its value, as it has been convincingly shown (Telfer, 199) that Hegesippus knew nothing of conditions in Judea. Mark's conflict with such tradition is not a means of dating his gospel.

4. Perrin (156, p 49) makes a case for the view that Mark himself composed his 9:1, using the saying he has in 13:30 (which he took from earlier tradition) as a model.

5. 125, p 141. Kümmel refers here to Conzelmann (41, part 1). Haenchen also illustrates Luke's ignorance of Palestinian geography from the statement (Acts 23:31-2) that infantrymen not only took Paul from Jerusalem to Antipatris (62 km) in a single night's march, but then immediately did the return journey to their barracks. Luke's general ignorance of conditions in Palestine is also suggested by his statement (Acts 4:1-3) that the Sadducees arrested and imprisoned the apostles. Although the Sadducees did form an important element in the council of Jerusalem before AD 70, they were not a body with authority to make arrests. At Acts 5:21 the high priest "called together the council and all the senate of Israel." Luke apparently did not know that the "council" was none other than the senate.

6. We saw (p 4) how Luke's ignorance is at one point corrected by his Western reviser.

7. Luke, although familiar with Roman persecution, had no desire to encourage Christians to seek martyrdom nor to stress its necessity, and he tones down some of Mark's references to persecution, perhaps in the hope that the stormclouds had passed, at least temporarily (Haenchen, 92, p 131). Mark's Jesus had said (8:34): "If any man would come after me, let him deny himself and take up his cross and follow me." Luke rewords this as: "take up his cross daily and follow me" (Lk. 9:23), thus replacing a reference to martyrdom with one suggesting the frustrations to which Christians are exposed in daily living.

8. *Luke* ends with Jesus leading his disciples on Easter day, after numerous appearances to them, from Jerusalem to the neighboring locality of Bethany, where he solemnly blesses them with uplifted hands before "he parted from them and was carried up into heaven"—on that same day. Some manuscripts have only "he parted from them" because copyists deleted the remaining words in order to represent the parting as only temporary and thus avoid contradicting the only other NT narrative of the ascension, in Acts 1, which dates it forty days later. The author was glad to utilize this latter tradition (even at the price of contradicting his own gospel) because, while occasional appearances of the risen one might be dismissed by skeptics as hallucinations, a sojourn of forty days, during which he presented "many proofs," was more substantial. Acts 13:31 repeats that there was a period of "many days" after the resurrection during which Jesus "appeared to those who had come up with him from Galilee to Jerusalem." This reiteration shows that the earlier statement about the forty days in 1:3 is not an interpolation or an editor's gloss as some (worried by the obvious contradiction between Acts and *Luke* here) have supposed.

9. That Herod died in 4 BC is undisputed. For a recent discussion of the evidence, see van Bruggen (28).

10. It may be that the story had already assumed two slightly different forms in the tradition and that Matthew drew on one version and Luke on the other.

11. Robinson also argues that, if Matthew's insertion in the parable had been written from knowledge of the events of AD 70, one would expect not merely the statement that the city was burned, but a more accurate account of its sack. It was, he says, the temple that perished by fire, whereas the walls of the city were thrown down (164, p 20). A little later, however (p 27), he seeks support for another argument by quoting Dodd to the effect that "a large part of the city," and not only the temple, was in fact burned in 70.

12. Robinson thus "fails to see any motive for preserving, let alone inventing, prophecies long after the dust had settled in Judaea" (p 23). Earlier, however (p 14), he quotes Moule to the effect that one *would* expect the evangelists, had they been writing at the end of the century, to "make capital out of the fact that they, and not non-Christian Judaism, were the true Israel." His argument here is that this expectation is not fulfilled: "our traditions are silent," and the evangelists therefore wrote before 70. So on the other hand there are gospel predictions about 70 (some of which represent it as God's judgment on the Jews) and these would not have been invented after 70; while, on the other hand, post-70 writers would be expected to make capital of 70, whereas the evangelists fail to do so.

CHAPTER 5

1. Barrett is among those who still think it probable that John knew *Mark*. But he allows that "anyone who prefers to say . . . 'not Mark, but a written source on which Mark drew,' may claim that his hypothesis fits the evidence equally well" (10, p 45).

2. Barrett notes that John does not expressly deny that there will be a "last day" when those who believe in Jesus will be "raised" (Jn. 6:39–40; cf. vss. 44 and 54). He "may have recognized that apocalyptic language was unavoidable" because established in the tradition, and that "to give it up would be to falsify the Christian faith." So "he retains it and reworks it" (9, pp 73–4).

3. Barrett notes that, as *John* was written with knowledge of the "putting" of Jewish Christians "out of the synagogue," which occurred 85–90, it "is quite a credible product of any date between 90 and 140. None of the attempts made to shift either date is successful" (10, p 128).

4. That John took some of the miracles he records from a short written collection in which they were numbered is betrayed when he calls the Cana miracle (where Jesus turns water into wine) "the first of Jesus' signs" (2:11) and the healing of the official's son "the second sign" (4:54)—even though he has narrated other "signs" which Jesus gave between these two occasions. He does not carry the numbering any further.

CHAPTER 7

1. The *we* disappears at Philippi at Acts 16:17 and reappears—after years of missionary travel—at this same locality at 20:5. This gave the Church fathers the idea that Luke had remained at Philippi (and not gone on to Macedonia and Greece with Paul) in order to practice his profession of medicine. This would be strange behavior on the part of one who had only just joined a missionary group—the *we* entered the narrative only at 16:10—and stranger still on the basis of 16:10 itself, which reads: "And when he [Paul] had seen the vision, immediately we sought to go into Macedonia, concluding that God had called us to preach the gospel to them."

2. The Greek verb in the original, which I have rendered *follow* (in the sense of "investigate") can sometimes mean "participate in." But in this context, that meaning is excluded by the adverb *accurately*. One can "investigate" a series of events "accurately," but one cannot "participate in them accurately" (cf. Haenchen, 91, p 263).

3. In 2 Tim. 3:10 ff, the writer (who poses as Paul) tells of "persecutions and sufferings that I went through at Antioch [in Pisidia], at Iconium, at Lystra." The passage

shows that, in some Pauline communities, a tradition was preserved about persecution of Paul in these three places. This tradition was obviously known to Luke, who makes Paul visit them (Act 13:14 ff) in the order specified in 2 Timothy (Haenchen, 94, p 374). That Luke stresses Paul's superiority over his opponents rather than his suffering does not alter the fact that his narrative has some basis in pre-existing tradition.

4. For details see Haenchen, 94, p 190 and Dibelius, 51, pp 127–8. One of Dibelius' examples is the summaries at Acts 2:44 and 4:34–5. These tell of organized communism, which required that every property owner should give up his possessions. But "in the story relating to this subject, we are told that Ananias kept back part of the proceeds and that he was reproached on the grounds that he should have brought all the money or none at all, since the surrender of goods was voluntary. And when a little earlier . . . Barnabas is praised for putting the proceeds of the sale of his field at the apostles' disposal, we can see that he did so of his own free will and not in accordance with some rule which was binding for all." Thus "Luke used the individual instances he knew of in order to compose a picture of an ideal."

5. Having recorded Paul's arrival in Rome (28:14), Acts represents (v. 15) Christians as setting out from Rome to meet him (still on his way there) at Forum Appii and Tres Tabernae (two well-known stopping places on the Via Appia between Rome and Naples, 63 and 49 kms. respectively from the city). That verse 15 was inserted by Luke into a story drawn from one of his sources is betrayed by the fact that the following verse reverts to the situation reported at the end of v. 14 (Paul's arrival in Rome). In the insertion Luke briefly acknowledges the existence of Christians at Rome, but he never mentions them again, saying nothing of an organized church there, and proceeds to make Paul summon (such a person of authority is he for Luke) the leading Jews of the city, who ask him to explain Christianity to them, since they know nothing about it, except that it everywhere meets with opposition (28:22). From Paul's own letter to Roman Christians, it is clear that a sizable Christian community existed there, and the leading Jews of the city could not have remained indifferent to and ignorant of Christian Messianism, as Luke suggests.

6. Luke is certainly aware that the Christian message is capable of being misunderstood as the proclamation of "another King Jesus" as the rival to Caesar (Acts 17:7). This passage reproduces the voice of Luke, not historical facts; for it forms part of a context where Christianity has only just been brought into Europe (by Paul from Asia Minor) and where Christians are nevertheless described by Thessalonian Jews as "men who have turned the world upside down" (v. 6). Luke is clearly envisaging the situation of his own times, when Christianity had in fact permeated the Empire.

7. This is Agrippa II (AD 27–100), the great-grandson of Herod the Great. Luke does not call him Herod, and reserves that appellation for those descendants of Herod the Great who were hostile to Christians.

8. The scene is imagined, since Paul has just appealed to Caesar (to be tried at Nero's court in Rome), so that the case was no longer in Festus' hands and he is left with no intelligible motive for inquiring further into Paul's guilt or innocence. The procurator did not, in reality, need to formulate charges, but only to render an account of the proceedings up to the prisoner's appeal, and, according to Acts itself, Festus had all the information needed for that purpose (Haenchen, 94, p 604). Nevertheless, he is represented as bringing Paul before Agrippa because he as yet has "nothing definite to write" to Nero about him, and finds it "unreasonable, in sending a prisoner, not to indicate the charges against him" (Acts 25:26–7).

234   *Notes*

9. Robinson notes that Paul's speech to the elders at Miletus is the only one in Acts where he is addressing Christians (as he is in his letters) instead of Jews or pagans, and that here, if anywhere, some trace of the ideas expressed in his epistles is to be expected. He claims to discern in the speech "some remarkable parallels with the later Pauline writings" (164, p 87). The writings thus designated are principally the pastoral epistles, regarded by most scholars as early 2nd-century works produced in Pauline Christian communities. In any case, the parallels with Acts are hardly "remarkable." Robinson mentions (pp 80–1):(1) the language of "completing the race." In the speech at Miletus Paul says: "I set no store by life: I only want to finish the race and complete the task which the Lord Jesus has assigned to me, of bearing testimony to the Gospel of God's grace" (Acts 20:24). The same metaphor is used in 2 Tim. 4:7: "I have run the race, I have completed the course." (2) Themes common to the speech in Acts and the epistle to Titus, namely warnings to elders concerning heretics, and "an insistence on the example of honest work."

10. Paul's own account (1 Cor. 15:5–7) makes the risen Jesus' appearance to him the very last of a series; and Peter and James will perhaps have needed convincing that a former persecutor of Christianity had in fact been vouchsafed any such appearance. For their part, they could have informed him of a few "words of the Lord" (that is, words spoken by the spirit to early Christians, cf. p 30) which will have been useful to him in his missionary work. (It is perhaps on such a basis that Paul is able to tell the Corinthians of "the Lord's" instructions concerning marriages with unbelievers: 1 Cor. 7:12.) It is commonly held that Paul could not have emerged from this fortnight in Jerusalem without detailed knowledge of Jesus' life. If Peter and James had been companions of a recently executed Jesus, then this inference is just. But its premise is precisely what I am calling in question. Haenchen (who of course does not question that Jesus existed, nor that Peter and James knew him personally) says, apropos of what Peter and James had to say to Paul, that the way Paul speaks of Jesus' incarnate life (as lived obscurely and in humiliation) does not suggest that they gave him detailed biographical information (91, p 57).

11. Thus the story of the ascension, as told at the end of *Luke,* is not compatible with the version given at the beginning of Acts (cf. p 231, note 8). In Acts itself the story of Paul's conversion is reported three times, and on each occasion is adapted to suit its context. (For details, see Haenchen, 91, pp 212 ff, 218.)

12. Luke works Paul into the story of Stephen's martyrdom by interpolating into his source material the words: "And the witnesses laid down their garments at the feet of a young man named Saul" (Acts 7:58). That this statement has been interpolated is betrayed by the fact that it is preceded by the words "and they stoned him" and followed by a repetition of almost the same words, which enable the author to resume the interrupted narrative of the martyrdom. Having made Paul present on the occasion, Luke adds that he "was consenting" to Stephen's death (8:1, reiterated at 22:20), and then makes him "lay waste" the church and "drag off" men and women to prison (8:3). From this point he alone is named as the Christians' persecutor, and when he is converted the church (which in the meantime had spread beyond Jerusalem) "had peace" (9:31). Luke later (26:10 ff) reveals how he envisaged Paul as persecutor: as one of the judges at Christian trials and as always voting for the death sentence (cf. Haenchen, 92, p 320).

13. "Was a man called with the marks of circumcision on him? Let him not remove them. Was he uncircumcised when he was called? Let him not be circumcised" (1 Cor. 7: 18–19, NEB). "If we are in union with Christ Jesus, circumcision makes no difference

at all, nor does the want of it: the only thing that counts is faith active in love" (Gal. 5:6, NEB). "There is no question here of Greek and Jew, circumcised and uncircumcised. . . . But Christ is all and is in all" (Coloss. 3:11, NEB).

14. He was far from feeling sure that the money would be acceptable (Rom. 15:31). He may well have feared that the Jewish authorities would regard him as a renegade and that James might in consequence hesitate to accept money from him for fear of jeopardizing his own relationship with them.

15. It is hinted even in Acts that Paul's second missionary journey (that is, the first he made without Barnabas) was not financed by Antioch; for on this second journey he is represented as having to earn his own living (Acts 18:3).

16. Admittedly, the four ordinances do not clear all obstacles from table-fellowship. They would not, for instance, have guaranteed that none of the wine had come from a libation, nor that forbidden meat (pork) was served. But agreement could easily have been reached on such matters once fellowship had, in principle, been conceded, as according to the agreement recorded in Acts it was. Pious Jews could, for instance, have brought their own food (cf. Schmithals, 172, pp 97–100).

17. The phrase "yoke of the Law," which Luke (Acts 15:10) understands as a complaint concerning its burdensomeness, has no such connotations for Jews, and for them refers only to the duty of keeping this privileged means whereby Israel attains to righteousness.

18. One of Robinson's arguments for dating *Luke* and Acts earlier than AD 62 is that Acts is silent about an incident which took place in that year, and which Luke would have been glad to mention had he known of it. Josephus tells that, during the absence of a Roman procurator after the death of Festus, a Jewish high priest exceeded his competence and had one "James and certain others" executed in AD 62. James is here further designated as "the brother of Jesus." Let us suppose, with Robinson, that this designation is not a Christian interpolation and identify this James in Josephus with the Christian James who, according to Acts, was one of the leaders of the Jerusalem church (even though this James is never, in Acts, called the brother of Jesus). Then we have Josephus telling of the martyrdom of this James in 62 at the hands of the intemperate high priest when there was no Roman governor to control him, whereas Luke says nothing about it. Robinson argues that, had the incident already occurred, Luke would have found in it ideal material for one of his major apologetic concerns, namely to show that the Jews, not the Romans, were the real enemies of Christianity. But this argument overlooks the fact that, for the author of Acts, Jewish Chrisitianity becomes of less and less interest in later chapters.

19. Luke's treatment of the Pharisees in his gospel is consistent with his attitude to them in Acts, in that his overall tendency is to soften the opposition between Jesus and the Pharisees in incidents he has drawn from *Mark* (see Ziesler, 222, pp 150–3).

20. Käsemann shows (114, pp 61–3) that when Paul mentions miracles he has worked (2 Cor. 12:12), he does so in order to stand up to rival Christian teachers who stressed their own capacities in this direction. That is, his appeal to his own miracles is part of the "folly" of "boasting," which he says he is forced into in order to show that he is as good an apostle as the "superlative" ones who have criticized him. At 1 Cor. 12:28–9 he says that working miracles is not to be expected of all those whom God has "appointed" in the church, and he goes on to list a number of alternative Christian activities which he regards as at least equally important. And at 1 Cor. 1:22 he declares himself unwilling to support his missionary preaching with miracles.

21. Lindemann thinks that Justin was in fact acquainted with Pauline letters and used ideas from Gal. 3 about the cross. But nowhere did Justin indicate the sources of his hermeneutic, since he accepted as authorities only the Septuagint and the words of Jesus and was not interested in other Christian tradition (232, pp 362–6).

CHAPTER 8

1. The oldest extant copy of this section of *Mark* (P^{45} from the first half of the 3rd century) has, not Jesus "the carpenter, the son of Mary," but Jesus "the son of the carpenter." Both readings are well-attested and either could be the original one (see Nineham, 148, p 166). If Mark wrote "the son of the carpenter," it is intelligible that a later copyist, familiar with the virgin-birth story (which is unknown to Mark) changed this to "the carpenter" and added "the son of Mary" (Taylor, 198, p 300). Morton Smith, however, finds such a change "incredible," as "son of Mary was certain to be understood as implying Jesus' illegitimate birth" (184, p 26). In Jewish custom, to describe a man as the son of his mother would carry this implication. But we cannot be sure that Mark — let alone a later copyist — appreciated what Nineham has called "such niceties of Jewish usage." (Morton Smith simply takes it for granted (p 28) that Mark was a Jew. But this is not generally agreed, and Nineham (p 41) thinks him more likely to have been a Gentile.) Taking "son of Mary" as the original reading, Morton Smith infers, from his premises, that Jesus was in fact an illegitimate child.

2. The fourth gospel consistently represents Jesus as from Galilee and makes no mention of any connection with David's Bethlehem. It also represents the Jews as saying that he cannot be the Messiah because he comes from Galilee and not from David's village, Bethlehem (Jn. 7:41–2), and the evangelist makes no attempt to refute this charge. His idea seems to be that Jesus, although from Galilee, is the Messiah, and that the Jewish categories of thinking about the Messiah are totally inadequate.

3. For a discussion of the infancy narratives in *Matthew* and *Luke* as a whole, see JEC, ch. 1. Even on the Catholic side, it is now admitted that it is "quite impossible" to harmonize the two narratives (Brown, 25, p 497). Brown believes that the stories of Jesus' ministry "depend, in part at least, on traditions that have come down from the disciples who accompanied him during that ministry," and he concedes that, in contrast, "we have no reliable information about the source of the infancy material" (p 7). He holds that the infancy narratives are nonetheless "worthy vehicles of the gospel message" (p 8).

4. Rahab, says Johnson, was "at some point in the Jewish tradition considered a proselyte belonging to the tribe of Judah" (112, p 164). In two Talmudic passages a section of the genealogy of Judah (as given in 1 Chron. 4:21–3) is applied to Rahab by a play on words.

5. Morton Smith does not mention this explanation of the presence of the four women in the genealogy. He thinks they are there because Jesus was an illegitimate child (cf. note 1 above for his evidence) and that the author of the genealogy, knowing this, "wanted to excuse Mary by these implied analogies" (184, p 26).

6. Burger also notes that, nevertheless, Matthew does not expressly link Jesus' birth in Bethlehem (the subject of his ch. 2) with his doctrine of ch. 1 that Jesus is a son of David. These are two originally independent traditions concerning his birth, and Matthew has simply arranged them in a sequence. A place of birth is not mentioned in

ch. 1, and ch. 2 seems to mark a new beginning and to represent an account of his origin which knew nothing of his virgin birth. ("When Jesus was born at Bethlehem in Judea in the reign of Herod," and so forth, on to Herod's slaughter of the Innocents, with no mention of David.)

7. Burger notes Mt. 9:27 as an instance where Jesus is addressed as "son of David" in a passage *not* deriving from *Mark*. Here two blind men cry: "Have mercy on us, Son of David." This, he says, is clearly a duplicate of *Mark*'s Bartimaeus incident. Although Matthew includes the latter in its proper place later (20:29–34), he needed to duplicate it here at 9:27 in order to justify Jesus' statement at 11:5 that, as a result of his activities "the blind receive their sight."

8. In Luke's version of the triumphal entry, it is only the disciples who hail Jesus with shouts of acclamation (19:37, reiterated in verse 39), not the whole crowd as in Mk. 11:9. Admittedly, Luke's Jesus is greeted as "the king that comes in the name of the Lord" (v. 38), but the disciples themselves supply the interpretation of this their acclamation: they mean it as thanks to God for all the miracles they had witnessed (v. 37, significantly added by Luke to *Mark*). And the altogether nonpolitical character of Jesus' kingship is underlined when their acclamation continues: "Peace in heaven and glory to the highest." (This again is not in *Mark*.) So instead of the Marcan hope for "the kingdom of our father David that is coming" (Mk. 11:10), Luke puts a reminiscence of what he has made the heavenly hosts say at Jesus' birth: "Glory to God in the highest, and on earth peace" (Lk. 2:14).

CHAPTER 9

1. Flusser, 66, p 216. For more recent accounts of the shroud, see the 1978 booklet edited by Jennings (110) and the one by Sox (185), with a foreword by Sir Steven Runciman.

2. The shroud's advocates have seen great significance in the fact that the evidence of the cloth is compatible with nail wounds in the wrists, rather than in the palms of the hands. I will not repeat what I have said elsewhere on this (208, pp 31–2).

3. The original Old French is quoted by Blinzler, 19, p 39. Runciman doubts whether the shroud mentioned by Clari is the one that can be accurately traced from the mid-14th century; for a shroud that depicted the face and body of Jesus was never mentioned by the Byzantines (even though they claimed to have Jesus' shroud) nor by any of the pilgrims who came to see the famed relic-collections of Constantinople (185, p 10).

4. For example, by Bulst, 29, pp 22–3. I have discussed elsewhere (208, pp 27–8) fanciful attempts to find pre-medieval evidence for the shroud. Wilson (218) has identified it with an icon discovered at Edessa in 543 (cf. my criticism of this theory, 210, p 12). Runciman comments (185, p 10) that all such attempts to identify the shroud with an earlier known relic have not been successful.

5. A forger could, however, have deliberately secured an old piece of linen from the East on which to work, "just as modern forgers of icons choose pieces of old wood" (Runciman, 185, p 10).

6. Sox, like Wilson, describes Joseph of Arimathea as a "wealthy disciple" of Jesus (185, p 23). This is not, as Sox suggests (p 22), one of the matters on which all three synoptics agree, but is peculiar to *Matthew*. Sox will perhaps not find this disconcerting, as "it has been observed that the Aramaic text of Matthew is older than Mark" (p 21).

There is, in fact, no Aramaic text of *Matthew,* only a Greek text. Sox is presumably alluding (in this highly misleading way) to Semitisms in the Greek. On the value of these, as indicators of material of early date and general reliability, see ch. 6.

7. Robinson says that Luke, having recorded (23:53) Jesus' burial in a "shroud," nevertheless goes on (24:12) to say that Peter saw "the cloths" by themselves in the empty tomb; and that this shows that, for Luke, the two words are identical in meaning. But Robinson knows quite well that Lk. 24:12 is absent from some manuscripts, and is printed only as footnote (not as part of the text) of the RSV. He discreetly alludes to the possibility of interpolation when he says that "Luke or his scribe" wrote 24:12 (110, p 70). This verse is widely regarded as a gloss influenced by Jn. 20:6 (where Peter sees the cloths in the empty tomb), or as a non-Marcan tradition (in conflict with the Marcan one Luke assimilated when he wrote of the shroud), which Luke himself introduced into his Marcan material and which had grown and developed somewhat by the time it reached John. It is in conflict not only with what Luke has earlier said about the shroud but also with what he goes on to say, namely that not only Peter but *a number of disciples* had gone to the tomb and found it empty (24:24). Robinson says (p 72) that Lk. 24:12 is omitted by "only one Greek manuscript" (that is, it is also absent from Old Latin translations). One sees how the evidence for its authenticity grows in less scholarly hands when Sox declares that the verse is "part of the original text according to all manuscripts except one" (185, p 23).

CHAPTER 10

1. Although Perrin is right to say that Mark records no resurrection appearances, this evangelist seems to imply that appearances in Galilee (of the type alleged by Matthew) will occur; for he makes Jesus say, at the Last Supper: "After I am raised up, I will go before you into Galilee"; and at the empty tomb the women are instructed to "tell his disciples . . . that he is going before you into Galilee." Perrin supposes (following Lohmeyer and Marxsen) that "going before them into Galilee" means leading them (in spirit) as missionaries into the Gentile world (of which Galilee is a symbol) where they will "see" him—not at a brief appearance as in *Matthew,* but at his second coming when he will judge the world.

2. See the article "Goldene Regel" in Galling et al. (75).

3. Crossan goes on to claim that the actual parable, ending in the rhetorical question "which of the three do you think proved neighbor to the man who fell among the robbers?" (Lk. 10:36), stemmed "from the historical Jesus" on the ground that its idealization of a Samaritan is not what one would have expected to be attributed to a 1st-century Jewish teacher; and also because parables are rare in the early church and therefore not part of its "creativity" (48, p 291). He admits, however, that the content of this parable "would not be at all uncongenial to the Samaritan interests of . . . *Luke*-Acts." It is not present in any other gospel.

4. For a detailed account of this matter, see my article on miracles (209).

5. On Q, see DJE, pp 84, 104–5, 114, 116. There would be no need to posit the existence of Q if one could explain the non-Marcan material common to *Matthew* and *Luke* by supposing that Luke drew it directly from Matthew (or Matthew from Luke). But there are well-known difficulties in supposing that either of these two evangelists had read the gospel of the other (cf. p 28). Nevertheless, the view is gaining ground that *Luke* is dependent on *Matthew*. See, for instance, the article by M. E. Boismard, "The Two-Source Theory at an Impasse" in *New Testament Studies* 26 (1979), 1–17.

References

A work listed below is referred to in this book by its number in the list. The following abbreviations as well as those on pp ix f, are used.

Black	*Black's New Testament Commentaries,* ed. by H. Chadwick
CBC	*The Cambridge Bible Commentary on the New English Bible,* ed. by P. R. Ackroyd et al.
CUP	Cambridge University Press
DJE	*Did Jesus Exist?* (no. 207 in the list)
HTR	*Harvard Theological Review*
JEC	*The Jesus of the Early Christians* (no. 206 in the list)
JTS	*Journal of Theological Studies*
NCB	*New Century Bible,* ed. by M. Black et al.
Nov Test	*Novum Testamentum*
NTD	*Das Neue Testament Deutsch,* ed. by G. Friedrich
NTS	*New Testament Studies*
Perspectives	*Perspectives on Luke-Acts,* ed. by C. H. Talbert (196, p 246)
RGG	*Die Religion in Geschichte und Gegenwart,* ed. by K. Galling et al.
TLS	*Times Literary Supplement*
trans.	English translation
ZNW	*Zeitschrift für neutestamentliche Wissenschaft*
ZthK	*Zeitschrift für Theologie und Kirche*

1 Abel, E. L., "The Psychology of Memory and Rumor," *The Journal of Religion* 51 (1971), 270–82.
2 Anderson, H., *The Gospel of Mark,* NCB (London, 1976).

239

3 Bailey, J. A., "Who Wrote 2 Thessalonians?", NTS 25 (1979), 131-45.
4 Barclay, R., *And Jesus Said* (Edinburgh, 1970).
5 Barnard, L. W., *Studies in the Apostolic Fathers* (Oxford, 1966).
6 ——, *Justin Martyr* (Cambridge, 1967).
7 Barrett, C. K., "Christianity in Corinth," *Bulletin of the John Rylands Library*, 46 (1964), 268-97.
8 —— (ed.), *The New Testament Background: Selected Documents* (London, 1974).
9 ——, *The Gospel of John and Judaism* (London, 1975).
10 ——, *The Gospel According to St. John*, 2nd ed. (London, 1978).
11 Bauer, W., *Orthodoxy and Heresy in Earliest Christianity*, trans. (London, 1972).
12 Beare, F. W., *The Earliest Records of Jesus* (Oxford, 1962).
13 ——, *The Epistle to the Philippians*, Black, 3rd ed. (London, 1973).
14 Best, E., *1 Peter, NCB* (London, 1971).
15 ——, "Mark 3:20-21, 31-35," NTS 22 (1976), 309-19.
16 Beyer, K., *Semitische Syntax im NT, Bd. 1 (Satzlehre)*. Vol. 1, (Göttingen, 1962) No further volumes published.
17 Black, M., "The Semitic Element in the New Testament," *The Expository Times* 77 (1965), 20-3.
18 ——, *An Aramaic Approach to the Gospels and Acts*, 3rd ed. (Oxford, 1967).
19 Blinzler, J., *Das Turiner Grablinnen und die Wissenschaft* (Ettal, 1952).
20 Boers, H., "The Form Critical Study of Paul's Letters, 1 Thessalonians as a Case Study," NTS 22 (1976), 140-58.
21 Bornkamm, G., *Paul*, trans. (London, 1971).
22 Bouquet, A. C., "Freedom and Responsibility in Christian Commitment," *The Modern Churchman* 15 (1971), 65-85.
23 Brandon, S. G. F., *The Fall of Jerusalem and the Christian Church* (London, 1951).
24 Braun, H., "Der Sinn der NT Christologie," in *Gesammelte Studien zum NT und seiner Umwelt*, 3rd. ed. (Tübingen, 1971), 243-82.
25 Brown, R. E., *The Birth of the Messiah. A Commentary on the Infancy Narratives in Matthew and Luke* (London, 1977).
26 Bruce, F. F., *The Acts of the Apostles. The Greek Text with Introduction and Commentary*, 2nd ed. (1952).
27 ——, *Jesus and Christian Origins Outside the New Testament* (London, 1974).
28 Bruggen, J. van, "The Year of the Death of Herod the Great," in *Miscellanea Neotestamentica, Supplements to Nov Test* 48 (1978), 1-15.
29 Bulst, W., *Das Grabtuch von Turin* (Frankfurt, 1959).
30 Bultmann, R., *Die Geschichte der synoptischen Tradition*, 8th ed. (Göttingen, 1970).
31 Burger, C., *Jesus als Davidssohn* (Göttingen, 1970).
32 Burkill, T. A., "The Condemnation of Jesus: a Critique of Sherwin-White's Thesis," *Nov Test* 12 (1970), 321-42.
33 ——, *New Light on the Earliest Gospel* (Ithaca, N.Y., 1972).
34 Caird, G. B., *The Gospel of St. Luke* (The Pelican New Testament Commentaries) (1963).
35 Calvert, D. G. A., "An Examination of the Criteria for Distinguishing the Authentic Words of Jesus," NTS 18 (1974), 209-18.

36 Campenhausen, H. von, *Ecclesiastical Authority and Spiritual Power in the Church of the First Three Centuries,* trans. (London, 1969).

37 Catchpole, D. R., *The Trial of Jesus. A Study in the Gospels and Jewish Historiography from 1770 to the Present Day* (Leiden, 1971).

38 Cerfaux, L., "Le titre Kyrios," *Revue des sciences philosophiques et théologiques* 12 (1923), 125–53.

39 Clarke, W. K. Lowther (ed.), *The First Epistle of Clement to the Corinthians* (London, 1937).

40 Cohn, H., *The Trial and Death of Jesus* (London, 1972).

41 Conzelmann, H., *Die Mitte der Zeit, Studien zur Theologie des Lukas,* 5th ed. (Tübingen, 1964).

42 ———, "Historie und Theologie in den synoptischen Passionsberichten" in *Zur Bedeutung des Todes Jesu* (by several hands) (Gütersloh, 1967), 35–53.

43 ——— and Dibelius, M., *A Commentary on the Pastoral Epistles,* from the 4th ed. of *Die Pastoralbriefe,* 1966 (Philadelphia, 1972).

44 ———, *Der Brief an die Kolosser,* NTD, vol. 8, rev. ed. (Göttingen, 1976), 176–202.

45 Corwin, Virginia, *St. Ignatius and Christianity in Antioch* (New Haven, Ct., 1960).

46 Cranfield, C. E. B., *Commentary on Romans,* vol. 1, in the series *International Critical Commentary* (Edinburgh, 1975).

47 Creed, J. M., *The Gospel According to St. Luke* (London, 1930, reprinted 1965).

48 Crossan, J. D., "Parable and Example in the Teaching of Jesus," *NTS* 18 (1971–2), 285–307.

49 Davies, D. P., "Christianity and the Appeal to History," *Question* 12 (1979), 28–50.

50 Davies, W. D., *The Setting of the Sermon on the Mount* (CUP, 1963).

51 Dibelius, M., *Studies in the Acts of the Apostles,* ed. H. Greeven, trans. (London, 1956).

52 Dinkler, E. (ed.), *Zeit und Geschichte,* Festschrift for Bultmann's 80th birthday, articles by D. Georgi (263–93) and E. Haenchen (235–54) (Tubingen, 1964).

53 Dodd, C. H., *The Apostolic Preaching* (London, 1936).

54 ———, *Historical Tradition in the Fourth Gospel* (CUP, 1963).

55 ———, *The Interpretation of the Fourth Gospel* (CUP, 1970).

56 ———, *The Founder of Christianity* (London, 1971).

57 Dupuis, C. F., *L'origine de tous les cultes,* vol. 5 (bound as 9), (Paris, 1795).

58 Ellis, E. E., *The Gospel of Luke,* NCB (London, 1966).

59 Enslin, Morton S., "How the Story Grew — Judas in Fact and Fiction," *Festschrift for F. W. Gingrich,* ed. E. H. Barth and R. E. Cocroft (Leiden, 1972), 123–41.

60 ———, "John and Jesus," ZNW 66 (1975), 1–18.

61 Epp, E. J., *The Theological Tendency of Codex Bezae Cantabrigiensis in Acts* (CUP, 1966).

62 Evans, C. F., *Resurrection and the New Testament* (London, 1970).

63 ———, "The New Testament in the Making," in *The Cambridge History of the Bible,* vol. 1 (CUP, 1970), 232–84.

64 ———, *Explorations in Theology,* vol. 2 (London, 1977).

65 Farmer, W. R., *The Last Twelve Verses of Mark* (CUP, 1974).

66 Flusser, D., "Jesus in the Context of History," in *The Crucible of Christianity* (London, 1969), 216–34.

67 Fornberg, T., *An Early Church in a Pluralistic Society: A Study of 2 Peter* (Lund, 1977).
68 Forer, R., *Die Zeugdrucke der byzantischen . . . Kunstepochen* (Strassburg, 1894).
69 ———, *Die Kunst des Zeugdrucks vom Mittelalter bis zur Empirezeit* (Strassburg, 1898).
70 Franklin, E., *Christ the Lord. A Study in the Purpose and Theology of Luke-Acts* (London, 1975).
71 Frend, W. H. C., *Martyrdom and Persecution in the Early Church* (Oxford, 1965).
72 Friedrich, G., ed. of 1 and 2 Thessalonians in NTD, vol. 8, rev. ed. (Göttingen, 1976).
73 Fuchs, E., *Studies of the Historical Jesus*, trans. (London, 1964).
74 Fuller, R. H., *The Foundations of New Testament Christology* (London, 1965).
75 Galling, K., et al. (eds.), *Die Religion in Geschichte und Gegenwart* (cited as RGG), 3rd ed., 7 vols. (Tübingen, 1957–65).
76 Garland, D. E., *The Intention of Matthew 23* (Leiden, 1979).
77 Gerhardsson, B., *Memory and Manuscript, Oral Tradition and Written Transmission in Rabbinic Judaism and Early Christianity* (Uppsala, 1961).
78 Goetz, K. G., *Petrus als Gründer und Oberhaupt der Kirche* (Leipzig, 1927).
79 Goodspeed, E. J., *A History of Early Christian Literature*, rev. ed. by R. M. Grant (Chicago, 1966).
80 Goppelt, L., *Christentum und Judentum im ersten und zweiten Jahrhundert* (Gütersloh, 1954).
81 ———, *Der 1. Petrusbrief* (Göttingen, 1978).
82 Goulder, M. D., *Midrash and Lection in Matthew* (London, 1974).
83 ——— (ed.), *Incarnation and Myth*, articles by D. Cupitt (31–40, 166–9), M. Goulder (51–9, 142–6), J. Rodwell (64–73), and G. Stanton (151–65) (London, 1979).
84 Grant, F. C., and Rowley, H. H. (eds.), *Dictionary of the Bible*, 2nd ed., articles by W. Förster (on 2 Peter), J. Knox (on 1 Thessalonians), and O. J. F. Seitz (on James) (Edinburgh, 1963).
85 Grant, R. M., *Miracles and Natural Law in Graeco-Roman and Early Christian Thought* (Amsterdam, 1952).
86 Grässer, E., "Das Heil als Wort. Exegetische Erwägungen zu Hebr. 2:1–4," in *NT und Geschichte*, Festschrift for O. Cullmann, ed. H. Baltensweiler et al. (Tübingen, 1972), 261–74.
87 Grayston, K., and Herdan, G., "The Authorship of the Pastorals in the Light of Statistical Linguistics" NTS 6 (1959), 1–15.
88 Grayston, K., *Letters of Paul to the Thessalonians and the Philippians* (CUP, 1967).
89 Greenlee, J. H., *Introduction to New Testament Textual Criticism* (London, 1976).
90 Guthrie, D., *New Testament Introduction: Hebrews to Revelation* (London, 1964).
91 Haenchen, E., *Gott und Mensch* (a collection of essays, including ten on the NT) (Tübingen, 1965).
92 ———, *Die Bibel und Wir* (a collection of essays, including eight on the NT) (Tübingen, 1968).

93 ——, *Der Weg Jesu*, 2nd ed. (Berlin, 1968).
94 ——, *Die Apostelgeschichte*, 6th ed. (Göttingen, 1968).
95 Hagner, D. A., *The Use of the Old Testament and the New Testament in Clement of Rome* (Leiden, 1973).
96 Hamerton-Kelly, R. G., *Pre-Existence, Wisdom and the Son of Man* (Cambridge, 1973).
97 Hanson, A. T., *The Pastoral Letters*, CBC (CUP, 1966).
98 Harrison, P. N., *Polycarp's Two Epistles to the Philippians* (CUP, 1936).
99 Hengel, M., *Crucifixion*, trans. (London, 1977).
100 Hennecke, E., *New Testament Apocrypha*, ed. W. Schneemelcher, trans. R. McL. Wilson, vol. 2 (London, 1965).
101 Hick, J. (ed.), *The Myth of God Incarnate*, articles by Frances Young (13–47, 87–121), M. Goulder (48–86), and an Epilogue (186–204) by D. Nineham (London 1977).
102 Hook, N., *The Eucharist in the New Testament* (London, 1964).
103 Hoskyns, E., and Davey, N., *The Riddle of the New Testament* (London, 1958).
104 Houlden, J. L., *Johannine Epistles*, Black (London, 1973).
105 ——, *The Pastoral Epistles* (The Pelican NT Commentaries) (1976).
106 Hull, J. M., *Hellenistic Magic and the Synoptic Tradition* (London, 1974).
107 Hunter, A. M., *According to John* (London, 1968).
108 Hunzinger, C. H., "Babylon als Deckname für Rom" in *Gotteswort und Gottesland*, ed. H. Reventlow (Göttingen, 1965), 65–77.
109 Hughes, G., *Hebrews and Hermeneutics* (CUP, 1979).
110 Jennings, P. (ed.), *Face to Face with the Shroud* (Oxford, 1978).
111 Jeremias, J., *New Testament Theology, Pt. 1. The Proclamation of Jesus*, trans. J. Bowden (London, 1971).
112 Johnson, M. D., *The Purpose of the Biblical Genealogies* (CUP, 1969).
113 Josephus, Flavius, *Antiquities of the Jews*, trans. by H. Thackeray, Loeb Classical Library, 6 vols. (London, 1930–65).
114 Käsemann, E., "Die Legitimität des Apostels," ZNW 41 (1942), 33–71.
115 ——, "The Problem of the Historical Jesus," in *Essays on New Testament Themes* (London, 1964), 15–47.
116 ——, *New Testament Questions of Today*, trans. (London, 1969).
117 Kee, H. C., *Community of the New Age. Studies in Mark's Gospel* (London, 1977).
118 Kelly, J. N. D., *The Pastoral Epistles*, Black (London, 1963).
119 ——, *The Epistles of Peter and of Jude*, Black (London, 1969).
120 Kenyon, Kathleen, *Jerusalem: Excavating 3000 Years of History* (London, 1967).
121 Klein, G., "Die Verleugnung des Petrus," in *Rekonstruktion und Interpretation, Gesammelte Aufsätze zum NT* (Munich, 1969), 49–98.
122 Klijn, A. F. J., *A Survey of Researches into the Western Text of the Gospels and Acts* (Utrecht, 1949).
123 ——, *A Survey of the Researches into the Western Text of the Gospels and Acts, Pt. 2 (1949–69)* (Leiden, 1969).
124 Köster, H., *Synoptische Überlieferung bei den apostolischen Vätern* (Berlin, 1957).
125 Kümmel, W. G., *Introduction to the New Testament*, rev. ed., trans. (London, 1975).

126 Larcher, C., *Etudes sur le livre de la Sagesse* (Paris, 1969).
127 Leaney, A. R. C., *The Letters of Peter and Jude*, CBC (CUP, 1967).
128 Lindars, B., *New Testament Apologetic. The Doctrinal Significance of the Old Testament Quotations* (London, 1961).
129 ———, *Behind the Fourth Gospel* (1971).
130 ———, *The Gospel of John*, NCB (London, 1972).
131 Lindemann, A., "Zum Abfassungszweck des zweiten Thessalonicherbriefes," ZNW 68 (1977), 35–47.
132 Linton, O., "The Third Aspect. A Study in Gal. 1-2 and Acts 9 and 15," *Studia Theologica* 3 (1950–51), 79–95.
133 Loisy, A., *La Naissance du Christianisme* (Paris, 1933).
134 ———, *Histoire et Mythe apropos de Jesus-Christ* (Paris, 1938).
135 Martin, R. P., Review of JEC in *Christian Graduate* 25 (1972), 9.
136 Menoud, P. H., "The Western Text and the Theology of Acts," *Bulletin of the Studiorum Novi Testamenti Societas* 2 (1951, published Cambridge, 1963), 19–32.
137 Merrill, E. T., *Essays in Early Christian History* (London, 1924).
138 Metzger, B. M., *The Text of the New Testament*, 2nd ed. (Oxford, 1968).
139 ———, *A Textual Commentary on the Greek New Testament* (London, 1971).
140 ———, *The Early Versions of the New Testament* (Oxford, 1977).
141 Mitton, C. L., *The Epistle to the Ephesians* (Oxford, 1951).
142 ———, *Ephesians*, NCB (London, 1976).
143 Montefiore, H. W., *The Epistle to the Hebrews*, Black (London, 1964).
144 Moody Smith, D., Jr., "Johannine Christianity," NTS 21 (1975), 222–48.
145 Morton, A. Q., and McLemon, J., *Paul the Man and the Myth* (London, 1966).
146 Moulton, J. H., and Milligan, G., *The Vocabulary of the Greek Testament* (London, 1930, reprinted 1972).
147 Nickell, J., "The Shroud of Turin–Solved," [American] *Humanist* 38 (1978), 30–2.
148 Nineham, D. E., *The Gospel of Mark* (The Pelican NT Commentaries) (1972).
149 ———, *Explorations in Theology*, vol. 1 (London, 1977).
150 O'Neill, J. C., *The Theology of Acts in Its Historical Setting* (London, 1961).
151 ———, *The Recovery of Paul's Letter to the Galatians* (London, 1972).
152 ———, *Paul's Letter to the Romans* (Penguin Books, 1975).
153 ———, Review of DJE in *New Humanist* 91 (1975), 45–6.
154 Pearson, B. A., "1 Thess. 2:13-16. A Deutero-Pauline Interpolation," HTR 64 (1971), 79–94.
155 Perrin, N., *Rediscovering the Teaching of Jesus* (London, 1967).
156 ———, *What Is Redaction Criticism?* (London, 1970).
157 ———, *The Resurrection Narratives. A New Approach.* (London, 1977).
158 Petzke, G., "Die historische Frage nach den Wundertaten Jesu," NTS 22 (1976), 180–204.
159 Riesenfeld, H., *The Gospel Tradition and Its Beginnings: A Study in the Limits of "Formgeschichte"* (London, 1957).
160 Rinaldi, P. M., *The Man in the Shroud* (London, 1974).
161 Robertson, J. M., *Jesus and Judas* (London, 1927).
162 Robinson, James M., *A New Quest of the Historical Jesus* (1959).
163 Robinson, John A. T., *The Body. A Study in Pauline Theology* (London, 1952).
164 ———, *Redating the New Testament* (London, 1976).

165 ———, Review of DJE, JTS 27 (1976), 447-9.

166 ———, Review of D. Nineham's *The Use and Abuse of the Bible,* TLS (April 8, 1977), 429.

167 Roloff, J., *Das Kerygma und der irdische Jesus. Historische Motive in den Jesus-Erzählungen der Evangelien* (Göttingen, 1970).

168 ———, "Der mitleidende Hohepriester. Zur Frage nach der Bedeutung des irdischen Jesus für die Christologie des Hebräerbriefes," in *Jesus Christus in Historie und Theologie,* Festschrift for H. Conzelmann, ed. G. Strecker (Tübingen, 1975), 143-66.

169 Ruef, J., *Paul's First Letter to Corinth* (The Pelican NT Commentaries) (1971).

170 Sanders, E. P., *The Tendencies of the Synoptic Tradition* (Cambridge, 1969).

171 Sanders, J. T., *Ethics in the New Testament* (London, 1975).

172 Schmithals, W., *Paul and James,* trans. (London, 1965).

173 ———, "Der Markusschluss, die Verklärungsgeschichte und die Aussendung der Zwölf," ZThK 69 (1972), 379-411.

174 ———, *Jesus Christus in der Verkündigung der Kirche* (Neukirchen, 1972).

175 Schonfield, H. J., *For Christ's Sake* (London, 1975).

176 Schulte, K. J., "Der Tod Jesu in der Sicht der modernen Medizin," *Berliner Medizin* 14 (1963), 210-20.

177 Schürer, E., *The History of the Jewish People in the Age of Jesus Christ,* New English version revised by G. Vermes et al., vol. 1 (Edinburgh, 1973).

178 ———, vol. 2 of no. 177 (Edinburgh, 1979).

179 Schweitzer, A., *Die Geschichte der Leben-Jesu Forschung,* 2nd ed. (Tübingen, 1913).

180 ———, *The Quest of the Historical Jesus,* 3rd ed., trans. (London, 1954).

181 Sherwin-White, A. N., "The Trial of Christ," in *Historicity and Chronology in the New Testament* (London, 1965), 97-116.

182 Sidebottom, E. M., *James, Jude and 2 Peter,* NCB (London, 1967).

183 Smith, Morton, *The Secret Gospel* (London, 1974).

184 ———, *Jesus the Magician* (London, 1978).

185 Sox, H. D., *File on the Shroud,* with a foreword by Sir Steven Runciman (London, 1978).

186 Sparks, H. F. D., "Some Observations on the Semitic Background of the New Testament," *Bulletin of the Studiorum Novi Testamenti Societas,* vol. cit. in no. 136, 33-4.

187 Stanton, G., "Form Criticism Revisited," in *What About the New Testament?,* Evans Festschrift, ed. M. Hooker (London, 1975), 13-27.

188 ———, Review of DJE, TLS (August 29, 1975), 977.

189 Stephenson, A. M. G., "On the Meaning of . . . 2 Thessalonians 2:2," *Studia Evangelica* 4 (*Texte und Untersuchungen zur Geschichte der altchristlichen Literatur,* 102) (1968), 442-51.

190 Strathmann, H., *Das Evangelium nach Johannes,* NTD, vol. 4 (Göttingen, 1968).

191 Strauss, D. F., *Der alte und der neue Glaube* (Leipzig, 1872).

192 Streeter, B. H., *The Four Gospels* (London, 1936).

193 Sturdy, J. V. M., Review of J. A. T. Robinson's *Redating the New Testament,* JTS 30 (1979), 255-62.

194 Sweet, J., *Revelation* (SCM Pelican Commentaries) (London, 1979).

195 Swinburne, R., *The Concept of Miracle* (London, 1970).

196 Talbert, C. H. (ed.), *Perspectives on Luke-Acts,* articles by F. L. Horton, Jr. (1–23), A. J. Mattill, Jr. (76–98), V. K. Robbins (215–42), and J. B. Tyson (24–39) (Edinburgh, 1978).
197 Tannehill, R. C., *Dying and Rising with Christ. A Study in Pauline Theology* (Berlin, 1967).
198 Taylor, V., *The Gospel According to St. Mark,* 2nd ed. (London, 1966).
199 Telfer, W., "Was Hegesippus a Jew?", HTR 53 (1960), 143–53.
200 ———, *The Office of a Bishop* (London, 1962).
201 Thrall, Margaret, *1 and 2 Corinthians,* CBC (CUP, 1965).
202 Trocmé, E., *Jesus and His Contemporaries,* trans. R. A. Wilson (London, 1973).
203 Vielhauer, P., "Franz Overbeck und die NT Wissenschaft," in *Aufsätze zum NT* (Munich, 1965), 235–52.
204 Vignon, P., *The Shroud of Christ,* trans. (London, 1902).
205 Weiss, J., *Jesus von Nazareth, Mythos oder Geschichte* (Tübingen, 1910).
206 Wells, G. A., *The Jesus of the Early Christians* (London, 1971).
207 ———, *Did Jesus Exist?* (London, 1975).
208 ———, "The Holy Shroud of Turin," *Question* 9 (1975), 24–37.
209 ———, "Miracles and the Nature of Truth," *Question* 10 (1977), 30–41.
210 ———, "More on the Holy Shroud," *New Humanist* 94 (1978), 11–15.
211 Werner, M., *Der protestantische Weg des Glaubens,* vol. 2 (Bern and Tübingen, 1967).
212 Whale, J., Review of DJE, *Sunday Times* (March 30, 1975).
213 Whiteley, D. E. H., *Thessalonians in the RSV* (Oxford, 1969).
214 Wilcox, M., *The Semitisms of Acts* (Oxford, 1965).
215 ———, Review of DJE in *Trivium* 14 (1979), 169–70.
216 Williams, R. R., *The Letters of John and James,* CBC (CUP, 1965).
217 Williamson, R., "The Eucharist and the Epistle to the Hebrews," NTS 21 (1975), 300–12.
218 Wilson, I., *The Turin Shroud* (London, 1978).
219 Windisch, H., *Paulus und Christus* (Leipzig, 1934).
220 Winter, P., "Tacitus and Pliny: the Early Christians," *Journal of Historical Studies* 1 (1967), 31–40.
221 Woods, G. F., "The Evidential Value of the Biblical Miracles," in *Miracles: Cambridge Studies in their Philosophy and History,* ed. C. F. D. Moule (London, 1965), 19–32.
222 Ziesler, J. A., "Luke and the Pharisees," NTS, 25 (1979), 146–57.

ADDENDA

223 Best, E., review of no. 81 in JTS 30 (1979), 539–42.
224 Brox, N., "Zu den persönlichen Notizen der Pastoralbriefe," in *Pseudepigraphie in der heidnischen und jüdisch-christlichen Antike,* ed. N. Brox, *Wege der Forschung,* vol. 484 (1977), 311–34.
225 Clark, K. W., "Worship in the Jerusalem Temple After AD 70," NTS 6 (1959–60), 269–80.
226 Feuillet, A., *Le Christ Sagesse de Dieu* (Paris, 1966).
226a Gager, J. G., "The Gospels and Jesus: Some Doubts about Method," *The Journal of Religion* 54 (1974), 244–72.

227 Gerhardsson, B., *The Origin of the Gospel Traditions* (London, 1980).
227a Gittings, R., *The Older Hardy* (London, 1978).
228 Haenchen, E., *Das Johannesevangelium,* ed. U. Busse (Tübingen, 1980).
228a Halson, R. R., "The Epistle of James," *Texte und Untersuchungen* 102 (1968), 308-14.
229 Hanson, A. T., *The New Testament Interpretation of Scripture* (London, 1980).
230 Hill, D., *The Gospel of Matthew,* NCB (London, 1972).
231 ———, "On the Evidence for the Creative Role of Christian Prophets," NTS 20 (1974), 262-74.
231a Laws, Sophie, *A Commentary on the Epistle of James,* Black (London, 1980).
232 Lindemann, A., *Paulus im ältesten Christentum* (Tübingen, 1979).
233 Pagels, Elaine, *The Gnostic Gospels* (London, 1980).
233a Theissen, G., *Untersuchungen zum Hebräerbrief* (Gütersloh, 1969).
234 Vielhauer, P., *Geschichte der urchristlichen Literatur* (Berlin, 1975).
235 Ziesler, J. A., *The Jesus Question* (London, 1980).

Index of New Testament References

General Index

(References readily inferable from the Table of Contents are not included)

259